NORTH CARO
NEW HANOVER COUN

D1547057

Southern Biography Series
William J. Cooper, Jr., Editor

William Woods Holden
Firebrand of North Carolina Politics

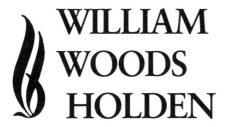

WILLIAM WOODS HOLDEN

Firebrand of North Carolina Politics

William C. Harris

Louisiana State University Press

Baton Rouge and London

Copyright © 1987 by Louisiana State University Press
All rights reserved
Manufactured in the United States of America

Designer: Diane Batten Didier
Typeface: Linotron Sabon
Typesetter: G & S Typesetters, Inc.
Printer: Thomson-Shore, Inc.
Binder: John Dekker and Sons, Inc.

10 9 8 7 6 5 4 3 2 1

Library of Congress Cataloging-in-Publication Data

Harris, William C. (William Charles), 1933–
    William Woods Holden : firebrand of North Carolina politics.

    (Southern biography series)
    Bibliography: p.
    Includes index.
    1. Holden, W. W. (William Woods), 1818–1892.
2. North Carolina—Governors—Biography.   3. North
Carolina—Politics and government—1775–1865.
4. North Carolina—Politics and government—1865–1950.
5. Reconstruction—North Carolina.   I. Title.   II. Series.
F259.H72H37   1987   975.6'041'0924 [B]   87-2699
ISBN 0-8071-1325-5

To Nelson, Frances, and Sehoya

Contents

Illustrations

Acknowledgments

I am indebted to many persons for aid and encouragement in writing this book. Archivists, custodians of manuscript collections, and librarians have been exceedingly helpful in the research phase of the study. I am particularly grateful for the assistance of Carolyn Wallace and Richard Shrader of the Southern Historical Collection, University of North Carolina Library, Chapel Hill, and Mattie Russell and Patricia S. Webb of the Manuscript Department, William R. Perkins Library, Duke University. On a regular basis the staff of the North Carolina Division of Archives and History, headed by Thornton Mitchell and Frank Gatton, extended a helping hand. Joe A. Mobley of the same agency provided intelligence on relatively obscure but valuable source materials, and he also tracked down census data and other information on Holden. Joe and Stephen E. Massengill, also of the Division of Archives and History, located and arranged for the reproduction of important illustrations for the book. The staffs of the D. H. Hill Library, North Carolina State University, and the North Carolina Collection, University of North Carolina Library, Chapel Hill, also provided generous assistance in the research on the book. In addition, I received important Holden materials from Donald Lennon of the East Carolina University Manuscript Collection, Sem C. Sutter of the University of Chicago Library, Watt P. Marchman of the Rutherford B. Hayes Memorial Library in Fremont, Ohio, Dianne M. Gutscher of the Bowdoin College Library, and Tom Hargrove of Raleigh, North Carolina.

Numerous historians and friends have discussed Holden with me and have read parts of the manuscript. Although they might not always agree with me, Otto H. Olsen, Richard L. Zuber, and Allen W. Trelease offered valuable insights into Holden's career and into the history of North Carolina during the Civil War–Reconstruction era. In several long conversations

Marc W. Kruman shared his thoughts about Holden and the political context in which he operated. Marc also read the first part of the manuscript and offered trenchant criticisms of it. Thomas B. Alexander has encouraged me in the project and, as he has done since 1958, when he took me under his wing as a graduate student, provided a model for my efforts as a historian. Catherine Alguire expertly prepared a map of North Carolina for the book, and John Easterly of the Louisiana State University Press provided able and generous assistance in the final preparation of the manuscript for publication.

I am also indebted to North Carolina State University for a semester's leave to advance the work. In addition, history department typists, namely Terri Anderson, Annette Tomlinson, and Amy Hosokawa, prepared the drafts and the final copy of the manuscript. I am indebted to my colleagues Gail W. O'Brien, John David Smith, Carolyn Pumphrey, and John deTreville for reading parts of the draft and making suggestions for improvements. Other colleagues rendered assistance in a variety of ways. Joseph P. Hobbs, Ronald Sack, and Burton F. Beers, although offering encouragement, frequently gave me a needed respite from Holden by reminding me of my current responsibilities in academe. If physical activity aids the mind, then my opponents on the tennis court, Kenneth P. Vickery, John M. Riddle, Michael Novak, and Collins Kilburn, made a major contribution to this study; indeed, their assistance was so thorough that on occasion it was counterproductive.

My family contributed in numerous ways to the preparation of the book. In addition to suffering from my preoccupation with Holden, my wife, Betty, and our daughters, Frances and Sehoya, assisted in the collection and arrangement of materials. My son, Nelson, did the heavy work around the house when I conveniently retired to my desk to study Holden. Without the encouragement and affection of my family, this book could not have been written.

Abbreviations

CWH	*Civil War History*
DU	Manuscript Department, William R. Perkins Library, Duke University, Durham, North Carolina
JSH	*Journal of Southern History*
LC	Manuscript Division, Library of Congress, Washington, D.C.
NA	National Archives, Washington, D.C.
NCHR	*North Carolina Historical Review*
NDAH	North Carolina State Division of Archives and History, Raleigh
OR	*The War of the Rebellion: A Compilation of the Official Records of the Union and Confederate Armies* (73 vols., 128 parts; Washington, D.C., 1880–1901).
Raleigh *Register*	*Register and North Carolina Gazette* (Raleigh)
Raleigh *Standard*	*North Carolina Weekly Standard* (Raleigh). Full titles of the daily and semiweekly editions will be cited in the notes.
SHC	Southern Historical Collection, University of North Carolina, Chapel Hill

William Woods Holden
Firebrand of North Carolina Politics

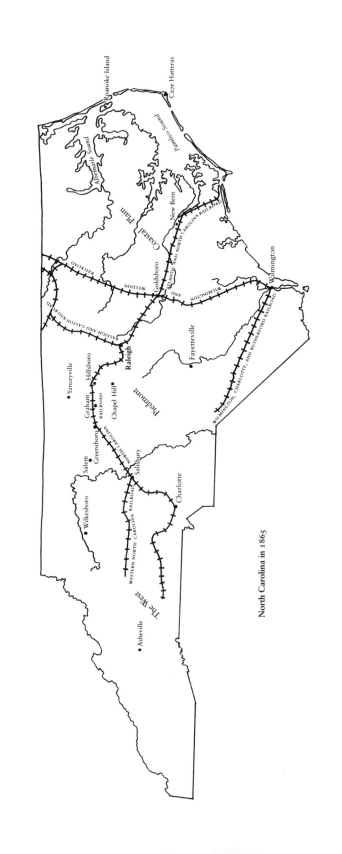

North Carolina in 1865

Roanoke Island
Cape Hatteras
Albemarle Sound
Pamlico Sound
Coastal Plain
New Bern
WELDON
Goldsboro
ATLANTIC AND NORTH CAROLINA RAILROAD
Wilmington
WILMINGTON AND
RAILROAD
RALEIGH AND GASTON RAILROAD
AND
Fayetteville
Yanceyville
Hillsboro
Graham
RAILROAD
Chapel Hill
Raleigh
Piedmont
WILMINGTON, CHARLOTTE, AND RUTHERFORD RAILROAD
Salem
Greensboro
NORTH CAROLINA RAILROAD
Salisbury
Wilkesboro
Charlotte
WESTERN NORTH CAROLINA RAILROAD
The West
Asheville

Introduction

William Woods Holden stood at the center of the political turmoil in Civil War and Reconstruction North Carolina. As editor of the Raleigh *North Carolina Standard* during the late 1840s and the 1850s, he revitalized the Democratic party in North Carolina and provided the leadership for its political control of the state before secession and war brought down the curtain on an era. In 1858 he sought his party's gubernatorial nomination but was denied it after a bitter struggle in the state convention. Holden was also the leading North Carolina defender of southern rights during the antebellum period, and though his critics, including later historians, dubbed him "the father of secession" in North Carolina, it was not until the Civil War began that he actually called for the state to leave the Union. Indeed, till then he repeatedly proclaimed his support for the Union. In order to save it, he paradoxically advocated southern rights under the protective umbrella of the national Democratic party. Then, after Lincoln's election, he led the unionist forces that checked the fever of secession in the state. But when Lincoln called for troops to suppress the rebellion after Confederates had fired on Fort Sumter, he reversed his position, and as a delegate to the state convention of May, 1861, he voted to take North Carolina out of the Union.

Although he supported the southern war effort, Holden soon became disillusioned with the state and Confederate administrations. In 1862 he almost single-handedly organized the state's Conservative party, which, with young Zebulon B. Vance as its candidate for governor, won control of North Carolina. After the battle of Gettysburg in July, 1863, Holden organized a peace movement in the state while continuing to proclaim his loyalty to the Confederacy. When Vance refused to support the call for a state convention to protect North Carolina from Confederate oppression and to initiate peace negotiations, Holden in 1864 ran against him for governor. He suffered a humiliating defeat.

After Appomattox, President Andrew Johnson appointed him provisional governor of North Carolina. Holden's main duty was the implementation of the president's mild plan of reconstruction. In the fall, 1865, election he suffered another bitter setback when his Union party, with himself as its candidate for governor, was soundly defeated. Because of the return of his old enemies to power and the failure of the southern states to be restored to the Union under Johnson's program, Holden repudiated the president's leadership and endorsed the congressional or Republican settlement for the South. The congressional plan included the southern ratification of the Fourteenth Amendment and the adoption of black political equality, a radical and potentially revolutionary step. In 1867 he organized the North Carolina Republican party, consisting of much-maligned southern whites called "scalawags," transplanted northerners known as "carpetbaggers," and blacks. In 1868 members of this party drew up a new constitution for the state and subsequently won control of North Carolina. Holden was elected governor, and for almost three years he worked to establish a permanent foundation for the new political order. In the end he failed. When the Ku Klux Klan threatened the Republican ascendancy in 1870, Holden dispatched state military forces into two Piedmont counties to suppress the terrorists and restore the rule of law. The so-called Kirk-Holden War that followed further aroused militant opposition against him and contributed to the Republican defeat in the legislative elections of August, 1870. When the Conservative (or Democratic) General Assembly convened in late 1870, it moved quickly to impeach and remove him from office. In March, 1871, Holden became the first governor in American history to suffer the indignity of expulsion.

Most contemporaries characterized Holden as a bitter, unscrupulous, and arrogant demagogue who frequently changed his political stripes to advance his own political ambitions. Writing in 1883,

North Carolina editor Josephus Daniels remarked that Holden had made "bitterer enemies than any other man in our history." Daniels admitted, however, that the former *Standard* editor and scalawag governor was "one of the foremost men in intellectual power and daring that was ever born here." He also predicted, "Whatever people in the future may think of him, one thing is certain—they will think of him." [1]

For many years most people who thought or wrote about Holden simply followed the early denunciatory accounts. Democratic politicians and editors, with elections to win, kept the Holden legend alive as part of their campaign to maintain white unity at the polls by recalling the "horrors" of Reconstruction. At the turn of the century Thomas Dixon in his popular novel *The Leopard's Spots* even used Holden as the model for his unscrupulous scalawag governor, Amos Hogg, and castigated him for suppressing the Ku Klux Klan. [2] Nevertheless, Holden continued to have his defenders, though by the twentieth century they had become only a corporal's guard of survivors from his Civil War–Reconstruction following.

Despite his prominence Holden has not received the careful and judicious attention of historians. Because of the unpopularity of Reconstruction and the causes for which he stood, historians during the first three decades of the twentieth century—and in some cases even later—reinforced the distorted contemporary interpretation of Holden. The Holden legend received its most indelible treatment at the hands of J. G. de Roulhac Hamilton. In two books, one of which, *Reconstruction in North Carolina*, is still the standard account of the postwar history of the Old North State, Hamilton portrayed Holden as an extremely ambitious and weak leader whose political deviation and unscrupulous conduct could be traced to his rejection for governor by the Democratic party in 1858. According to Hamilton, when Holden during Reconstruction finally achieved

1. Clipping from Raleigh *State Chronicle*, 1883, Scrapbook, William Woods Holden Papers, DU.

2. Thomas Dixon, Jr., *The Leopard's Spots: A Romance of the White Man's Burden, 1865–1900* (1902; rpr. Ridgewood, N.J., 1967), 69–71, 156–58, 160–62, 164. For the rare exception to the early anti-Holden theme, see William K. Boyd, "William W. Holden," *Trinity College Historical Society Papers*, Ser. III (1899), 39–130.

his ambition to be governor, he presided over "a highly partisan administration which was characterized by the most brazen corruption, extravagance, and incompetency" in the history of the state. Although Hamilton did not charge Holden with personal profit from the Reconstruction scandals, he claimed that the scalawag governor surrounded himself with "incompetent sycophants and highly skilled plunderers who robbed the state through the issuance of fraudulent railroad bonds." When their schemes were jeopardized by a Democratic resurgence in 1870, the corruptionists, according to Hamilton, influenced Holden to institute a "reign of terror" to carry the state elections.[3]

Other historians and writers soon picked up on the Hamilton theme and embroidered it. Claude G. Bowers in *The Tragic Era: The Revolution After Lincoln* (1929), an extremely popular account of Reconstruction, portrayed Holden as the epitome of the unscrupulous southern scalawag. "Here was a man on whose overweening ambition for place and distinction a wretched period played to its undoing," Bowers indignantly wrote. Holden "was essentially an opportunist" who aligned himself "with parties and causes" to advance himself and who was "neither keen enough nor strong enough to cope with the machinations of the party leaders about him." E. Merton Coulter, writing the Reconstruction volume in the prestigious History of the South series, opined that Holden "had an itch for office" and believed that "co-operation with the Radicals was [the] easiest and quickest road to success." Then, as governor he "ran wild in his irresponsible attempt to break up the Ku Klux Klan in the so-called Kirk-Holden war."[4]

As Civil War and Reconstruction revisionism developed during

3. J. G. de Roulhac Hamilton, *Reconstruction in North Carolina* (New York, 1914), 6, 343–44, 371, 413; Hamilton, *Party Politics in North Carolina, 1835–1860* (Durham, 1916), 188; Hamilton's biographical sketch of Holden in *Dictionary of American Biography*, IX, 139. See also Robert D. W. Connor, *North Carolina: Rebuilding an Ancient Commonwealth* (4 vols.; Chicago, 1928–1929), II, 156, 281, 291, 326–27, and Samuel A'Court Ashe, *History of North Carolina* (2 vols.; Raleigh, 1925), II, 521, 833.

4. Claude G. Bowers, *The Tragic Era: The Revolution After Lincoln* (1929; rpr. Boston, 1957), 312–14; E. Merton Coulter, *The South During Reconstruction* (Baton Rouge, 1947), 124, 170. The view of Holden as essentially an unscrupulous opportunist has been retained in Carl N. Degler, *The Other South: Southern Dissenters in the Nineteenth Century* (New York, 1974), 144. See also Glenn Tucker, *Zeb Vance, Champion of Personal Freedom* (Indianapolis, 1965), 149, 427, 429.

the 1930s and after, most historians dropped the popular canard of Holden as an unscrupulous opportunist. Nevertheless, they generally retained the view that he was an exceedingly ambitious man who was unstable in his political views and party allegiances. But unlike the traditional historians, the revisionists attributed his strong desire for position and power to his lower-class origins and his determination to replace aristocratic rule in the state with a truly democratic order. According to biographer Horace W. Raper, first in a 1951 dissertation and recently in a published study, Holden, after being thwarted in 1858 by the landed gentry, joined with the Radical Republicans in Congress during Reconstruction to seek the realization of his cherished dream of a progressive yeoman democracy in North Carolina. In this respect, Raper claims, Holden "was a positive and fairsighted leader" who "placed principle ahead of power." Raper, who devotes only fifty-eight pages in his biography to Holden's antebellum and wartime career, concludes that if Holden had sacrificed principle and practiced demagoguery, "undoubtedly he could have gained the approbation of the ruling class" and avoided later abuse. In office during Reconstruction Holden "failed to live up to the promise of being a strong and popular leader" mainly because "he allowed personal animosities to get in the way of political harmony."[5]

Otto H. Olsen in a revisionist essay on North Carolina Reconstruction also identifies Holden "with the common man and the western, urban, nonslaveholding" class, whose interests he sought to serve after his 1858 rejection for high office by the Democratic party's "controlling and largely slaveholding gentry." Olsen asserts that Holden, instead of being truly radical, failed during Reconstruction because he was too willing to appease the new political order's critics in what proved to be a futile effort to win acceptance.[6] James L. Lancaster in a 1974 dissertation on North Carolina's scalawags also stresses the class consciousness of Holden,

5. Clarence C. Norton, *The Democratic Party in Ante-Bellum North Carolina, 1835–1861* (Chapel Hill, 1930), 211, 225, 231, 233; Joseph Carlyle Sitterson, *The Secession Movement in North Carolina* (Chapel Hill, 1939), 162–64 and note; Connor, *North Carolina*, II, 291, 305–306; Dan T. Carter, *When the War Was Over: The Failure of Self-Reconstruction in the South, 1865–1867* (Baton Rouge, 1985), 47, 54; Horace W. Raper, *William W. Holden: North Carolina's Political Enigma* (Chapel Hill, 1985), ix.

6. Otto H. Olsen (ed.), *Reconstruction and Redemption in the South* (Baton

which, he writes, became "sharply-etched" after his failure to win the 1858 Democratic nomination. After the war, Lancaster asserts, Holden "envisioned a social and economic revolution . . . which would permanently elevate the common whites." But, this historian concludes, Holden failed because his political ambition and his desire for social approval outweighed his commitment to reform.[7]

A biography of Holden by Edgar Estes Folk and Bynum Shaw, published in 1982 and based on Folk's 1934 doctoral dissertation, provides a variation to the class-consciousness thesis of the revisionists. This biography, which is concerned mainly with Holden's prewar editorial career, emphasizes the influence on him of his lowly origins (his was an illegitimate birth) and the early slights that he received from North Carolina aristocrats, culminating in his 1858 rejection for governor.[8] The authors, however, do not demonstrate how his personal or social sensitivities influenced his position on various issues or how Civil War and Reconstruction issues affected his political attitude and behavior.

Holden did not neatly fit into any of the categories that historians and others have assigned him. He was too much a product of the diverse interplay of political rivalries and events, too much a man shaped by the common political culture of all classes and the trauma of the Civil War ordeal, to be so easily classified. In this book I seek to provide the reader with a comprehensive and balanced account of the life of this complicated man. I attempt to place him in the context of the times while avoiding the temptation to write a history of the period. A more difficult task has been in measuring Holden's influence on men and events, though I cautiously make the effort and hope that I do not exaggerate his importance or distort the history of the period. I also hope that the book, at

---

Rouge, 1980), 157, 174, 180. See also Olsen, "Reconsidering the Scalawags," *CWH*, XII (1966), 307.

7. James L. Lancaster, "The Scalawags of North Carolina, 1850–1868" (Ph.D. dissertation, Princeton University, 1974), 13–14, 68, 77, 225. An important exception to the class-conflict approach is Marc W. Kruman's *Parties and Politics in North Carolina, 1836–1865* (Baton Rouge, 1983). Although Kruman does not seek to explain and evaluate Holden's career, he emphasizes the role of party politics and republican ideology in the bitter political battles of the period.

8. Edgar E. Folk and Bynum Shaw, *W. W. Holden: A Political Biography* (Winston-Salem, 1982). See also Edgar E. Folk, "W. W. Holden and the Election of 1858," *NCHR*, XXI (1944), 294–318.

least in a small measure, will increase the reader's understanding of North Carolina and the South during the turbulent Civil War era and, especially, shed a ray of light on the history of southern unionism, wartime dissent, racial adjustment, and postwar southern Republicanism. The centrality of Holden in the North Carolina of the Civil War and Reconstruction period gives the biographer an excellent state and local vantage point from which to view the history of a young, confident republican people in a time of crisis and civil war. It was at the state and local level where most of the political action in nineteenth-century America took place and where the impetus for national history occurred.

I
Poor and Unknown and Very Ambitious

William Woods Holden was born on November 24, 1818, in a log cabin near the historic town of Hillsboro, North Carolina. He was born out of wedlock to Priscilla Woods, from whom came his middle name, and Thomas Holden, a relatively prosperous mill owner in Orange County. Before he sold out and moved to Milton, North Carolina, during the mid-1840s, Thomas had developed on the Eno River a small industrial complex consisting of a sawmill, a flour-and-corn mill, two wool-carding machines, four houses (including the Holden home), and various outbuildings. Thomas also farmed the surrounding land and in 1820 owned at least eighteen slaves whom he had inherited from his father. In public affairs he became "a man of considerable influence in Orange County," according to a contemporary, and beginning in 1822 served as a justice of the peace in the county. The history of William Holden's mother is largely unknown, though in adulthood he assumed some responsibility for her and after the Civil War gave her a tract of land in Orange County.[1]

The fact of William Holden's illegitimacy carried no enduring

1. Mrs. Henry Murdock, "Recollections of W. W. Holden" (MS by Holden's stepsister in William Woods Holden Papers, NDAH); Thomas Hargrove to the author, June 14, 1982; clipping from the Hillsboro *Recorder,* February 13, 1845, provided to the author by Thomas Hargrove of Raleigh, North Carolina; Priestly H. Mangum to William A. Graham, May 12, 1842, in J. G. de Roulhac Hamilton and Max R. Williams (eds.), *The Papers of William Alexander Graham* (7 vols. to date; Raleigh, 1957–), II, 310.

stigma, and it did not impede his rise to prominence in the state. Most North Carolinians never knew of his illegitimate birth, and it was not publicly used against him. During the antebellum period he occasionally referred to his "obscure origins," but his purpose was hardly to call attention to the circumstances of his birth. Most North Carolinians held the doctrine of equal opportunity as an article of faith and believed that upward mobility was the reward for those who worked hard. In recalling his humble origins, Holden sought to establish his empathy with the great majority of the people while appealing to their democratic instincts. Still, he was sensitive about his illegitimacy, a sensibility that at least on one occasion he publicly expressed, though in a coded fashion. In 1858 he alluded not only to the hardships of his youth but also to his birth when he complained of "those who would punish me on account of my origins, and because I had the energy and ambition to struggle upwards in life, who if they had been born in the same conditions in which I was, would have been there yet."[2]

Two or three years after William's birth, Thomas Holden married another woman, Sally Nichols, and when William was six or seven years old, Sally, without consulting her husband, brought William to live with them. She raised him like one of her own children, and his childhood, which was shared by several half brothers and half sisters, was moderately happy and fulfilling.[3] Like other Americans of rural origins who achieved prominence in maturity, Holden later took pride in his early struggles and probably exaggerated the hardships.

Nevertheless, compared with the affluent merchant and lawyer classes of the towns and with the large planters, life was hard for young Holden, but not because his family suffered material deprivation. Although William was "a willful boy who did not like to be bossed," his father exercised strict discipline over him in his work and social habits, giving him little time to attend the local "field school." In the year or two in which he studied at the school, he learned to read and write and also gained a deep appreciation for books. When William was nine or ten years old, his father sent

2. Raleigh *Standard,* October 20, 1858.
3. Murdock, "Recollections of W. W. Holden," in Holden Papers, NDAH. Thomas and Sally Holden ultimately gave birth to ten children, one of whom died in infancy.

him to Hillsboro to become an "irregular" printer's apprentice in the office of Dennis Heartt, the Whig editor and proprietor of the *Recorder*. He spent six years under the tutelage of Heartt, who had trained a number of editors in the robust skill of political journalism.[4]

At age sixteen, Holden, after being flogged by a supervisor for leaving his printing case to attend a Fourth of July celebration, quit his apprenticeship. With Heartt's approval, he went to nearby Milton, where he obtained employment on a local newspaper. After living in Milton for four months, he took a printer's job on a Danville, Virginia, newspaper. In Danville he wrote and published his first newspaper article, which filled him with intense satisfaction and spurred his ambition for editorial renown.[5]

Lonesome for home, he soon returned to Hillsboro and to the *Recorder*. But he became restless and, believing that the commercial world offered a quicker road to success than the newspaper business, obtained employment as a clerk in a Hillsboro store. While tending the store, he spent a great deal of time, as he later recalled, "in studying and reading the standard authors." He also maintained his interest in political journalism by writing several articles for the Raleigh *Star*. After a year as a clerk, Holden, now seventeen years old, wrote *Star* editor Thomas J. Lemay and asked for a job on the newspaper. Lemay replied, offering him work as a typesetter at eight to ten dollars per week, provided he could prove "as successful at the case as with the pen." Holden was ecstatic with the offer; the salary that Lemay proposed was at the highest rate printers then received in North Carolina. In preparation for his move to Raleigh he purchased on credit a broadcloth coat and a gold watch—status symbols of the time.

On October 7, 1836, young Holden took the stage for Raleigh. Arriving on a beautiful moonlit evening with only seven dollars in his pocket, he marveled at the splendor of the state capital, with its broad, oak-lined avenues radiating from the square in the center of town where a stately new capitol was being constructed. Years later he recalled the moment. "Poor and unknown and very ambitious,"

4. *Ibid.*; Edgar Estes Folk, "W. W. Holden and the *North Carolina Standard, 1843–1848*: A Study in Political Journalism," *NCHR*, XIX (1942), 24.
5. Raleigh *Semi-Weekly Standard*, February 5, 1862; Raleigh *Daily Standard*, August 25, 1868.

as he characterized himself, he could hardly conceal his delight in being at the center of political activity in North Carolina.[6] He expected eventually to be a part of it, though his position as a typesetter offered little immediate prospect for political preferment.

Actually, the Raleigh that Holden came to in 1836 was not much larger than Hillsboro, and it still possessed many of the raw elements of a young and fluid community. With a population of about two thousand people, including three hundred free blacks, the town could boast of a few fashionable mansions and a larger number of neat, white-framed houses. The most impressive features of Raleigh were the unfinished state capitol, three hotels, and seven boardinghouses, where the mighty and the politically knowledgeable met and conducted the affairs of state. But many residents still kept cows, horses, and hogs in their yards, grazing them on Capitol Square and in the dense woods that began abruptly at the end of the town. Furthermore, residential log cabins could still be seen only one block from the capitol. Into one of these log huts, owned by editor Lemay, Holden moved upon his arrival in Raleigh.[7]

The young printer was soon hard at work setting type for the *Star,* one of two powerful Whig newspapers at the capital. He frequently worked from sunrise until late at night, sometimes seven days a week. Lemay occasionally permitted him to write editorials for the newspaper. Holden's commentaries stressed support for the doctrines of states' rights and continental expansion, especially toward the Southwest, a position he believed that the Whig leadership held. His affiliation with the Whig party was made easier by his dislike for Democratic President Martin Van Buren, whose "aristocratic pretensions" offended young Holden. In the 1840 hard-cider presidential campaign of William Henry Harrison, he made his first political speeches, proclaiming at Whig "log cabins" in Wake County the virtues of "Tippecanoe and Tyler too." Later, when he became a Democrat, he would minimize his youthful commitment to the Whig party and deny that he had been an active participant

6. Raleigh *Daily Standard,* August 25, 1868; William W. Holden, *Memoirs of W. W. Holden* (Durham, 1911), 94–95.

7. Guion Griffis Johnson, *Ante-Bellum North Carolina: A Social History* (Chapel Hill, 1937), 121, 152; Elizabeth Culbertson Waugh, *North Carolina's Capital, Raleigh* (Raleigh, 1967), 10, 80; Raleigh *Standard,* September 4, 1845; Moses N. Amis, *Historical Raleigh* (Raleigh, 1913), 75; Raleigh *Daily Standard,* August 25, 1868.

in the 1840 campaign. He then insisted that he had never sub-scribed to the national or "American System" of Whig leader Henry Clay, which called for the rechartering of the Bank of the United States, a protective tariff, and federal support for internal improvements. He admitted, however, that he had been attracted to Clay by his remarkable rise from obscurity to wealth and political greatness, a course Holden himself hoped to follow.[8]

Soon after the Whig victory of 1840 Holden became alarmed by the centralizing tendencies of the party's national leadership. When Whigs in Congress aggressively pushed for the enactment of the American System, only to be foiled by President John Tyler, Har-rison's successor, Holden began to suspect that the party "was not the Republican party of the country" and would not "restore the government to its original purity." His disillusionment with the party increased when in early 1842 he unsuccessfully sought the support of the North Carolina Whig delegation in Congress for his proposal to become the coeditor of the *Star*, a plan that Lemay had approved provided Holden could raise the money to purchase an interest in the newspaper. Already, as a result of study during his few spare moments while working for the *Star*, Holden had ob-tained a license as an attorney. When his attempt to become the *Star*'s coeditor failed, he left the newspaper to practice law, further separating him from Whig politics.[9]

His absence from the political wars was brief. In June, 1843, he assumed control of the *North Carolina Standard*, the struggling Democratic newspaper in Raleigh. He immediately attracted a crowd of Whig detractors who instinctively girded their loins for battle with "the little political renegade" who had been placed in control of the state "Loco Foco" organ. The Greensboro *Patriot* greeted the news by commenting, "Mr. Holden is a very smart young man; but the integrity of a renegade is always more or less doubted, and the proverbially hot zeal of a proselyte is looked upon by the more sensible portion of mankind with many grains of al-lowance." Whig opponents did not look far to find the reason for

8. Raleigh *Standard*, October 19, 1843, June 28, 1854; Raleigh *Daily Stan-dard*, August 25, 1868.
9. Raleigh *Standard*, June 28, 1854; W. W. Holden to William A. Graham, January 18, 1842, in Hamilton and Williams (eds.), *Graham Papers*, II, 252; W. W. Holden to John H. Bryan, July 13, 1842, in John H. Bryan Papers, NDAH.

this remarkable and sudden turn of events. They charged that supporters of southern rights' leader John C. Calhoun were behind the
move to place Holden in charge of the *Standard*. Calhounites, they
contended, needed an organ at the state capital, and they sought
out young Holden with promises of money and influence if he assumed control of the newspaper and made it into a Calhoun propa-
ganda sheet.[10]

Although some Democratic leaders were taken aback by Holden's
elevation, they remained silent, hoping that the hard-working, ambitious young editor could revive the *Standard* and with it the fortunes of the party in North Carolina.[11] The party had not controlled
the state since the mid-1830s; its only success since then had been
its victory in the legislative elections of 1842. Democratic leaders
blamed the party's decline on the inept editorial policies of retiring
Standard editor Thomas Loring. To hopeful Democrats, the Whig
characterization of Holden as a renegade was viewed simply as the
venting of party spirit against a potentially formidable opponent.
Such exaggerated charges and feigned outrage, Democrats knew,
constituted the staples of North Carolina political tilting. Democrats denied that Holden had ever had a hand in Whig affairs or
edited a party newspaper, and they insisted that there had not been
any irregularities in his assumption of control of the *Standard*.

The Democratic account of Holden's conduct in the affair was
closer to the truth than that of the Whigs. His decision to join the
Democratic party was made before the opportunity to purchase the
Standard had occurred. For several months prior to the purchase
he had consorted with Wake County Democratic leaders, including
Loring and James B. Shepard. He had developed a strong friendship with Shepard, who took Holden under his wing and encouraged him to join the party that closely reflected his states' rights
and intensely republican views. Holden's failure to secure political
preferment at the hands of state Whig leaders also must have influenced his decision to affiliate with the Democrats. He later insisted

10. Raleigh *Register,* July 7, 1843; Greensboro *Patriot,* quoted in Edgar Estes
Folk, "W. W. Holden, Political Journalist" (Ph.D. dissertation, George Peabody
College for Teachers, 1934), 104; Raleigh *Standard,* June 7, 1843; J. G. de Roulhac
Hamilton, *Party Politics in North Carolina, 1835–1860* (Durham, 1916), 103.
11. Raleigh *Daily Standard,* August 25, 1868; Holden, *Memoirs,* 96–97;
Hamilton, *Party Politics in North Carolina,* 90.

that before the purchase of the *Standard* "it was well known" to his
friends that he "was out and out with the Democratic party." By
April, 1843—two months before the *Standard* deal was struck—
Holden had announced his political conversion. "I am thoroughly
democratic in my sentiments, and I have been for some time," he
wrote at this time. He also indicated that he had declined an offer
to establish and edit a Calhoun newspaper in Raleigh. In turning
down this proposition, Holden cleverly calculated that, though he
admired Calhoun, he would risk failure by tying himself to the support of this faction of the Democratic party, particularly since most
North Carolinians deeply resented South Carolina's leadership.[12]

When Loring intimated that he desired to sell the *Standard*,
Shepard, after consulting with a few Democrats in the capital, proposed to Holden that he purchase the newspaper. Seizing on the
suggestion, the young printer rushed to the Bank of North Carolina and brashly sought financial support for the purchase. He arrived at the right time. The Loring-managed *Standard* had recently
aroused the ire of Duncan Cameron, the powerful president of the
bank, by advocating soft money and attacking the bank for attempting to control state financial policy. Although Cameron, a
Whig, knew that Holden, as a converted Jacksonian Democrat,
could hardly be a friend of a financial corporation, he also understood that Holden favored hard money and, along with most Democrats, believed that state banks were preferable to the "Monster"
Bank of the United States. Holden, though impecunious at the moment, seemed also to the shrewd Cameron to be a good financial
risk. Two years earlier the young printer had married Ann Young,
the favorite niece of the wealthy planter-merchant William Peace,
who now lived with the young couple and would endorse the loan
for the *Standard*.[13]

Cameron quickly agreed to lend Holden two thousand dollars,
and that, along with a five-hundred-dollar loan from his friend
Shepard, permitted him to purchase the *Standard*. In turning over
the direction of the newspaper to the twenty-four-year-old printer,

12. Raleigh *Standard*, June 28, 1854, Raleigh *Daily Standard*, August 25,
1868; W. W. Holden to William A. Jeffreys, April 14, 1843, in William A. Jeffreys
Papers, NDAH.
13. Raleigh *Daily Standard*, August 25, 1868; Hamilton, *Party Politics in
North Carolina*, 88; Folk, "Holden, Political Journalist," 27, 46.

Loring praised him as "well qualified to fill the station" and "a young man of great moral worth." Holden, for his part, sought to assure surprised Democrats that he was "and ever has been a Democratic Republican" in the tradition of Thomas Jefferson. He supported the Democratic party, he said, because its leaders had always been "the friends and supporters of equal rights . . . the advocates of the *many* against the combinations of the few," and the guardians of "the freedom, sovereignty and independence" of the states. Not surprisingly, he attacked the Whig party for its violation of the people's trust and declared that he was opposed "to all projects, measures and principles" of that party, including Clay's American System. Finally, he announced that he would support no candidate for state or national office until nominated by the appropriate Democratic convention.[14] In laying down this policy—a rule that in the future he would stretch but not violate—Holden shrewdly recognized that early endorsements of candidates could create bitter intraparty opposition to him and seriously damage his standing as a spokesman for all state Democrats.

Holden acted immediately to establish his credentials as a party editor in the highly charged political atmosphere at the state capital. In early issues of his newspaper, he lashed out at members of "the little Federal Whig Clique" in Raleigh who "have for a moment crept up from the dirt to opulence" to dominate the state. More of the same was to follow, and the columns of the *Standard* soon groaned with recriminating attacks on Whigs. In adopting this style of journalism, Holden, who wrote almost all of the editorials in the *Standard*, was following common editorial practices.[15] Only the suddenness and shrillness of his thrust against the Whigs was surprising. Newspapers existed for an avowedly par-

14. Raleigh *Daily Standard*, August 25, 1868; Raleigh *Standard*, May 31, 1843.

15. *Ibid.*, June 7, 21, July 5, 1843. During his long tenure as proprietor and editor of the *Standard* Holden rarely permitted another person to write the political commentaries for the weekly or main edition of the newspaper. When absent, he assigned the task to a member of his staff or a local political associate. The words of the *Standard* editorials were literally the words of Holden. I have been careful to avoid attributing opinions in the *Standard* to Holden when it was clear, as during his infrequent absences from Raleigh, that he did not write the column. For his close attention to the editing of the newspaper, see Raleigh *Standard*, December 2, 1859, and the deposition of Mrs. L. V. Holden before a Wake County commissioner, March 12, 1891, in Holden Papers, DU.

tisan purpose. Indeed, much of the space in mid-nineteenth-century American newspapers was devoted to partisan political commentaries, not only from the pen of the editors but also from party activists who wrote long articles for the press or sent in speeches to be printed by their party newspaper organs. Holden knew that the *Standard*, which had suffered under the timid management of Loring, could not gain much attention unless it followed an aggressive editorial policy that gave no quarter to the opposition party and its newspapers, particularly those in Raleigh. The most effective tactic was to personalize the issues and portray opponents as haughty, evil conspirators against the public interest and republican institutions.[16]

The young editor early established himself as a master of devastating ridicule, virulent innuendo, eye-popping epithets, and biting sarcasm. By the 1850s he had no peer in North Carolina—and few in the United States—in the use of such editorial tactics. He frequently insisted, however, that his attacks on opponents were political and not personal, but the distinction was hardly real. Like other editors, he questioned the honesty and motives of his opponents. This style of recriminating journalism could have easily backfired, but in the hands of a clever practitioner like Holden, who, though possessing rough edges, was skilled in the use of the English language, it proved exceedingly effective. The targets of his editorial wrath replied in kind, principally through the columns of the leading Whig newspapers. But, except for the able Edward J. Hale of the Fayetteville *Observer*, they usually found themselves overmatched.

Holden also became skilled in demonstrating—and exaggerating—the differences between the Democrats and their Whig opponents. In the beginning Holden trumpeted the class differences between himself and the Whig "aristocrats." Although an appeal to the laboring class's distaste for privilege and aristocracy had been employed by earlier editors to discredit the opposition, he used it in a peculiarly personal way. He cited his "obscure ori-

---

16. Several recent accounts of antebellum American politics reveal the important partisan tactic of branding opposition leaders as enemies of republican government. See Michael F. Holt, *The Political Crisis of the 1850s* (New York, 1978), 5, 38, 244; Marc W. Kruman, *Parties and Politics in North Carolina, 1836–1865* (Baton Rouge, 1983), 5.

gins" and contrasted his struggle to succeed with the indolent life of the aristocracy, which he equated with the Whig leadership and not the slavocracy. He found no aristocrats in a Democratic wigwam, though in historical lore that party has become associated with the interests of the slaveholding class. Little significant correlation existed between slaveholding and party affiliation in pre–Civil War North Carolina. For leadership at all levels both parties naturally turned to men of education and property. These individuals usually held slaves, but not necessarily in large numbers; many of them, like Holden (who owned six slaves by 1850), had risen from the yeoman or lower classes to positions of influence in public affairs. Holden had no objection, as he said soon after assuming control of the *Standard*, to "wealth in its place. We delight to see a *good man* in the possession of it; for him it is a source of comfort, and he makes it a fountain of refreshment for the poor. But the mean rich man—heaven preserve us from his influence, and our country from the influence of his gold." [17]

He also disliked "pretensions of aristocracy," but this was a sentiment with which a true aristocrat could also agree. When he denounced "aristocrats" during the antebellum era, it normally was in an abstract or general way and associated with North Carolina Whiggery. Like many others, including Whigs, he had a special sympathy for the white working classes and wanted the door of opportunity to remain open for every white person, which was hardly a new idea in the Age of the Common Man. His appeal had a distinctly political purpose. It was designed to discredit the Whig leadership in a political culture that hated aristocratic pretensions and elitism. [18]

Whigs worried that Holden's vigorous campaign to associate their party with a state aristocracy would succeed among a populace that was ever alert to class discrimination. Instead of engaging Holden in a debate over which party better reflected the interests of the

17. See Raleigh *Standard*, June 7, 21, July 12, 1843, July 15, 1846; Kruman, *Parties and Politics in North Carolina*, 14–15. Five of Holden's slaves were females, one of whom was ninety years old; the youngest was an eight-year-old girl. Seventh Census of the United States, 1850, Slave Schedule, Raleigh, Wake County, North Carolina (on microfilm, NDAH).

18. Holden's surviving private correspondence is free of attacks on the aristocracy, and he twice married into families that could claim aristocratic ties. See Chapter III for an account of his family relations.

common people, Whig editors attempted to make "the little renegade editor of the *Standard*" the issue. Weston Gales of the Raleigh
Register denounced Holden for the "extraordinary audacity which
characterized his editorial calumnies" and acidly charged that in
his forays against the Whigs he did not have "the slightest pretensions to political truth and honesty." Edward J. Hale of the Fayetteville *Observer* sniffed that "people talk about a Mr. William W.
Holden in a very ugly manner hereabouts. They charge him with
having bartered his conscience for filthy lucre; of suddenly crossing
over to the enemy in broad day-light and belying his whole past
life. . . . No man of any party here regards or respects him." Many
North Carolinians "loathe him, as being diseased with a vile moral
leprosy, that has not left a single virtue unconsumed amid his thousand meannesses and vices."[19]

For almost two decades Hale and other leading Whig editors re-
lentlessly vilified Holden. In extreme moments they "appealed to
decency" for an end to the *Standard* editor's "unprincipled and
malignant assaults." Yet it is difficult to measure precisely how
bitter and serious were these editorial and political calumnies. In
an age when hyperbolic recrimination characterized the American
press, the exaggeration of the opposition's failings was fair game,
and ridicule and satire were the favorite weapons of the political
editor. Nevertheless, the battles between Holden and his Whig adversaries frequently went beyond the bounds of accepted practices
and became sordid examples of journalism gone awry at a time in
the history of the Republic when a dispassionate treatment of public issues was most needed.

Despite the vigor of Holden's attacks and his success in arousing
Whig ire, subscriptions to the *Standard* remained constant at about
eight hundred patrons during the first six months of his proprietor-
ship. Subscriptions among Democrats began to increase in late 1843
after Holden led a successful congressional campaign in his district
against a heavily favored Whig candidate. The hard-working Holden
also proved to be a good businessman, and as a "practical printer"
he understood the nuances of the newspaper guild better than most
editor-proprietors. In an age when the management of a newspaper

19. Raleigh *Register* July 7, August 4, 1843; Fayetteville *Observer*, quoted in
Clarence C. Norton, *The Democratic Party in Ante-Bellum North Carolina, 1835–
1861* (Chapel Hill, 1930), 25.

was frequently a short road to bankruptcy for an ambitious young man, Holden's close attention to the financial affairs of the *Standard* office helped to ensure his success. By 1845 *Standard* subscriptions had almost doubled, and Democratic editors and politicians throughout North Carolina read the newspaper and took their cues from it.[20] Local party newspapers frequently copied Holden's articles, indicating their source and praising the author.

Having gained the confidence of Democratic leaders, Holden in 1845 took stock of his situation and concluded that perhaps he had been overzealous in his early editorial tactics. He blamed his errors on youthful inexperience and promised his readers to atone for his mistakes through "industry and assiduity."[21] Although Holden failed to indicate what editorial changes he would make, it was already very clear that he would moderate his personal attacks on "Whig aristocrats" and focus on the state and national issues that divided the two parties. At the same time, he sought a more vigorous and unified state Democratic effort by encouraging the publication in the *Standard* of reports of local party meetings and letters from leaders at all levels. He knew that such a central role for the *Standard* would also increase his own influence in the party.

He focused his attention mainly on state issues and specifically those that promised to dislodge the Whigs from political power. Since 1836 Whigs had dominated the state, though their margin of victory at the polls was never large. Political stability characterized North Carolina elections during this period, as voters identified with one of the two parties and continued to support that party at the ballot box. To overcome the Whig advantage, Democratic leaders had to obtain a high turnout of party faithful and at the same time persuade a few thousand Whigs to switch their party allegiance. To do this, they needed state issues that could appeal to voters throughout North Carolina. In 1844 Holden chose the state debt question as the main domestic issue likely to cut into Whig strength. Most of the debt, which he claimed had reached "hundreds of thousands of dollars" by the mid-1840s, had been largely acquired in aid of the Wilmington and Raleigh and the Raleigh and

20. Holden, *Memoirs*, 97; Raleigh *Standard*, September 10, 1845. Not until 1848, however, did the newspaper make a profit. Raleigh *Standard*, August 25, 1868.

21. Raleigh *Standard*, September 10, 1845.

Gaston railroads. In his editorials Holden criticized the idea of state aid for internal improvements and cleverly indicated the financial burdens that Whig legislatures, in assisting these troubled companies, had imposed on the state and its taxpayers. He reminded North Carolinians that Democrats had traditionally opposed heavy public debts, which stood mainly to benefit corporations. Holden charged that Whigs had further schemes afoot, which if adopted would absorb all of the revenues of the state and would ultimately oppress the taxpayers. Even after the Whigs had retreated from their support of state aid for the railroads, Holden continued to denounce their extravagance and call for a return to "Democratic simplicity and economy."[22]

At the same time he raised the state debt issue, Holden launched a Democratic offensive to undermine Whig strength in the West. He contended that during their eight years in power, Whigs, despite their dependence on western votes, had done nothing for the region. "Guilford is as far west as many of them ever extend their vision, when benefits are to be conferred, but when votes are to be obtained they go to the other side of the western streams to rally their forces."[23] In the gubernatorial campaign of 1844, Holden joined with Senator William H. Haywood, Jr., to write and circulate anonymously a series of tracts entitled *Plain Thoughts for the West*. The purpose of the tracts was to discredit the Whigs in the area and promote Democrat Michael Hoke as the "western candidate" for governor. Holden in this case abandoned his practice of reprinting Democratic tracts in the *Standard*, since he knew that some of the party's promises to the West contained in the *Plain Thoughts* would offend eastern Democrats.[24] He grasped quite early the significance of sectional divisions in North Carolina and the need to reconcile Democratic political strategies with the interests and predilections of the people of each of the three regions (the West, the Piedmont, and the East or Coastal Plain).

22. Kruman, *Parties and Politics in North Carolina*, 27–29; Raleigh *Standard*, July 24, September 18, 1844, November 26, 1845, June 10, 1846; W. W. Holden to J. M. Bullock, June 10, 1846, in E. V. Howell Papers, NDAH.

23. Quoted in Thomas Edward Jeffrey, "The Second Party System in North Carolina, 1836–1860" (Ph.D. dissertation, Catholic University of America, 1976), 289.

24. Only one of these tracts has been found. It is reprinted in Hamilton and Williams (eds.), *Graham Papers*, II, 503–506.

Holden's western strategy did not succeed in 1844. Whig strength in the region declined in the election but not enough to defeat the party in that area or in the state. Whig William A. Graham won the governor's race, jolting Holden's hopes for an early Democratic return to power in the state. That same year a presidential contest occurred that changed the complexion of national politics and gave Holden and North Carolina Democrats an important new issue to use against their Whig opponents—territorial expansion.

II
Democratic Stalwart

The American desire to expand its borders was not new, but the effort of the John Tyler administration in 1843–1844 to annex Texas posed ominous difficulties for the nation. Not only would annexation raise the possibility of war with Mexico, which had never recognized Texan independence, but it would also threaten to revive the controversy over the expansion of slavery. Expansionist southerners, who were lodged mainly in the Democratic party, however, were determined to have Texas. Antislavery northerners, primarily Whigs, were just as determined to prevent it. They charged that the demand for Texas was a southern plot to extend slavery and increase the power of the slavocracy. Although Secretary of State John C. Calhoun suggested that the security of slavery was at stake in the annexation of Texas, most southern expansionists argued their case on national grounds, specifically the mission of the United States to establish its republican institutions in an area threatened by decadent Great Britain. In their desire for expansion they found enthusiastic allies in midwestern Democrats, whose principal interest was "the re-occupation of Oregon."[1]

On the eve of the 1844 presidential contest, Calhoun drew up an annexation treaty with Texas and sent it to the Senate for ratification. As the leading candidates for the presidential nomination of their parties, Henry Clay (Whig) and Martin Van Buren (Demo-

1. Glyndon G. Van Deusen, *The Jacksonian Era, 1828–1848* (New York, 1949), 177–82; Frederick Merk, *Manifest Destiny and Mission in American History: A Reinterpretation* (New York, 1963), 40–42.

crat) were expected to take a position on this important national issue. Both, however, sought to avoid the question. Soon after the signing of the treaty, Clay visited North Carolina in what became as much a Whig celebration of his greatness as a campaign trip. When he arrived in Raleigh for a six-day stay, thousands of Whigs, joined by many Democrats, greeted him with massive demonstrations.[2]

Not everyone expressed pleasure in Clay's visit. Holden and local Democratic leaders clearly saw a political setback for their party in the exuberant reception for the Whig hero. Ignoring the risk of being charged with inhospitality toward a prominent American, Holden attempted to bring Clay down from his pedestal and show North Carolinians how the Whig leader differed from them on crucial national issues. He especially sought to draw Clay out on the Texas issue. "We desire to know," he wrote in the *Standard*, "what are the sentiments of Mr. Clay in relation to it? Is he for or against annexation? We call upon his Whig friends here to have this question answered when he makes his speech in this city."[3]

Holden accompanied his query with his own ringing endorsement of annexation. He had not taken a position on the issue prior to the signing of the Texas annexation treaty, and he did so only after a public expression of support for ratification by the aging Andrew Jackson. Denying the northern Whig argument that the United States had no legal claim to the area, Holden contended that the Louisiana Purchase had given the country a perfect title to Texas, and British intrigue now made it necessary for America to "have Texas very soon, or lose her forever."[4]

Clay's speech on Capitol Square ignored the Texas issue and, for that matter, Holden's sniping. But while in Raleigh the Whig candidate wrote his famous letter to the *National Intelligencer* opposing annexation. What influence Holden's demands had upon Clay's decision to take a public stand against annexation is impossible to say. But we do know that while Clay was in town, he read the *Standard* and was concurrently pressed by North Carolina Whigs to respond to increasing public pressure for a statement on annexation.[5]

2. On Clay's North Carolina visit, see issues of the Raleigh *Register* for April, 1844, and the Raleigh *Standard*, April 10, 1844.
3. Raleigh *Standard*, April 10, 1844.
4. *Ibid.*
5. Raleigh *Daily Standard*, August 25, 1868.

Actually, during Clay's visit the *Standard* focused most of its attention on the Whig leader's American System and not the annexation issue. Holden repeatedly charged that Clay's economic program was "an imitation of the enormous corruption and oppressions of Great Britain." He also warned that the royal treatment Clay had received in Raleigh would lead, if he became president, to the trappings of monarchy and the consolidation of power in his hands.[6]

The Raleigh editor's outburst against Clay reveals more about the bitter partisan spirit in antebellum North Carolina and the republican suspicion of power than it does about Whig purposes. Each party repeatedly charged the other with being a threat to republican liberties. Whigs, with a stronger emphasis on order and harmony in society, argued that if Holden and the Democrats, or, as the Whigs preferred to call them, the "loco-focos," gained power, republican institutions and the rights of the people would be destroyed.[7] Overwhelmingly, North Carolinians feared power and the dissolution of the republican virtues that they associated with the Founding Fathers. Public spokesmen of both parties reflected this fear, and for political purposes they also exaggerated it. Holden was especially clever in the use of rhetoric and hyperbole to arouse fears regarding the exercise of arbitrary power by the opposition party.

Along with most Americans in 1844, Holden believed until the meeting of the national convention that Van Buren would be the party's candidate for president against Clay. Party loyalty required that he defend the Little Magician from Whig assaults. Even after the publication of Van Buren's March 27 letter to the Washington *Globe* opposing the immediate annexation of Texas, he maintained his public pose of confidence in Van Buren, contrasting the former president's stand with Clay's unequivocal opposition to expansion. "Clay is opposed to annexation either immediately or hereafter," Holden argued, "whilst Mr. Van Buren, though opposed to it as an

6. Raleigh *Standard,* April 17, 24, 1844.
7. Marc W. Kruman, *Parties and Politics in North Carolina, 1836–1865* (Baton Rouge, 1983), 3–6. John Mayfield, in his *Rehearsal for Republicanism: Free Soil and the Politics of Antislavery* (Port Washington, N.Y., 1980), 42, describes the Whig emphasis on order and harmony as crucial to the preservation of republican institutions. A sampling of the issues of the Raleigh *Register* for the mid-1840s bears out this contention.

immediate step, is nevertheless in favor of it, provided the voice of the people should clearly call for it, and the grounds of difficulty between Mexico and Texas should, in the mean time, be fairly surmounted or removed." Van Buren, Holden claimed, would never tolerate a British dependency in Texas, whereas Clay would.[8]

Holden obviously was disappointed with Van Buren's equivocation on Texas. But like Van Buren, he did not want to see the issue "break up and destroy the democratic party . . . stir up strife and inappeasable [sic] discontent among members of the Union, or impair the value or terminate the existence of the Union itself." If the annexation of Texas led to disunion, "better had it been for us all if Texas had been smitten by the hand of Providence into a barren and neglected desert." Four months later the state Democratic executive committee expressed a similar sentiment when it published a letter—perhaps written by Holden—reaffirming the party's support of annexation but not at the expense of the Union.[9]

Meanwhile, the national Democratic convention abandoned Van Buren and selected James K. Polk of Tennessee to run on a platform calling for the "re-annexation" of Texas and the "re-occupation" of Oregon. Holden could not conceal his relief and "inexpressible pleasure" at the turn of events. "Our delegates left us amid darkness," he exclaimed. "They have come back in light, TEXAS and POLK—Democratic principles and action will now be the words, until the standard of democracy shall float in triumph from the national battlements."[10]

Despite strong support in North Carolina for the Democratic platform on expansion, Whigs were still the dominant party in the state. Holden, however, galvanized Democrats into a vigorous campaign against "the profligate demagogue," Clay, that almost carried North Carolina for Polk in November. When the national returns indicated a victory for the party of Jackson, Raleigh Democrats, including Holden, surged into the streets in a wild celebration, punctuated with huzzahs for Polk, Texas, and Oregon.[11] The spirit of Manifest Destiny had triumphed, and young Holden was thrilled

8. Raleigh *Standard*, May 8, 1844.
9. *Ibid.*; Kruman, *Parties and Politics in North Carolina*, 111.
10. Raleigh *Standard*, June 5, 1844.
11. W. W. Holden to David S. Reid, October 30, 1844, in David S. Reid Papers, NDAH; Raleigh *Standard*, November 13, 20, 1844.

to be a part of it. In the process, he had gained a reputation as a relentless and hard-hitting combatant who could be expected to play an important role in future party politics in North Carolina. Although only twenty-six years of age, Holden had emerged as the state party's leading propagandist and an important Democratic strategist at the capital.

Historians have written that the desire for the expansion of slavery underlay the Manifest Destiny impulse of the South in the mid-1840s.[12] But if this were true of Holden, it was carefully concealed. In justifying expansion, Holden ignored the issue of slavery, which Calhoun and his antislavery antagonists of the North had moved to the forefront of the Texas debate. Not until late 1846—several months after the Wilmot Proviso had ignited in Congress the controversy over slavery in the territories to be gained from Mexico—did he pay much attention to the antislavery movement or the issue of slavery expansion. His support for American expansion, with or without slavery, can also be seen in his insistence after Polk's inauguration that the Democratic party honor its pledge to annex Oregon as well as Texas. When in 1845 the Raleigh *Register* and state Whig leaders demanded that Polk avoid an adventurous Oregon policy that could erupt into war with Great Britain, Holden lashed out at "the Federalists and their British allies" and called for a policy that would provide "full security to Oregon," an area uncongenial to slavery. He carefully avoided, however, the question of Oregon's territorial limits, since the Polk administration had not defined the area.[13]

The Whig charge that "our people are dangerously influenced by a love of conquest" especially offended Holden. He argued that under the Constitution "it is impossible" for the republic to "extend its boundaries by force," though he did not say how the Constitution could prevent national aggression. In typical Manifest Destiny fashion he contended that the new territories were "attracted to [the United States] by its remarkable adaptation to the wants of mankind, and by its wise and liberal forms of government. Not by the sword of conquest does it make its way, but by the spirit of freedom pervading all its parts, and by that fraternal affection

12. See, for example, Charles S. Sydnor, *The Development of Southern Sectionalism, 1819–1848* (Baton Rouge, 1948), 321–22.
13. Raleigh *Standard*, November 19, 1845.

which unites and binds together common sympathies and common hopes."[14]

A few months later Holden supported the American declaration of war against Mexico with a similar high-sounding rationalization. North Carolina "will not be backward now," he exclaimed, "when the soil of our Republic is invaded and the blood of our brave defenders is flowing upon the banks of the Del Norte." The outpouring of volunteers, he insisted, was "the voice of a free people" girding to fight the "military aristocracy" of Mexico. He referred to those Whigs who opposed the war as "Tories" and declared that any "man who refuses to defend Texas, now that she is a member of the Union, *is* a foe to the Union of the States."[15]

North Carolina Whigs, however, continued to oppose "Mr. Polk's War," though they advocated full support for American troops in the field. Holden quickly sensed that most North Carolinians either agreed with the Whig position on the war or did not want the issue to intrude into state politics. In the 1846 gubernatorial campaign, Holden, after securing the Democratic nomination for his friend James B. Shepard, turned his party's attention away from the Mexican War issue and focused the Democratic campaign on the old economic and financial issues separating Whigs and Democrats. No matter, the Whigs won again, this time by a larger margin than before. Instead of blaming himself and other Democratic leaders for the party's setback, a frustrated Holden lashed out at the Whigs for their "slanders and falsehoods" in the campaign, charging that they had deliberately poisoned the minds of the people against their true interests. Worse still, he declared that the election meant the continued ascendancy of unprincipled Whig politicians who "violate the law and trample on the Constitution whenever it suits their unhallowed purposes."[16]

After the bitter 1846 contest the goal of destroying the Whig hegemony in North Carolina consumed Holden's enormous energies. His contacts with local Democratic leaders increased, not only

14. *Ibid.*
15. *Ibid.*, May 27, June 10, 1846.
16. Kruman, *Parties and Politics in North Carolina*, 112–13; W. W. Holden to David S. Reid, March 20, 1846, in Reid Papers; Raleigh *Standard*, June–July, *passim*, August 19, 1846; W. W. Holden to J. M. Bullock, June 10, 1846, in E. V. Howell Papers, NDAH.

through the columns of the *Standard* but also by means of private correspondence and one-to-one talks in Raleigh. He later claimed that he sometimes wrote a hundred letters a week to Democratic friends.

Holden's grasp for party leadership came at an opportune time. The second American party system was relatively new and still dependent largely on grass-roots leadership, while leadership at the state level was rather loose and informal. This was especially true of North Carolina because of its overwhelmingly rural character, which made communications difficult and accentuated localism (only 2.4 percent of the population lived in towns in 1850; none of these towns had a population of more than ten thousand). Furthermore, the interior of the state before the emergence of the railroads was virtually isolated from the political center at Raleigh. Since the Whigs had long controlled the state government and had sponsored state economic measures that appealed to interior residents, they managed to achieve a greater degree of party unity than the Democrats, whose state leadership was weak until the rise of Holden. By the late 1840s local Democratic politicians, who had suffered successive humiliating defeats at the hands of the Whigs, were anxious to follow the lead of anyone who offered hope for victory in the state elections. Holden shrewdly realized the opportunity for political leadership and seized it.

By the time of the 1848 elections Holden had assumed direction of the state Democratic party, though his control was rather tenuous and would likely disintegrate if the party continued to lose at the polls. In the 1848 state Democratic convention his influence was clearly paramount. He wrote the party's platform, which emphasized Democratic complaints against the state Whig administration but also condemned the Wilmot Proviso, though Holden had not yet fully realized how to use the slavery issue in state political contests. He also secured the nomination for governor of Congressman David S. Reid of Rockingham County.[17]

Holden immediately urged Reid to come to Raleigh in order

17. William W. Holden, *Memoirs of W. W. Holden* (Durham, 1911), 3; Clarence C. Norton, *The Democratic Party in Ante-Bellum North Carolina, 1835–1861* (Chapel Hill, 1930), 154; W. W. Holden to David S. Reid, April 19, 1848, in Reid Papers.

to plan a vigorous stump-speaking canvass of the state.[18] A few days later he received a startling letter from Reid indicating that because of poor health and his inability to campaign extensively, he probably would decline the nomination. A dumbfounded Holden rushed a message to Reid's home, pleading with him to come to Raleigh and discuss the matter. Reid consented to the meeting, and when he arrived, he was whisked into a room in the Guion Hotel where the *Standard* editor and several local politicos persuaded him to accept the nomination. His acceptance carried with it the unsettling demand that he be permitted to campaign on a platform calling for the elimination of the fifty-acre property qualification for voters in state senatorial elections. Holden was not philosophically opposed to the principle of "equal suffrage," as Democrats called the proposal. But along with other Democrats in the Guion meeting, he feared that by raising the issue, Democrats risked defeat in the election. Support for equal suffrage, Holden knew, might injure the party in the conservative East. He also understood that a greater danger was the Democratic embarrassment and confusion that would follow Reid's rejection of the nomination. With this in mind, Holden and his Democratic associates accepted Reid's terms, pledged their hearty support to him and equal suffrage, and sent him east to confront Charles Manly, the Whig nominee.[19]

Reid found Manly at New Bern. In the first joint debate the Democratic candidate called for a constitutional amendment ending the property qualification for voting in state senatorial elections. Surprised by Reid's proposal, Manly instinctively pronounced the principle of equal suffrage a revolutionary doctrine. Almost immediately the issue ballooned in importance, heartening Democrats who had been demoralized by repeated Whig victories and causing Manly supporters to squirm lest they lose key support among equalitarian westerners.[20]

18. W. W. Holden to David S. Reid, April 19, 1848, in Reid Papers.

19. Holden's reminiscence of the events surrounding Reid's acceptance of the nomination (Holden, *Memoirs*, 3–5) differs somewhat from the contemporary *Standard* reports (Raleigh *Standard*, May 3, 10, 1848) and from Reid's later explanation (Raleigh *Standard*, June 28, 1850). My account is pieced together from all three sources.

20. Raleigh *Standard*, May 17, 1848; Raleigh *Register*, May 20, 1848; W. W. Holden to David S. Reid, June 23, 1848, in Reid Papers.

As he had promised, Holden vigorously promoted the equal-suffrage campaign. One week after Reid had hurled his thunderbolt at Manly, Holden announced in the *Standard* that "we have always thought that there ought to be no distinction between the voters in this State for the Senate and the Commons." He justified his position on the ground that property interests had no special claim to be represented in a republican government. "In all free Governments," he argued, "mind is the test of merit, not property." Those with intellectual ability should "hold chief sway in the public councils." Nevertheless, property "is entitled to protection; and this protection it will always have, for it is only one among many interests in the State, and the people of the State, the original source of all power, will always see to it that no one class is oppressed or injured for the benefit of others."[21]

Manly persisted in his attack on equal suffrage, and he was soon joined by his party's state newspaper organ. The Raleigh *Register* branded the proposal "rank agrarianism," which to the mid-nineteenth-century mind meant an attack on property rights. The paper also called equal suffrage "a species of miserable political clap-trap" and a "demagogical cry" to "array the poor against the rich." The *Register* editor and other Whigs seemed sincerely to believe that the adoption of equal suffrage would be the first step toward the destruction of the constitutional rights of individuals and would ultimately lead to social leveling or "agrarianism." Holden, however, repeatedly denied that its success would open the floodgates of radicalism. The Reid proposal, he insisted, was not designed "to 'level' down the landed interests" or to encourage class conflict; its purpose was simply "to establish equality in political rights among free white men."[22]

Because of the excitement generated by the suffrage issue, Holden fully expected his party to win the election. He should have realized that, as Marc Kruman has pointed out, in a state like North Carolina, where party divisions were bitter and long-standing, "no election served as a referendum on any particular issue." It was primarily "a voter's identification with his party [that] determined the

21. Raleigh *Standard,* May 17, 1848.
22. Raleigh *Register,* May 20, 27, 1848; Raleigh *Standard,* June 14, 21, 1848. For a good account and analysis of the Whig reaction to the equal-suffrage proposal, see Kruman, *Parties and Politics in North Carolina,* 87–89.

way he voted."[23] Other issues, such as state aid for internal improvements, which Whigs but not Democrats supported, also had
an influence on the 1848 election. Although each party charged the
other with having abolitionist friends in high places and "Wilmot
Provisoists" on the national ticket, the emerging slavery controversy
did not cause voters in 1848 to change their political allegiances.

Following traditional voting patterns, Manly won the election.
His victory was a narrow one, a difference of only 854 votes of
84,218 cast. The election results made it clear to Holden that, despite the popularity of the equal-suffrage issue, Democratic opposition to state aid for internal improvements hung like an albatross
around the neck of the party. This was especially true in the Piedmont and the West, areas that also exhibited strong sympathy for
the principle of equal suffrage. Democrats, he concluded, could not
break the hold of the Whigs on these areas unless the party abandoned its negative position on railroad development.

On November 8, 1848, Holden astonished many Democrats by
coming out in favor of state aid for railroad development. Actually,
he had never opposed railroad construction or even local and state
aid to finance it. But during the mid-1840s he had criticized Whig
extravagance and mismanagement in aiding the troubled Raleigh
and Gaston Railroad. At the time he had insisted that "we are not
ourselves hostile to [railroad] improvement, prudently conducted.
But we are opposed to any increase of our State Debt" until "the
existing Rail Road debt be paid off first." As early as 1844 he was
willing, at least in principle, to support aid to any railroad in which
the state owned stock and shared in the management and profits.[24]

Despite his desire to rid the Democratic party of its opposition to
internal improvements and advance the party's chances in 1850,
Holden's motive in calling for such projects was not merely political. Like other North Carolinians, he resented the Rip Van Winkle
image of the state as backward and economically stagnant. "Is it
not high time that we had all waked up to the importance of doing

23. W. W. Holden to David S. Reid, June 23, 1848, in Reid Papers; Marc W.
Kruman, "Parties and Politics in North Carolina, 1846–1865" (Ph.D. dissertation, Yale University, 1978), 124.

24. Raleigh *Standard*, September 18, 1844, October 1, 22, 1845, November 8,
1848; Thomas E. Jeffrey, "Internal Improvements and Political Parties in Antebellum North Carolina, 1836–1860," *NCHR*, LV (1978), 132n.

something for North Carolina, in the way of Internal Improvements?" he asked. "Party spirit and party interests have nothing to do with this work." The General Assembly, he insisted, must act before the state fell too far behind other states in the development of transportation for the interior. He was shocked by the migration of North Carolinians to the more fertile lands of the Deep South and argued that the only way to reverse the trend before the state suffered irreparable economic loss was for the legislature to initiate "a bold, a general, and a vigorous system of Internal Improvements."[25]

Holden at first left the specific plans for the system to those knowledgeable in such matters. But it soon became clear that he had a few ambitious projects of his own to advance. The young editor's program entailed state involvement in the construction and control of a railroad from Goldsboro on the Wilmington and Raleigh Railroad to Charlotte and also the completion of two lengthy turnpikes, one from Salisbury to the Georgia line and the other, a plank road, from Fayetteville to Salisbury. Holden was especially interested in the construction of the Goldsboro to Charlotte trunk line, which became known as the North Carolina Railroad.[26] The completion of this road, via Raleigh, Greensboro, and Salisbury, would dramatically boost the Piedmont economy, give interior communities easy access to the sea, and herald future railroad construction in the West.

The showdown for the proposed North Carolina Railroad occurred during the General Assembly session of 1848–1849. Holden realized that some Democratic support was essential for the success of a bill chartering the railroad and subscribing, on the part of the state, two million dollars of the three million dollars of the company's capital stock. Under such an arrangement, the state would assume a controlling interest in the road, as well as in the turnpikes that were simultaneously advanced to gain logrolling support for the railroad. This plan of state control was consistent with Holden's earlier position regarding public assistance for railroad development. In an extremely close vote, in which twenty-three Democrats abandoned their traditional party position on internal improve-

25. Raleigh *Standard*, November 8, 1848.
26. *Ibid.*, January 24, 31, 1849.

ments, the North Carolina Railroad bill was enacted. Holden's advocacy of what he termed "the greatest measure which has ever received the legislative sanction of North Carolina," though probably not decisive in every case, had a significant influence in the voting of these Democrats. The Raleigh editor also brought along with him the support of eight of the eleven major Democratic newspapers in the state.[27]

Democratic opponents of internal improvements, however, lashed out at Holden's political "apostasy" on the issue. Although stunned by the criticism, the Raleigh editor, instead of retreating, became even more determined in his advocacy of internal improvements. He refrained, however, from attacking antirailroad Democrats, because he feared that such criticism would permanently alienate them from the party. As the state election of 1850 approached, he began to play down the railroad issue in order to avoid a Democratic division that could destroy the gains achieved by the equal-suffrage issue. Some damage, however, had already been done. But when the state Democratic convention met, Holden rallied sufficient support to keep Democratic railroad opponents at bay and prevent the adoption of a platform denouncing state aid for internal improvements.[28]

An additional reason existed for his desire to minimize the railroad issue: his candidate for governor, David S. Reid, was an opponent of the North Carolina Railroad. The Democratic wire-puller believed that Reid, who came close to victory in 1848, could win in 1850 on a platform emphasizing "State Reform," which included not only equal suffrage but also the popular election of judges. But three weeks before the Democratic convention met, Reid wrote Holden that because of the intraparty criticism he had received as a result of his opposition to the North Carolina Railroad and to the proposed Nashville convention on southern rights, he would not further divide the party by running for governor.[29]

27. *Ibid.*, January 31, February 14, 1849; Cecil K. Brown, *A State Movement in Railroad Development: The Story of North Carolina's First Effort to Establish an East and West Trunk Line Railroad* (Chapel Hill, 1928), 69. The trunk-line bills were also enacted.
28. Raleigh *Standard*, February–March, 1849; Kruman, *Parties and Politics in North Carolina*, 70–71.
29. Norton, *The Democratic Party in Ante-Bellum North Carolina*, 157–58.

His best-laid plans for a Democratic victory in 1850 in jeopardy, Holden pleaded with Reid to reconsider his decision. He assured Reid that the railroad issue would not damage his candidacy among those Democrats like himself who supported state aid for internal improvements. Railroad Democrats, Holden cleverly argued, understood his position on the North Carolina Railroad, and as governor he could not injure them, since they "have nothing further to ask in the way of appropriations. . . . Besides, being for the Road, I have a right to require them by every honorable consideration, to sustain you. They will do it." Regarding the Nashville convention issue, he informed Reid that it "is a dead question," though he himself had supported the movement. "It would be madness to make either the Central Road or the Nashville Convention a test. I have never done so; but directly the contrary."[30]

Holden confidently told Reid that Governor Manly, who was expected to run for reelection, could be defeated. "For the last two months I have carefully kept back from the Standard all evidences of Manly's unpopularity, in the hope that he would be again the candidate; there is now no doubt that he will be; and I have all these evidences filed away, to be used as soon as he is nominated." Holden reported to Reid that "the universal opinion of our friends" throughout the state was that he could defeat the governor; even "Whigs have told me that you would certainly beat Manly. . . . So far as I am concerned, I am for you against the world; and if you consent to run, I will omit neither expense, nor labor, nor pains, so far as they go, to insure your success." Holden assured Reid that with him heading the ticket Democrats for the first time in fourteen years could go confidently into the campaign with an assurance of victory. "What a honor for a young man to redeem poor old Whig-ridden North Carolina," Holden exhorted Reid in an effort to induce him to become the party's standard-bearer.[31]

When he did not receive an answer, Holden, on the day before the meeting of the Democratic convention, published Reid's letter declining the nomination. But he advised the delegates to make a leap of faith and nominate Reid anyway on a "State Reform" platform that skirted the issues dividing the party, a recommendation

30. W. W. Holden to David S. Reid, June 1, 1850, in Reid Papers.
31. *Ibid.*

that the convention followed. A few days later news arrived in Raleigh that Reid had accepted the nomination.[32] For Holden the last piece was now in place for a hard-hitting campaign that he believed would bring Democrats to power in North Carolina.

As before, Holden from the *Standard* office on Fayetteville Street directed the Democratic canvass. He sent numerous letters of advice to stalwarts in the field and frequently consulted with them when they visited Raleigh. Through the columns of his newspaper he provided campaign information and inspiration to Democratic workers. True to his promise to Reid, Holden published the material that he had "filed away" on Governor Manly and began to issue the *Standard* twice a week, evidently at a financial loss. The campaign focused on Reid's support of equal suffrage and Manly's continued opposition to it. Manly soon saw that sentiment, even among Whig editors, was running against him on the issue, and in a speech at Wentworth he announced that he would support equal suffrage provided it was accompanied by a change from the federal basis of representation in the House of Commons to one based solely on the white population. The federal basis permitted counties to count three-fifths of their slaves for representative purposes. Easterners, with the heaviest concentration of blacks, were certain to oppose such a change, since they stood to lose political power by it. Many westerners, though supporting an end to the federal basis, saw Manly's move as a desperate political ploy to undercut equal suffrage.[33]

Seizing upon another Manly mistake, Holden went for the Whig candidate's jugular vein. THE FACT IS SO! Holden exclaimed in the *Standard*. The white basis of representation, "the very measure [Manly] opposed and deprecated two years since, and which he falsely charged to be a part of Equal Suffrage, HE NOW COMES

32. Raleigh *Standard*, June 12, July 3, 1850.
33. Norton, *The Democratic Party in Ante-Bellum North Carolina*, 163; W. W. Holden to David S. Reid, July 7, 1850, in Reid Papers; W. W. Holden to Weldon N. Edwards, July 15, 1850, in Katherine C. P. Conway Papers, NDAH. Actually, Manly raised the issue as a hypothetical proposal designed to show that if Democrats were really sincere in their declaration of support for democratic reform, they would advocate the white basis, which would provide a meaningful redistribution of political power and not the facade that equal suffrage seemed to offer. Manly supported neither the white basis nor equal suffrage. Kruman, *Parties and Politics in North Carolina*, 93.

OUT FOR AND ADVOCATES, hoping thereby to retrieve his fallen fortunes in the Western counties, and thus demagogue himself a second time into the office of Governor!" Jubilantly, he wrote Reid that "Manly's opposition to the Federal basis falls like a bomb shell in the middle and East" and predicted that Democratic success in the election was inevitable. He encouraged Reid to "give it to him" because "a baser demagogue than Charles Manly never lived."[34]

Simultaneous with the excitement generated by Manly's "bomb shell," the slavery issue assumed major importance for the first time in a North Carolina political contest. To be sure, both state political parties had agreed all along that slavery must be defended from the strident assaults of antislavery "fanatics." Each party also had tried to portray the other as weak on southern rights and submissive to the leadership of its northern wing, which presumably was antislavery. By the sectional crisis of 1849–1850 Holden had emerged as the leading defender of southern rights in the state, with his skill in the use of innuendo and hyperbole to discredit Whigs on the slavery question. Despite his use of the issue against the Whigs, Holden fundamentally did not see the slavery controversy as a matter for political division. He perceived the defense of the South as also a defense of the Union, a cause that, he believed, transcended party politics. But predictably for this rigidly partisan editor, he quickly discovered that national Democratic leaders were more sympathetic to southern interests than northern Whigs and that state Democrats were more alert to antislavery plotting than their Whig counterparts.

As the storm clouds gathered in 1849 over the question of slavery in the Mexican cession, Holden devoted more and more attention to sectional issues. Both publicly and privately he castigated North Carolina Whigs for their presumed indifference to the danger posed by northern antislavery efforts to deny the South its rights in the territories. The exclusion of slavery from the common territories, as the Wilmot Proviso proposed, exceeded the authority of Congress and violated the equality of the states established by the Constitution, he asserted in the *Standard*. The antislavery forces,

34. Raleigh *Standard*, July 10, 13, 17, 1850; W. W. Holden to David S. Reid, July 7, 10, 1850, in Reid Papers.

Holden charged, planned for the Wilmot Proviso to be the foot in the door for a campaign against the institution in the South. "They intend to agitate, and to pursue a system of measures calculated and designed to abolish Slavery throughout the United States." Those "miserable fanatics" were the real enemies of the Union, and the Republic could only be preserved by standing firm and united against them, he maintained. North Carolina Whigs, by advocating compromise, were preparing the minds of the people for the Wilmot Proviso, he told a friend. "What baseness, what humiliation," Holden stormed. "What treachery and deception! As a just God lives and disposes of the affairs of nations, as the American people possess common sense and reason, to say nothing of common honesty, such a course of policy must and will be blasted."[35]

When the slavery controversy in Congress threatened the Union in early 1850, Holden called for a united southern front in the crisis. He urged the dispatch of state representatives to the Calhoun-inspired southern convention that would assemble in Nashville in June for the purpose of developing a plan of resistance. The Nashville convention, Holden declared, "is the only course, in this emergency, to preserve the Union and to save the South from accumulated aggression and insult." The North Carolina editor, however, still demanded that Congress settle the crisis, implying that it should do so before the Nashville convention met.[36]

Despite his support for the Nashville convention, Holden was not a southern fire-eater of the Calhoun school. He found much in Calhoun to admire; when he died in March, Holden wrote a poem eulogizing him. He also owed a great deal to the South Carolinian's elaborate arguments in defense of southern rights, though he made no attribution to him. But in actuality Holden, unlike Calhoun and his radical followers, was prepared to accept a compromise on the slavery issue, even to the extent of acquiescing in California's admission to the Union as a free state, which Calhoun maintained would be sufficient cause for the South to leave the Union.[37] Also,

35. Raleigh *Standard,* May 23, June 20, August 15, 22, September 12, 1849; W. W. Holden to Henry T. Clark, June 21, 1849, in Henry T. Clark Papers, DU.
36. Raleigh *Standard,* February 6, 27, 1850.
37. *Ibid.,* February 20, 1850. For the view of the Calhounites and the division among southern Democrats, see William J. Cooper, *The South and the Politics of Slavery, 1828–1854* (Baton Rouge, 1978), 287–88, 296–97, and David M. Pot-

unlike Calhoun, who believed that political parties were a danger to southern well-being, Holden saw the Democratic party as the best hope for the preservation of southern rights and the Union. This conviction on Holden's part became stronger as the 1850s progressed and Democratic ascendancy in both Washington and Raleigh became a reality.

As news of the compromise effort led by Henry Clay reached Raleigh in February, 1850, Holden began to disassociate himself from the southern-rights extremists. He applauded Daniel Webster's conciliatory March 7 address as "statesmanlike in a high degree," and he expressed general approval of Calhoun's brooding address to the Senate, which, however, did not directly respond to Clay's compromise resolutions. But Holden also found reason to criticize Calhoun's speech. "Mr. Calhoun attaches too much importance to 'the equilibrium' of power between the sections," he wrote, "and we regard his allusion to an amendment of the Constitution [creating a dual sectional executive] as unfortunate. . . . The people of the South have always contended for the Constitution as it is fairly, equitably, and honestly administered. They will not abandon this ground." [38]

It was at this point that the sectional controversy became important in the 1850 gubernatorial contest. The Whig press charged that North Carolina Democrats, led by Holden, were plotting secession. The Raleigh *Register* likened the Nashville convention to the discredited Hartford convention of 1814 and charged that if the Democrats prevailed in the election, they would take North Carolina out of the Union despite the fact that Reid, their gubernatorial candidate, opposed the Nashville meeting.[39] Holden could ignore the Whig attacks, but Democratic division on the issue, as well as strong evidence that a substantial majority of North Carolinians disapproved of the southern rights convention (the legislature rejected a proposal to send a state delegation to Nashville), caused him to abandon his support for it. As previously indicated,

ter, *The Impending Crisis, 1848–1861*, completed and edited by Don E. Fehrenbacher (New York, 1976), 100–101, 104–105.

38. Raleigh *Standard*, March 13, 1850. See also the issue of May 22, 1850.

39. For the North Carolina reaction to the Nashville convention, see Kruman, *Parties and Politics in North Carolina*, 126–27.

Holden at the time of the state Democratic convention assured Reid that the question of the Nashville convention was a dead issue. He told the Democratic candidate that "we are all for the Union."[40]

On the defensive, Holden during the 1850 campaign sought to demonstrate his devotion to the Union by carrying a memorable Jacksonian slogan on the masthead of the *Standard*: "The Constitution and the Union of the States—They must be preserved." He also launched a counterattack against the Whigs. Ignoring Clay's compromise proposal regarding slavery in the New Mexico Territory, he attacked Whig President Zachary Taylor for his willingness to exclude the institution from the area. He charged that Whig congressmen who supported Taylor, like Edward Stanly of New Bern, were tools of northern antislavery interests and friends of Senator William H. Seward, who in the minds of many North Carolinians was the evil genius behind the president. When Taylor died in July and was succeeded by Millard Fillmore, Holden immediately shifted his attack to the new president, whom he facilely labeled an abolitionist. In catering to Fillmore, Holden charged, Governor Manly and state Whigs were "giving aid and comfort to Abolitionists." Conveniently overlooking his own willingness to accept the compromise settlement, he denounced Manly for presumably favoring the admission of California as a free state, and he insinuated that the governor's position on this issue was connected to his advocacy of the white basis of apportionment in the House of Commons. "It was not enough for him to strike at the basis of representation in the Legislature, but he must [also] deliberately propose to yield up the common Territories to the enemies of Southern rights!"[41]

How much effect the slavery issue had on the election is difficult to gauge. In a state where most elections during the 1840s and early 1850s were close, Reid swept to victory by a margin of 3,345 votes, and fellow Democrats gained a slim majority in the General Assembly. Some Whig voters probably voted for Democratic candidates because of the charge that Manly and state Whig leaders were

40. W. W. Holden to David S. Reid, June 1, 1850, in Reid Papers.
41. Raleigh *Standard*, July 27, 31, 1850; W. W. Holden to David S. Reid, June 1, 7, 10, 1850, in Reid Papers.

soft on southern rights. But on the other hand the spirit of national conciliation was strong when the election was held on August 1, and this fact worked to the advantage of the Whigs, since North Carolinians correctly perceived them as friends of compromise who at the same time were devoted to southern rights. Furthermore, Holden's charge that the new president was an abolitionist had little foundation in fact and was easily brushed aside when Fillmore announced his wholehearted support of the sectional settlement. The president's appointment of four southerners, including William A. Graham, to his seven-member cabinet also helped defuse the slavery issue in the contest.[42]

Holden himself did not expect his party to gain many Whig votes by his campaign of innuendo and exaggerated charges. But as he told Reid, the stabbing accusations "must produce lukewarmness in the Whig ranks . . . which cannot fail to diminish Manly's vote." Many Whigs, he said, would remain at home rather than vote for either candidate. The reduction in the Whig strength from the 1848 election was only five hundred votes, suggesting that the Holden strategy failed to persuade Whigs to go fishing on election day. The main reason for the Whig defeat was the large turnout of non-Whig voters who had previously remained away from the polls but were now aroused to participate by the equal-suffrage campaign and Manly's perceived failures. State issues and personalities, as before, determined the election of 1850, despite the seriousness of the slavery controversy and the vigorous efforts of both parties to portray the other as the enemy of the South and the Union.[43]

After seven years of trying, Holden had finally led his party to victory in North Carolina. Although only thirty-one years of age in 1850, his successful management of the Reid campaign, including the delicate handling of the candidate himself, revealed a masterful political leader at work. His quiet and effective behind-the-scenes direction of the Democratic campaign contrasted with his grow-

42. See Cooper, *The South and the Politics of Slavery*, 314–15, for the popular effect of Fillmore's policies upon the South.
43. W. W. Holden to David S. Reid, June 1, 1850, in Reid Papers. On the decisiveness of North Carolina issues in the election, see James Graham to William A. Graham, August 10, 1850, and Charles L. Hinton to William A. Graham, August 22, 1850, both in J. G. de Roulhac Hamilton and Max R. Williams (eds.), *The Papers of William Alexander Graham* (7 vols. to date; Raleigh, 1957–), III, 354, 365–66, and Holden to Reid, July 19, 24, 1850, in Reid Papers.

ing reputation as a dictatorial party leader. Despite his strong southern-rights sentiments and his belief that some North Carolina Whigs had allied themselves with northern antislavery "traitors," Holden understood the limitations of the sectional issue in a state where the overwhelming majority of the people preferred moderation and compromise to sectional excitement and possible disunion. In 1850 he shrewdly concluded that North Carolina Democrats should emphasize their devotion to the Union while maintaining their support for southern rights and castigating Whigs for their presumed infidelities. The political necessity for such an approach also influenced his private view that support for the Union should take precedence over southern rights, though there was a point in defense of the Union that neither Holden nor most North Carolinians would go beyond. That point had not been reached in 1850.

In leading the Democrats to victory, Holden saw himself as the facilitator of the party's success rather than its kingpin. He seemed genuinely more gratified with the "glorious and unprecedented" triumph of the party over "Federalism" than with his own emergence as a powerful political leader, though he obviously basked in the accolades of the faithful for his leading role in the party's success. "We have the high and rare gratification of announcing to the Democracy everywhere," he exulted as the 1850 election returns decreed victory, "that we have a DEMOCRATIC GOVERNOR and a DEMOCRATIC LEGISLATURE; and that North Carolina is at last completely and gloriously redeemed."[44] But the significance of that redemption would not prove to be as great as Holden believed.

44. W. W. Holden to David S. Reid, August 7, 1850, Asa Biggs to David S. Reid, August 23, 1850, both in Reid Papers; Raleigh *Standard*, August 7, 1850.

III
Champion of
Southern Rights

As soon as the 1850 election was over, Holden turned his attention to the compromise on slavery that was nearing approval in Congress. No longer bound by the restraints imposed by the state campaign, and incensed by the glowing Whig defense of the compromise, he lashed out at Senator George E. Badger and other North Carolina Whig leaders, who, he repeatedly charged, were willing to submit to antislavery aggression against the South. A Badger speech in the Senate admitting in principle the authority of Congress to prohibit slavery in the territories was branded by Holden as "the very quintessence of craven submission and federal consolidation." The Whig senator's "theory of government is monstrous and most dangerous," Holden exclaimed, and if logically applied would convert the states into mere counties of the federal government. As his Whig defenders were quick to indicate, Badger supported slavery. But that was not the point, Holden said, since on the preservation of slavery "we all agree." He told his readers that the issue of "slavery in the States furnishes no test of Abolitionism, for [Joshua] Giddings and [John P.] Hale profess to respect it, and say they will stand by it. Abolitionism seeks, by act of Congress, to circumscribe Slavery and starve it out; Mr. Badger voluntarily admits the power, but begs Congress not to exercise it." In essence, Badger "yields advantage after advantage, and draws the enemy still closer on the main works, with the vain hope of saving the magazine after the fire shall have reached it."[1]

1. Raleigh *Standard*, August 7, 28, September 25, 1850.

When the compromise was enacted, Holden grudgingly and bitterly yielded an advantage to the "enemy" rather than see the Union destroyed. "The storm has been lulled," he announced, "but a great wrong has been afflicted upon the South in the admission of California" as a free state. "The South submits, and further discussion or controversy is, therefore, useless. We have done our duty. When the 'evil day' [disunion] comes, as come it must, we shall have no heart" to reproach any southerner for his failure in 1850 to see the danger. If the South cannot develop "a common platform upon this vital subject, there must be a point, which, when reached by our assailants, will force secession and rend the bonds" of the Union. "We know of no man in the South who desires dissolution for dissolution's sake," Holden claimed. The disruption of the Union would be "among the greatest of evils; but not the greatest— there is one greater—submission to a government of unlimited authority" that would attack slavery and violate the constitutional rights of southern whites. He warned northerners that if they valued the Union, they should "let this question of Slavery alone— take it out and keep it out of Congress; and respect and enforce the Fugitive Slave Law as it stands. If not, WE LEAVE YOU!"[2]

While state legislatures met during the winter of 1850–1851, the debate raged in the South over whether to accept the parts of the compromise that conceded southern rights on slavery. In North Carolina the debate centered on a set of resolutions, introduced in the state Senate by Holden's friend James B. Shepard, affirming the right of secession as "an extreme remedy" and one that might be used if Congress repealed or altered the Fugitive Slave Law. The resolutions, which stopped perilously short of advocating disunion, ignited a heated debate over the right of secession. Whigs denied that such a right existed, and they charged that the Democrats in advancing the Shepard resolutions plotted "practical disunion" and the establishment of "a southern confederacy."[3] In addition to

2. *Ibid.*, August 28, September 11, 25, October 16, November 13, 1850.
3. David M. Potter, *The Impending Crisis, 1848–1861*, completed and edited by Don E. Fehrenbacher (New York, 1976), 125–30; J. G. de Roulhac Hamilton, *Party Politics in North Carolina, 1835–1860* (Durham, 1916), 143–44; Marc W. Kruman, *Parties and Politics in North Carolina, 1836–1865* (Baton Rouge, 1983), 130; Raleigh *Register*, December 4, 14, 18, 1850. The Shepard resolutions were similar to the Georgia Platform adopted at this time and later labeled a moderate Unionist document by historians. Potter, *The Impending Crisis*, 128.

a genuine desire to sustain the Union in the crisis, Whigs also saw an opportunity to avenge their defeat in the 1850 state elections, since most North Carolinians seemed to oppose the extreme southern-rights position.

Again on the defensive, Holden characteristically searched history for evidence to show the legitimacy of his position, in this case the right of secession. Not surprisingly, he found it. He claimed that the principle of secession had its roots in the American Revolution, the Articles of Confederation, and the Constitution, the latter of which had "reserved" the right to the states. Whenever the Constitution "is palpably violated" by the federal government, he argued, a state could legitimately sever its ties with the other states. "One violation of that instrument, if acquiesced in, would speedily lead to others, ending only in the complete overthrow of State sovereignty, and the establishment of a central, consolidated despotism."[4]

Holden, having endorsed the right of secession, recoiled at the thought of its application. "Heaven forbid," he declared, "that such an extreme resort should be presented to us as the only alternative against aggressions upon our rights! We trust it may not, but the bare probability of the contingency should nerve our public men to look the danger boldly in the face" and try to avert it through a unified position, one that the antislavery North would clearly understand. He insisted that "before any State can be justified in severing the bonds" of Union, "all reasonable ground for hope of returning justice must depart, and dishonor and ruin must rise up before us as inevitable."[5]

After the sound defeat of the radical Shepard resolutions, followed by the Whig victories in the 1851 congressional elections, Holden retreated even further from his brinksmanship stance. With Democratic control of the state in jeopardy, the politically sensitive Holden assured North Carolinians that "it is one thing to contend for the abstract right of secession in the last resort, and quite another thing to insist that the right shall be exercised now." He was also quick to denounce the spirit of secession that stirred in neighboring South Carolina, characterizing it as suicidal. Holden even proposed that the Democratic General Assembly pass a reso-

4. Raleigh *Standard,* December 4, 1850, January 15, 1851.
5. *Ibid.,* December 4, 1850, March 5, 1851.

lution supporting the Compromise of 1850. Such a statement of policy, he told an associate, would have immediate political value for the party, since it would undercut the repeated Whig claim that the Democrats favored secession. At the same time, he predicted that the Democratic party "will gain, in the long run, by our southern Rights, or rather *State's* Rights position, which grew out of it." By supporting the compromise, as he briefly explained to another friend, Democrats would be viewed as the saviors both of "the public liberties and of the Union." [6]

In moderating his rhetoric and emphasizing Democratic devotion to the Union, Holden was clearly looking ahead to the state and presidential elections of 1852. Now a veteran of several hard-fought political campaigns, Holden had developed a scale of values that weighed heavily toward Democratic unity, the welfare of the party, and an end to the sectional agitation threatening party stability. In explaining his conversion to moderation, he candidly reminded an associate that "we all live more or less by party," a truism for those who sought political success in nineteenth-century America.[7]

Holden's ascendancy in the party was clearly revealed in the state Democratic convention of 1852. The convention routinely renominated Governor Reid, "Holden's man Friday," as the Whigs dubbed him, and, following the *Standard* editor's recommendation, adopted resolutions supporting the Compromise of 1850 and emphasizing old differences between Whigs and Democrats. As in 1850, Holden focused the attention of the Democrats on state issues, mainly the equal-suffrage question, which had not yet been settled. When Whigs suggested that a state convention be called to change representation in the General Assembly from the federal basis to a basis of white population alone, which would have been a more meaningful democratic reform than equal suffrage in state Senate elections, Holden denounced the proposal as one designed to destroy

6. *Ibid.*, September 3, October 1, 1851; Hamilton, *Party Politics in North Carolina*, 86–93; W. W. Holden to Abraham W. Venable, December 24, 1851, in Abraham W. Venable Papers, SHC; W. W. Holden to John W. Ellis, January 8, 1852, in Noble J. Tolbert (ed.), *The Papers of John Willis Ellis* (2 vols.; Raleigh, 1964), I, 106.

7. W. W. Holden to Abraham W. Venable, February 7, 1852, in Venable Papers; W. W. Holden to John W. Ellis, January 8, 1852, in Tolbert (ed.), *Ellis Papers*, I, 105–106.

the regional compromise arranged by the constitutional convention of 1835. Publicly insisting that the Democratic party was the party of all the state and "neither makes sectional appeals nor panders to sectional prejudices," he knew that though the white formula was popular in the West, the party's support of the reform could ruin it in the East.[8] The latter region, the heartland of Democratic strength in the state, benefited from the federal basis of representation. In the difficult task of balancing regional political interests, Holden shrewdly calculated that it would be wiser to risk losing some Democratic votes in the West than alienating more numerous and powerful eastern Democrats. Like many of his allies and opponents, he believed in the doctrine of white equality but was not anxious to risk electoral defeat to achieve it.

The Democrats again rode the equal-suffrage issue to victory. Holden's strategy of supporting the Compromise of 1850 had also partly robbed the Whigs of the Union issue that they had effectively used against the Democrats in the 1851 elections. Those southern-rights Democrats who felt uneasy with a compromise that excluded slavery from California and left the issue dangling in New Mexico could take comfort in the fact that Holden and the party hierarchy expressed a determination to continue their resistance to federal encroachments on states' rights and the liberties of the people. Whigs, however, gained a partial success in the 1852 elections. They won a slim control of one house of the General Assembly, causing Holden to despair not only for the success of equal suffrage in the new legislature but also for the election of a Democratic United States senator to succeed Whig Willie P. Mangum. Indeed, for two years the divided General Assembly could not elect a new senator, leaving the seat vacant in Congress.

With political control of North Carolina virtually on dead center, presidential politics assumed more importance than before. Holden knew that another Democratic failure to carry North Carolina for the party's standard-bearer could demoralize state Democrats, give the edge to their opponents in local contests, and cause party stalwarts to question his leadership. But if their candidate captured the White House, Holden, as the leader of the state party, could expect to have a major role in the distribution of fed-

8. Raleigh *Standard,* February 12, 1851, May 19, June 23, 1852.

eral patronage in North Carolina. Contributing to Holden's intense interest in the campaign was the fact that the national Whig party was in disarray over the slavery issue and Democratic hopes for victory were bright. As a delegate to the national Democratic convention, he supported James Buchanan, a northerner with a favorable view toward southern rights, for the presidential nomination. But when it appeared that Buchanan could not win the nomination, Holden led a movement to swing the North Carolina delegation to Stephen A. Douglas, hoping that such action would create a bandwagon effect. However, as Holden observed, "the combinations [were] too strong . . . against the 'little Giant,'" and when Franklin Pierce's star began to rise, the North Carolinians threw their support to him. After forty-nine ballots the convention nominated the relatively obscure New Hampshire politician.[9]

The Democratic platform was all that Holden and other moderate southern-rights men could desire. And well it should have been, since it followed the plank in the North Carolina Democratic platform endorsing the Compromise of 1850 and opposing any renewal of the agitation over slavery. Although mildly disappointed in the nomination of Pierce, Holden returned home to extol the New Englander's virtues and to proclaim the candidate's soundness on southern rights. As was the custom of every political editor, he exaggerated the achievements and good qualities of the party's standard-bearer.[10]

When Pierce won the election, Holden proclaimed it a great victory for the Union and a decisive defeat for the sectionalizing tendencies of the William H. Seward–led Whig party. "Confidence in the republic has again been restored," he exclaimed, "and we look to the future with pride and exultation." The republic, he declared, was now safely in the hands of a man with "the iron of Jackson."[11]

The future also seemed bright for Holden personally. Thirty-four years of age in 1852, he was the most powerful political leader in

9. W. W. Holden to Abraham W. Venable, March 26, 1852, in Venable Papers; Raleigh *Standard,* June 16, 1852; W. W. Holden to John W. Ellis, June 16, 1852, in Tolbert (ed.), *Ellis Papers,* I, 114.

10. W. W. Holden to John W. Ellis, June 16, 1852, in Tolbert (ed.), *Ellis Papers,* I, 115; Raleigh *Standard,* June 16, 23, 30, September 1, October 13, 1852; W. W. Holden to Abraham W. Venable, July 8, 1852, in Venable Papers.

11. Raleigh *Standard,* November 10, 1852.

the state. He had good reason to believe that he was destined for high public office, though at this time he seemed content with his role as party editor and manager. The *Standard* also prospered, showing a handsome profit of about eight thousand dollars per year during the 1850s. Appointed state printer in 1850, Holden installed one of the first steam-powered presses in the state, naming it the Little Giant after Stephen A. Douglas. He later claimed that his newspaper, after the installation of this press and other modern equipment, "presented the finest appearance of any sheet in North Carolina." [12] He was probably not exaggerating.

Raleigh was a pleasant town to raise a family and experience the amenities of antebellum life. The society of the state capital was unpretentious and fluid; most of the town's 4,500 inhabitants, including 400 "free coloreds" and 1,400 slaves, had been born elsewhere. Political party loyalties and personal rivalries, instead of wealth or cultural distinctions, divided Raleigh society. The completion of the Yarborough House in 1852, not far from the *Standard* office, gave the state capital an excellent hotel that not only provided a meeting place for politicians but also attracted theatrical troupes, musicians, and important visitors to the town. [13]

As a young married couple during the 1840s, William and Ann Holden lived in a house provided by William Peace, Ann's uncle. About 1850 Holden purchased a two-acre Raleigh lot bounded by Hargett, McDowell, Martin, and Salisbury streets, and there he built a large colonial frame house. Completed in 1852 at a cost of five thousand dollars, a portion of which was provided by his wife's estate, the Holden house was one of the finest antebellum homes in Raleigh. The sunken flower garden that Holden developed on the lot became his pride and joy as he grew old, and it was also a delight to visitors. Although proclaiming himself the champion of the common man, his material and cultural tastes, like those of his idol Thomas Jefferson, were hardly the simple stuff of the lower classes. During the next twenty years, except for the Civil War and early

12. William W. Holden, *Memoirs of W. W. Holden* (Durham, 1911), 97–98; clipping from the Raleigh *Times*, December 19, 1925, in Scrapbook, William Woods Holden Papers, DU.

13. W. W. Holden to Thomas Settle, February 13, 1856, in Thomas Settle Papers, No. 2, SHC; Moses N. Amis, *Historical Raleigh* (Raleigh, 1913), 118; Raleigh *Standard*, November 17, 1858; Frederick Law Olmsted, *A Journey in the Seaboard States, with Remarks on Their Economy* (New York, 1856), 318.

Reconstruction periods, he spent approximately five thousand dollars on house furnishings, including extensively carved mahogany furniture and a bathtub. His home reputedly was the first one in Raleigh to be supplied by running water, which came from a tank on top of the house. By 1860 Holden's assets amounted to thirty-three thousand dollars, of which eight thousand dollars was invested in Raleigh real estate.[14]

Soon after the completion of the house Ann died suddenly, leaving Holden with four children, shattering his domestic life, and sending him into a state of "unutterable bereavement." "I have realized for the first time that all words, and forms of grief are unavailing," he wrote a friend. "Nothing sustains me but a sense of duty to those behind, and an unshaken confidence in God and the assurance of meeting her hereafter."[15] The death of Ann drew him closer to his children and to his Protestant religion. He wrote to his daughter, whom he had sent to a girls' academy in Salem, that "nothing, my dear child, gives me greater satisfaction than to know that you are living with reference to the next life. Religion is a matter of principle—not cold and formal, but lively, earnest, and of the heart. It consists in 'ceasing to do' or think evil, and in 'learning to do well.' It is no matter of whim or fancy, to be thought of to-day and forgotten to-morrow; but it should be a part of our daily lives, always paramount, and manifesting itself in all we say or do." In this letter Holden also indicated his aspirations for his offspring and gave an insight into his own set of values. "I desire most ardently to see all my children happy here and saved hereafter. I may not have much to give them; but if they should be well educated and should be moral, just, courteous, honest, industrious, gentle and yet spirited when occasion really requires it, I will esteem this as infinitely better for them than dollars and cents."[16] Although his

14. Testimony of Mrs. Henrietta R. Mahler, August 5, 1904, in *F. L. Mahler* et al. v. *W. R. Henry and wife*, Wake County Estate Records, W. W. Holden Folder, NDAH; unidentified newspaper clipping entitled "Another Landmark Gives Way to the Parade of Progress," in Scrapbook, Holden Papers, DU; Eighth Census of the United States, 1860, Schedule I, Free Inhabitants, Wake County, North Carolina (on microfilm, NDAH).

15. W. W. Holden to Abraham W. Venable, July 8, 1852, in Venable Papers.

16. W. W. Holden to Laura Holden, April 4, 1858, in William Woods Holden Papers, NDAH. See also W. W. Holden to Thomas Settle, February 13, 1856, in Settle Papers.

neighbors came to recognize these virtues in Holden, his political enemies, who grew in number as the years passed, knew a different man.

In 1854 Holden married Louisa Virginia Harrison, a twenty-four-year-old descendant of the prestigious Harrison family of Virginia and the second cousin of William Henry Harrison. Louisa brought into the marriage four slaves, whom she had inherited from her father. Three of the slaves—a painter, a baker, and a dining room servant—were hired out for work in town. Louisa managed the slaves, including the income from their work, a sum of $150 a year in the case of the painter. In 1858 or 1859 she inexplicably sold two of the slaves to masters in the Deep South. Including slaves that Holden held before his marriage to Louisa, the family owned six blacks in 1860, only one of whom was a male adult.[17]

Louisa also assumed control of the home, which now included her mother and William Peace, the aging uncle of Holden's first wife. She subsequently gave birth to four more Holden children. All eight of Holden's children lived to adulthood, a somewhat remarkable achievement in nineteenth-century America. Holden provided them with the formal educational advantages that he had missed. All of them, including the girls, attended private schools and Charles, the youngest son, obtained a degree from Yale during the 1870s. In the home Holden made available to his children the best works of literature.

His affection for Louisa and his children was deep and constant. He disliked leaving home unless in the company of his family; and the rarity with which he made political appearances outside of Wake County—even when running for governor during Reconstruction—was partly due to his reluctance to leave his family. When he visited eastern North Carolina to mend political fences in 1857, he lamented to Louisa that "it is a great deprivation to me to be away so long . . . but I think that it would be much to my interest to go to Wilmington. I think of you and my children, many, many times. But words are no avail—you know how I love my dear,

17. A. F. Phillips to E. W. Halford, March 18, 1889, and Deposition of Mrs. L. V. Holden, March 12, 1891, before the Wake County commissioners, in Holden Papers, DU; Eighth Census of the United States, 1860, Slave Schedule, Wake County, North Carolina (on microfilm, NDAH).

dear wife." Three years later, while attending the crucial national Democratic convention in Charleston, Holden, though shaken by the impending sectional division of his party, could not keep his family out of his mind. He wrote Louisa, "I think of you very often, in the throng, in the Hotel, in my room, every where, your sweet face and kind voice are remembered." [18]

At the height of his manhood during the 1850s, Holden had the appearance and manner of a gentleman. He was of average size (five feet nine inches in height) with thick, black hair, dark eyes and eyebrows, and a relatively long nose. [19] He spoke softly and was a good conversationalist. His conversations, in contrast to his editorials, rarely gave offense. A former apprentice in the *Standard* office recalled that Holden was "kind and generous to his employees, always treating them with the utmost consideration." Although busy during the 1850s, he still found time to read poetry, a diversion that owed much to the influence of his first wife, whose literary interests were extensive. John H. Boner, a prominent late-nineteenth-century literary editor who grew up in Raleigh, later wrote that Holden "had fine poetic taste; he was a good critic, though inclined to favor religious verse." His favorite poet was Milton, but he was also familiar with Shakespeare, Burns, and Byron. He occasionally wrote and contributed poems to the *Standard*, his most noteworthy effort being his ode to Calhoun. In 1854 two of his poems were published in a popular collection of North Carolina poetry compiled by Mary Bayard Devereaux Clarke. [20]

Holden's private gentleness and refinement rarely surfaced in his public role as the editor of the state's leading Democratic newspaper. His training and experience in the school of political combativeness, combined with his narrow dedication to the republican

18. W. W. Holden to Louisa Holden, November 8, 1857, April 24, 1860, in Holden Papers, DU.

19. This description is based largely on one given to Claude G. Bowers by an unidentified Holden daugher. Claude Bowers, *The Tragic Era: The Revolution After Lincoln* (1929; rpr. Boston, 1957), 313.

20. Raleigh *State Chronicle*, March 2, 1892; Susan Hutchinson to W. W. Holden, July 6, 1852, John H. Boner to "My dear Hill," March 10, 1892, both in Holden Papers, DU; clipping from the Raleigh *Times*, December 19, 1925, in Scrapbook, Holden Papers, DU; Tenella [Mary Bayard Devereaux Clarke] (comp.), *Wood Notes; or, Carolina Carols: A Collection of North Carolina Poetry* (2 vols.; Raleigh, 1854), I, 166–69.

ideology of the new nation, did not permit him in public affairs to exercise those traits of gentility and kindness that were so prized by southern society. On the dubious grounds that he put principle, truth, and concern for the Republic and the state ahead of appeasement and conciliation, he filled the columns of the *Standard* with harsh condemnation of presumed enemies of these virtues. He almost invariably identified the transgressors with the Whig party. Holden could be unremitting in his vilification of opposition leaders, a style that was hardly new, but in the hands of such a powerful editor it could not be ignored. Whig editors, who were guilty of the same practices, minced few words in criticizing him for his aggressive and intolerant brand of journalism. Holden scorned such criticism and promised, as he wrote on one occasion, to "continue to perform his duty . . . fearlessly, firmly, unshrinkingly, without reference to personal considerations or personal consequences."[21]

As every antebellum political editor knew, the "personal consequences" could mean a violent confrontation in the streets. Many editors went armed when expecting trouble. Holden, however, professing to be a man of peace, refused to carry a weapon, though he had no intention of avoiding a fight and being branded a coward. At the same time, he denounced the ready resort to violence or dueling to redress supposed wrongs. "It is the duty of the press, as one of the conservators of law and morals, to bear its testimony against the 'code of honor,'" he declared. "We counsel no one to submit to personal insult; but . . . in our opinion, the custom of dueling is founded in wicked principles—is contrary to the laws of man and awfully at war with the laws of God."[22]

Only on a few occasions during his twenty-four years as editor of the *Standard* did Holden have a violent encounter with an irate adversary. The most famous incident involved Kenneth Rayner, a powerful Raleigh Whig and the leader of the Know-Nothing party in the state. Beginning in 1855 and continuing into 1856, Holden had conducted an unrelenting campaign of ridicule and abuse of Rayner. On one occasion Holden labeled a Rayner speech as "the most complete compound of billingsgate misrepresentation and low slang ever delivered in this community." Meeting by chance in

21. Raleigh *Standard*, November 15, 1856.
22. *Ibid.*, May 14, 1856.

a Raleigh store, the antagonists argued and came to blows. Although Rayner "endeavored to wield, with some effect, a heavy stick," neither combatant was injured. Holden's sensibilities, however, were wounded by the praise that Rayner received from Whigs and others for the assault. He credited this support not only to partisan spirit but also to the hatred of "the old and exclusive Whig aristocracy, against whom the Editor of the Standard has been contending for nearly fourteen years and who are . . . closely associated with Mr. Rayner." In professed self-pity, Holden complained, "We have no family influence, no great amount of wealth, no venerable and time-honored aristocracy to sustain us." He ended his lament with his usual claim that the people were his source of strength. "We rely upon and belong to the masses of the people, and before God we believe they are our friends."[23] The Holden-Rayner vendetta was soon forgotten, and after the war the two men briefly cooperated in Reconstruction politics.

Despite Holden's claim that Pierce's election and the Democratic ascendancy in the federal government would bring sectional peace, the reverse proved to be the case. The administration's prosouthern policies, highlighted by its support of the Kansas-Nebraska bill in 1854, aroused bitter opposition in the North. At first Holden viewed the Kansas-Nebraska controversy in strictly political terms, believing that the northern wing of the Whig party and its "lackeys" in the South had raised the issue in order to embarrass the Democrats and gain a political advantage. He could see nothing that the South could gain from the Kansas-Nebraska bill, which repealed the Missouri Compromise line and permitted the people of the Platte River country to decide whether they wanted slavery. When antislavery opposition to the measure mounted, Holden began to view the bill in a favorable light and announced after passage that it represented "the progress of just sentiment and free principles" on slavery in the territories.[24]

Although he continued to defend southern rights in the territories, Holden was no radical on the issue. Astutely reflecting the relatively moderate sentiment of the Upper South on the question,

23. *Ibid.*, July 14, 1855, December 3, 1856.
24. *Ibid.*, February 1, March 8, May 31, 1854.

he was content to follow the popular-sovereignty policies of national Democratic leaders Pierce and Douglas, the author of the Kansas-Nebraska bill. He mainly feared the impact of the agitation on North Carolina slaves and the political impetus that it would give to the antislavery forces in the North. In May, 1854, while the debate over the Kansas-Nebraska bill raged, he visited New York and was alarmed to discover that Democrats in the Northeast had been reduced to only a "gallant minority." The passage of the Kansas-Nebraska bill relieved some of his distress, but he still worried that the revival of the slavery issue would sectionalize politics in America and destroy the Democratic party, the last hope of the Union, as he saw it.[25] Holden never recognized that the sectional polarization over slavery owed more to the failure of national Democratic leadership and the intransigence of southerners on slavery in the territories than it did to the aggressions of antislavery northerners.

There was also a state election in 1854, and state issues still had a way of taking precedence over national (or sectional) concerns in local contests. Although nationally the Whig organization had been shattered by the slavery issue, the party was very much alive in North Carolina and anxious to challenge the Democrats on matters unrelated to slavery. Holden, however, tried to use the slavery question against the Whigs; he specifically condemned those North Carolina Whig congressmen who had voted against the Kansas-Nebraska bill. But he soon discovered that the Democrats could make little headway with the issue. Instead, Whigs, reflecting traditional local interests, had seized the initiative in the campaign by adopting a platform promising liberal state aid for internal improvements and also state constitutional reform.[26] Frightened by the success of the Whigs on the former issue, Holden told Democratic gubernatorial candidate Thomas Bragg, whose nomination he had arranged, that he must "come out boldly and emphatically" for state aid for railroad construction or risk defeat in the election. Bragg, as well as other Democratic candidates, heeded Holden's advice, and when the votes were counted in August, the party had retained control of the governor's mansion (though barely) and had won a clear major-

25. *Ibid.*, May 17, 31, June 7, 14, 1854.
26. *Ibid.*, May–July, 1854; Kruman, *Parties and Politics in North Carolina,* 100–101.

ity of the seats in the General Assembly.[27] The central direction that the *Standard* editor had given to the Democratic campaign was decisive in the victory.

With the internal-improvements issue preempted by the Democrats and the national Whig party disbanded, North Carolina Whigs looked for a new identity. Many of them found it in the Know-Nothing movement of 1855–1856. Led by Kenneth Rayner, Holden's Raleigh antagonist, this faction of Whigs endorsed nativism and organized the American (or Know-Nothing) party in the state. Holden was alarmed by this new threat to the Democratic hegemony, and predictably, he sought publicly to identify it with the growing antislavery movement in the North. He charged that "the most noted Abolitionists of the Free States," allied with embittered North Carolina Whigs, were conspiring in the Know-Nothing party to subvert southern rights and destroy republican liberties. He also attacked the party's nativism as contrary to the republican principles of the Founding Fathers. He claimed that Know-Nothingism had "been hatched from the foul brains of designing [antislavery] demagogues" who wanted to close the doors of America "to the oppressed of all nations" and demand that all citizens "worship God in a particular way." Paradoxically, Holden mixed, in about equal portions, his criticism of Know-Nothing nativism and religious intolerance with his attack on the national party's antislavery leanings.[28] He evidently never recognized the contradiction.

Holden was not far off the mark in claiming a close relationship between northern nativists and that section's antislavery devotees. By 1855 this combination within the Know-Nothing party seemed to be the wave of the future, prompting the New York *Herald* to predict that it would win the presidency in 1856.[29] As Holden saw it, such an insidious threat to the South, a threat that, he repeatedly claimed, had the support of demoralized North Carolina Whigs

27. Holden, *Memoirs,* 9; Kruman, *Parties and Politics in North Carolina,* 77–78; Raleigh *Standard,* June 7, July 5, 12, 1854; Thomas E. Jeffrey, "Internal Improvements and Political Parties in Antebellum North Carolina, 1836–1860," *NCHR,* LV (1978), 146.
28. Raleigh *Standard,* January 24, February 7, March 7, 14, 21, April 18, June 6, July 4, 11, 1855.
29. Potter, *The Impending Crisis,* 251–52, 256, 258.

like Rayner and Seaton Gales of the Raleigh *Register*, necessitated a militant southern campaign to arrest its growth before it was too late. He was wrong, however—and he probably knew it—in charging the existence of an alliance between state Whigs and northern antislavery nativists. Actually, Rayner and his associates, in launching the North Carolina Know-Nothing movement, were attempting to escape the antislavery and sectional politics of northern Whigs, a fact that the partisan Holden would cleverly avoid mentioning.[30]

The campaign against the Know-Nothings proved successful, perhaps less because of Holden's vilification than local revulsion to the party's intolerance and secrecy. In 1856 the party abandoned its nativism and secrecy, and by the state election that summer it had become little more than a diluted version of the old Whig party.

Meanwhile, in the North, as the controversy over slavery in Kansas raged, the Know-Nothing coalition was replaced by the avowedly antislavery Republican party. It was with gloomy forebodings that southerners watched its emergence. Holden quickly labeled Republicanism "the largest installment of perdition [from Hell] that ever came up to afflict this planet." When the "black Republicans" nominated John C. Fremont for president, he predicted that the Pathfinder's election "would inevitably lead to a separation of the States. Even if no overt or direct act of dissolution should take place, [Fremont] could not carry on the government in the South. No true or decent Southern man would accept office under him; and our people would never submit to have their post-offices, their custom-houses and the like, filled with Fremont's Yankee abolitionists."

As before, he believed that only the national Democratic party and its presidential candidate, this time James Buchanan, whom Holden had long favored for the office, could prevent the dissolution of the Union. Holden, however, found hope for victory in the North. "Democratic speakers and writers, by the thousands, in all the free states," he noted, were "exerting themselves with a power and a will never before witnessed" in an effort to defeat the forces of disunion. He pleaded with North Carolinians to shun the Know-Nothing (third-party) candidacy of Millard Fillmore, which, he argued, could only help the Republicans by dividing the vote of those

30. For an excellent account of the Know-Nothing movement in North Carolina, see Kruman, *Parties and Politics in North Carolina*, Ch. 7.

opposed to the antislavery fanatics. Holden worried that a Fillmore victory in North Carolina would rob Buchanan of the necessary electoral votes to defeat Fremont. For the first time in a political contest he actively sought Whig support. He appealed to those old Whigs who, he said, put constitutional rights ahead of party to join in the Democratic crusade to elect Buchanan and save the Union.[31]

As tensions mounted with the approach of the presidential election, Holden discovered a "black Republican" at nearby Chapel Hill. In mid-September, evidently without a specific college in mind, he had wondered aloud if any professors in North Carolina's institutions of higher learning might be guilty of teaching heretical antislavery doctrines. He declared in the *Standard* that "the expression of black Republican opinion in our midst is incompatible with our honor and safety as a people. . . . Let our schools and seminaries of learning be scrutinized; and if black Republicans be found in them, let them be driven out." In response to the editor's concern, "An Alumnus" of the University of North Carolina wrote him, "We have been reliably informed that a professor at our State University is an open and avowed supporter of Fremont, and declares his willingness—nay, his desire—to support the black Republican ticket." This writer demanded the unnamed professor's ouster. Holden published the letter in the October 1 issue of the *Standard*. Immediately, Benjamin S. Hedrick, professor of agricultural chemistry and a graduate of the university, wrote the *Standard*, identifying himself as the offending faculty member and justifying his antislavery views and support for Fremont on moderate grounds. Holden found Hedrick's explanation "ingenious, impudent, and highly objectionable" but "not seditious." Nevertheless, he took "it for granted that Prof. Hedrick will be promptly removed."[32]

After copies of the *Standard* containing Hedrick's letter were circulated in Chapel Hill, students burned the professor in effigy. Hedrick immediately accused Holden of instigating the incident, a charge that the latter denied with the sanctimonious comment that he had "studiously refrained from uttering any thing calculated to

31. The quotations in this paragraph and the preceding one appear in two editorials, both in the Raleigh *Standard*, September 17, 1856. Other issues also reflect the intensity of Holden's anti-Republican views in the 1856 campaign.

32. Raleigh *Standard*, September 17, October 1, 8, 1856.

excite students against him; and we regret that they burned him in effigy." The Raleigh editor backhandedly called on the students to "let the Professor be—he feels acutely enough his indiscretion, his sin, without hisses and effigies." But he also expressed confidence that the executive committee of the university's board of trustees "will perform their whole duty" and remove Hedrick from the faculty.[33]

A few days later, as popular opposition to the professor mounted, the executive committee of the trustees dismissed him. Holden greeted the news "with much gratification" and gloated over ridding "the University and the State of an avowed Fremont man." He announced that no antislavery proponent "ought to be allowed to breathe the air or to tread the soil of North-Carolina." Incredibly, Holden assured his readers that Hedrick had not been dismissed "because he had avowed himself for a geographical, disunion candidate for the Presidency, but because, having taken part in politics" with the publication of his defense in the *Standard*, "he had ceased to be useful as a professor." Holden facilely claimed that the university in the affair had preserved its nonpartisan integrity.[34]

Actually, North Carolina had become a closed society on the issue of slavery. Although he repeatedly proclaimed the sacredness of constitutional liberties and the Republic, Holden in the Hedrick affair (and on other occasions also) contributed immensely to the climate of intolerance and insecurity that weakened North Carolina's ties to the Union. A sectional champion himself, though not a secessionist, Holden could not see that his crusade for purity on southern rights worked inexorably to defeat the very cause that he professed to serve—the perpetuation of the Union.

Two weeks after Hedrick's dismissal Holden had additional cause for rejoicing. With many North Carolina Whigs shunning the third-party candidacy of Fillmore and voting Democratic out of a fear of a "black Republican" success, Buchanan easily won the state and the presidency. In announcing the victory, Holden proclaimed that "the Democratic party has again saved the Union. Abolitionism has been rebuked, and . . . we shall have peace and harmony again." Sectionalism, he declared, now "writhes in mor-

33. *Ibid.*, October 15, 1856.
34. *Ibid.*, October 22, November 5, 1856.

tal agony, with the iron tramp of the Democratic hosts upon its body." [35]

A careful study of the election returns, however, produced a sobering reality for Holden as well as for others who feared the ultimate fruits of sectional polarization. The division between Buchanan and Fremont in key northern states had been close, placing the new antislavery party in a position to capture the national government in 1860. "I have serious fears that the black Republicans will succeed in the [next] Presidential struggle," he wrote John W. Ellis. "The future is indeed gloomy. The indications are that Mr. Seward will almost surely carry New York, Pennsylvania, and Ohio; and the lesser free State stars, with one or two exceptions, must follow in such a train: God defend and preserve the Republic." [36] Holden's despair proved temporary. In a few months, when a relative calm returned to the national political scene, his spirits revived, and he regained his confidence in the saving power of the Democratic party.

35. *Ibid.*, November 5, 1856.
36. W. W. Holden to John W. Ellis, January 19, 1857, in Tolbert (ed.), *Ellis Papers*, I, 162. Holden, as well as most political observers, expected William H. Seward of New York to be the Republican candidate for president in 1860.

IV
The Pope of
Hargett Street

The rise of the antislavery Republican party and the threat that it posed to the South impelled Holden to contemplate anew the value of the Union. His reflections, which were far more penetrating than his emotional response to the crisis of 1850, led him to a firmer commitment to the Union than he had previously held. By 1856 Holden was no longer an impetuous young editor, as he had been during the earlier crisis. He was now seasoned by his leading role in the state's dominant political party and influenced by the need to satisfy the various elements in the organization. Like many southern moderates, he sought to rationalize southern rights within the context of the Union and to find reasons why the Republic would survive the slavery furor. In a nonpartisan Fourth of July oration in Raleigh, which was subsequently published in pamphlet form, he developed an elaborate and clever defense of the Union, which, though reflecting in part what other moderates had expressed, was the reasoned product of his own thinking. He especially took pains to show the historical greatness of the Republic and the interdependence of the sections. He also sought to isolate the "miserable fanatics" of the free states from the majority of northerners, who, he said, felt a bond of nationality with southerners.

Echoing the exuberant spirit of Manifest Destiny, Holden in the address declared that the federal government "was wisely formed, not only for the common defense, the protection of State rights, and the preservation of individual freedom, but for expansion and duration." He maintained that the Union created by the Founding

Fathers was "an admirable and fortunate combination of federal power and State sovereignty. What individual freedom!—what an exemption from taxation and the evils of class legislation! what developments in science, in arts, and in arms! and what capabilities of improvements and advancement in all that concerns the moral, the physical and the intellectual condition of mankind!" The masses of the Old World, who still suffered from "the hand of the oppressor," look to America, he boasted, "and take new courage from the light which burns so steady and glorious a lustre in this Western hemisphere."[1]

The key to the success of the Union was the federal Constitution, Holden told his Fourth of July audience. Coming after the nearly disastrous failure of the Articles of Confederation, the Constitution created a Union of liberty that "would leave to the States supreme control over all their domestic concerns, while it undertook for them the direction and management of their general interests and exterior relations. . . . If this Constitution shall be palpably broken, or shall utterly fail in its objects, as the Articles of Confederation failed, then there will be no more Union. The Constitution is the bond of the Union, and the attachment of the people of *all* the States to the Constitution is the life of the Union."[2]

But the life of the Union, Holden declared, was threatened by the antislavery agitation. He then outlined to his audience a history of slavery in the United States and declared that many northerners simply did not understand their material interest in slavery. Northeastern merchants, Holden cogently argued, controlled southern trade and reaped profits from the export of its staple crops, which were produced mainly by slave labor. Furthermore, he said, the South "contributes largely to support the North with her breadstuffs, her rice, and her sugar." As the free states became more industrial, they would become even more dependent on southern agricultural products, including cotton, which, he claimed, already gave employment to one million northerners in the emerging textile industry and trades.[3]

Northerners, Holden insisted, had no practical reason to oppose

1. William W. Holden, *Oration Delivered in the City of Raleigh, North-Carolina, July 4th, 1856* (Raleigh, 1856), 6–7.
2. *Ibid.*, 8.
3. *Ibid.*, 9–11.

southern rights regarding slavery in the territories. The institution of slavery could not "take root and flourish in any territory where the great staples of cotton, tobacco, rice, sugar and hemp are not cultivated"; thus in most of the territories nature would exclude slavery and reserve the West for "those fields and departments of labor and industry which are best suited to the white race." He was confident, however, that the "solid men of the North" would recognize their true interests, assert themselves against "the incendiaries and traitors in their midst," and prevent the dissolution of the Union.[4]

Come what may, Holden looked to North Carolina for succor. He declared that "the disastrous darkness which even now seems to be settling on" states like Massachusetts would not affect North Carolina, whose heritage of liberty and republicanism predated the Revolution. He claimed that North Carolinians, having made considerable progress in public education, internal improvements, and material development during the past twenty years, had a bright future ahead in the Union. Holden, perhaps as well as any nineteenth-century American, merged loyalty and pride in the Union with loyalty and pride in his state. He maintained that for North Carolinians to divide these loyalties and dissolve their ties with the other states, a political upheaval destroying the constitutional basis of the government and subverting the liberties of the people would have to occur. He did not expect any such catastrophe to happen.[5]

Throughout the 1850s and until the crisis of 1861 Holden maintained that the preservation of the Union depended upon the continued ascendancy in Washington of the Democratic party. Democrats, he claimed, "were essentially national, and in every section they war against sectionalism and fanaticism." Democratic recognition of southern rights on slavery was a unionist position, he argued, and those who opposed the party were the real sectional agitators. If the national Democratic party was overthrown, Holden predicted that "fanaticism will run riot over the Constitution, and

4. *Ibid.*, 10–11, 13.
5. *Ibid.*, 14, 16–19. In a letter to a prominent Democrat Holden also privately expressed confidence at this time that the Union would survive the sectional storm. W. W. Holden to Weldon N. Edwards, February 2, 1856, in Katherine C. P. Conway Papers, NDAH.

when that is done the Union will be deservedly dissolved." It was imperative, he contended, that the Democratic party maintain its strength in the South, thereby encouraging northern Democrats to stand firm in the face of the antislavery onslaught. He denied that such an arrangement had led to the virtual subservience of the northern wing of the party to the interests of southern slaveholders and had reduced its strength in the North. Indeed, he viewed Democratic Presidents Pierce and Buchanan, both northern "doughfaces," as able leaders. He insisted that they were statesmen whose firm commitment to the Constitution would eventually restore the northern people to their senses and check the antislavery fever.[6]

During the period of relative calm after Buchanan's election in 1856 Holden saw encouraging signs in the North that tended to confirm his view. "In the municipal and other elections which have occurred there since the Presidential struggle last fall," he reported in June, 1857, "the demon of abolition has . . . been trodden under foot by a returning sense of justice. . . . Towns, counties, and even States that Fremont swept with a tornado of Black Republicanism, have since faced about and taken steps to the music of a constitutional Union by giving good national Democratic majorities and electing good national Democrats to office." But "the people of the South should not be lulled into confident security by these favorable omens." It was important for southerners to adopt and sustain "a firm, decided and united position, and say to the North: 'We prefer the Union provided the Constitution is maintained in its integrity; but we prefer disunion to a Union with a broken Constitution.'"[7]

When he wrote those words, Holden was at the zenith of his power and influence in antebellum North Carolina. His success as a state political leader brought with it an increasing involvement in nonpolitical affairs and simultaneously a broadening of his view of the criteria for progress. He had earlier emphasized political virtue and internal improvements as essential elements in the state's shedding of its Rip Van Winkle image. Holden now insisted on educational

6. Raleigh *Standard*, March 4, June 17, 22, 1856.
7. *Ibid.*, June 24, 1857. The fall, 1857, elections also provided Holden with additional evidence "of a returning sense of justice" in the North toward the South. *Ibid.*, October 21, 1857.

improvements and economic diversification as important parts of the equation for progress. He also took an active interest in the care of unfortunates in society, an important concern of Americans during the 1850s. He served as a director of both the state insane asylum and the Institution of the Deaf and Dumb in Raleigh, and he was a warden for the poor of Wake County. Like other southern reformers of the late antebellum era, Holden stopped short of advocating the more advanced reforms, such as women's rights, then being considered in the North. Southern reforms, he insisted, should not incorporate the "isms" of the North, which were designed "to overturn social systems, to uproot or change religions, and to remodel the world on some utopian and impracticable basis." The "head and front" of these isms, he declared, was abolitionism, and this meant that those reforms linked with it would never be acceptable to southerners.[8]

During the middle and late 1850s Holden became a prominent crusader in the campaign for public schools then fitfully beginning in North Carolina. In 1857 he gave the main address at the annual meeting of the newly formed state education association, a speech that the historian of public schools in North Carolina has labeled "one of the strongest addresses on the subject of education ever delivered in the state." For almost two hours he held the attention of the 143 delegates while he reviewed the history of North Carolina education, related its importance to the freedom of the people, and outlined the needs of the infant public school system. "There is no cause more important to a free people than that of education," he told his sympathetic audience. Holden associated the cause of education with his often-expressed political theme regarding the rights of the people. "No free people can hope to perpetuate their liberties without constant and general mental and moral culture," he maintained. To improve the public schools, he called for more and better teachers, uniformity of textbooks (written if possible by North Carolinians), and establishment of school libraries. The Raleigh editor insisted that rising property values in the state warranted an increase in taxes to support improvements in the school system. He approvingly cited northern educational progress, but, reflecting his animosity toward the growing antislavery movement in the North,

8. *Ibid.*, September 14, November 9, 1859.

he warned members of the education association that their children "must learn to be North-Carolinians in deed and in truth."[9] The association immediately published Holden's address and distributed it throughout the state.

Inspired by the favorable reception of his speech, Holden joined state Superintendent of Common Schools Calvin H. Wiley in a campaign to secure the publication of a journal of education. Something must be done to disseminate information and promote the cause of public schools, he wrote Wiley. "The Association must have an organ that will go to the 3,500 [?] districts of the State." Wiley, who earlier had unsuccessfully attempted to start such a journal, agreed to try again, and in 1858 the first issue of the *North Carolina Journal of Education* appeared. In an article published in the new journal, Holden gave education a broader purpose than the political one of preserving liberty that he had emphasized in his 1857 address. Children, he wrote, should be educated "in the ways of virtue and knowledge . . . not only in mind, but *morally*, in all the exalted and saving affections of the heart." History, he declared, "is full of examples showing the paramount importance of moral instruction to the young. . . . Without this moral instruction . . . mental strength is but the strength of the savage or of an insane giant. . . . As ignorance is the parent of most degrading vices, so mere human learning without morals is the prolific source of materialism, spiritualism, scepticism, and infidelity."[10]

Holden's treatise on moral instruction was hardly unique as a rationale for education in the nineteenth century, but he deftly expressed the arguments and provided North Carolinians a more coherent philosophy for public schools than the complex discourses of unimaginative organizers like Wiley. In the 1859 annual meeting of the state education association, attended by many prominent men of the state, Holden was rewarded for his efforts. He was selected president of the organization. Governor Ellis himself, Holden's 1858

9. William W. Holden, *Address Delivered Before the State Educational Association of North Carolina, at Warrenton, July 1st, 1857* (Raleigh, 1857), 3, 12–13, 32; Marcus C. S. Noble, *A History of Public Schools in North Carolina* (Chapel Hill, 1930), 170–71.

10. W. W. Holden to Calvin H. Wiley, July 3, 1857, in Calvin H. Wiley Papers, SHC; Raleigh *Standard*, November 18, 1857; Edgar W. Knight, *Public School Education in North Carolina* (Boston, 1916), 177; William W. Holden, "Importance of Moral Instruction," *North Carolina Journal of Education*, I (1858), 56–57.

rival for the governorship, in "a few very appropriate and eulogistic remarks" nominated the Raleigh editor for the position.[11] Soon the sectional crisis diverted Holden's attention from educational reform, but his interest would be rekindled after the war.

Holden's new vision for North Carolina also included the fullest possible development of its resources and land. In the tradition of William Gaston and other early state promoters, he was a firm believer in the idea of progress.[12] Educational reform was only one part of this mosaic of progress. The expansion of the railroads, which he had had a hand in initiating, was another. As the east-west trunk line took shape during the late 1850s, Holden and his family visited the emerging resorts in the mountains and on the coast. He was greatly impressed by train travel, and what he saw and heard on these trips broadened his vision of North Carolina's needs and prospects. He could see at first hand the prosperity of the 1850s that flowed from the state's booming agricultural economy and from the promising beginnings of small industries. Holden attributed this growth largely to the extension of the railroads into the interior and the relatively convenient access to markets for North Carolina's products. Indeed, like other nineteenth-century Americans, he used the railroad as a symbol of material progress. "The day is not distant," he lyrically predicted in 1859, "when the iron horse, with thundering hoof and lungs of flame, will dash through the Swannanoa gap [near Asheville], and thus unite together, and unite forever, the people of the East and the West."[13]

In the columns of the *Standard*, Holden emphasized the prosperity that would flow from economic diversification, especially agricultural, while largely shunning the arguments of southern economic nationalism that characterized this late antebellum crusade. In lengthy addresses to well-attended county fairs in Kenansville and Fayetteville he elaborated on this theme. In these speeches,

11. Excerpt from the New Bern *Progress,* in Raleigh *Standard,* June 22, 1859. During the late 1850s Holden was also appointed to the board of trustees of the University of North Carolina at Chapel Hill.

12. On the growth of the idea of progress in North Carolina, see Elgiva D. Watson, "The Pursuit of Pride: Cultural Attitudes in North Carolina, 1830–1861" (Ph.D. dissertation, University of North Carolina, Chapel Hill, 1972), 73–83.

13. William W. Holden, *Address Delivered Before the Cumberland County Agricultural Society, at Fayetteville, November 3rd, 1859* (Fayetteville, 1859), 18.

which were later published, he urged farmers and planters to produce more grain and fruit, though he admitted the wealth of the state would continue to depend mainly upon the cultivation of staple crops, principally cotton. He applauded the recent emergence of tobacco farming in North Carolina and predicted that with the opening of Oriental markets and the anticipated reduction of European tariffs on the staple, the state's production of it would mushroom.[14]

Holden's vision for North Carolina retained a large measure of the Jeffersonian ideal. Like Jefferson, he believed that "agriculture is the safest and most pleasant of all pursuits. I can imagine no situation more desirable than that of the farmer, living on his own land . . . independent, out of debt, relying on the earth and on nature for support and comfort." Not only did "the smile of God" rest on the independent farmer, but good government depended upon him. "A government based on thrifty and virtuous [farm] households is best prepared to resist dangerous innovations, the allurements of luxury, and the wear of time," he told his Kenansville audience. Holden admonished "bright young men" to remain on the farm, where satisfaction and success could be found. Too many of them, he said, "are engaging, or seeking to engage, in mercantile or professional pursuits," leaving "dull boys" to farm or engage in mechanical trades. "This is a great mistake, and one peculiar to the Southern country."[15]

Despite his commitment to the agrarian creed, Holden conceded a greater importance in the life of the community to transportation, commerce, and the "mechanic arts" than did pure Jeffersonians. Although "agriculture is the chief pursuit of man," he told his Fayetteville audience, "it is dependent on, and indissolubly connected with the mechanic arts. They exist together, they flourish together, or they languish and decline together." Both agriculture and the mechanic arts—by which he meant small industries and domestic handicrafts—"have been greatly stimulated in this State

14. *Ibid.*; William W. Holden, *Address Delivered Before the Duplin County Agricultural Society, November 6, 1857* (Raleigh, 1857). The Duplin County address was also published in Holden's *Standard*, December 9, 1857.

15. Holden, *Address Delivered Before the Duplin County Agricultural Society,* 14–15.

during the last six or seven years." Nevertheless, much still needed
to be done to connect the interior with markets and apply steam
power, "the mighty agent" of material progress, to the development
of factories in the state.[16]

Holden deplored the emergence of cities in the North, which,
like Jefferson, he pronounced "sores upon the body politic." Taking
his cue from George Fitzhugh and other southern apologists for
slavery, he indignantly contrasted the treatment of laboring whites
in the antislavery centers of the North with that of the working
class in the South. In the heartless North, Holden asserted, while
"the fashionable and the wealthy crowd to their splendid churches,
in shining broad cloth and rustling silk," to worship God and hear
"scores of ministers dilate upon the negroes' wrongs, and foment
contention, hatred, and fratricidal war," the needs of the poor went
unanswered. These self-righteous northerners, Holden bitterly complained, had doomed "whole multitudes to a condition more forlorn than any single slave in all these States ever heard of, much less
endured."

In the South, Holden claimed, "the white race, the master race,
have not only the necessaries but the luxuries of life; and the black
race have not only enough in food and clothing, but something to
waste, and luxuries also suited to their taste and fancy. We have no
acres here covered with paupers—no soup-kitchen, surrounded by
clamoring and starving hosts." [17]

Except to place his reliance upon individual virtue, Holden
seemed never to have confronted the issue of how the South, and
North Carolina specifically, could achieve economic progress without the evils that accompanied it in the North. But one thing was
clear to Holden: continued progress required the perpetuation of
"the Union under the Constitution." The Union provided individual liberty and a vast territory for the development of "all varieties
of human industry and human skill." "Every true patriot and believer in material progress," he declared, "must hope" that the
Union would be "immortal." [18]

16. *Ibid.*, 18; Holden, *Address Delivered Before the Cumberland County Agricultural Society*, 20.

17. Holden, *Address Delivered Before the Duplin County Agricultural Society*,
23–24.

18. *Ibid.*, 27–29.

During the late 1850s the immortality of the Union did not appear to Holden to be seriously threatened, despite the continued agitation in Congress over slavery in Kansas. State political issues and rivalries again occupied his main attention, as well as that of other North Carolina political leaders. After the disintegration of the nativist Know-Nothing party in 1857, North Carolina Whigs looked for a new platform on which to defeat the Democrats. They seized upon the old issue of federal land distribution to the states. Holden and other Democratic politicians had vehemently opposed distribution in the past, but in the fall of 1857 frustrated Whig journals whiffed discontent among Democrats on the issue. Highly publicized reports of the squandering of public land beyond the Mississippi and also the pressing need for additional revenue to meet increased state expenses had made the notion of distribution attractive. Whig newspapers announced their intention to support any "patriotic Democrat" who would defy his party's leadership and demand North Carolina's share of public-land revenues.[19]

Whigs did not have to wait long before a "patriotic Democrat" took their bait. In a public letter Duncan K. McRae, a prominent Cumberland County Democrat, declared that he would raise the issue in his party. He claimed that he had found "leading Democrats in every county" endorsing distribution and insisted that "it only needs organization, a press and a leader, to secure its triumph in the democratic party." Holden could hardly miss the challenge contained in the next sentence of McRae's letter: "There is no better opening for a young man of talent than to take charge of a paper at Raleigh advocating [distribution]—a sufficient fund is already in hand to place such an enterprize beyond danger, and a commanding subscription list could soon be obtained for a democratic administration paper on this basis."[20]

As expected, McRae's letter provoked the wrath of Holden. The editor of the *Standard* lashed out at this "enemy to the party which has promoted and honored him," who was now seeking an alliance with the remnants of the discredited Know-Nothing party. Holden

---

19. Raleigh *Standard.*, December 9, 1857; Clarence C. Norton, *The Democratic Party in Ante-Bellum North Carolina, 1835–1861* (Chapel Hill, 1930), 185–86.
20. Holden published the full text of the McRae letter in the Raleigh *Standard*, December 9, 1857.

warned fellow Democrats against cooperating with the "renegade" McRae and lectured them on the virtues of party unity. "Parties are indispensible in all free governments," he reminded Democrats. "Every public man who is useful is a member of some one party; and as soon as he sets up for himself and becomes 'independent,' he ceases to be useful. No public man can serve two parties. He must either be a Democrat or a co-operator with the opposition, no matter by what name the opposition may be known." [21]

In January, 1858, McRae, though still unannounced as a gubernatorial candidate, took his distribution campaign to the major eastern towns. Inflamed by Holden's assaults, the eloquent McRae spent as much time denouncing his detractor as he did urging Democrats to select prodistribution delegates to the forthcoming state convention. Indeed, the feud with the Raleigh editor strengthened McRae's resolve to pursue the distribution issue, even if it meant bolting the Democratic party and running as an independent gubernatorial candidate in 1858. He reported to a friend that "the prospects are so encouraging that I can not bear to lose the opportunity of establishing a great principle and breaking down [the] despotic dynasty" headed by the *Standard* editor. Holden, sarcastically professing that "we would be wanting in courtesy if we did not reciprocate the attention thus bestowed upon us," intensified his attacks on the "Democratic disorganizer" and repeatedly charged him with being the "victim of disappointed ambition." [22]

It was soon clear that Holden had beaten back "the cloven foot of disorganization." But he had paid a high price for it. After a decade of managing Democratic campaigns, the powerful Raleigh editor in 1858 was himself seeking the state's highest office, and on the eve of delegate selections by county conventions his tilt with McRae and other Democrats who favored distribution had unwisely reminded party activists of his hot partisan temper. Instead of enhancing his political appeal, Holden's success as editor and party leader had created the impression of an ambitious politician whose real source of strength lay with his control of the "Raleigh clique" and not the Democratic masses.

21. Raleigh *Standard*, December 9, 1857.
22. Duncan K. McRae to Archibald H. Arrington, February 16, 1858, in Archibald H. Arrington Papers, SHC; Raleigh *Standard*, March 3, 1858. See also the issues of late March–May, 1858, *passim*.

On February 15 the Wake County Democratic convention dutifully—and unanimously—nominated him for governor. In endorsing Holden for the nomination, a political friend in the Wake convention claimed that the gubernatorial "nomination could not
exalt that gentleman—could be hardly a feather in his cap—but if
he wanted the office, he was justly entitled to it, and in God's name
let him have it."[23]

Holden's candidacy immediately aroused opposition within the
party. Historians have usually assumed that the main resistance to
him came from aristocratic elements in the party who resented his
lower-class origins and feared his power with the common people.[24]
Actually, class divisions had little, if anything, to do with the movement. Political and personal considerations lay at the heart of the
intraparty opposition to his candidacy.

Even before Wake County Democrats had unfurled Holden's
banner, friends of Judge John W. Ellis of Salisbury were touting
their man for governor. In 1854 Ellis had been Holden's first choice
for the office, but after he refused to become a candidate, Holden
ceased to tempt him with the prize. By 1858 Ellis had acquired a
taste for the position, and though no real differences on political
issues separated him from Holden, a strong rivalry soon emerged,
fueled by the friends of the two men.[25]

Because of Holden's great influence in the party, the Ellis forces
had to move cautiously in promoting their hero. They saw an opportunity in Holden's war on McRae and other prodistribution
Democrats. Although Ellis also opposed distribution, his supporters carefully depicted Holden as too controversial on the issue for
the good of the party. Former Whigs who had joined the Democrats
after the collapse of their party also expressed opposition to his
nomination. There were few old Whig activists who did not bitterly

23. Raleigh *Standard,* February 17, 1858.
24. J. G. de Roulhac Hamilton, *Party Politics in North Carolina, 1835–1860*
(Durham, 1916), 183; Norton, *The Democratic Party in Ante-Bellum North Carolina,* 231; Horace W. Raper, "William Woods Holden: A Political Biography"
(Ph.D. dissertation, University of North Carolina, Chapel Hill, 1951), 43; Edgar
Estes Folk, "W. W. Holden and the Election of 1858," *NCHR,* XXI (1944), 297–
98, 317–18.
25. John W. Ellis to William F. Dancy, November 20, 1857, Edward P. C. Cantwell to Ellis, January 27, 1858, in Noble J. Tolbert (ed.), *The Papers of John Willis
Ellis* (2 vols.; Raleigh, 1964), I, 168, 177–79.

resent the role that the Pope of Hargett Street, as Holden's enemies frequently referred to him, had played in the decline of their party and the defamation of their state leaders. Local Democratic leaders knew that Holden's nomination for governor would drive many co-operating Whigs back into the opposition party. Furthermore, his severe attacks on the principle of distribution, which Whigs had traditionally supported, were unnecessarily partisan, further alienating Whigs and threatening to restore the old political alignments in the state. Indeed, a Holden candidacy on a strong antidistribution platform, many Democratic devotees believed, would reunite North Carolina Whigs, and with the support of dissidents such as McRae they would sweep the state in 1858, destroying the Democratic ascendancy. Under the circumstances many Democratic stalwarts, who otherwise were friendly with Holden and appreciated his unmatched contributions to the party's success, were not willing to make him their standard-bearer in the election. As one of them expressed it: "Holden has done a great deal for the Democratic Party and is certainly very deserving. Still I think he will meet with stronger opposition [for governor] than any man that we could start, as he is most heartily despised by the other side."[26]

Still, he had many devoted political friends who were anxious to test the gubernatorial waters for him in 1858. These friends knew that, despite Holden's vehemence in attacking McRae and other Democratic "disorganizers," he had a history of faithfully defending party candidates and officeholders and in the campaign would receive the vigorous support of these important local leaders. He had also maintained an extensive correspondence and personal contacts with Democratic activists, further enhancing his party standing. Holden partisans believed that, despite the threat of division in the party, their man had waited long enough to claim the governorship. Throughout the state in February and March, 1858, numerous meetings were held endorsing him for governor, and several prominent Democratic newspapers, representing all three sections of the state, announced their support for him. Concurrently, the opposition in the party rallied to Ellis, and by the time of the state convention the contest between supporters of the two candi-

26. John W. Cunningham to Calvin H. Wiley, October 10, 1857, in Wiley Papers.

dates had become intense, with no apparent winner. In the *Standard* Holden maintained a strict impartiality, even to the point of publishing the proceedings of meetings that endorsed Ellis.[27]

The state Democratic convention, which assembled in Charlotte on April 14, was the most imposing political gathering held in North Carolina during the antebellum period. Of the 454 delegates many were recent Whig converts, causing Holdenites to sense early that their candidate might be in trouble. Their fears seemed to be justified when the convention selected C. M. Avery, a former Whig from the West, as its president and accorded 1852 Whig gubernatorial candidate John Kerr, who had been pilloried by Holden, a prominent role in the convention. W. J. Houston, the Holden floor leader, later bitterly lamented that "the most violent opposition to [Holden] in the Charlotte contest had come from recent converts to Democracy—an opposition which resulted in 'snowing under' the champion of Democracy in North-Carolina."[28]

The voting strength of each county in the convention was based on its Democratic vote in the preceding gubernatorial election. Nevertheless, a county could be represented by any number of delegates. Mecklenburg, with a majority for Ellis, had 102 delegates in the convention, which was more than twice the number of the county with the next highest number. Many counties had only one delegate, and ten eastern counties were not represented in the convention. The sheer numbers and lobbying presence of the large Mecklenburg delegation, though its actual voting strength was no greater than that of Wake and several other counties, contributed to the undermining of Holden's candidacy. The last-minute withdrawal of a third candidate, W. W. Avery of Buncombe, did not appreciably improve Holden's chances, though many of Avery's western friends threw their support to the Raleigh editor. Even a stirring nomination speech by John Walker, a prominent Democrat, in which he proclaimed that Holden "has done more for the Demo-

27. Proceedings of these meetings may be found in the Raleigh *Standard*, February–March, 1858. The *Standard* made no comment on the meetings. For the intensity of feeling between the friends of the two candidates and the manipulations at Charlotte from Ellis' point of view, see John W. Ellis to H. M. Shaw, April 1, 1858, in Thomas M. Pittman Papers, NDAH.

28. Proceedings of the state Democratic convention as reported by the Charlotte *Western Democrat*, April 20, 1858; remarks of W. J. Houston, as reported in the Raleigh *Standard*, April 21, 1858; Raleigh *Register*, April 21, 1858.

cratic party of the State *than any other five men in it*," failed to rally additional support for him. Seeing the handwriting on the wall, Holden leaders desperately sought the passage of a resolution requiring a two-thirds vote for the nomination, a hurdle, they believed, that Ellis could not overcome and that would eventually swing the convention to their candidate.[29]

The resolution failed, and Ellis won the nomination by a vote of 25,051 to Holden's 21,594. Ellis carried forty county delegations to Holden's twenty-seven. The Raleigh editor's strength lay in the northern Piedmont and in the counties of the far West that would benefit from the extension of the North Carolina Railroad, a project that Holden had supported and Ellis had opposed. Holden won only six eastern counties while Ellis carried eighteen.[30] Ellis' impressive success in the East and in the southern Piedmont decided the contest in his favor. Slaveholders as well as nonslaveholders, town dwellers as well as rural residents, supported both candidates. Political preferences, forged by perceptions of the candidates' ability to win and to maintain party unity, as well as personal ties, determined the outcome of the 1858 Democratic convention. As the proceedings ended, Holden received another blow when convention president Avery refused to reappoint him to the powerful state party executive committee.

Although his friends bitterly charged that their candidate had been sacrificed at Charlotte to preserve party harmony, Holden accepted the defeat with good grace. In the *Standard* he praised the work of the convention, especially the platform that included an antidistribution plank, and he proclaimed Ellis "a worthy and deserving" nominee. Since the convention "has spoken," he wrote, "it is the duty of every good Democrat to spring with alacrity to the support of its nominee." Holden also privately congratulated Ellis and assured him that he would vigorously "promote your success as the nominee of the Democratic party." "I have no disposition to complain," he wrote Ellis. "My nature is to look on the bright side.

29. Charlotte *Western Democrat*, April 20, 1858; Raleigh *Standard*, April 21, 1858; Norton, *The Democratic Party in Ante-Bellum North Carolina*, 229–30; Folk, "Holden and the Election of 1858," 306–307; John W. Ellis to H. M. Shaw, April 19, 1858, in Pittman Papers.

30. Charlotte *Western Democrat*, April 20, 1858; Raleigh *Standard*, April 21, 1858.

I bow to the decision of the Convention, and shall work for the party with as much ardor as I shall have worked for myself." [31]

Meanwhile, McRae had announced his independent candidacy. He was soon endorsed by Whig leaders, who in the nadir of their political despair wanted to keep the Democratic pot boiling until they could reorganize and regain their strength. Editor John Syme of the Raleigh *Register*, who had never had a kind word for Holden, observed that the *Standard* editor had served "as the ladder up which Democratic aspirants climb, and which, when the object is reached, is unceremoniously kicked out." Syme professed to see a conspiracy against Holden in the Democracy's denying him the nomination. "The lawyers and upper crust are for Ellis," the *Register* editor disingenuously remarked, "while the unwashed multitude are for Holden." [32]

Actually, Syme's commentary was a typical one for mid-nineteenth-century editors, including North Carolina journalists of both parties, who were imbued with the egalitarian political doctrine of the Jacksonian era. The charge that the opposition party was aristocratic and hostile to the rights of the people was frequently used to arouse sympathy and gain a political advantage. Democrats, who had Holden as their chief propagandist, were more adept than Whigs in evoking antiaristocratic sentiment in North Carolina. Although some historians have judged otherwise, the appeal to the liberty and rights of the people against an amorphous "aristocracy" did not reflect a significant class division but was a common political strategy; in this case it was designed to arouse Democratic support for Holden and create a fatal schism in the party. [33] Even Holden became weary of the Whig campaign to portray him as a "very proper man" who had been wronged by the Democratic convention. "Many tears were shed over the result at Charlotte by sundry persons of the opposition," he wrote, "and the Convention has been compared to an assemblage of birds of the most opposite natures, by whom 'Holden' was hustled out of the

31. Raleigh *Standard*, April 21, 28, 1858; W. W. Holden to John W. Ellis, April 19, 1858, in Tolbert (ed.), *Ellis Papers*, I, 187–88.

32. Raleigh *Register*, April 14, 21, 1858.

33. For the prevailing social- or class-conflict interpretation of the division between Holden's and Ellis' supporters, see Edgar E. Folk and Bynum Shaw, *W. W. Holden: A Political Biography* (Winston-Salem, 1982), 98–103.

nest and forced into the bleak, unwholesome air. Nevertheless, 'Holden' is just what he was, both in heart and in action; and the answer he makes to [the Whigs] is the earnest support which he is extending, and extending with pleasure, to John W. Ellis."[34]

The Whig effort to exploit the Democratic division failed. True to his promise to Ellis, Holden threw himself into the 1858 campaign and was soon his old political self in advising and encouraging the Democratic gubernatorial candidate. He supplied Ellis with a wealth of material on McRae's past political sins and gave him suggestions on campaign strategy. "Mr. McRae is a bold campaigner," Holden warned Ellis, and you should "put him all the time on the defensive." He explained to Ellis how that might be done, providing historians also with an insight into the shrewd mind of this expert in political warfare.

[McRae's] denunciation of taxation, though not so intended, can be shown to be a sort of preparation of the hearts of the people for repudiation; his opposition to Kansas with Lecompton places him side by side with the black Republicans and against the administration; his censures upon Governor Bragg for appointing [Thomas L.] Clingman and upon the President for appointing [Asa] Biggs, places him among our enemies and in front of the disorganizers; and his intention is, if he can secure a balance-of-power party in the legislature, to throw his whole influence against the party here, against our Northern brethren, in favor of Douglas and the new party now forming for 1860, and of course against the administration and the Democratic party generally.[35]

Ellis, who was hardly the aristocrat that historians have portrayed, followed Holden's advice. As the campaign progressed, he also agreed with Holden to support unequivocally the westward extension of the North Carolina Railroad, a position that McRae had hesitated to take. For Democratic eyes, Holden in the *Standard* constantly identified McRae with the defunct Know-Nothing party. The success of this tactic dumbfounded McRae, who had to win a fairly large number of Democratic votes to carry the election. In the

34. Raleigh *Standard,* July 14, 1858.
35. W. W. Holden to John W. Ellis, May 4, 5, 18, June 1, 1858, in Tolbert (ed.), *Ellis Papers,* I, 191–96. See also Raleigh *Standard,* April 28, May 5, July 7, 14, 21, 1858. Asa Biggs resigned from the United States Senate to accept a federal judgeship, whereupon Governor Bragg appointed Clingman to fill the Senate vacancy.

election Ellis soundly defeated the independent candidate, and Democrats won a commanding majority in the General Assembly.[36]

The votes had hardly been counted when intrigue began to swirl around the selection of the two United States senators, which would be the first order of business for the new legislature. The incumbents were the "renegade" Whig Thomas L. Clingman, who had recently been appointed by Governor Bragg to the Senate vacancy created by the resignation of Asa Biggs, and incumbent David S. Reid, who did not make a vigorous effort to retain his seat. Clingman naturally appreciated the high favor that Bragg had bestowed on him, and friends of the two men intrigued to keep him in the Senate and also to put the governor in Reid's seat.[37] Returning from a three-week vacation at Beaufort, Holden discovered that some of his friends, who were still rankled by his defeat at Charlotte, were testing the senatorial waters for him. Holden immediately announced that "we shall take no part in these elections" and warned his supporters to "refrain from any expressions calculated to engender ill feeling or a spirit of recrimination" among Democrats. Later he emphatically denied that he sought a senatorial seat, insisting that he had repeatedly told his friends that he would not become a candidate for the position.[38]

Despite Holden's strong denials, friends of Governor Bragg and other senatorial candidates charged him with duplicity in the affair. Chagrined by these attacks, Holden on the eve of the legislative session signaled his supporters to enter him in the contest for the seat held by his old ally Reid. Although most observers did not believe that Reid had a chance to retain his seat in the face of the Clingman-Bragg alliance, Holden's candidacy mortified the former governor's friends in the General Assembly. On the first ballot in the Democratic legislative caucus, which actually decided the winner, the

36. Archibald H. Arrington to Duncan K. McRae, May 1, 4, 1858, Arrington to James C. Cooper, May 20, 1858, Duncan K. McRae to Arrington, June 2, 1858, in Arrington Papers; Raleigh *Standard*, August 4, 11, 1858.

37. William V. Geffroy to David S. Reid, August 30, September 28, 1858, in Lindley S. Butler (ed.), "The Papers of David Settle Reid" (MS in Historical Publications Section, NDAH); Weldon N. Edwards to Thomas Ruffin, September 4, 1858, in Joseph G. de Roulhac Hamilton (ed.), *The Papers of Thomas Ruffin* (4 vols.; Raleigh, 1918–20), II, 609.

38. Raleigh *Standard*, September 8, October 20, 1858.

vote stood Bragg 40, Holden 36, Reid 18. On the second ballot Reid's supporters turned on Holden and gave their votes and the election to Bragg. Clingman easily won the other Senate seat.[39]

As before, Holden put the best face possible on his defeat and praised the selections of Bragg and Clingman for the Senate. He insisted, however, that he had been "a victim of entanglement" in the affair. He added that since the senatorial elections were over, "we trust that all ill feeling growing out of the contest will subside, and that party harmony will be thoroughly restored. Personal interests and feelings must always be subordinated to the good of the party." The fact that some Democratic politicians were predicting that he would be the party's gubernatorial candidate in 1862 softened the impact of the 1858 defeats for him.[40] Only forty years of age in 1858, Holden had plenty of time to reach the highest political office in the state.

Although careful to mask his disappointment, Holden became increasingly sensitive to local Democratic challenges to his influence. A procedural dispute in the Wake County Democratic convention on April 5, 1859, between his supporters and those of Congressman Lawrence O'Bryan Branch, followed by the publication of the meeting's minutes in the Raleigh *Register* rather than in the *Standard*, triggered a sharp public outburst by Holden. He charged that "pretended Democrats, self-seekers, and office seekers," whom he identified as Edward Cantwell and editor Robert H. Whitaker of the supposedly nonpolitical Raleigh *Live Giraffe*, were plotting against him, and he warned them that "it will not do to slight us and put upon us politically." He specifically claimed that the young Wake upstarts planned to establish a rival Democratic newspaper in Raleigh to replace the *Standard* as the state party organ. Holden pointedly reminded them that his newspaper "speaks the sentiments, and has the confidence of the Democratic masses of the State, and *because* of this, and for no other reason, it can kill and make alive."[41]

39. William J. Yates to David S. Reid, November 25, 1858, in Butler (ed.), "Reid Papers"; John W. Ellis to David S. Reid, January 1, 1859, in Tolbert (ed.), *Ellis Papers*, I, 212; Hamilton, *Party Politics in North Carolina*, 190.

40. Raleigh *Standard*, December 1, 1858, J. J. Martin to J. A. Waugh, November 15, 1858, in Lindsay Patterson and Edmund Jones Papers, SHC; Raleigh *Live Giraffe*, November 18, 1858.

41. Raleigh *Standard*, April 13, 1859.

Cantwell and Whitaker contemptuously defied Holden by founding the *Democratic Press* at the state capital. Labeling Holden "a
consummate ass," they seized upon his "kill and make alive" pronouncement as conclusive proof of his "wicked vanity and sinful
arrogance." "It is time you were learning, Mr. Holden," they thundered, "that you are not the Democratic Party—that you are not
able to 'kill and make alive'" political opponents. The young hotspurs were quietly encouraged in their challenge of Holden by Congressman Branch, who believed that the *Standard* editor had plotted
to replace him as the district's representative in Congress. Governor
Ellis, who resented Holden's power in the party, nonetheless remained discreetly aloof from the conflict. He evidently was prepared to support the insurgency against Holden only if the revolt
spread throughout the state Democratic party and demonstrated
good prospects for success.[42]

Reacting like a wounded lion, Holden called on "Old Guard"
Democrats to save the party from the "self seekers and disorganizers." He assured local Democratic leaders that, despite the furor
in Raleigh created by Cantwell and Whitaker, "there is really no
division among prominent Democrats at the centre." In response to
the charges of the insurgents, he begged Democrats to believe that
he was not "disposed to be dogmatic or dictatorial" in party affairs. "If we have now and then spoken freely and severely," he told
Democratic activists, "the language was not meant for them, or for
true Democrats, but was the result of the most ardent desire to do
our part in defending the principles and maintaining the organization of the party."[43]

Holden's appeal for Democratic support against the insurgents
achieved impressive results, especially among party editors. Eight of
the thirteen Democratic newspapers denounced the *Democratic
Press* for its campaign against Holden; the other five journals, Holden claimed, quietly supported him. The Tarboro *Mercury* provided

42. Raleigh *Live Giraffe*, April 16, 23, 30, 1859; Raleigh *Democratic Press*,
May 21, 28, 1859; Lawrence O'Bryan Branch to his wife, February 6, May 29,
1859, in Mrs. Lawrence O'Bryan Branch Papers, NDAH; Raleigh *Standard*, September 7, 14, 1859. Years later Whitaker wrote a sympathetic article on Holden.
He also gave an account, from Holden's perspective, of the newspaper war of 1859.
Robert H. Whitaker, "William W. Holden, the Governor and the Man," newspaper
clipping in Scrapbook, Holden Papers, DU.

43. Raleigh *Standard*, April 13, May 25, September 7, 14, 1859.

the most vigorous defense of Holden, informing concerned Democrats that "there are always some ready to impugn his motives, and as far as we have seen, without cause." The *Mercury* editor claimed that he had never read anything in the *Standard* warranting the assertion by critics that Holden "was disposed to require those occupying less responsible positions in the Democratic party to submit to his dictation. Why there are so many objections urged against Holden we confess we are unable to divine. He has always acted, in our opinion, with the utmost consistency."[44]

Holden easily survived the challenge of 1859. But his increasing sensitivity to intraparty opposition led many Democrats to believe that he had grown petulant and arrogant in the management of party affairs. The conflict with McRae in 1858 and with the Wake County hotspurs in 1859 strongly suggested to these Democrats that Holden was more anxious to protect the *Standard* from competition, including the lucrative state printing contract, than in advancing the Democratic cause in North Carolina. His willingness to enter the senatorial race in late 1858, despite the conflict that it was sure to cause, appeared to confirm the charges of his detractors that he did so only to satisfy his blighted ambition for high political office. Instead of contributing to party unity, which he always professed to support, Holden, according to his Democratic critics, had become a major source of contention in the party. In 1858–1859 the discord generated by Holden was relatively harmless, since the Whig opposition was in disarray and posed no real threat to the Democratic ascendency in the state. But the imminent revival of the Whigs (under the name Opposition party) and the forthcoming state and national elections—the latter with vital sectional issues at stake—placed a premium on Democratic unity and on the stifling of intraparty conflict. The tensions created by the 1860 presidential contest would heighten the desire for party unity among state Democrats. The decline in Holden's position in the party meant that his influence in the campaign was certain to be less than in earlier contests. If he found cause to dissent from the Democratic mainstream, which he might do partly in reaction to his critics, he would lose

44. The quotation from the Tarboro *Mercury* and the data on newspaper support for Holden are in *ibid.*, September 28, 1859.

his remaining power in the party and become politically adrift. Such a development could not only influence the course of party politics in North Carolina, it could also go far toward determining the state's position in the event that a "black Republican" won the presidency in 1860.

V

Defender of the Union

The intensification of the sectional conflict did not await the 1860 presidential campaign. In late 1859 North Carolinians, as well as others, were electrified by the news of John Brown's raid on Harpers Ferry to liberate slaves. Holden at first, like other state political leaders, concluded that, since Brown's violent incursion into the South appeared to be the work of a few fanatical "incendiaries," it would actually contribute to reducing antislavery agitation. He explained to his readers that "at the North this Harpers Ferry movement should produce more sound reflection on the subject of slavery than heretofore, and should dispose every just and fair-minded citizen to set his face against a party [*i.e.*, the Republicans] whose doctrines lead inevitably to insurrection and dissolution of the Union."[1]

But when evidence began to appear linking prominent northern abolitionists with Old Ossawatomie and when antislavery zealots like Joshua Giddings called for more violent assaults on the institution of slavery, Holden became excited and thundered against Brown's northern defenders. He proposed—perhaps only partly rhetorically—that a harsh punishment be meted out to leading antislavery fanatics. "If about one thousand of the prominent abo-

---

1. Raleigh *Standard*, October 26, 1859. For the North Carolina reaction to Brown's raid, see Victor B. Howard, "John Brown's Raid at Harpers Ferry and the Sectional Crisis in North Carolina," *NCHR*, LV (1978), 396–420, and William A. Walsh to Lawrence O'B. Branch, December 12, 1859, January 15, 1860, in Branch Family Papers, DU.

litionists could be hanged by the neck until they were dead," he exclaimed, "the country would be benefitted, and all good men everywhere would be more assured of a continuance of concord between the States." Despite the efforts of "black Republican journals to palliate the wickedness of old Brown . . . by declaring that he is a madman, and that they are not responsible for his conduct," Holden vehemently contended that "*his* acts are the legitimate fruits of *their* doctrines, which teach that slavery is a monstrous evil to be 'extirpated' by every means under the 'higher law' which its enemies can command." Turning to the grave political implications of the raid, Holden warned northerners that after the Harpers Ferry raid the election to the presidency of William H. Seward, the Republican leader, "with his odious doctrines . . . would be regarded as a deliberate and final declaration of the North against the South, and would sound the death-knell of the union of the States." "The people of the South will never consent that that man shall rule over them," he declared. "This is no idle threat. . . . Their minds are already made up" in the event of a Seward victory in 1860.[2]

The sympathetic reaction to Brown by many antislavery men shook Holden's confidence in the ability of northern Democrats to check the Republican juggernaut in their section and preserve the Union. He still expected the Democrats to prevail in 1860; "but what of 1864, of 1868, of 1872, of the next fifteen years? Who can penetrate the gathering gloom before us? Let the South be ready for any emergency. Let North Carolina be ready. Let her be put on a war footing at the next session of the Legislature, whatever may be the result of the contest of 1860."[3]

Holden also called for increased domestic vigilance against black unrest. He alerted North Carolinians to antislavery "emissaries" in the state who "are travelling on various missions, but the true mission of many of them is to excite slaves against their masters. . . . Let every person of doubtful character be questioned and watched." He maintained that "if suspicious people are found tampering with slaves or heard uttering incendiary expressions," they should be driven from the state. Holden, who in the past had rarely commented on the "peculiar institution" per se, probably because he

2. Raleigh *Standard*, October 26, November 2, 16, 1859.
3. *Ibid.*, November 30, 1859.

took it for granted, now urged slaveholders to exercise proper discipline over their blacks. He warned against "too much liberty, too
much indulgence" in the slaves, and he advised masters that if the
treatment of blacks "be strict, but kind and reasonable, it will
produce good results; but if it be loose, and careless, and vicious,
the worst consequences may be anticipated."[4]

In common with other white North Carolinians, whose commitment to slavery was as strong as that of other southerners, Holden
found the presence of free Negroes disturbing and a source of po-
tential trouble.[5] Some of the thirty thousand free blacks in the
state, he said, "are worthy and industrious; but, as a general rule
they are idle, improvident, and vicious. Their presence among us is
injurious to slave property, while they no doubt consume more
than they produce." He called on the legislature to prohibit future
manumissions, but it was not in session and would not meet again
until November, 1860. For those blacks already in freedom Holden
advised "nothing . . . of a harsh or unjust character; but it is apparent to every reflecting person that something should be done either
to reform them and render them useful to society and to the State,
or to banish them from among us." The influential editor declared
that he had "always maintained the opinion that there should be
but two classes in the slaveholding States—the master white, and
the subjugated black or colored race." True liberty, he insisted, was
for the white race only.[6]

In addition to the excitement of a presidential contest, Holden and
North Carolina Democrats in 1860 had to wage a divisive state
campaign. The Whigs had reorganized in 1859, and the new party
met in a state convention in February, 1860, to adopt a platform
and choose a gubernatorial candidate for the August election. Des-
ignating themselves the Opposition party in order to attract dissident Democrats, they nominated John Pool, a prominent eastern
planter, as their candidate for governor and adopted a platform

    4. *Ibid.*, November 9, December 7, 1859.
    5. For the conclusion that North Carolinians were as determined as other
southerners to preserve slavery, see Marc W. Kruman, *Parties and Politics in North
Carolina, 1836–1865* (Baton Rouge, 1983), 180–81.
    6. Raleigh *Standard*, December 7, 21, 1859.

calling for the *ad valorem* taxation of property, including slaves.[7] In unfurling the banner of tax reform, the Whigs sought to emulate the earlier Democratic success with equal suffrage. Such a platform, if properly managed, could effectively challenge the Democrats' claim to be the party of the people.

The *ad valorem* issue was not new to North Carolina politics. But by 1860 it had become important, given the increasing demand for state revenues to support internal improvements and expanded government functions. Perceiving the issue's divisiveness among Democrats, Holden, though sympathetic in principle to the reform, refused to take a public stand on it until the state Democratic convention had acted. Instead he opened the columns of the *Standard* to both its advocates and its opponents. At the same time, he gave quiet encouragement to the Wake County Workingmen's Association's support of *ad valorem* taxation. His straddling of the issue further damaged his influence among Democrats, especially among Governor Ellis' friends, who sought any excuse to undermine Holden's position in the party. Many eastern Democrats criticized him for supporting the principle of *ad valorem* taxation, which if enacted would fall heavily on the planters of their section. On the other hand, in the West, where Democrats supported the reform, a growing dissatisfaction with Holden set in because of his vacillation on the issue.[8]

When the state Democratic convention met in March, 1860, Holden urged the adoption of the *ad valorem* principle. But the majority of the delegates disagreed, and they approved a resolution denouncing the Opposition party's *ad valorem* plank and charging that if it became law, no property, including the "tin cups" of workers, would be exempt from taxation.[9] To placate Holden, the convention selected him as a delegate at large for the national Democratic convention.

7. On the role of the *ad valorem* taxation issue in the 1860 state campaign, see Donald C. Butts, "The 'Irrepressible Conflict': Slave Taxation and North Carolina's Gubernatorial Election of 1860," *NCHR*, LVIII (1981), 44–66. My interpretation of the issue's significance and Holden's position, however, differs from that of Butts.
8. Raleigh *Standard*, February 1, 1860; William A. Walsh to Lawrence O'B. Branch, March 1, 1860, in Branch Family Papers.
9. Raleigh *Standard*, July 11, 1860; Butts, "Slave Taxation," 51.

Holden swallowed his disappointment with the platform and immediately entered the campaign against what he dubbed the Whigs' "cunningly devised fables" on *ad valorem* taxation and other state issues designed to entrap voters. He claimed that "the present revenue law of North-Carolina is, for the most part, an *ad valorem* law" and should not be changed except to reduce the tax on "professional and laboring men." Furthermore, he declared, the General Assembly did not have the power to tax slave property according to value, as suggested by the Opposition party platform. "To confer this power on the Legislature the Constitution must be changed," he said. "Is *this* a time to change the State Constitution? Is it wise to dispute about the burdens which should be placed on negro property, when our very existence as a people is threatened because we own negro property?"[10]

Although a suspicious Governor Ellis privately charged him with a lack of interest in the state campaign, Holden actually displayed remarkable vigor in support of the governor, who had been renominated. Even when he disagreed with Ellis and mainstream Democrats over presidential politics, he still admonished party members to work and vote for the governor.[11]

Holden's plea for Democratic unity in the state contest was partly motivated by the desire to cover up intraparty divisions over *ad valorem* taxation. He also felt compelled, lest his influence be further eclipsed, to demonstrate to the Democratic faithful that, despite the divisions of 1858–1859, he was still loyal and could still be counted on to provide ideological leadership for the party. Publicly, he insisted that the state contest carried too much significance for the critical fall presidential election to permit Democrats to divide. "The approaching contest for the Presidency will be the most important which has taken place since the formation

10. Raleigh *Standard*, March 28, 1860. See also the issues of March 14, April 18, May 16, 1860. Holden was essentially correct in saying that a change in the state constitution was required before the General Assembly could enact an *ad valorem* tax on slaves. After the Civil War began, the state convention of 1861, in need of increased revenues to finance the war, approved a constitutional ordinance authorizing such a tax. John L. Cheney (ed.), *North Carolina Government, 1585–1979: A Narrative and Statistical History* (Raleigh, 1981), 823, 827.

11. John W. Ellis to William H. Thomas, April 17, 1860, in Noble J. Tolbert (ed.), *The Papers of John Willis Ellis* (2 vols.; Raleigh, 1964), II, 415; Raleigh *Standard*, March 14, May 16, July 11, 1860.

of the government," he told fellow Democrats. "Upon its result will depend the existence of the Union, the safety of our property, and it may be the lives of our families and the destinies of unborn generations." The early state election in North Carolina, he predicted, "will tell for good or for injury to the cause in every State in the Union. If we falter or lose ground here, our allies in the non-slaveholding States will be disheartened, and we may lose every one of them in November."[12]

With more than 80 percent of North Carolina's white male population going to the polls and voting largely along old party lines, Governor Ellis defeated Pool by a margin of six thousand votes. Democrats also won a slender majority of the seats in the General Assembly. Wake County polled a majority for the Opposition party and elected an independent pro–*ad valorem* Democrat to the state Senate, a turn of events that caused Democratic activists to question further Holden's usefulness. Nevertheless, Holden put the best face possible on events and declared that North Carolinians could now give their full attention to the momentous presidential contest that was already under way.[13]

When the national Democratic convention met at Charleston in April, 1860, Holden, along with other representatives from the Upper South, arrived with the firm belief that the northern and southern wings of the party would resolve their differences over slavery in the territories and nominate a candidate for president who would have strong support in both sections. He soon saw that he had been mistaken. Although Holden enjoyed the hospitality of the town, he discovered on the first night that Charleston, the stronghold of the southern fire-eaters, was a poor site for a convention that desperately needed an atmosphere of sectional harmony. "The outside pressure on the delegates was against the Union—against the nationality of the Democratic party, and therefore unfavorable to calm deliberation and fortunate results," he lamented a few days after the convention met. "The disunionist, Mr. [William L.] Yancey, was at home in Charleston. Night after night large crowds as-

12. Raleigh *Standard*, March 14, 1860.
13. Kruman, *Parties and Politics in North Carolina*, 195–96; Raleigh *Standard*, August 15, 1860.

sembled to hear speeches from delegates and others, Mr. Yancey and his followers being conspicuous among the speakers. Nearly all the speeches which we heard were ultra Southern in their tone and denunciatory of Mr. [Stephen A.] Douglas." Holden, who preferred a southern moderate to Douglas for the presidential nomination, nevertheless woefully complained that supporters of the Little Giant, a majority in the convention, "were either hissed or their voices drowned by the hooting of the crowd." At a meeting of southern delegates that he attended, Holden was alarmed to hear Bedford Brown of North Carolina ridiculed for warning southerners against demanding federal protection of slavery in the territories, a demand that was the cornerstone of the Yanceyites' "Alabama Platform." When he returned to his hotel, he was further appalled by the chants of a crowd denigrating the American flag.[14]

The Charleston convention climaxed with the bolt of the delegates from the Lower South after the Alabama Platform was rejected by the majority and the Douglas plank, leaving open the question of slavery in the territories, was adopted. The delegates from the Upper South, including the North Carolinians, were divided over the issue, with a majority actually supporting the Alabama Platform but not willing to leave the convention when it was defeated. After the bolt, pressure mounted on the North Carolinians to walk out also. Uncertain of their course, they obtained permission from the convention president to retire for consultation among themselves. In the meeting Holden, though maintaining a remarkable ambivalence on the platform issue, made an impassioned speech attacking the Yanceyites for their secessionist proclivities and announcing that he would not contribute to the destruction of "the bonds of Union" by quitting the convention. Holden's strong statement had a salutary effect on confused members of the delegation, and they returned to the hall, avowing their determination to remain in the convention. The action of the North Carolinians, Holden later claimed, also encouraged wavering delegations from the other states of the Upper South to stand firm against the bolters.[15] The convention, however,

14. Raleigh *Standard,* February 26, May 9, 1860; William W. Holden, *Memoirs of W. W. Holden* (Durham, 1911), 10–12; W. W. Holden to his wife Louisa, April 22, 1860, in William Woods Holden Papers, DU.
15. Holden, *Memoirs,* 12–14; Raleigh *Standard,* May 16, 1860. For excellent summary accounts of the Charleston convention, see Roy F. Nichols, *The Disrup-*

could not nominate a candidate for president, and it adjourned to
meet again six weeks later in Baltimore.

The Charleston convention profoundly affected Holden's out-
look on the unfolding sectional crisis. After more than a decade of
defending southern rights as the only truly national position, he
came to the startling conclusion that extremists in the South shared
a major responsibility with the antislavery North for the political
polarization of the nation. The disruption of the Democratic party,
which he blamed entirely on the Yanceyites, was "a national calamity" placing the Union "in imminent peril," he wrote a friend.
"God forbid," he cried, "that the madness of the North, and our
own blindness, prejudice and folly should compel the destruction
of the republic. From what I saw and heard at Charleston I am convinced that the [bolters] are disunionists *per se*. We must check this
movement," he told his friend. In the *Standard* he expressed the
hope "that a re-union will be effected at Baltimore—that all the
States will be there again . . . and that a ticket will be presented
which will prevail in the contest over the black Republicans." A
somber Holden announced that Douglas was "probably the only
man with whom we can defeat the black Republicans," though he
acknowledged that he had opposed the Little Giant's candidacy at
Charleston.[16]

Prior to departing for the Baltimore convention, Holden introduced and secured the unanimous approval by a Wake County
Democratic meeting of a resolution endorsing Douglas for the
presidency. The meeting also approved resolutions introduced by
him deploring the sectionalizing of the Democratic party and denouncing "all movements, the design or tendency of which is to
'precipitate the cotton States into a revolution' and to involve North
Carolina in a premature, and perhaps bloody struggle with her sister States of the North and Northwest." He sent Douglas a copy of

---

tion of the American Democracy (New York, 1948), Chs. 15–16, and David M.
Potter, *The Impending Crisis, 1848–1861,* completed and edited by Don Fehrenbacher (New York, 1976), 407–12. Holden's role in the convention, though not
major, has largely been ignored. See, for example, Owen M. Peterson, "W. W. Avery
in the Democratic National Convention of 1860," *NCHR,* XXI (1954), 463–78.

16. W. W. Holden to Calvin H. Wiley, May 9, 1860, in Calvin H. Wiley Papers,
SHC; Holden to Thomas Goode Tucker, May 19, 1860, in Stephen A. Douglas
Papers, University of Chicago Library; Raleigh *Standard,* May 9, 30, 1860.

the resolutions and predicted that most of the North Carolina delegation would vote for him at Baltimore.[17]

The Baltimore convention proved a bitter disappointment to Holden and other national Democrats who longed for the reunification of the party. The convention's rejection of a number of delegates who had bolted at Charleston triggered another division. This time most of the representatives from the Upper South left the hall, including all but three members of the North Carolina delegation. Holden was one of the three, but as he later explained, though he remained on the floor, he declined to participate in the proceedings "out of respect for the opinions of the fifteen delegates" who had departed. He also stayed because he wanted "to do nothing which would prevent us from cordially co-operating with our [Douglas] Democratic friends in the [forthcoming] Gubernatorial, Legislative, and Presidential campaigns."[18] He thus sat mute during the balloting that nominated Douglas for the presidency.

When he returned home, Holden found himself under severe attack by many North Carolina Democrats for his refusal to walk out of the Baltimore convention. Since the Charleston convention the position of most Democratic spokesmen in the state, in contrast to Holden, had hardened on the territorial issue and against Douglas. The nomination of John C. Breckinridge by the Southern Rights Democratic party immediately received the support of these Democrats, including Governor Ellis, who earlier had supported Douglas on a moderate platform. The governor's commitment to southern rights, which would grow as the election of a "black Republican" appeared imminent, was mainly dictated by the winds of state Democratic opinion, but his stance probably also was influenced by the contrary position of his powerful rival. Conversely, Holden's moderation, though primarily motivated by his fear of secession, owed something to Ellis' vigorous support of southern rights.

In assuming a moderate position, Holden realized that his political influence, already shaken by Ellis' intrigues and by his own intemperate reaction to local challengers, was endangered. Instinc-

17. Raleigh *Standard*, May 30, June 6, 1860; W. W. Holden to Thomas Goode Tucker, May 19, 1860, Holden to Stephen A. Douglas, June 1, 1860, in Douglas Papers.

18. Potter, *The Impending Crisis*, 412–13; Raleigh *Standard*, July 4, 1860.

tively he trimmed his sails, but he was not willing to propose a political course that would lead to North Carolina's abandonment of the national Democratic party or the dissolution of the state party. In his first editorial after his return from Baltimore he retreated from his earlier endorsement of Douglas while still defending the Little Giant and his own position in the crisis. "We are striving to put out the fires of sectionalism, which, if permitted to burn on, will consume the very temple of the Union. We are neither for the South against the North, nor for the North against the South, *but for an undivided country, and against sectionalism and disunion.*"[19]

In the same issue of the *Standard* Holden for the first time warned of the tragic consequences of secession. "While we would surrender no right of our State," he decried the disruption of the Union because it would produce "fraternal strife, civil and servile war, murder, arson, pillage, robbery, and fire and blood through long and cruel years. It would unsettle all business, diminish the value of all property, put the lives of both sexes and all ages in peril, and launch the States on a sea of scenes which no eye has scanned and no navigator sounded. It would bring debt, and misrule, and oppressive taxes, to be followed, perhaps, by the military rule of titled tyrants."

Holden, however, insisted he was not charging that Breckinridge or "any considerable portion of the Democracy of this State are disunionists." His criticisms, he said, were directed at "Mr. Yancey and his followers *in States south of us.*" Holden did not believe that Breckinridge or Joseph Lane, his running mate, "would do anything knowingly" to destroy the Union. "But we object to the manner of their nomination," he went on, "and to *some* of the company in which they find themselves." Indeed, he claimed that Breckinridge, Buchanan's vice-president, had been his first choice for president in 1860.[20]

Holden, along with seven other men who had served in the national Democratic convention, urged the state party's executive committee to call a meeting "for the purpose of harmonizing the action of the party in the Presidential election." He announced that

19. Raleigh *Standard,* July 11, 1860.
20. *Ibid.,* July 18, 1860.

his newspaper would "support either Breckinridge or Douglas, as a State Convention may determine; or leave the Electors free to cast the vote of the State in any way so as to defeat Lincoln."[21]

Since Democratic support for Breckinridge seemed overwhelming, the committee refused to call a convention, forcing Holden to decide on his own which candidate his newspaper would endorse. With emotions so high, a decision against Breckinridge would probably have destroyed his position as the leading spokesman for the state Democratic party, a sacrifice he was not prepared to make. On July 18 he reluctantly endorsed the Kentuckian for the presidency. "A public man must deal with things as they are, and not as he would have them," he candidly explained. *"The Democratic people, whose voice is above all committees, conventions, and caucuses, have commanded us to raise the names of Breckinridge and Lane, and we obey."* But he supported the ticket on the condition, as he proclaimed on the masthead of every issue of the *Standard*, that the victorious state presidential electors "will vote for the strongest man, Breckinridge or Douglas as the case may be, against Lincoln. That is, if the vote of this State will elect either of them over Lincoln, or will put either of them in the House [of Representatives], it is to be cast accordingly." Editorially, he told his readers, "With Breckinridge in the South and Douglas in the North, let us make common cause against the great common enemy, black Republicanism." Professing to see signs nationwide that such a course would succeed, he called on North Carolinians to "render available all the Democratic strength in the hour of need." Holden, despite his endorsement of the Democratic Southern Rights ticket, continued to believe that only the reunification of the national Democratic party, either with Douglas or Breckinridge as its candidate for president, could save the Union.[22]

Having announced his position, Holden, though suffering from "neuralgia" during the summer, launched a campaign to win over Douglas men to the support of Breckinridge. He wrote his vacationing wife that "between the Douglas and Breckinridge men my position is a critical one"; his office, he reported, was constantly thronged with visitors discussing the presidential contest. When

21. *Ibid.*, July 11, 1860.
22. *Ibid.*, July 18, 25, 1860.

Douglas Democrats met in Raleigh in late August, Holden pleaded with them to endorse the Breckinridge ticket in order to prevent John Bell, the Constitutional Union (Whig) candidate, from winning the state's electoral vote. A Bell victory in North Carolina, he contended, would severely damage the chances for the national success of a united Democratic party. He also pleaded with both Democratic factions to cease their abuse of each other. "We must unite, or all is lost," Holden warned. "By our divisions we strengthen Lincoln. If he is elected it will be our own fault, and we must reap the fruits of our folly, either in submission to Black Republican sway, or in the blood and conflagration of civil war, a disruption of the Union, and the loss—the irretrievable loss—of the last hope of liberty, the last hope of man!" Holden also feared that a divided state party would open the door for the restoration of Whigs to power in North Carolina. Shall Democrats, he asked, "by the indulgence of passion and ill feeling, cast away the fruits of long years of anxiety and toil?"[23]

State Democratic unity, however, could not be achieved. The Douglas convention, which met in Raleigh in August, listened to "an ultra Union" speech by the candidate himself and announced that it would offer an electoral ticket in the fall. The convention, consisting mainly of diehard supporters of the Little Giant, also endorsed the use of force against states attempting secession. Although Holden printed Douglas' speech, he announced his bitter disappointment with the action of the convention. Still, he urged the state Democratic executive committee "to make some tender of compromise to the Douglas men." He also refused to attack the Douglasites, a policy that brought him under renewed criticism from the extreme advocates of southern rights, who labeled him an outright Douglas supporter. He reminded his critics, mostly followers of his rival Governor Ellis, that he had never bolted the regular state party and insisted that his course of conciliation and Union was approved of by most North Carolina Democrats.[24]

He also refuted the charge of both Douglas and Bell supporters

23. W. W. Holden to Lulu (Louisa) Holden, September 1, 1860, in Holden Papers, DU; Raleigh *Standard*, August 22, September 5, 29, 1860.
24. Raleigh *Standard*, August 22, September 5, 1860; W. W. Holden to D. M. Barringer, September 2, 1860, in Daniel Moreau Barringer Papers, SHC.

that Breckinridge was a secessionist. The charge, he declared, was "unfounded and absurd." He cited Breckinridge's September 5 speech at Ashland, Kentucky, as proof that the candidate was loyal to the Union. In this speech Breckinridge affirmed his unionism but never indicated precisely the extent of his commitment to the Union. Holden's unionism at this time was less qualified than Breckinridge's and less committed to southern rights. "We are the advocate of the Constitutional Union and opposed to secession and disunion, and yet we are not afraid to trust Breckinridge and Lane to the fullest extent," Holden declared.[25]

Still suffering from neuralgia and following his doctor's advice, Holden visited the Atlantic coast in early September. While away from the *Standard* office, he asked Daniel M. Barringer, a prominent Democrat, to write an editorial on the political situation. The editorial, entitled "The Crisis," appeared in the September 12 issue of the *Standard* and went further than Holden would have gone in support of southern rights. Barringer even suggested that separation from the Union was inevitable if Lincoln won the fall election.[26]

Holden was stunned by the Barringer editorial. When he returned to Raleigh, he attempted to undo the damage of the editorial and counteract the rising tide of secession sentiment, especially among fellow Democrats. He backed off from his earlier insistence that the South should contemplate secession if an antislavery candidate won the presidency. Three weeks before the election he plainly told a Breckinridge rally in Raleigh that a Lincoln victory would be insufficient cause for secession. In a series of editorials before the election he followed up on this theme and declared that only if Lincoln as president sent military forces into the South to coerce a seceded state should North Carolina consider leaving the Union. "If so great a calamity as his election should befall the South, it will be the part of wisdom to wait and see what he will recommend in his Inaugural, and what he will attempt to do." Lincoln, Holden reminded his readers, would control only the presidency; the other two branches of the federal government would remain in the hands of anti-Republicans and would check any rash southern policy he might attempt. "It will not do for [North Carolinians] to abandon

25. Raleigh *Standard*, September 12, 19, 1860.
26. W. W. Holden to D. M. Barringer, September 2, 1860, in Barringer Papers; Raleigh *Standard*, September 12, 1860.

their *own* government—a government under which they have as many rights, and in which they have as deep an interest as the North—because one of its three departments has been turned against them. Neither will it be wise to make threats or give way to passion." Furthermore, "Lincoln has enough common sense to know . . . that it would be a most daring and dangerous act in him, or in any President, to touch in the slightest respect the vital interests of the slaveholding States."[27]

Election day brought the bitter fruits of Democratic division, as Holden interpreted the results. Lincoln won the election without carrying a single southern state. Immediately, the states of the Lower South, led by South Carolina, prepared to leave the Union. In keeping with his promise, Holden acquiesced, though cautiously, in Lincoln's triumph. He reiterated his preelection position that "while determined *not* to submit to the administration of the government on black Republican principles, it would be our duty to give Mr. Lincoln a trial, and to preserve the government, if possible, from disruption and destruction." His main fear was that Lincoln's election would cause "bad white men" to incite blacks to rebellion. For that reason, as he had done after John Brown's raid, he called for increased security in the country and the thorough organization and arming of the militia to meet any "aggressions" that might be launched.[28]

The majority of North Carolinians agreed with Holden and other leaders who advised a "watch and wait" policy toward the Illinois rail splitter.[29] Ironically, his main allies in the effort to keep North Carolina in the Union were old Whigs whom he had hotly denounced for many years. Among members of his own party secessionist sentiment was strong, though by no means universal. When the General Assembly met two weeks after Lincoln's election, the lines were drawn between radical Democrats who wanted to move toward secession, perhaps in cooperation with other southern states, and conservatives of both old parties who followed Holden's

27. Raleigh *Standard*, October 17, 24, 31, November 7, 1860.
28. *Ibid.*, November 14, 28, 1860. Breckinridge won North Carolina with a vote of 48,533 to Bell's 44,039 and Douglas' 2,690. Cheney (ed.), *North Carolina Government*, 1331.
29. Dennis R. Lawson, "The Ending of an Era: North Carolina and Secession" (M.A. thesis, North Carolina State University, 1977), 79–82.

lead. The radicals gained temporary advantage when Governor Ellis in his opening message to the legislature seemingly threw his support behind secession by calling for North Carolina's participation in a southern convention that would be immediately followed by a state convention to deal with the crisis. Holden immediately attacked the governor's proposal as a plan to take the state out of the Union without permitting the people to vote on the issue.[30]

While the debate raged on this issue and other proposals, the radicals quickly moved to remove Holden from the position of state printer and replace the *Standard* as the party newspaper organ in Raleigh. By a majority of five votes they secured the Democratic caucus's approval of John Spelman for state printer, and the next day the legislature, with Ellis' tacit backing, dutifully ratified the decision. Holden's claim a few weeks later that he "could easily have beaten John Spelman for State Printer, if [he] had made an effort" was probably only an attempt to put the best face possible on a humiliating defeat.[31]

Holden did not pretend to conceal his anger at his replacement by Spelman, a recently naturalized citizen who only two years earlier had worked in the *Standard* office and had since become a protégé of Governor Ellis. Abandoning his customary practice of not publicly criticizing Democratic leaders, he inveighed against the combination of disunionists and spoilsmen, including Ellis, who had engineered his defeat. He specifically attacked the policy of the Ellis faction "that no man is a true Democrat or a friend of his country who is opposed to secession and disunion. . . . We declare that we are a better Democrat than John W. Ellis. Our Democracy have [sic] never before been questioned," he said, though the governor's had.[32]

Holden warned that Ellis and other "ambitious and designing

30. Raleigh *Standard*, November 28, 1860. Ellis, ever quick to find fault with Holden, privately placed Holden "without the pail [sic] of the party" when the *Standard* editor criticized his message. John W. Ellis Journal, November 24, 1860, in Tolbert (ed.), *Ellis Papers*, II, 473.

31. Jonathan Worth to [J. J. Jackson?], letter fragment written in late 1860, in J. G. de Roulhac Hamilton (ed.), *The Correspondence of Jonathan Worth* (2 vols.; Raleigh, 1909), I, 125–26; W. W. Holden to the Charlotte *Democrat*, February 11, 1881, newspaper clipping in Scrapbook, Holden Papers; DU; Raleigh *Standard*, January 9, 1861.

32. Raleigh *Standard*, November 28, 1860. In the same issue Holden also for the first time publicly charged Ellis with political chicanery in defeating him for the

men," because of Lincoln's election, were determined to commit North Carolina "to revolution, anarchy, and civil war." North Carolina Democrats should know, he declared, "that their Governor is thoroughly committed to disunion schemes; that the control of the party at this point has been usurped by a few ambitious and aspiring men, whose Democracy never was of the best stamp; that renegade Know Nothings, old line Whigs, and naturalized foreigners, under the lead of Governor Ellis, are shaping the policy of the party and ignoring the 'Old Guard' who stood by Jackson and elected Reid" governor. In the winter crisis of 1860–1861 Holden repeatedly appealed to the Democratic masses to rescue the party from the disunionist usurpers and restore the "Old Guard . . . to full standing and influence."[33]

Many "Old Guard" Democrats did rally to Holden's defense, probably in most cases because of his unionist stance rather than because of any strong personal loyalty to him. In the General Assembly a corporal's guard of outraged Democrats joined with Union Whigs in an attempt to elect Holden to the United States Senate in place of Thomas L. Clingman. But Ellis Democrats, not all of whom, despite Holden's claim, were secessionists, beat back the challenge. From all over the state, Democratic "friends," whom Holden did not identify except to say that most of them had voted for Breckinridge, flooded the *Standard* office with letters expressing their strong approval of his stand against the "disunion demagogues" of the Ellis faction. As an Alamance Democrat expressed it: "You have always been true to [the] Democracy. You are one of those who, with Reid, stood by the flag and sustained it in the dark days years ago. They have put a naturalized Englishman [Spelman] over you, who has done nothing of consequence for the party, and they did it because you would not go for disunion; but hurrah for Holden!— they cannot put you down. Let the fire-eaters fume and rage, but expose them, and we, the people, will sustain you."[34]

<hr>

Democratic gubernatorial nomination in 1858. Ellis had obtained the nomination, the disappointed editor asserted, "by a resort to means which would be considered unfair even by New York politicians."

33. *Ibid.* Despite Holden's charges, Governor Ellis, though favoring a southern convention on the crisis, had not at this time committed himself to the immediate secessionist position. He would take this step in January, 1861.

34. C. B. Harrison to Lawrence O'B. Branch, December 2, 11, 1860, in Branch

Despite a great deal of support for Holden and his "watch and wait" policy toward Lincoln, the Ellis faction consolidated its control over the Democratic organization and gained the endorsement of several important Democratic newspapers for its strong southern-rights stance. After South Carolina's secession in late December and the North Carolina General Assembly's authorization of a convention election to determine the state's position in the crisis, a political transformation occurred. Governor Ellis, fearing the coercive power of a Lincoln government and goaded by Holden's attacks, in January embraced immediate secession, and from behind the scenes he turned the Democratic party into the party of separation. Holden, unable to regain control of his old party either for the cause of the Union or for what now seemed relatively minor—his own political vindication—called for the establishment of a "Constitutional Union" party to resist the designs of the secessionists. "The old parties are extinct," he declared, and he urged the formation of a bipartisan coalition of unionists to save the state from the "demagogues." Holden insisted that he had not abandoned true Democratic principles; the fire-eaters, who had usurped the party organization in their hell-bent desire to take the state out of the Union, were the ones who "are *outside* of Democratic principles and who, in assuming to expound Democratic doctrines, are guilty of brazen presumption. . . . Secession at the mere whim or caprice of a State, is utterly undemocratic." Democratic principles, he contended, consisted of "a strict construction of the Constitution; the reserved rights of the States; opposition to oligarchies and aristocracies; and the greatest good [for] the greatest number." These principles, he repeatedly declared, did not conflict with North Carolina's continuance in the Union. Indeed, he predicted that the constitutional rights of the state, the liberties of the people, and the institution of slavery would ultimately be destroyed if North Carolina followed the rash lead of the lower southern states and left the Union. Secession "on account of Lincoln's election," he insisted, "would end in civil war, in military despotism, and in the destruction of slave property. *Let us give the Northern people time. . . .*

Family Papers; Raleigh *Standard,* December 26, 1860. See also issues of December 5, 1860, January 2, 9, 23, 1861.

The Constitution will be restored, and Mr. Lincoln and his party will be hurled from power in 1864."[35]

At Holden's urging, Constitutional Union party rallies were held throughout the state in preparation for the February 28 election on the convention question. These meetings adopted resolutions favoring Holden's "watch and wait" policy and also selected candidates for delegates to the convention in case it was approved. Such a state convention might take North Carolina out of the Union, just as conventions were doing throughout the Lower South. Although he had initially opposed the convention bill, preferring instead a national convention of the states to resolve the sectional differences, Holden took no public position on whether unionists should vote for the state convention. Nevertheless, he entered the campaign with confidence that a majority of unionist delegates would be elected to such a convention, and they would vote down the demon of secession. Most unionist leaders, however, opposed the convention, believing that if it met, it might be swayed "to subvert and destroy the government" without submitting the question of secession to the people for ratification.[36]

Recognized as the inspiration behind the state's movement for the preservation of the Union, Holden found himself with strange bedfellows. Old Whig leaders like George E. Badger, William A. Graham, Alfred Dockery, and John A. Gilmer joined with him and conservative Democrats to rally the voters for the Union. Holden must have felt particularly strange in printing, without biting ridicule, the commentaries of Whigs whom he had vehemently assailed for almost two decades. After a Wake County Union party convention nominated Holden and Badger for seats in the convention, the two former antagonists canvassed the county together, holding joint debates with the secessionist candidates.[37]

35. Raleigh *Standard*, January 23, 1861. See also the issues of February 6, 13, 1861. For evidence that Ellis had abandoned his equivocation on secession and had cast his lot wholeheartedly with the disunionists, see his letter to Governor Joseph E. Brown of Georgia, January 21, 1861 in Tolbert (ed.), *Ellis Papers*, II, 564–65.

36. Kruman, *Parties and Politics in North Carolina*, 204–205; Lawson, "The Ending of an Era," 126–27.

37. Raleigh *Standard*, January–February, 1861, *passim;* William H. Battle to his wife, February 10, 1861, in Battle Family Papers, SHC.

The briefness of the campaign required an intensive effort by spokesmen on both sides. To aid the cause of the Union party, Holden began the publication of a triweekly edition of the *Standard*, though without the state printing contract the expansion of the newspaper probably resulted in a financial loss for him. Even though the circulation of the *Standard* did not exceed three thousand copies, the position of the newspaper in the campaign had a significant influence among conservative Democrats, including those who had supported Douglas in 1860 and many who had voted for Breckinridge on Holden's assurance that he was not a secessionist.[38] Holden's well-phrased arguments in favor of the Union and his "watch and wait" position regarding Lincoln also reassured "floating" voters and even many wavering old Whigs, some of whom had previously made it a point never to believe anything they read in the *Standard*.[39]

As the brief campaign climaxed, Holden happily reported a moderation of northern sentiment toward the South. He predicted that a compromise would be worked out in Washington to save the border states for the Union and perhaps secure a reversal of secession in the Lower South. Despite the failure of the Crittenden compromise in Congress in January, Holden expressed confidence that the so-called peace conference of "old gentlemen," mainly from the border states and meeting in the national capital in February on the eve of the North Carolina convention election, would arrange a favorable settlement. He also eagerly reported a strong momentum for the Union in the states of the Upper South. Virginia had elected a majority of unionists to its convention, Tennessee had voted down a convention, and Kentucky, Missouri, and Maryland had shown no disposition to secede, he informed his readers. "Let us be watchful, patient, and hopeful. The lights of concord, of justice, and reconciliation are streaming along the Northern heavens. Never despair of the Republic!"[40]

38. For the paper's circulation figures, see Raleigh *Standard*, May 13, 1863.

39. On the importance of the floating vote in the campaign, especially in the West, see Tod R. Caldwell to William A. Graham, February 11, 1861, in J. G. de Roulhac Hamilton and Max R. Williams (eds.), *The Papers of William Alexander Graham* (7 vols. to date; Raleigh, 1957–), V, 232–33.

40. Raleigh *Standard*, February 6, 1861. See also issues of January 22, 30, February 13, 1861.

The success of Holden's leadership in the Union party campaign was evident on election day. North Carolinians rejected the call for a convention, though by only a slim margin. But because many unionist leaders had supported the convention—privately including even Holden, who foresaw that unionists would easily control it—the vote was not a true indicator of unionist strength in the election. A more accurate reflection of unionist sentiment can be found in the selection of delegates to the convention, which took place in the same election. According to Marc Kruman, who has made a careful examination of the election, unionists won 81 of the 120 delegate seats in the convention, polling 60.1 percent of the votes. In Wake County the Union party ticket, including Holden, almost tripled the vote of the secessionists; in Raleigh the victory was even more overwhelming with the Union party candidates winning more than 700 of the 800 votes cast.[41]

Holden gloated over the triumph of the Union party and the defeat of the secessionist "conspirators." The people by their votes, he exulted, had been "true to themselves, to their State, to their section, and at the same time to the Union." He declared, however, that unionists "must not be understood as saying that they will submit to the administration of the government on sectional or black Republican principles." The election meant "that they are anxious to preserve the Union on a Constitutional basis, and to obtain such guarantees as will lead to a permanent re-construction of the Union. The Unionists entertain hopes, and nearly all of them strong hopes that the Union can and will be preserved."[42]

As Holden knew, Abraham Lincoln, who would become president four days after the convention election in North Carolina, held the key to the continued success of unionism in the state. All political elements looked to Lincoln's inaugural address for an indication of his policy toward the seceded states, now the Confederate States of America; most of them interpreted the message in light of their

41. Kruman, *Parties and Politics in North Carolina*, 210–11; W. W. Holden to Raleigh *News and Observer*, March 16, 1887, newspaper clipping in Scrapbook, Holden Papers, DU. The Wake County and Raleigh election returns are in Raleigh *Standard*, March 6, 1861.
42. Raleigh *Standard*, March 6, 1861.

own predilections. Secessionists naturally found cause for alarm in the new president's statement that he intended to maintain a federal presence in the Lower South, a policy that could be implemented only by armed force. Even some North Carolina unionists, who had argued during the convention campaign that Lincoln would not attempt to suppress the seceded states, believed that his inaugural remarks meant coercion, and coercion meant war and the secession of their state.[43]

Holden, on the other hand, perceived no threat in Lincoln's remarks. The new president's address, he told his readers, "*is not a war message*. . . . It is not unfriendly to the South. It deprecates war and bloodshed, and it pleads for the Union." Holden indicated, as historians since then have generally confirmed, that "so far as coercion is concerned, Mr. Lincoln occupies the very ground occupied by Mr. Buchanan," a policy of nonrecognition of secession combined with the intention to enforce the laws. Like Buchanan, Lincoln "virtually omits the cotton States" in his policy, "for the simple reason that he has no officers in those States and cannot execute" the laws there. Holden argued that "if Mr. Lincoln were mad enough to attempt to subjugate the Southern States, or even if he were disposed to do so—as his Inaugural shows he is not—he has no army at his command" except a few thousand troops mainly on the distant Indian frontier. Furthermore, he had no money or authority to raise an army for the suppression of the South. "His party is already demoralized, and in addition to this, the great body of the Northern people will never consent to an aggressive war on the South." The Raleigh editor also pointed out that the new president recognized the perpetuity of slavery in the South, and he claimed that Lincoln favored a national convention "to reconstruct the Union on an enduring basis" or, that failing, to provide for a peaceable separation of the states of the Lower South.[44]

Although sanguine in print, Holden sensed that the reaction of most North Carolinians to Lincoln's inaugural was one of despair. During March, political momentum swung dramatically toward

43. Joseph Carlyle Sitterson, *The Secession Movement in North Carolina* (Chapel Hill, 1939), 231–32; Potter, *The Impending Crisis*, 568.

44. Raleigh *Standard*, March 13, 1861; Potter, *The Impending Crisis*, 569. Although he did not publicize it, Holden wrote Lincoln recommending Charles Henry Foster of North Carolina, "a consistent Union man," for a federal position.

the disunionists, and while the iron was hot, they held mass meetings throughout the state, climaxing with the formation of the Southern Rights, or secessionist, party at Goldsboro on March 22.[45] Holden quickly sought to arouse lethargic unionists and win back the support of the faint-hearted. He called for the thorough organization of the Union party at the grassroots and for the selection by district conventions of congressional candidates for the August election. He declared that the Union party, as it had done in February, should be able to defeat the "Disunion party," provided its local leaders campaigned vigorously. He vehemently defended the unionists from charges that they were "submissionists" in the struggle for southern rights, claiming that the real submissionists were those who had succumbed to the inflammatory harangues of the Ellis "oligarchy"in favor of disunion. When a secessionist critic referred to Raleigh and Wake County as "abolition holes," Holden indignantly announced that of the seven hundred unionists in the state capital he had "never heard one even breathe a word against slavery," and the Union party, he declared, was as committed as the fire-eaters to the preservation of the peculiar institution.[46]

His strongest outburst against his secessionist critics occurred when the Goldsboro *Rough Notes* branded him an ally of Abe Lincoln. Although the editor of the *Rough Notes* was hardly an oligarch, Holden made the connection and in an appeal for support grimly invoked the old aristocrat—laboring man dichotomy. "The oligarchs who instruct their minions when and at whom to groan," he thundered, "hate Lincoln, not because he is a black Republican, but because he split rails for his daily bread when a young man; they hate Douglas because he worked at the cabinet-maker's trade for his daily bread when a young man; they hate Andrew Johnson because he worked at the tailor's trade for his daily bread when a young man; and they hate Holden because, being only a printer, he dared to be Governor of North Carolina. . . . They know that he is as true to the South as they are, but they seek to ruin him by associat-

W. W. Holden to Abraham Lincoln, April 6, 1861, in Presidential Papers of Abraham Lincoln, LC (microfilm).

45. Lawson, "The Ending of an Era," 146–47; Sitterson, *Secession Movement in North Carolina*, 234–36.

46. Raleigh *Standard*, March 6, 27, April 10, 1861.

ing him with a black Republican." Holden obviously was sensitive about his lowly origins, but it was a rather low-level sensitivity that, as in his response to the attacks by the *Rough Notes*, was invoked at critical and emotional times for the main purpose of eliciting narrowly political sympathy.[47] As a prominent editor and political leader in a society that honored public leaders who had risen by pulling up their own bootstraps, Holden could hardly have believed that people hated him because he was "only a printer." He must have been aware of his solid standing in Raleigh society and the fact that no real stigma attached to his unpretentious background.

In his effort to reverse the postinaugural losses suffered by the unionists, Holden appealed to the traditional, fundamental concerns of North Carolinians regarding governmental authority. He attacked the recently formed Confederate States as antidemocratic, the offspring of oligarchs, such as Yancey of Alabama, who were in the process of suppressing opposition in the Lower South. "There is no Democracy in the action of the Southern oligarchs," Holden told North Carolinians. The people of the Lower South "were rushed out of the Union without the privilege of being heard at the polls." Moreover, he charged, the Confederate constitution itself included provisions that were "dangerous to the liberties of the people" in those states. "The Confederate experiment," he predicted, "will end either in anarchy or despotism."[48]

Holden professed to see the same tyrannical pattern emerging in the disunionist administration of Governor Ellis. Despite the overwhelming defeat of the secessionists in the February election, he charged the governor with continuing his oligarchical schemes to take the state out of the Union. Ellis, he said, was determined to subvert the will of the people and establish a Confederate-style despotism in North Carolina. He found additional evidence of this tendency in the governor's refusal to appoint unionists as officers in the beefed-up state military force. The lesson seemed clear to Holden: if the secessionists succeeded in their deception, the freedom of the people would be extinguished.[49]

47. *Ibid.*, March 20, 1861.
48. *Ibid.*, March 13, 1861. See also the issues of March 20, April 3, 1861.
49. *Ibid.*, March 13, 20, 27, April 10, 17, 1861.

For Holden and thousands of other North Carolina unionists the debate over secession ended in mid-April when Lincoln, after the Confederate firing on Fort Sumter, called for troops to suppress "the rebellion" in the South. Branding war "a terrible evil," Holden sadly announced that the time for "watching and waiting" had passed, and North Carolinians must unite to prevent their state from being "polluted by the tread of armed men sent to make war on the 'Confederate States.'" Lincoln's decision to coerce the Lower South, Holden roared, was a "gross usurpation" of power, arrogantly violating the Constitution and portending the destruction of republican government in America. The shaken Raleigh editor reflected the attitude of most members of the North Carolina Union party when he sternly declared that the proclamation "has left no alternative but resistance or unconditional submission. The Southern man who would quietly submit to the doctrines enunciated in that document, is fit only for a slave." He also expressed a willingness to forgo "partisan discussion," drop his quarrel with Governor Ellis, and come "forward to sustain him in his day of trial."[50]

Holden soon announced his candidacy for a seat in the convention called for the purpose of taking North Carolina out of the Union. He avowed his intention to resist "to the last extremity the usurpations and aggressions of the federal government." Elected to the convention, he voted on May 20 for the ordinance of secession, and in the *Standard* he proclaimed that North Carolina should give her "last dollar and her last man" to win the war for southern independence. Despite these expressions of enthusiasm for the southern cause, the complete history of Holden's role in the crisis of 1860–1861 strongly suggests, as he insisted years later, that his signing of the secession ordinance "was the saddest and most reluctant act of his life."[51] Such lukewarmness in support of southern nationalism, combined with his position of leadership in a party hostile to the

50. *Ibid.*, April 17, 24, May 8, 1861.
51. *Ibid.*, May 8, 22, 1861, March 14, April 4, 1866; Holden, *Memoirs*, 17. Supposedly Holden bought a gold pen for the purpose of signing the ordinance of secession and exuberantly remarked when he signed, "This is the greatest act of my life." Horace W. Raper, *William W. Holden: North Carolina's Political Enigma* (Chapel Hill, 1985), 40; William K. Boyd, "William W. Holden," in *Trinity College Historical Society Papers*, Ser. III (1899), 65–66; J. G. de Roulhac Hamilton, *Reconstruction in North Carolina* (New York, 1914), 32.

secessionist state administration, meant that Holden would be quick to find fault with the Confederate leaders and would train his editorial guns on them early. Furthermore, his sensitivity regarding traditional American liberties, which he already believed the secessionist leaders were trying to subvert, and his strong, almost myopic attachment to the rights and interests of North Carolina, made it virtually inevitable that he would play a major dissident role during the Civil War.

VI
Confederate Dissident

Despite strong professions by Holden and other North Carolina leaders that they would shun party politics and unite against the common enemy, political rancor in the state never really took a holiday. Two weeks after the firing on Fort Sumter, the *Standard* editor charged that John Spelman's *State Journal*, the newspaper organ of Governor Ellis, was attempting to provoke him "into a partisan discussion" by claiming that the "old Union men" (*i.e.*, those who had opposed secession until Lincoln's call for troops) were lukewarm in their support of the southern cause. Holden hotly warned that, though he deplored party spirit, "at this time of crisis" he would "insist on justice to our late Union associates and ourselves."[1]

A few days later he became further agitated when Spelman announced a "compromise slate" of candidates to oppose the local Holden-Badger ticket in the new state convention election. In proposing his ticket, Spelman renewed his characterization of the *Standard* editor and Badger as "submissionists" who deserved public ignominy rather than election to office in the new order. The old Union party slate, however, won the contest in Wake County, causing Holden to exult that despite the "whole power of the State gov-

1. Raleigh *Standard*, May 1, 1861. See also Jonathan Worth to John B. Troy, May 21, 1861, in J. G. de Roulhac Hamilton (ed.), *The Correspondence of Jonathan Worth* (2 vols.; Raleigh, 1909), II, 150, and Zebulon B. Vance to Harriet Vance, May 18, 1861, in Frontis W. Johnston (ed.), *The Papers of Zebulon Baird Vance* (1 vol. to date; Raleigh, 1963), I, 100.

ernment" being "brought to bear against him," he had crushed his opponents. He promised that in the future he would "strike back when assailed" and would fearlessly expose and denounce governmental actions "prompted by selfish or partisan aims, damaging to the public interests and dangerous to the peace, the harmony and the success of our people in the conduct of the war."[2]

While North Carolina and the Upper South grappled with the momentous issues of secession and war, the bitter personal feud between Holden and Spelman intensified. The quarrel approached a violent stage in early May when Spelman demanded that Holden "assume a responsibility for his slander" by meeting him on the field of honor. This invitation to duel was only the second such challenge that Holden had received in his long, stormy career as editor of the *Standard*. As before, he refused the invitation, explaining that "the code now-a-days is a farce" and it was proper not to recognize it. "We think proper [also] to show ourselves a law-abiding citizen as long as we honorably can," he added. Furthermore, Spelman was not "a fit person to correspond with on any subject," including arrangements for a duel. Holden, however, warned Spelman and his friends that his refusal should not be construed to mean that he would not fight under any circumstances.[3]

Spelman was determined to create the circumstances. In the *State Journal* he scorned his rival as "a despicable character" and "an unscrupulous politician—the most selfish man we ever knew—revengeful—without gratitude or a sense of obligation—truthless, shameless and cowardly." Neither these epithets nor a more cautious challenge a few days later by editor John W. Syme of the Raleigh *Register* could arouse Holden to violence. But when William Robinson, assistant editor of the *State Journal*, called him a "poltroon," Holden sought him out on the streets and assaulted him with a cane. During the melee Robinson attempted to stab his assailant with a sword cane, but bystanders separated them before blood was spilled. Both combatants were arrested and ordered to appear in county court at its next term; neither was punished. Although

2. Raleigh *State Journal*, May 4, 8, 1861; Raleigh *Standard*, May 22, June 5, 1861.
3. Raleigh *State Journal*, May 8, 1861; Raleigh *Standard*, May 22, 1861.

Holden had insisted that he deplored violence, after this incident few questioned his willingness to fight when provoked.[4]

North Carolina had hardly left the Union on May 20 when Holden discovered that the Ellis administration was derelict in its preparations for war. On May 29 he chided state authorities—and North Carolinians in general—for assuming that the war would be short and easy. He specifically criticized Ellis and the state military board for not being "sufficiently alive to the imminent hazard" of a Federal invasion of the North Carolina coast. To meet the needs of local defense, the old unionist faction in the state convention demanded, but to no avail, that state officials raise several regiments for coastal defense. The *State Journal* denounced the attempt on the grounds that such a policy was too exclusively for the benefit of one state in the Confederacy. Warming to the issue, Holden became more critical of the administration's neglect and demanded that North Carolina's security receive top priority from the state administration.[5] The fall of Cape Hatteras to Federal forces in August provided a dramatic exoneration of his campaign for a stronger coastal defense.

Holden also soon found purely political reasons for criticizing the Ellis administration. On June 12 the *Standard* teemed with a denunciation of the governor's policy of discriminating against old unionists in his selection of state military officers. Holden charged that of the twenty-two military appointments, excluding former regular army officers, none had supported the unionist position in the February convention election. Along with other former unionists, or "conservatives," as Holden sometimes dubbed them, he claimed that the policy was a deliberate attempt by the precipitators of disunion to use the war as a means to consolidate their power in the state.

In June he renewed his pre–Fort Sumter charge that the secessionist state authorities were plotting against the constitutional rights of the people. When reports of government seizure of provi-

---

4. Raleigh *State Journal*, May 11, 15, 1861; Raleigh *Standard*, May 22, December 11, 1861.
5. Raleigh *Standard*, May 29, June 12, 19, 1861.

sions and buildings for military purposes reached Raleigh, Holden stormed: "Will the free people of North Carolina submit to such despotism?" Martial law, which included the seizure of private property, could be imposed only "under circumstances of imminent hazard to the State," he asserted. Such an instance should be "exceedingly rare, and should never be exercised, but with the greatest caution and under the most solemn conviction of its absolute necessity." Conditions in the state at that time, he insisted, did not warrant a resort to extraordinary measures. He reminded North Carolinians that they "are at war with Lincoln, a military despot, for the protection and maintenance of [the] *very rights*" that the state administration was violating. "We shall resist [Lincoln] with all the force and the means God has given us. But the war will be a fruitless one indeed, when we conquer, as we believe we shall, our Northern foes, if the Governors of North Carolina are to be invested with so arbitrary a power. . . . We warn the people of North Carolina to look closely to your *home* interests—watch narrowly the conduct of your rulers."[6]

In order to "watch narrowly the conduct" of North Carolina's rulers, Holden quietly set about organizing an opposition bloc of conservatives in the state convention.[7] In late May or early June he hosted at his home a caucus of old Union party delegates, most of whom were former Whigs. William A. Graham, a longtime Whig antagonist of Holden but now a nominal ally, presided over the caucus. The group agreed to support a vigorous prosecution of the war, but they also resolved to resist the usurpations of the secessionists. In addition, they approved a slate of candidates for election by the convention to the provisional Confederate Congress. The conservatives won four of the ten seats in the Congress. With a solid Union-Whig base, the conservative faction, strengthened by the *Standard*'s punishing criticism of the state administration, gradually gained the support of disaffected Democrats in the convention. When the state convention met for its second session, it was controlled by the conservatives.[8]

6. *Ibid.*, June 19, 1861.
7. The state convention continued to meet after secession and into the summer of 1861. It dealt with a number of issues involving the war and the state constitution.
8. John G. McCormick, "Personnel of the Convention of 1861," in *James Sprunt Historical Monographs*, No. 1 (Chapel Hill, 1900), 6–8; Kemp P. Battle,

Governor Ellis, who was always quick to believe the worst about his opponents, especially Holden, reacted in cold fury to the conservative challenge in the convention. On June 20 he wrote Confederate Secretary of Treasury Christopher Memminger that "the convention is filled with partisans—late submissionists and they give us much trouble. There are those among them who would make terms with Lincoln upon the first reverse of our arms."[9]

Two weeks later Ellis was dead, prompting Holden and other conservatives to still their criticism of the governor. As part of an expression of sympathy for his fallen rival, the *Standard* editor exonerated Ellis from the frequent charge that he had conspired to subvert the will of the people immediately after Lincoln's election by taking the state out of the Union, a charge that Holden had earlier cleverly exploited. The new governor, Henry T. Clark, however, continued Ellis' policies of ignoring former unionists in his appointments and encouraging the secessionist majority in the General Assembly to resist the convention's designs.[10]

In defiance Holden announced on October 9 a conservative electoral ticket pledged to support Jefferson Davis for president. Referring to his slate as the "People's Ticket," he claimed that his purpose in advancing it was "to do justice to the old parties" and "put down the hydrahead of party now raised for selfish purposes in our midst."[11]

One week later the *State Journal*, the "depraved oracle of the destructives in this city," as Holden characterized it, responded by coming out with a prosecessionist Davis ticket (Davis was unopposed in the election). Supporters of this ticket charged that the success of Holden's slate would give aid and comfort to the enemy by causing northerners to believe that a resurgence of unionist sentiment was occurring in North Carolina. Furthermore, they insisted that the Holden ticket was "designed to crush out the men

---

"Legislation of the Convention of 1861," in *James Sprunt Historical Monographs*, No. 1 (Chapel Hill, 1900), 126.

9. John W. Ellis to Christopher G. Memminger, June 20, 1861, in Noble J. Tolbert (ed.), *The Papers of John Willis Ellis* (2 vols.; Raleigh, 1964), II, 851.

10. Raleigh *Standard*, July 17, August 22, 1861; Charles Jeffrey Bailey, "North Carolina Politics During the Civil War, 1861–1865" (M.A. thesis, North Carolina State University, 1975), 37–38.

11. Raleigh *Standard*, October 9, November 6, 1861.

who foresaw our present dangers and gave timely warnings of their approach, and to reward the men who cried 'peace, peace,' till the enemy was at our door. . . . It is another of Holden's low party tricks, concocted in his usual underhanded manner." A soldier was more to the point. He wrote home that if Holden and "the old Union men" succeed in the election, "N.C. is sold out to Lincoln." [12]

Confused by two tickets supporting the same presidential candidate, most voters failed to see the significance of the state political divisions in the 1861 election. The voter turnout was low, with the secessionist ticket winning about 58 percent of the vote. Holden attributed the conservatives' defeat to the refusal of thousands of former unionists to vote because the slate contained secessionists. In some counties, he claimed, two-thirds or more of these disenchanted conservatives did not go to the polls. Holden, however, found comfort in the fact that five outright conservatives and five moderates were elected to the Confederate Congress. The results of the contest, he confidently announced, "clearly foreshadows the doom" of the original secessionists in the 1862 state election. [13]

Despite his postelection bravado, Holden's desire to organize a conservative party was frustrated by the popular aversion to "politics as usual" while the war raged. In an editorial on December 11 he seemed on the verge of calling for the formation of a new party in North Carolina. "Proscribed, crowded out and crowded down, suspected, maligned, and almost crushed," he thundered, "the old Union men are determined *now* to make a stand, and to appeal to the people. This course has been forced upon them. They will not submit to be proscribed any longer." [14] But shrewdly, Holden still hesitated to act. He waited for public opinion to crystallize against the "Destructives," meanwhile hoping that the opposition could be provoked into making the first move toward party organization.

In early 1862 the course of the war provided Holden with ample ammunition with which to attack the secessionists and expand his following. The fall of Roanoke Island, New Bern, and adjacent areas

12. *Ibid.*, October 16, 23, 1861; Marc Kruman, *Parties and Politics in North Carolina, 1836–1865* (Baton Rouge, 1983), 229; Raleigh *State Journal*, October 19, 1861; Bailey, "North Carolina Politics During the Civil War," 51.

13. Kruman, *Parties and Politics in North Carolina*, 229; Raleigh *Standard*, November 27, December 4, 1861.

14. Raleigh *Standard*, December 11, 1861.

to Federal forces shocked North Carolinians and gave Holden a tangible issue to use against the state administration. He also had a personal reason for scoring the Confederate failures in the East. His son Joseph W. Holden, who had volunteered for the army at age seventeen, was captured by the enemy when Roanoke Island fell and would remain a prisoner of war until 1863.[15]

Holden also began to lump the Davis government in Richmond with his foes at home. Recent military reverses in eastern North Carolina, he contended in the *Standard*, "can be chargeable to nothing so much as the imbecility and inefficiency of the State and National [Confederate] authorities." He claimed that "far more interest has been manifested by those in power to distribute the offices of the government among pets and favorites, than in the security of our defences and the procurement of men and means to resist the invader. . . . The whole course of the government has been dilatory and time-serving from the beginning."[16]

He soon found additional cause to criticize Richmond authorities. The proposal by the Davis administration to conscript men into the army caused him, as well as others, to bristle with indignation. In North Carolina he became the most vocal—and perhaps the most influential—critic of conscription. "Such a power was never before exercised or claimed in this country," he declared, and if enacted by Congress would create a strong army and lead to a military despotism. "The heel of a domestic despot would bear as heavily upon us as a foreign one," he told his readers. "This is the people's war, and not a war to be waged by forced levies. If the people will not volunteer in sufficient numbers to carry it on, and to repel the invader, then let them bear the consequences." The Confederacy "cannot be saved by a palpable disregard of the rights of the states, and by the establishment of a great military consolidation."[17]

After the conscription bill passed Congress in April, 1862, Holden continued to denounce it as oppressive and unconstitutional, but significantly he did not call on North Carolinians to resist the law.[18] In his early opposition to conscription, he developed

15. *Ibid.*, August 3, 1864; Grady Lee Carroll, *They Lived in Raleigh: Some Leading Personalities from 1792 to 1892* (2 vols.; Raleigh, 1977), I, 157–58.
16. Raleigh *Standard*, February 12, March 5, 1862.
17. *Ibid.*, April 9, 1862. See also issues of January 22, April 16, 1862.
18. *Ibid.*, April 23, 1862.

an approach that he would use repeatedly in his criticism of Confederate war policies, an approach that was consistent with his past position on measures he considered wrong. He criticized the Confederate administration on the grounds that it threatened the traditional rights of North Carolinians and if tolerated would lead to a military despotism.

Nevertheless, he denied—and would continue to deny—that he was disloyal or even lukewarm in his support of southern independence. When northern newspapers took notice of Holden's "unionism" and when state opposition newspapers charged that he wanted to abandon the war, he denounced such attention as a "vile slander" on his name and vigorously reaffirmed his intention "to stand to the last by the new government." "A revolution of madness," he declared, had engulfed the North, and the people there were submitting like slaves to "the Lincoln despotism." Having gained control of the North and its resources, the Lincolnite purpose in the war, he insisted, was "to subjugate the South, to confiscate, emancipate and destroy Southern property, and to reduce us, if possible, to utter vassalage." He maintained that "we are fighting against tyranny and despotism—for liberty and independence—for our rights and our homes. Let us fight as never men fought before," contesting every inch of southern soil. "We scorn the traitor who in this hour of peril is untrue to the South." [19]

The success of "our great Southern revolution," Holden wrote, depended upon more than the valor of arms and the people's determination to win the war. It also depended upon "a careful abstinence by all in authority from any unnecessary coercion, whether physical or mental, [and] upon the active, punctual, and intelligent exercise by the people of their right of suffrage. If a majority of the people do not vote, the experiment will fail, a faction will control, and the inevitable result will be a destruction not only of the forms but the substance of freedom." [20]

Already, in 1862, Holden saw the erosion of the constitutional liberty and self-government that he cherished. He seemed genuinely to believe that the original secessionists, who controlled the state

19. *Ibid.*, February 5, April 30, June 25, December 18, 1862.
20. *Ibid.*, December 11, 1861.

government, in their hell-bent proscription of the old unionists were rapidly imposing a political despotism on the state. "Reckless of the property or the persons of the people," these "Destructives," he charged, would force North Carolina "through the purgatorial fires of mobocracy and despotism in order to gratify their hatred towards the late Union men" and preserve their offices.[21]

For Holden and other conservatives, the state election of August, 1862, assumed a greater significance than most previous political contests. Nothing less, they insisted, than the redemption of North Carolina from the bitter partisan domination of the secessionist "cormorants" and the restoration of self-government were at stake. The nomination of William Johnston for governor by a meeting of Mecklenburg "Destructives"—an action that was quickly endorsed by several secessionist newspapers—gave Holden the excuse he needed to challenge his antagonists without being viewed as the instigator of wartime party politics. He denounced Johnston as "an ultra and bitter partisan secessionist" and called upon "the people" to hold local "primary meetings" for the purpose of indicating their choices of conservatives for governor and other state offices.[22]

At first the response to Holden's call was slow. Few prominent conservatives wanted to risk the stigma of running for office and participating in party politics while North Carolina troops were engaged in a desperate struggle to repel the northern invaders. Secessionists had sought to brand the old unionists as disloyal, and, as Holden admitted, if the conservatives dared "move a finger, it will create a fuss." Furthermore, some prominent former Whigs, like William A. Graham and John A. Gilmer, who would be natural choices to head a ticket dependent mainly upon Whig votes, were reluctant to seek a nomination controlled by their old nemesis Holden. When the Raleigh editor suggested Graham for the governorship, the secessionist press, including a few Whig newspapers, printed excerpts from earlier issues of the *Standard* pointedly reminding Graham and his friends of Holden's long record of abusing them. Holden disingenuously responded by explaining that his earlier assaults on Graham occurred "in the heat of party strife, and

21. *Ibid.*, April 9, May 28, 1862.
22. *Ibid.*, March 19, May 14, 1862.

for party purposes. Then we were influenced by party prejudice, and now we are in an atmosphere above party, where we can see men and things as they really are."[23]

Although Graham, citing personal reasons, refused to become a candidate for governor, most conservative Whigs, having cooperated with Holden in the Union party of early 1861, were ready to join with him in a campaign to redeem the state from the proscriptive secessionists. Holden's control of a powerful state newspaper and his influence among former unionist Democrats could not be ignored by pragmatic Whig leaders, though some of them never really trusted him.[24] In 1862 the *Standard* editor was the recognized spokesman of the conservative forces in the state, and Whigs realized that too much was at stake in the August election for them to challenge his leadership and thereby create a division among anti-"Destructives."

In mid-April about thirty prominent conservatives, including Holden, met in Raleigh to select a candidate for governor. Since they wanted to avoid the appearance of holding a party convention, which Holden had publicly opposed earlier and which the secessionists would be certain to attack, the meeting was held in secret. The participants planned to recommend a gubernatorial candidate for consideration by local "primary meetings," which, Holden said, would make the actual nomination. Holden himself had been mentioned for the governorship; indeed, his enemies charged that his whole purpose in the conservative movement was to get himself elected governor. But Holden, as well as other members of the state conservative conclave, realized that his candidacy would not appeal to Whig voters, without which the election could not be won. Conservative leaders understood that they needed a candidate who could attract both Whigs and Democrats; young Zebulon B. Vance, a former Whig congressman who was serving in the Confederate army, was such a man.[25]

23. *Ibid.*, May 14, April 16, 23, 1862; Raleigh *Register*, April–May, 1862.
24. Kruman, *Parties and Politics in North Carolina*, 232; William A. Graham to Rufus L. Patterson, April 17, 1862, in J. G. de Roulhac Hamilton and Max R. Williams (eds.), *The Papers of William Alexander Graham* (7 vols. to date; Raleigh, 1957–), V, 383.
25. Kruman, *Parties and Politics in North Carolina*, 232–33, departing from the traditional story of the Vance nomination, first revealed the existence of this

A few weeks after the Raleigh caucus, county primary meetings, as arranged, nominated Vance for governor, and Holden quickly followed suit by hoisting the candidate's name to the masthead of the *Standard*. Although Holden sought to leave the impression that the gubernatorial nomination came from the grass roots— and he only followed the dictates of the people—the source of Vance's good fortune was not lost upon the young westerner. From his army camp, Vance wrote Holden consenting to the nomination and asking him and other Raleigh conservatives to read the draft of his public letter of acceptance and suggest any changes that they thought appropriate.[26]

By past standards, the campaign was lackluster and conducted almost entirely by the partisan press. Holden, whose experience and skill in attacking his opponents gave him a distinct advantage in a newspaper war, was remarkably effective in the 1862 campaign. He heaped a torrent of malediction on the secessionists, generally repeating the shopworn charges of the past year. When some of his opponents adopted the name Confederate party during the campaign, Holden labeled them "Stallfederates" because, as he explained, "they have been stall fed until they have grown fat at the expense of the people" while neglecting the defense of the state and other public interests. Once again, he referred to the conservative slate, which also included candidates for Congress and the state legislature, as "the People's Ticket." Denying that he had organized a political party, he called on "old Jackson Democrats" and "Old Henry Clay Whigs" to rise up without benefit of party organization and join the crusade "to reform the government and vindicate popular rights."[27]

Spokesmen for the so-called Confederate party, including a number of old unionist Whigs, spent more time attacking Holden than

---

meeting. My account elaborates somewhat upon Kruman's, mainly regarding the meeting's secrecy and Holden's prospects for the nomination. See Raleigh *Standard*, February 26, March 26, 1862, and James T. Leach to Zebulon B. Vance, March 5, September 22, 1864, in Zebulon B. Vance Papers, NDAH.

26. Raleigh *Standard*, June 4, 25, 1862; Bailey, "North Carolina Politics During the Civil War," 70–71. Holden and other conservative leaders recommended no significant changes in the address.

27. Raleigh *Standard*, June 4, 11, 18, 25, 1862.

they did Vance, who was largely invisible during the campaign. They routinely referred to the Vance coalition as the "Holden-Conservative party" and declared that "every vote for Vance was a vote for Holden." The Raleigh *Register*, once the moderate newspaper organ of the Whig party but now a bitter anti-Holden journal, professed astonishment that old Whigs could be hoodwinked by such an unscrupulous demagogue as the *Standard* editor. The Salisbury *Watchman*, hoping also to detach Whig voters from Vance, referred to the conservatives as "Holdenites," a label that many Whigs resented and, the *Watchman* believed, would persuade them either to vote with the secessionists or stay at home on election day.[28]

The main charges against Holden were that he was lukewarm toward the Confederacy and that his criticism of state secessionists and the Davis administration was giving aid and comfort to the northern enemy. The secessionist press ran damning excerpts from the New York *Herald*, the Philadelphia *Inquirer*, and eastern North Carolina newspapers now under northern editors. These statements indicated that the *Standard*, "in defiance of the Rebel powers, plants itself beside the old and honored Union." Opponents of the conservatives gleefully repeated the comment in the Philadelphia *Inquirer* that the issue in North Carolina "was squarely secession against anti-secession."[29]

Holden answered such charges by insisting that he and other conservatives were truer to southern independence and the interests of the state than the "Destructives." He asserted that, while late Union men were fighting in the ranks around Richmond and in eastern North Carolina, original secessionists were remaining at home and profiting from the war. These stay-at-home "cormorants," he claimed, were the same ones who were charging him with disloyalty to the Confederacy. William Johnston, the secessionist candidate for governor and president of a South Carolina railroad, was, unlike Vance, "a party man" and a promoter of the Palmetto State, Holden declared. When reports reached Raleigh that the Richmond *Enquirer* was trying to persuade North Carolina troops

28. *Ibid.*, September 3, 1862; Raleigh *Register*, June 18, 21, 25, 1862; Bailey, "North Carolina Politics During the Civil War," 80.

29. Raleigh *Register*, June–July, 1862; J. G. de Roulhac Hamilton, *Reconstruction in North Carolina* (New York, 1914), 42–43.

to vote for Johnston, Holden warned outsiders against interfering in North Carolina politics. Touching the exposed nerve of state pride, he exclaimed: "We now say to Virginia and South-Carolina, let *North Carolina alone!* She is *not* a narrow strip of land between you, but a sovereign, self-governing State."[30]

Holden would not be intimidated by the opposition's assaults on his loyalty or influenced to curtail his criticism of the administration by pressure from well-meaning friends. His old friend William J. Yates of the Charlotte *Western Democrat*, while acknowledging Holden's loyalty, unsuccessfully pleaded with him to cease his partisan abuse of the secessionists lest the cause of southern independence suffer. Even Vance became perturbed with Holden. He complained to a Raleigh associate that "the tone of Holden's paper is too ultra; it will do harm, you may depend upon it." He asked his friend to talk to the *Standard* editor and, without offending him, "try and teach him moderation. . . . As sure as you live, moderation, no partyism, harmony and deprecation of strife constitutes [*sic*] our true tactics" in the campaign.[31]

Long a practitioner of the invective style of political journalism, Holden could not be persuaded by Vance's friend to temper his language. He continued to hiss scorn at the secessionists and their policy of denouncing and proscribing former unionists for their presumed disloyalty. The "real traitors" in North Carolina, Holden repeatedly charged, were those "Destructives," such as the editors

30. Raleigh *Standard*, July 2, 1862. The quotation from the *Standard* that historians have used to suggest that many North Carolinians, including Holden, had repented the act of secession was taken out of context. Holden's comment referred to those who sought to take the state out of the Union *before* Lincoln's call for troops after Fort Sumter. Hamilton (*Reconstruction in North Carolina*, 41) quotes Holden as saying, "All those who, with South Carolina, preferred to break up the government, and who have not repented for so doing, will vote for Colonel Johnston." But what Holden actually said was that Johnston had "showed his contempt for the people by refusing to submit to their voice in February, and he showed his bitter partisan feelings by denouncing those who would not go with *him* and his beloved South-Carolina in the work of disunion. Everyone, therefore, who with South-Carolina, preferred to break up the government, and who labored to do it before Lincoln's proclamation was issued, and who has not repented for so doing, will vote for Mr. Johnston." Raleigh *Standard*, June 25, 1862.

31. Raleigh *Standard*, June 18, July 2, 1862; Charlotte *Western Democrat*, July 22, 29, 1862; Zebulon B. Vance to George Little, June 1, 1862, in George Little Papers, Little-Mordecai Collection (filed under Miscellaneous Business Papers), NDAH.

of the Raleigh *Register* and the *State Journal*, who had joined the
Lincoln newspapers in spreading false stories of disloyalty in the
state. These accounts had confused and divided the people, creating an atmosphere of intolerance and political strife at a time when
North Carolinians should be united against the common foe.[32]

On the eve of the August election Holden predicted that the
conservative coalition would triumph by a margin of 20,000 to
25,000 votes. His prediction, it turned out, was unduly pessimistic.
The "Conservative party," as many of its supporters now labeled it,
won a sweeping victory at the polls. Vance defeated Johnston by
a vote of 55,282 to 20,813, and the Conservatives easily won control of the General Assembly. Holden extravagantly asserted that
30,000 "old, true blue, Jackson Democrats" cast Conservative ballots in the election. Most of the Conservative votes, however, came
from the ranks of the old Whig party, but Holden was probably
correct in claiming that a relatively large number of Democrats,
who had been suckled on the *Standard*, supported the new party's
candidates.[33]

Holden exuberantly proclaimed the Conservative success "the
most signal political victory ever achieved in this State." The voters,
he crowed, had completely vindicated the course of the old Union
men since Lincoln's election, had repudiated the proscriptive policy
of the original secessionists, and had checked the bent toward military power. He wrote that the "Destructives'" incompetence in
providing for North Carolina's coastal defense had also contributed to the Conservative victory.[34]

Holden's assessment of the election was only partly correct. It ignored voter discontent with Confederate policies, particularly conscription, an issue that had already elicited considerable concern in
the state but that Holden had rarely used in the campaign. The
Conservative victory also owed a great deal to Holden's leadership
in the organization of former unionists at the local level and his insistence that they conduct the campaign like a crusade. The admin-

32. Raleigh *Standard*, July 16, 23, 30, 1862.
33. *Ibid.*, July 23, 30, August 6, 1862; Kruman, *Parties and Politics in North
Carolina*, 238–39. For the election returns, see John L. Cheney (ed.), *North Carolina Government, 1585–1979: A Narrative and Statistical History* (Raleigh, 1981),
1400–1401.
34. Raleigh *Standard*, August 20, 1862.

istration party had no such inspiration from the top. As Kenneth
Rayner, a prominent "Confederate," admitted at the height of the
campaign: "The 'Conservatives' or Holdenites are thoroughly organized; they are working like beavers. The Southern-rights men
have no party organization; they are comparatively supine and
apathetic."[35]

Although the Conservatives did not adopt an official state platform, Holden's commentaries in the *Standard* provided the political doctrine for the new party, the main points of which were frequently repeated in the resolutions passed by local Conservative
meetings. In effect, Holden was the catalyst for the organization of
the Conservative party and the revival of the two-party system in
North Carolina. Without Holden's energizing leadership, discontent in North Carolina might have continued as an amorphous,
nonparty political force that, as was the case in other Confederate
states, could not marshal a strong challenge to Confederate war
policies.[36] Indeed, the new Conservative party was so successful
that the secessionist faction could not again mount a real challenge
to it, and when Conservatives divided in 1864, old secessionists
were impotent to take advantage of the schism.

After Vance's inauguration in late 1862, Holden and associates
moved quickly to cleanse the state government of their adversaries.
In addition, Conservatives in the General Assembly, with Holden
and Governor Vance looking over their shoulders but evidently not
interfering, sent William A. Graham to the Confederate Senate.
Holden was selected as state printer, which must have gratified him
immensely in view of his dismissal from the office by the upstart
secessionists in 1860. Nevertheless, at first he refused to accept this
lucrative position, "but at the urgent appeal of many friends," including Governor Vance, he claimed, he consented to it. When opponents bitterly complained that the Conservatives, in sweeping clean
the state administration, were motivated by partisan animus toward

35. Kenneth Rayner to Thomas Ruffin, July 12, 1862, in J. G. de Roulhac
Hamilton (ed.), *The Papers of Thomas Ruffin* (4 vols.; Raleigh, 1918–20), III,
253–54.
36. For the peculiarity of wartime North Carolina politics, see Thomas B. Alexander and Richard E. Beringer, *The Anatomy of the Confederate Congress: A
Study of the Influences of Member Characteristics on Legislative Voting Behavior,
1861–1865* (Nashville, 1972), 39, and Kruman, *Parties and Politics in North
Carolina,* 240.

the secessionists, Holden replied, "Every head that drops in the basket falls by way of retaliation *forced* upon the Conservatives." [37]

Although grateful to Holden for his leadership in the 1862 campaign, Whig Conservatives like Graham, State Treasurer Jonathan Worth, and Edward J. Hale, the editor of the Fayetteville *Observer* and a confidant of Governor Vance, never completely trusted Holden and were alarmed by his continuing vilification of the original secessionists. At first these Conservatives treated Holden with civility and, in the case of Governor Vance, with deference. Vance, for example, submitted his inaugural address to Holden for criticism before he delivered it. But privately they soon found fault with the *Standard* editor. Still, they were reluctant, during the critical early months of Conservative rule, to challenge him lest they fatally divide the party, especially since Holden showed no real disposition to control the new government.

Holden Democrats, whose political creed had been largely shaped by the *Standard*, were devoted to him and expected him to be the dominant person in the new order. Bitterly resentful of the secessionists who had destroyed the Democratic party, they supported Holden's unrelenting campaign against the "Destructives." They also wanted him to continue the fight for the interests and constitutional liberties of North Carolinians, which had been an article of faith of the antebellum Democratic party. These former Democrats, however, represented only a minority in the Conservative party; they probably numbered less than one-third. Old Whigs, whatever their view of Holden or the shifts in political loyalties that had occurred since 1860, were the dominant element in the new coalition. This fact, though difficult to gauge precisely, significantly influenced the course of North Carolina's political history for the remainder of the war. It also influenced the state's—and Holden's—response to the external threat posed by the war and by Confederate policies.

A public conflict between Whigs and Holdenites was carefully avoided during the first year of the Conservative ascendancy. Holden

37. Kenneth Rayner to Thomas Ruffin, November 23, 1862, in Hamilton (ed.), *Ruffin Papers*, III, 271; Raleigh *Standard*, August 20, December 10, 1862; W. W. Holden to Edward J. Hale, November 21, 1862, in Edward Jones Hale Papers, NDAH.

endorsed "every word" of Vance's lengthy first message to the General Assembly and applauded the governor's generally successful efforts in late 1862 to uphold civil authority when Confederate military officers sought to enforce conscription. Both Holden and Vance, while deploring the necessity for conscription, believed that until its repeal the law should be enforced, but only by state officials. Holden insisted that a conscript should have the right to "sue out his habeas corpus" in a state court if he felt himself wronged under the law. "We hold that every soldier and every conscript should stand by his colors and do his duty, but we hold also that a conscript has rights as well as a General, and he ought to insist on those rights."[38]

Despite Governor Vance's partial success in preventing Confederate infringements on the legal rights of conscripts and those charged with disloyalty, incidents of "military usurpations" continued to occur. Holden highlighted each incident in the *Standard*, usually accompanying his account with a long editorial comment on the threat it posed to the civil liberties of the people. When a Confederate army unit operating in the western mountains massacred thirteen Shelton Laurel unionists, including women and children, who were in their custody, he denounced the act as "both cowardly and wicked," and demanded "in the name of outraged humanity the punishment of the officer who is guilty of these murders." One month later he renewed his demand for the prosecution of the perpetrator or perpetrators. "We are not apologists for tories or traitors in our midst," he soberly declared, "but we do insist on the observance of the rules of civilized warfare, especially toward our own people, no matter how guilty they may be; and we intend to resist, as we have heretofore done, every encroachment by the military on the civil power." Governor Vance made a strong effort to bring the offending officer to justice, but the War Department in Richmond through evasive tactics permitted him to escape punishment.[39]

Military defiance of civil authority, Holden continued to remind his readers, was "the very essence of despotism." It smacked of

38. Raleigh *Standard*, September 17, 26, November 5, 26, 1862.
39. *Ibid.*, March 18, April 22, 1863; Phillip Shaw Paludan, *Victims: A True Story of the Civil War* (Knoxville, 1981), 104–106.

European monarchy and was grounded in "unadulterated Lincolnism," he declared. Exceeding Vance in his public outrage at the military arrests of those suspected of avoiding conscription, Holden claimed that such incidents were "a gross and palpable violation of the Constitution and Bill of Rights of this State, and of the first principles of liberty." When the Confederate Congress, at President Davis' insistence, in March, 1863, provided for the suspension of the writ of habeas corpus to deal with violators of the conscription law, deserters, and the disloyal, Holden reacted sorrowfully to this "gross usurpation" of civil authority. In permitting the violation of constitutional rights, many southerners, Holden contended, had succumbed to their passion. They "hate Lincoln so bitterly that in order to resist him successfully [they] must make slaves of [them]selves. The answer of our people is, *we will be slaves to neither Lincoln, nor Davis, nor France, nor England.*" Shockingly, he promised that North Carolina would "withdraw from the Confederacy rather than permit a Davis Dictatorship" and if necessary would "fight her way out against all comers."[40]

At the same time, the continued Federal occupation of the eastern counties and the refusal of the Confederate administration to send a military force capable of expelling the invaders gave Holden, as well as Vance and other Conservatives, additional cause to criticize the Davis government. Claiming that the Confederate War Department had admitted its inability to protect the East, Holden vigorously urged the approval of a proposal by the governor that would authorize him to recruit ten regiments to be deployed only for eastern defense.[41]

When the pro-Davis press, both inside and outside North Carolina, attacked the governor's bill for its narrow state purpose and its apparent conflict with Confederate conscription policy, Holden vigorously defended it and declared that the main priority for North Carolinians was their own military defense. "Self-preservation is the first law of nature. If the enemy should be allowed to occupy the Eastern Counties as far west as the Wilmington and Weldon Rail-

40. Raleigh *Standard*, December 10, 17, 1862, January 14, May 6, June 3, 1863.

41. *Ibid.*, November 26, December 17, 31, 1862; Richard E. Yates, *The Confederacy and Zeb Vance* (Tuscaloosa, 1958), 25–27.

road [at Goldsboro], *the State will be ruined,"* he maintained, since that area supplied a large quantity of foodstuffs for the people of the interior.[42]

For a variety of reasons the "Ten Regiment bill" failed to pass the General Assembly, leaving the East in Federal hands and leaving Holden fuming at the Confederate neglect of the state's defense. The Wilmington and Weldon Railroad, however, remained under Confederate control, and not until the last weeks of the war did the area fall to Federal forces.

With the approach of the crucial military campaign of 1863, which Holden predicted would determine the fate of the Confederacy, his criticism of President Davis and his supporters became shriller. He excoriated the Confederate administration for its anti–North Carolina bias and its appointment of Virginia and Maryland citizens to Confederate offices in the state. He especially expressed his resentment toward those "swarms of foreign mercenaries" who were dispatched from Richmond to collect taxes, impress supplies for the army, and administer the conscription law. "Our State is under the ban at Richmond," he told his readers, and such treatment was due to the "partyism or favoritism" of the Davis administration, aided and abetted by "Pharisaical Destructives" in North Carolina. Davis and his secessionist cronies, Holden asserted, felt threatened by the success of the Conservative party in North Carolina and were determined to prevent its spread. Through their newspaper organs they were endeavoring "to produce the impression, for party purposes, that a considerable portion of our Legislature and a majority of our people are friendly to Lincoln's government."[43]

Again he warned Richmond authorities: "North Carolina will never hew wood and draw water for those who slight or underrate her. She must be the equal of the other States of the Confederacy, or she will leave it and endeavor to take care of herself."[44]

Actually, Holden's threat to lead North Carolina out of the Confederacy was an empty one. In using such strong language, he sought to shock Richmond authorities into a fairer treatment of the

42. Raleigh *Standard*, November 26, 1862, January 21, February 1, 1863.
43. *Ibid.*, January 14, February 4, 11, March 11, 25, June 3, July 8, 1863.
44. *Ibid.*, February 11, June 3, 1863.

state and, not incidentally, spotlight in North Carolina the "Destructives" as a major source of the state's troubles. He vigorously
insisted that his criticism of the Davis administration was not evidence of disloyalty to the Confederacy but rather an expression of
dissatisfaction with the management of the war and the narrow
partisanship of Richmond authorities.[45] Nevertheless, when, beginning in mid-1863, his harsh criticism of the Confederate government was tied to efforts to bring peace, Holden gained notoriety,
both inside and outside North Carolina, as the South's leading
apostle of defeatism and its offspring, reconstruction of the Union.

45. *Ibid.*, August 12, 1863.

VII
Peace Leader

His bitter disaffection with the Davis government and his growing realization that the war was exacting a terrible toll upon the South and particularly upon North Carolina led Holden in mid-1863 to call for negotiations to end the war. Many southerners, of course, were war-weary by this time and desired an end to the conflict, but in most cases they rejected any state or local debate on peace for fear that it would demoralize the army and give encouragement to the enemy. They believed that peace efforts should only be initiated by Confederate authorities and only after the Lincoln administration had indicated a willingness to recognize southern independence.[1]

Although overwhelmingly in favor of Confederate independence, a relatively large number of North Carolinians rejected such logic. For more than a year they had been exposed to Holden's charges against the Davis administration and the "Destructives" who had brought on the war. Many of them, as their trepidations increased, accepted the truth of the Raleigh editor's charges. Evidence that Holdenism had entered the consciousness of thousands of North Carolinians is abundant. Newspaper editorials, letters to editors, speeches, and private correspondence all attest to the profound effect of Holden's arguments, though many, especially his old Whig

1. E. Merton Coulter, *The Confederate States of America, 1861–1865* (Baton Rouge, 1950), 533–35.

antagonists, would have denied that Holden had been the main-spring of their opposition to Davis and his allies.

Language that Holden had used in the *Standard* became common parlance in the anti-Davis and anti-"Destructive" campaign of 1862–1863 and the subsequent peace movement. In words remarkably similar to those appearing in the *Standard*, a Conservative of nearby Franklin County wrote Governor Vance in March, 1863, that the authorities in Richmond and their "die-hard secessionist" allies "will do any and everything in order to oppress and harass the Conservatives of this State." Theirs "is an organized movement . . . for military power," he charged. If they gained power, "the last vestage of human liberty" would be destroyed. Having "inaugurated our present calamities . . . they are resolved to rule or ruin," he concluded. Nathaniel Boyden, a prominent leader in the western Piedmont, wrote Vance in early 1863 that he feared a "military Tyranny" if North Carolina did not insist on its rights. Using terms and phrases that Holden had coined (for example, "Destructives" to refer to the original secessionists and "horrible Bastile" to refer to the Confederate prison in Salisbury where many North Carolinians were held), Boyden told the governor that he must be "extremely alive and sensitive to even the slightest encroachments of the military power upon the civil jurisdiction. This is the point now to be guarded with the utmost vigilance by all." Congressman Burgess S. Gaither also feared military power, and soon after the Boyden letter he wrote from Richmond that "the tendency of things here is towards a consolidated military despotism," phraseology that Holden had frequently used in his editorials.[2]

In early 1863 letters poured into Holden's office—and he published many of them—applauding his ringing denunciations of the "Destructives" and his defense of the people against "military encroachments." These and other letters depicted the deplorable economic and social conditions that were enveloping the state with the cream of its manpower in the army and its transportation facilities

2. C. D. Smith to Zebulon B. Vance, March 12, 1863, Nathaniel Boyden to Zebulon B. Vance, March, 1863, Burgess S. Gaither to Zebulon B. Vance, April 24, 1863, in Zebulon B. Vance Papers, NDAH. See also Edward J. Hale to William A. Graham, April 6, 1863, in J. G. de Roulhac Hamilton and Max R. Williams (eds.), *The Papers of William Alexander Graham* (7 vols. to date; Raleigh, 1957–), V, 471–72.

in disarray. Many communities, according to these accounts, were threatened with anarchy and severe suffering because of lack of food, clothing, and adequate housing. Bands of deserters, men fleeing conscription, bushwhackers, unionists, and Confederates roamed the western part of the state, preying upon the defenseless and attacking one another. Guerrillas, some of whom were black, operated in a similar fashion in the no-man's-land between the armies in the East.[3]

Reports that speculators and extortioners were growing rich while the families of soldiers grew poorer received wide circulation in the *Standard* and aroused Holden's indignation to a fever pitch. "The worst enemies of the Confederacy," he stormed, "are those who speculate upon salt, flour, bacon, corn, leather, cotton and woolen goods . . . and they have no concern except to keep the war raging that they may make money." In at least one instance he directly injected a class issue into the war, castigating planters who speculated in corn and kept it from the needy. As a slaveholder himself, he declared, he had a right to remind them "that this war was occasioned by slavery, and that they are bound by every consideration of justice and policy to see to it that the families of the non-slaveholders who are fighting our battles, are supplied with bread." He warned planters that unless they opened their storehouses to sufferers, they "will sow to the wind and reap the whirl-wind."[4]

Intentionally or not, Holden's shrill rhetoric heightened class consciousness among yeoman whites who had few resources to draw upon to escape the ravages of the war. The belief that the conflict was "a rich man's war but a poor man's fight" grew in strength as the hardships became greater and Holden's criticisms became more widely known. Yet, class divisions never reached the point where they threatened the traditional political order. A longtime participant in the political battles of the second American party system, Holden himself rejected a class orientation for his move-

3. Raleigh *Standard*, November, 1862–June, 1863, *passim*. See also J. A. Worth to Jonathan Worth, January 23, 1863, in J. G. de Roulhac Hamilton (ed.), *The Correspondence of Jonathan Worth*, (2 vols.; Raleigh, 1909), I, 224–25; Zebulon B. Vance to Weldon N. Edwards, September 18, 1862, in J. G. de Roulhac Hamilton (ed.), *The Papers of Thomas Ruffin* (4 vols.; Raleigh, 1918–20), III, 260; John G. Barrett, *The Civil War in North Carolina* (Chapel Hill, 1963), 174.

4. Raleigh *Standard*, November 5, 1862, February 4, 1863.

ment. Instinctively he kept the discontent channeled into the regular political current that reflected old political experiences and ideologies and cut across class lines.

Even in commenting on corn speculation, Holden found politics in the old sense more important than class. He claimed that nine-tenths of the "merciless speculators and extortioners" were original secessionists who had "skulled from the war which they were so anxious to bring on and remained at home to grow rich by grinding the faces of the poor." Exclaiming that such men "are worse than Lincolnites," the fiery editor asserted that "they will strangle liberty in its very cradle in order to put money into their filthy pockets."[5]

Holden found avarice among all classes of North Carolinians—merchants, farmers, manufacturers, professionals, and artisans. War-bred opportunism, he lamented, "is a viper gnawing at the vitals the country" and undermining the Christian morality of the people. "The war goes on, and blood gushes, and widows mourn, and orphans wail, and debt is piled on debt, and the poor unoffending slave is also a victim, and slavery itself is perishing, and schoolhouses and churches are closing, and the poor are made poorer, the rich richer, and the morals of the people are sinking to a level where God is forgotten and self alone is worshipped."[6]

In Raleigh, Holden observed first hand the suffering caused by the war, though neither he nor his family experienced privation. By mid-1863 the streets of the state capital were filled with refugees from the war, especially from eastern North Carolina, where many people had fled the Union-occupied areas and the no-man's-land between the armies. Housing and food were in great demand in the town, and though few actually died of exposure or starvation, prices soared and deprivation became the lot of hundreds of people there. Flour, for example, rose from an already inflated fifteen dollars a barrel in 1862 to more than a hundred dollars in 1864. Compounding the problems of shortages and inflation was the presence in Raleigh of army camps for recruits and conscripts, the latter of whom were sometimes brought to town under guard.[7] The pathos

5. *Ibid.*, February 25, 1863.
6. *Ibid.*, November 5, 1862, June 17, 1863.
7. Elizabeth Reid Murray, *Wake: Capital County of North Carolina* (Raleigh, 1983), 460–61, 485, 489; Raleigh *Standard*, June 27, 1866. Letters in the Alex-

of war was poignantly brought home to Holden by the scenes of suffering that he saw in the three military hospitals in Raleigh. His visits to these hospitals reinforced his longings for peace and heightened his concern for his son Jo who, after being released from a Federal prison in 1863, wanted to rejoin the troops in the field. Holden, however, persuaded Jo to enroll in the university at Chapel Hill, but the young man quickly tired of academic life. Much to the relief of his father, Jo agreed to join the *Standard* as a printer, an occupation that was covered by the exemption provisions of the conscription law.[8]

In mid-June, 1863, Holden came to the conclusion that the only way "to arrest this awful evil" and avert social chaos was to initiate peace negotiations. Encouraged by the emergence of peace sentiment among "national Democrats" in the North, he believed that "the people of both sections are tired of war and desire peace. We desire it on terms honorable to our section, and we cannot expect it on terms dishonorable to the other section." Since he was still unsure of his ground and probably anxious to weigh public opinion before advancing too far, Holden did not immediately indicate how negotiations should begin or what terms the South should accept. Two weeks later, the twin Confederate disasters at Gettysburg and Vicksburg, along with the strong local support that his tentative peace proposal had aroused, convinced Holden that he should strike a bolder blow for peace. But first he again denied the charge that he favored reconstruction or submission to Lincoln. Insisting that he advocated "no peace which will not preserve the rights of the sovereign States and the institutions of the South," he argued that "what the great mass of our people desire is a cessation of hostilities, and negotiations. If they could reach that point, they would feel that the conflict of arms would not be renewed and that *some* settlement would be effected which would leave them in the future

ander M. McPheeters, Sr., Papers, DU, also describe conditions in Raleigh during the war.

8. Raleigh *Standard*, December 18, 1861, August 3, 1864; Weymouth T. Jordan (comp.), *North Carolina Troops, 1861–1865: A Roster* (8 vols. to date; Raleigh, 1966–), VIII, 429, 454; Samuel A. Ashe (ed.), *Biographical History of North Carolina from Colonial Times to the Present* (8 vols.; Greensboro, 1905–17), VI, 321–22.

in the enjoyment of 'life, liberty, and happiness.'" Only the sovereign people, acting in local meetings, could launch the peace movement, he asserted. "The two governments are so inflamed by the
war spirit, and so intent on mere physical triumphs, that unless the
people of the two sections rise up and demand that mental and
moral means shall be resorted to to close the war, those means may
not be employed, and the war may be prolonged indefinitely." He
proposed that in the fall congressional contests the voters elect
peace candidates who would demand that Congress appoint commissioners to meet with Lincoln's representatives for the purpose
of arranging "an honorable adjustment" between the two sides.
The settlement that they reached, Holden said, should then be submitted to the people for ratification.[9]

Despite his assurance that he still favored Confederate independence, Holden announced that if the people of North Carolina
wanted reconstruction of the Union, "it would not be in our power
to prevent it, even if we could." He insisted, however, that if reunion occurred, he would "feel the humiliation as profoundly and
acutely" as the "Destructives." Meanwhile, he declared, "we cannot cease to fight" as long as northern armies were in the South
and the rights and interests of southerners were jeopardized.[10]

Holden's call for peace precipitated a bitter debate in North
Carolina and divided the citizenry to a greater extent than perhaps
any other issue in the state's history. Hurriedly organized "peace
meetings," many held in small crossroads communities, passed
resolutions supporting a vigorous effort to end the war and praising Holden for his defense of civil liberty. Almost all of the meetings
protested the Davis administration's unfair treatment of North
Carolina, its blatant partisanship, and its tendency toward military
despotism. The peace resolutions ignored Lincoln's Emancipation
Proclamation, suggesting that the fate of the "peculiar institution"
was not a primary consideration in the movement to end the war.
Nevertheless, most peace advocates, including Holden, expected
slavery to be preserved if an early end to the war could be arranged.[11]

9. Raleigh *Standard*, June 17, 24, July 22, 29, August 5, 1863.
10. *Ibid.*, July 29, 1863.
11. The Raleigh *Standard* (see issues of July–September, 1863) printed most of
the peace proceedings, though Holden later admitted that he did not agree with the
unionist tone of some of them. For Holden's appraisal of the meetings, see the *Stan-*

"Destructives," both inside and outside the state, charged that Holden and supporters plotted treason against the Confederacy. Catherine Edmondston, an ardent anti-Holdenite of Halifax County, exclaimed that "the Standard commenced by inveighing against President Davis. It has culminated in dishonor and treason." Governor Vance and Edward J. Hale, the editor of the Fayetteville *Observer* and the governor's chief political ally, were bombarded with reports that the real purpose of the peace movement was reconstruction of the Union and demanded that the state administration suppress Holden and the "submissionists." A staunch Raleigh Confederate reflected the alarm caused by the peace meetings when he wrote Hale that the *Standard* "is doing incalculable harm to our noble cause. Open treason, submission and reconstruction is the common talk of our streets, all the work of Mr. Holden, who has *in heart* never given in to the Confederate cause. Governor Vance must now take some position; he cannot idly stand by and see our cause lost in this State." An eastern secessionist feared that "Jacobinism [was] rampant in the land" and that Holden was playing the part of Murat as a reign of terror seemed imminent.[12] From the West reports also reached Vance that the peace movement threatened to ignite civil strife, and Confederate stalwarts demanded that the governor act against Holden before it was too late. A westerner wrote that the *Standard* was "a fire brand and a curse to the land" and that its editor "should be hung." Another westerner labeled Holden a "son of Belial" who ought to be "hewed in pieces before the Lord." [13]

---

dard, October 7, 1863. On the underlying belief that slavery might be saved or at least gradually extinguished by an early peace, see L. S. Gash to Governor Zebulon B. Vance, June 1, 1863, in Vance Papers. This belief may have reflected a better understanding of northern peace and reconstruction sentiment than many historians have assumed. Despite Lincoln's Emancipation Proclamation, as late as 1864 the basic northern commitment was not to emancipation but to the restoration of the Union as it had been before the war. V. Jacque Voegeli, *Free but Not Equal: The Midwest and the Negro During the Civil War* (Chicago, 1967), 147–52.

12. Beth Gilbert Crabtree and James W. Patton (eds.), *"Journal of a Secesh Lady": The Diary of Catherine Anne Devereaux Edmondston, 1860–1866* (Raleigh, 1979), 466; W. A. Harris to Edward J. Hale, August 24, 1863, Frederick Fitzgerald to Hale, July 24, 1863, Thomas Ruffin to Hale, August 17, 1863, Thomas S. Ashe to Hale, August 5, 1863, in Edward Jones Hale Papers, NDAH; Charles Jeffrey Bailey, "North Carolina Politics During the Civil War, 1861–1865" (M.A. thesis, North Carolina State University, 1975), 137–38.

13. Barrett, *The Civil War in North Carolina*, 196n; unidentified correspon-

Despite these attacks on him and the peace movement, Holden struck a sympathetic cord among thousands of war-weary North Carolinians. The circulation of the *Standard*, according to Holden, increased by 25 percent during the summer of 1863. It rose from about 7,000 weeklies and 1,500 semiweeklies in May to a total of more than 10,000 copies in August. Indeed, since late 1860, when Holden had become the chief promoter of conservatism in the state, the *Standard*'s circulation had increased more than 100 percent; some of this good fortune, however, resulted from the wartime collapse of numerous small newspapers that had operated on a shoestring and from the fact that the *Standard* could meet the local need for war news. Although the circulation of Holden's newspaper was general throughout Confederate North Carolina, it was especially large in the region west of Greensboro and in the Raleigh area. The newspaper was also read by North Carolina troops in Virginia and by sympathetic conservatives or former unionists in other southern states until it was suppressed during the summer of 1863. An ardent Confederate from western North Carolina complained to Hale that the administration underestimated the peace influence of Holden. He indicated that the Raleigh editor had the support of influential men as well as the masses in his section of the state and that a belief existed among the people "that he cannot be mistaken about public opinion. He is in truth, every way qualified to head a base enterprise & to give a terrible direction to events. You have no idea of the extent of his circulation. I have found his paper in every nook & corner of the mountains." [14]

Holden, however, discounted his preeminent role in the peace movement. He claimed that he had not organized or controlled the meetings. They were "the result of the spontaneous action of the people," and the variety of sentiment contained in the peace resolutions was proof of that fact, he said. He also defended the peace advocates against charges of disloyalty. "It is a gross slander to say that the public meetings in this State which expressed a desire for peace

dent to Edward J. Hale, August 29, 1863, in Hale Papers; Laura L. Norwood to James Gwyn, July 17, 1863, in James Gwyn Papers, SHC.

14. Raleigh *Standard*, October 30, 1861, May 13, August 5, October 21, 1863; unidentified correspondent to Edward J. Hale, August 29, 1863, P. W. Stanback to Hale, August, 1863, in Hale Papers.

were attended or held by disloyal persons. No doubt there were a few deserters at some of these meetings, and a few who would prefer to see the State separate from the Confederate government; but the great bulk of those who got up, attended, and shaped the action of these meetings are as true to the Southern cause as any men in the State. They are the fathers and brothers of thousands of our soldiers who are dedicating their very lives to the cause." [15]

Holden also denied that the peace movement was demoralizing the army or encouraging desertions, as his critics, including General Robert E. Lee, charged. He claimed that North Carolina troops would fight harder to improve the South's position at the peace table if they knew that negotiations with the North were imminent. The desertions were not inspired by the agitation for peace, he contended. The real causes were the Confederate hierarchy's mistreatment of the common soldier, the impoverishment of the soldier's family, and the failure of the Davis administration to seek peace. He even denied the frequent charge by Confederate authorities that North Carolina regiments had more deserters than those of other states. Since the fall of Roanoke Island in early 1862, he said, North Carolina, in the matter of army desertions, had "been made a scapegoat for the sins of others." [16] As for his own role, Holden declared that he had "never written, or uttered, or printed a word designed or calculated to cause desertion. On the contrary, we have written and printed more, perhaps to discourage desertions and to encourage volunteering than any Editor in the State." [17] Many Confederates, including Governor Vance, found such an assertion absurd.

Staunch Confederates soon reported to authorities in Richmond the disturbing developments in North Carolina. "Trouble is brewing here," one prominent citizen wrote President Davis in July, 1863, "and I fear we shall soon have open resistance to the govern-

15. Raleigh *Standard*, August 12, October 14, 1863.
16. *Ibid.*, August 17, September 9, November 25, 1863. A recent account suggests that Holden might have been correct in his claim that the desertion of North Carolina troops was no greater than that of other Confederate states. Richard Reid in "A Test Case of the 'Crying Evil': Desertion Among North Carolina Troops During the Civil War," *NCHR*, LXIII (1981), 253–55, argues that the desertion rate for North Carolina troops was exaggerated by people at the time and also by historians later.
17. Horace W. Raper, "William W. Holden and the Peace Movement in North Carolina," *NCHR*, XXXI (1954), 501.

ment under the leadership of that reckless politician, Holden."
General D. H. Hill, a North Carolinian, warned the administration
that Holden would welcome the Yankees to Raleigh if they succeeded in their eastern campaign. Federal officers in the area also
reported to their superiors that unionism was flourishing in North
Carolina. United States Assistant Secretary of War Charles Dana,
after talking to Governor Andrew Johnson of Tennessee, confidently
wrote that the Holdenites "will seize the first opportunity to free
themselves from the Confederate Government," a prediction based
on inflated hopes, not evidence. Such reports caused the northern
press to hum with rumors of rebellion against Confederate authority
in North Carolina.[18]

An alarmed Davis warned Vance of the gravity of the situation
and indicated that Holden's treasonable activities, if true, warranted
criminal prosecution. Vance, fearing Confederate dictation as much
as he feared civil strife, indignantly informed the president that "it
would be impolitic in the very highest degree to interfere with
[Holden] or his paper." The governor, however, did agree to a request by Davis that he go to Richmond to discuss the political crisis
in the state. In their conversations the president gave Vance assurances that Confederate authorities would redress North Carolina's grievances and would allow the governor free rein in dealing
with the peace movement.[19] Peace negotiations—a central concern
of the Holdenites—evidently were not discussed by the two leaders.

18. Richard E. Yates, *The Confederacy and Zeb Vance* (Tuscaloosa, 1958), 88;
General D. H. Hill to Secretary of War James A. Seddon, June 3, 1863, in OR, Ser. I,
Vol. XVIII, 1092. Two recent historians, citing only the Dana report to Secretary of
War Edwin M. Stanton, have concluded that Holden did establish contact with
northerners and with Federal authorities in the South. David D. Scarboro III, "An
Honorable Peace: The Peace Movement in Civil War North Carolina" (Ph.D. dissertation, Trinity College, Cambridge University, 1981), 118; William T. Auman,
"Bryan Tyson: Southern Unionist and American Patriot," *NCHR*, LXII (1985),
273. The Dana report indicated that Governor Johnson of Tennessee had received
"some communications" from North Carolina unionists, including "Holden of the
Raleigh Register." This document is of dubious value in establishing the unionism
of Holden in 1863. In addition, the Dana report is highly suspect in other particu-
lars. Incredibly, Dana claimed that "the people of the whole State" of North Carolina "are true to the Union." He also exaggerated the progress of unionism and
emancipation in Tennessee. Dana to Stanton, September 8, 1863, in OR, Ser. I, Vol.
XXX, Pt. 1, pp. 182–83.
19. Jefferson Davis to Zebulon B. Vance, July 24, 1863, Vance to Davis, July 26,
1863, in OR, Ser. I, Vol. LI, Pt. 2, pp. 739–40.

Impressed by what he heard in Richmond, the young governor returned to Raleigh determined to move against Holden and the peace movement. On August 11 Vance told Edward J. Hale that "the split with Holden is decreed of the gods." He added, "I have made up my mind to it," though he feared a major division in the Conservative party and the return of the "Destructives" to power if he initiated the break. He also feared that most Conservatives would view him as a "disorganizer" and rally to Holden if he launched a public attack on the *Standard* editor. So Vance demanded that Hale "pitch into" Holden in the editorial columns of the Fayetteville *Observer* with the purpose of provoking him to make a rash move. The governor, who bitterly distrusted the "Destructives," ironically had accepted their view of Holden as a unionist conspirator. "He is for submission, reconstruction or everything else that will put him back under Lincoln . . . and punish his old friends and co-laborers, the Secessionists," Vance charged. Holden really believed, the governor wrote, that "4/5 of the people are ready for reconstruction & says he is only *following* the people, not leading them." [20]

Hale, however, at first refused to "pitch into" Holden, and he advised the timid governor to speak publicly for himself. Vance finally agreed to draft an open letter to North Carolinians decrying the peace movement, but without mentioning Holden's role in it. Incredibly, he asked Holden's opinion of the letter before it was published. Holden, of course, opposed its release, whereupon the governor submitted the letter to William A. Graham, who gave him similar advice, emphasizing that such a public exposition would exacerbate political conflict in the state. Coming from a man of Graham's prestige in the Conservative party, the governor had no choice but to accept the advice and refrain from publishing his denunciation of the peace movement. [21]

Frustrated in his efforts to challenge Holden, Vance took a new tack. This time he called a "council" of several prominent Conservatives, including Graham and Holden, to meet with him in Raleigh and iron out a state policy on the peace movement. In the meeting a

20. Zebulon B. Vance to Edward J. Hale, July 29, August 11, 1863, in Hale Papers.

21. William A. Graham to Zebulon B. Vance, August 21, 1863, in Hamilton and Williams (eds.), *Graham Papers*, V, 522–23; W. W. Holden to Calvin Cowles, March 18, 1864, in William Woods Holden Papers, NDAH.

compromise proposed by Graham was reluctantly accepted by both Holden and Vance. It was agreed that the governor should issue a proclamation condemning resistance to Confederate authority in the state and discouraging, but not prohibiting, the peace meetings. Holden, though disappointed that the peace movement was not endorsed by the conference and concerned that force might yet be employed to suppress the meetings, agreed not to criticize the proclamation when it was published.[22]

On September 9, 1863, one day after the publication of the governor's proclamation calling for "public peace and tranquility," an event occurred that threatened to undo the Graham compromise and plunge the state deeper into civil conflict. The event was the sacking of the *Standard* office by Georgia troops passing through Raleigh.

Since the beginning of the peace movement in July, the Confederate army in Virginia had become a hotbed of anti-Holden sentiment. Army officers, especially in North Carolina units, had feared the effects of the *Standard* on troop morale and had sought unsuccessfully to suppress it in camp. Regimental meetings were held in which anti-Holden officers secured the passage of resolutions condemning the Raleigh editor and the peace movement. On August 12 a "general convention" of North Carolina troops, consisting principally of officers, met at the Orange County Courthouse in Virginia and demanded that the *Standard* be suppressed and the peace crusade dissolved.[23]

Holden, as might be expected, reacted in cold fury to the army meetings. He charged that they were purely political, the product of "a few destructive officers in the army" who desired "to divide the Conservatives of this State, and thus prostrate our people at the feet of central power." Holden further charged that "this political

22. Samuel F. Philips to David L. Swain, September 7, 1863, in Hamilton and Williams (eds.), *Graham Papers*, V, 529–30; Yates, *The Confederacy and Vance*, 91.

23. Robert D. Graham to William A. Graham, August 20, 1863, in Hamilton and Williams (eds.), *Graham Papers*, V, 522; Barrett, *The Civil War in North Carolina*, 196n; Raleigh *Standard*, August 19, 1863. Although Holden insisted otherwise, evidence exists that opposition to the peace movement was fairly widespread in North Carolina units serving under General Lee. See especially Charles Girard, *A Visit to the Confederate States of America in 1863: Memoir Addressed to His Majesty Napoleon III*, trans. William Stanley Hoole (Tuscaloosa, 1962), 66.

movement has the implied if not direct sanction of the President and the Secretary of War." He contended that the common soldiers and Conservative officers had no real voice in the meetings; indeed, he claimed, the majority in the army favored his course. He also predicted that if Confederate authorities attempted to carry out the resolutions, the worst days of the French Revolution would be re-enacted in North Carolina. "Civil Liberty," he extravagantly ex-claimed, "will expire in the blood of our own people, and we shall have a reign of terror such as the world has never witnessed." [24]

Inspired by the army meetings and, on their way to Raleigh, in-flamed by "Destructives" in North Carolina, Georgia troops under the command of General Henry Benning decided to carry out the resolutions calling for the suppression of the *Standard*. On the night of September 9, a mob of soldiers, including officers, broke into the *Standard* building, scattered Holden's papers, and dumped printing type and ink out of their cases. Amazingly, the printing presses were not touched, nor were the offices seriously damaged. The quick ar-rival of Governor Vance on the scene and his success in persuading the soldiers to return to camp probably saved the presses from de-struction, making possible the early resumption of publication by Holden. The shaken editor, after having a glass of brandy at the Governor's Mansion, returned home to spend a restless night. [25]

Early the next morning Raleigh friends of Holden retaliated against Spelman's *State Journal*, which had joined in the call for the suppression of the *Standard*. The pro-Holden mob sacked the offices of the newspaper and destroyed the presses. Vance again went to the scene of the disturbance and, accompanied by Holden, who had not been forewarned of the attack, persuaded the crowd to go home. [26]

Tension increased in Raleigh when word reached the citizens that "infuriated soldiers" from a passing Alabama brigade planned to enter the town and "mob" Holden. State Treasurer Jonathan Worth excitedly reported to a friend that "a large majority of this commu-

24. Raleigh *Standard*, August 19, 26, September 2, 1863.
25. Jonathan Worth to A. M. Tomlinson, September 10, 1863, in Hamilton (ed.), *Correspondence of Worth*, I, 261. For Holden's account of the incident, see Raleigh *Standard*, October 7, 28, 1863.
26. Yates, *The Confederacy and Vance*, 92; Raleigh *Standard*, October 28, 1863.

nity will fight for Holden" against the Confederate troops. Once again Governor Vance intervened, this time to prevent a bloody confrontation between the opposing sides. He also sent an urgent message to President Davis threatening to recall North Carolina's "troops from the field to the defense of their own homes" unless he "order immediately that troops passing through here shall not enter the city." "If you wish to save North Carolina to the Confederacy, be quick," the governor concluded. Although Davis did not halt the movement of army units through Raleigh, he did issue strict orders to the officers regarding the behavior of their men. Five days after the assault on the *Standard*, peace had been restored and Vance could report to Davis that "troops are now passing quietly" through the town.[27] Less than a month later the *Standard* resumed publication; its bitter rival, the *State Journal*, never published again.

On the surface Conservative unity in North Carolina had been restored by Vance's timely intervention in the crisis. Holden himself lauded the governor's conduct in maintaining the peace and defending civil liberty. He even indicated that he would support Vance for reelection in 1864 provided the governor continued to "adhere to Conservative principles." Holden appeared to be moving toward the war Conservatives when on November 4 he called for a more vigorous prosecution of the war and indicated that he would be willing to pay heavier taxes in order to restore confidence in Confederate finances. In addition, peace meetings ceased to be held. However, in the fall elections the peace faction of the Conservative party captured six of the ten seats in Congress. The virtually moribund secessionist faction, which would eventually merge with the Vanceites, won only one seat.[28]

Despite the relative political calm in North Carolina in late 1863, Holden's attacks on the Confederate administration intensified. His concern for the preservation of "liberty and law" grew as a result of the September excitement in Raleigh and continued Confederate encroachments, especially a more rigid enforcement of conscription and the impressment of food. Republican victories in the fall

27. Jonathan Worth to Archibald McLean, September 10, 1863, in Hamilton (ed.), *Correspondence of Worth*, I, 261; Yates, *The Confederacy and Vance*, 93–94; Raleigh *Standard*, October 28, 1863.

28. Raleigh *Standard*, October 7, 28, November 4, 11, 18, 1863; Bailey, "North Carolina Politics During the Civil War," 162.

elections in the North indicated to Holden that a hard war still lay ahead unless a concrete effort was soon made to secure peace. As another gloomy winter settled upon North Carolina, Holden and his supporters looked for a new approach to peace. They found it in the mechanism of the state convention. This instrument of the sovereign people had taken North Carolina and other southern states out of the Union; might it not be used to initiate peace negotiations? They knew, however, that the launching of such a movement would destroy the fragile unity of the Conservative party and produce a new wave of denunciation of the peace advocates. But as Holden publicly and privately indicated, thousands of North Carolinians were growing desperate for an end to the war before it was too late to save the liberties of the people and avert complete ruin.[29]

In December, 1863, Holden announced to his friends that he would demand the calling of a state convention to begin the peace process. "The power that made the war can alone close it—the power of the sovereign States"—he told Thomas Settle. "Our next election will turn on the question of a State Convention," he said, and he planned to be counted among those advocating the issue.[30] Although some Conservatives had already thought of the convention method for initiating peace negotiations and protecting North Carolina from Confederate encroachments, they waited for Holden to commit himself to it before organizing local peace meetings to endorse this approach. They realized that Holden's influence and his support in the *Standard* were necessary for the success of a convention campaign.[31]

Even before he publicized his decision to seek a state convention, Holden met with James T. Leach, a bold peace advocate in the Confederate Congress, and prepared a set of resolutions to be introduced by Leach at peace meetings in his home county. The resolutions, adopted by meetings in two Johnston County communities, asked state authorities to call a convention of the people for the

29. Raleigh *Standard,* October 21, November 18, December 2, 9, 23, 1863; W. W. Holden to Thomas Settle, December 22, 1863, in Thomas Settle Papers, SHC.

30. W. W. Holden to Thomas Settle, December 22, 1863, in Settle Papers; Curtis B. Brogden, "Biographical Sketch of William W. Holden" (Ms in William K. Boyd Papers, Department of History Division, Duke University Archives, DU).

31. See Thomas Settle to Martin Starbuck *et al.,* January 14, 1864, in Settle Papers.

purposes of protecting North Carolinians from "a military despotism" and seeking a peaceful solution to the war.[32]

Governor Vance was furious. He wrote William A. Graham, "I will see the Conservative party blown into a thousand atoms and Holden and his understrappers in hell . . . before I will consent to a course which I think would bring dishonor and ruin upon both State and Confederacy!" Upon a closer reading of the resolutions, the governor admitted to his friend Hale that "on the whole they are not particularly objectionable." (For example, they endorsed his administration and requested, not demanded, the meeting of a state convention.) His real objection to the resolutions was the direction the convention campaign would take under the leadership of Holden. Vance complained to another friend that "it is now a fixed policy of Mr. Holden to call a convention in May to take N.C. back to the United States."[33]

While Governor Vance at last girded on his loins to fight, Holden filled the columns of the *Standard* with a vigorous defense of the proposal for a state convention. He again denied that the peace proponents plotted treason to the Confederate States, and he lamented, "We are constantly prejudiced and injured by misrepresentations of our views and opinions by our political opponents." According to him, the South, with North Carolina in the lead, should act immediately to end the war while it was in a position to bargain for terms. "If the war should be continued twelve months longer negro slavery will be utterly and finally destroyed in these States, and it will be impossible to re-establish the institution. Its sudden destruction will involve the whole social structure in ruin." Furthermore, Holden claimed, by the end of the year "the rights of the States and the liberties of the people, by the very force of circumstances, to say nothing of the aggressive disposition and purposes of the government at Richmond, will have been blotted out, or will be at the mercy of the government." He insisted that his purposes in the peace movement were not diabolical. They were, he said, "first, to save human life and to prevent the impoverishment and ruin

32. Zebulon B. Vance to Edward J. Hale, January 1, 1863 [1864], in Hale Papers; Raleigh *Standard*, January 13, 20, June 29, 1864.

33. Yates, *The Confederacy and Vance*, 95; Zebulon B. Vance to Edward J. Hale, January 9, 1863 [1864], in Hale Papers.

of our people; secondly, to prevent the sudden abolition of slavery, the blighting effects of which would be seen on this continent for generations; and thirdly, to prevent the extinction of the State sovereignties, which, if it should take place, would reduce us to the condition of territorial dependents on the favor of some great central, despotic government."[34]

Holden contended that peace "can be obtained only by the sovereign states" acting in state conventions and cooperating with the Confederate government. "We are, therefore, for a Convention, and for a cooperation with our sister States of the South in obtaining an armistice, so that negotiations may be commenced." Such a state initiative, he argued, "will strengthen the Conservative sentiment" in the North and "compel Mr. Lincoln and the Abolition party to enter upon negotiations." The convention would not only seek peace, but it would also "protect the State against the encroachment of arbitrary power." Unlike other institutions of government, the convention could "speak and act for the State as a sovereign," and it could "demand that the [Confederate] Congress and the military respect [the] civil law and the inalienable rights of our people." Although he denied that the convention would "destroy or even embarrass the common government," he warned that North Carolina "would not be bound by a government which had lost its original character and had been perverted to despotic purposes."[35] Without explicitly stating it, Holden now favored separate state action if the Confederate government could not be persuaded to seek an immediate end to the war.

A grim President Davis in February, 1864, took what Holden and many of his supporters predicted would be the next step toward the imposition of a military despotism in the state. He secured congressional passage of a bill suspending the writ of habeas corpus in cases of persons resisting Confederate authority or "inciting others to abandon the Confederate cause." The measure exceeded the scope of the earlier suspension bills, and provocatively, Davis in securing its enactment had North Carolina in mind.[36]

34. Raleigh *Standard,* January 20, February 3, 1864.
35. *Ibid.,* January 20, February 10, 1864.
36. Kenneth Rayner to Thomas Ruffin, February 18, 1864, in Hamilton (ed.),

A storm of protest greeted the bill's passage. Although the outrage was not confined to North Carolina, the suspension of the
writ inflamed citizens in the Old North State more than any previous action of the Confederate government. Holden's two-year campaign to bridle Confederate authority had created an atmosphere
in the state that would not ignore such a direct assault upon a basic
civil right and upon North Carolina's dissidents. Suddenly the
Raleigh editor's political star was on the rise, and his rival, Governor Vance, who only mildly pleaded with Davis "to be chary of ex-
ercising the powers" under the law, was threatened with the loss of
considerable Conservative support. State Treasurer Jonathan Worth
believed that because of the suspension of the writ and other tyrannical acts by the Confederacy, three-fourths of the people of North
Carolina now supported the calling of a state convention to end
the war.[37]

In a dramatic demonstration of outrage at the passage of the
habeas corpus bill, Holden suspended publication of the *Standard*.
His private explanation for this action coincided with his public
one. He wrote a friend that since the writ had been suspended,
thereby "abolishing civil law, I felt that if I could not continue to
print as a freeman I would not print at all, and I could not bear the
idea of lowering or changing my tone." Contributing to Holden's
decision to cease publication was the unsettling news that a Confederate brigade under the command of General Robert F. Hoke
had been ordered to encamp near Raleigh. To Raleigh Conservatives, the purpose of this movement was clear: the Davis administration intended to arrest Holden and suppress his followers. The
troops, however, were never ordered to enter the town or seize the
Raleigh editor. Despite Holden's belief that Vance in late 1863 "had
made up his mind deliberately to go with Davis and the Destructives," it was probably the governor's warning to the president not

Ruffin Papers, III, 369–70; Paul D. Escott, *After Secession: Jefferson Davis and the Failure of Confederate Nationalism* (Baton Rouge, 1978), 202.

37. James T. Leach to Zebulon B. Vance, March 5, 1864, in Vance Papers; Marc W. Kruman, *Parties and Politics in North Carolina, 1836–1865* (Baton Rouge, 1983), 258; Zebulon B. Vance to Jefferson Davis, February 9, 1864, in OR, Ser. I, Vol. LI, Pt. 2, p. 818; Kenneth Rayner to Thomas Ruffin, April 1, 1864, in Hamilton (ed.), *Ruffin Papers*, III, 381; Jonathan Worth to Daniel L. Russell, February 16, 1864, in Hamilton (ed.), *Correspondence of Worth*, I, 297.

to make arrests in North Carolina under the habeas corpus law that saved Holden from the clutches of the military.[38]

While these stirring events were occurring, the astute Vance quietly mapped his reelection strategy, expecting Holden to offer the only opposition to him in the contest. He wrote Hale that the secessionists would not nominate a candidate, since "they are as dead as a door nail. They will be obliged to vote for me" in preference to Holden. The real danger in seeking the secessionist vote, Vance informed his friend, was that he might push "too big a slice of old union men" into Holden's camp. "The old union men are in a large majority, and without them we would be helpless." Vance planned to avoid "coming square out with the secessionists," but he proposed to run on a platform calling for a vigorous prosecution of the war and the defeat of the state convention movement. He believed that, despite the infringement of the Confederate administration on the rights of the people, most former unionists would support him on the convention issue. Let the "ultra Conservatives . . . abuse Jeff Davis and the Secessionists to their hearts content so they but oppose this convention movement and keep to their duty on the war question," he told Hale.[39]

On February 22, 1864, Vance boldly opened his campaign at Wilkesboro, in the heart of Holden country. He devoted a great deal of attention in his speech to the convention issue, claiming that if a convention met to withdraw North Carolina from the Confederacy a blood bath would occur. Violence would break out among North Carolinians, and contending Confederate and Union armies would penetrate the interior of the state. "We would catch the devil on all sides," he predicted. Furthermore, negotiations at this stage of the conflict would fail; they would contribute only to the defeat of the Confederacy. Vance, who believed that anarchy was more likely to occur than tyranny, appealed to North Carolinians to acquiesce in the obnoxious habeas corpus law, contending that "it may not be in contravention of the Constitution, for the courts have decided

38. W. W. Holden to Calvin J. Cowles, March 18, 1864, in Holden Papers, NDAH; Raleigh *Standard*, February 24, 1864; Jonathan Worth to [?], March 2, 1864, in Hamilton (ed.), *Correspondence of Worth*, I, 299–300; J. G. de Roulhac Hamilton, *Reconstruction in North Carolina* (New York, 1914), 58.

39. Zebulon B. Vance to Edward J. Hale, February 11, 1864, in Hale Papers. See also *ibid.*, December 30, 1863.

that Congress can suspend the writ within certain limits." Finally, the governor admonished the people to "remain true to the cause we have solemnly undertaken to support."[40]

Convention supporters, most of whom had voted for Vance in 1862, were outraged by his Wilkesboro declaration. "To all intents and purposes," Holden stormed, Vance had become "the Destructive candidate" for governor. If Holden had any reservations about running for the office—and evidence exists that he did—he abandoned them now.[41]

On March 3 he announced his candidacy, but not in the *Standard*, since he had suspended publication the previous week. On April 6, however, Holden brought out a special edition of the *Standard* giving his platform. He also indicated that he would not campaign, because, as he explained, "I am not disposed . . . [to] add to the excitement which prevails in the public mind by haranguing them for votes." The real, unmentioned reason for shunning an active campaign was the fact that he was a poor stump speaker and would lose support by his appearance. He also may have feared possible violence in some strong Confederate areas if he campaigned there. Claiming to be a "Conservative after the straitest sect," he announced a platform that was brief and ambiguous: "If elected," he said, "I will do everything in my power to promote the interests, the honor, and glory of North Carolina, and to secure an honorable peace."[42]

Not until May 18 did Holden resume the regular publication of the *Standard*, his campaign forum. The delay permitted Vance to steal the march on him precisely at the time when North Carolinian outrage at Confederate transgressions was at its height and could have been used to good effect against Vance. In March the aggressive governor even took his campaign to North Carolina troops in Virginia, where he won many supporters and received the

40. Yates, *The Confederacy and Vance*, 101–102; Jonathan Worth to W. W. Holden, April 23, 1864, in Hamilton (ed.), *Correspondence of Worth*, I, 306–307; Bailey, "North Carolina Politics During the Civil War," 185–87. Vance's Wilkesboro speech is in the Fayetteville *Observer*, March 3, 1864.
41. W. W. Holden to Calvin J. Cowles, March 18, 1864, in Holden Papers, NDAH; Samuel F. Phillips to William A. Graham, February 26, 1864, in Hamilton and Williams (eds.), *Graham Papers*, I, 33–34.
42. Zebulon B. Vance to William A. Graham, March 3, 1864, in Hamilton and Williams (eds.), *Graham Papers*, VI, 36; Raleigh *Standard*, April 6, 1864.

praise of Generals Robert E. Lee and J. E. B. Stuart for his remarks. In April he covered the state in a speaking tour that, according to a historian of the campaign, "left Holden all but helpless."[43]

Vance also established a newspaper organ, the *Conservative*, in the state capital, and it joined with the vitriolic Raleigh *Confederate*, the sheet of the "Destructives," to wage a vituperative campaign against Holden. The governor's strategy was to prevent his rival from securing the support of the bulk of the old Whig voters, many of whom favored Holden's position on peace and applauded his ardent opposition to the "Destructives" but were uneasy about his personal qualities and the direction that a state convention might take under his leadership. Vance and his lieutenants added to their apprehensions by portraying Holden as a "Lincolnite" who would use a state convention to restore North Carolina to the Union.[44]

When Holden finally got his campaign in the *Standard* under way, he focused on the same group of voters as did Vance—the Whig element in the Conservative party. Holden repeatedly claimed that Vance, in order to secure secessionist votes, had abandoned his old political friends and allied himself with leading "Destructives" like Thomas Bragg, Thomas Clingman, and Duncan K. McRae of the Raleigh *Confederate*. He warned Whig Conservatives that Vance's success in the election "would inure substantially to our political enemies, who now constitute the bulk of his supporters." In essence, Holden argued, Vance "is striking a fatal blow at his own party organization and playing into the hands of the Destructive leaders."[45]

43. Zebulon B. Vance to William A. Graham, April 9, 1864, in Hamilton and Williams (eds.), *Graham Papers*, VI, 56–57; Yates, *The Confederacy and Vance*, 102–103. In March reports reached Holden that "the Western Counties almost to a man was [sic] for him and the army supported him by a margin of four or five to one." By May this advantage had been lost. W. W. Holden to Calvin J. Cowles, March 18, 1864, in Holden Papers, NDAH; Jonathan Worth to J. J. Jackson, May 30, 1864, in Hamilton (ed.), *Correspondence of Worth*, I, 309.

44. Zebulon B. Vance to Edward J. Hale, March 6, 1864, in Hale Papers; Samuel F. Phillips to William A. Graham, February 26, 1864, in Hamilton and Williams (eds.), *Graham Papers*, VI, 35; Raleigh *Standard*, February 10, June 15, 1864; R. F. Hackett to W. W. Hampton, February 1, 1864, Hampton to Hackett, April 17, 1864, Gordon-Hackett Papers, SHC.

45. W. W. Holden to Calvin J. Cowles, March 18, 1864, in Holden Papers, NDAH; Raleigh *Standard*, May 25, June 15, 29, 1864.

Holden's association of Vance with the discredited secessionists had some effect among Whig Conservatives. When the governor's friends warned him that the issue could defeat him unless he put some political distance between himself and the "Destructives," he shifted his campaign tactics and began to assail the secessionists as much as he did Holden. Some secessionists reacted bitterly to Vance's vilification of them and the Confederate government, but the governor knew that most members of this faction would vote for him to prevent the election of the "low down scoundrel" Holden.[46]

From the beginning, Holden expressed confidence, both privately and publicly, that he would win the election. He believed that the differences between him and Vance on the peace and convention issues gave him the advantage in a state where virtually everyone proclaimed their desire for an end to the war. To make the distinction clear to the people, he repeatedly pictured Vance as the war candidate who had admonished North Carolina troops "to fight till hell froze over, and then fight upon the ice." He even charged that Vance and the "Destructives" whom he had appointed to office wanted "the war to go on until speculators, officials, and blockade runners who are their friends shall have amassed and secured their fortunes in gold." The issues in the election, he argued, could be narrowed to "Peace or War, and Liberty against Despotism. Those who may vote for Vance and the Destructives will vote for War and Despotism."[47]

Concerning his peace plan, however, Holden found himself increasingly on the defensive. He insisted that his state convention proposal, contrary to his critics' charges, was not a ruse to take North Carolina out of the Confederacy but, in cooperation with other states and the Confederate government, was designed to facilitate the search for an early peace. But a major weakness in Holden's plan was the fact that the convention movement had virtually no support in other southern states. Even Confederate nemesis Joseph E. Brown of Georgia discountenanced the convention method for

46. Charles Phillips to Kemp Battle, June 22, 1864, in Battle Family Papers, SHC; John A. Gilmer to Zebulon B. Vance, April 14, 1864, John D. Hyman to Vance, March 19, 1864, in Vance Papers; Bailey, "North Carolina Politics During the Civil War," 195–96; Kruman, *Parties and Politics in North Carolina,* 261–62.

47. W. W. Holden to Calvin J. Cowles, March 18, July 19, 1864, in Holden Papers, NDAH; Raleigh *Standard,* May 25, June 1, July 6, 27, 1864.

protecting states' rights and negotiating an end to the war. In late May the Conservative-dominated North Carolina legislature dealt Holden's campaign a further blow when it passed resolutions endorsing Vance's administration, pledging the state's continued support for the Confederacy, and announcing that only the Confederate government should enter into peace negotiations with the enemy.[48]

Holden quickly adjusted his peace proposal to accommodate the new reality. He endorsed the peace resolutions introduced into Congress by James T. Leach, a Holdenite, calling for a ninety-day armistice that would be followed by negotiations between Federal and Confederate commissioners. In supporting this plan, Holden did not indicate what role he thought the southern state conventions should play in the peace negotiations; he simply proposed that the states themselves appoint commissioners to make "common cause" with the Confederate representatives. The treaty emerging from the deliberations, he said, should be ratified by both Confederate authorities and the voters in each state. The Leach resolutions were tabled in Congress. Holden, however, continued to insist, even after the 1864 campaign, that the Leach plan offered the best hope for ending the war.[49]

Holden never understood that his capacity for leadership was also an issue in the election. Of course, old secessionists believed, as former Confederate Senator William T. Dortch reported, that Holden was "a wily and dangerous enemy whose policy is rule or ruin." But a large body of Conservatives, some of whom had supported the peace movement, questioned the Raleigh editor's ability to lead during a time of turmoil. Admittedly, most of these Conservative skeptics were former Whigs who in many cases still held political grudges against "the Pope of Hargett Street." Still, many of them were torn between their support of Holden's principles and the belief that his election as governor would make matters worse in the state and would not contribute to ending the war. Even prominent peace men like Chief Justice Richmond M. Pearson, State Treasurer Jonathan Worth, and Samuel F. Phillips, all former Whigs, agonized over their choice before endorsing Vance, though they

48. Raleigh *Standard*, May, 1864, *passim;* Joseph E. Brown to Zebulon B. Vance, January 16, 1864, in Vance Papers; Scarboro, "An Honorable Peace," 263–64.

49. Raleigh *Standard*, June 15, 22, July 13, 1864.

manifested concern that the "Destructives" might profit from the governor's reelection. Phillips, the scion of a prominent Chapel Hill family who would join the Republican party during Reconstruction, expressed the difficulty that many of this persuasion had with Holden's candidacy. "I can hardly anticipate the state of things which would make it proper that Mr. Holden should be Governor of North Carolina, at a time when spirit, coolness, singleness of purpose, & statesmanship, are so much required as now. Vance may lack the latter qualification, but I attribute the others to him. I do not regard Mr. Holden as possessing any one of them." [50]

Despite Holden's expectation that all who desired peace would rally to his banner, two months before the election most observers believed that he would be defeated. If there were any doubts, they vanished with the exposure of the Heroes of America society in North Carolina. This secret organization of militant unionists, though few in numbers until after the war, had penetrated the state by 1864. Its aim was simple—the overthrow of the Confederacy and the restoration of the Union. A month before the election the Vance Conservatives discovered the organization's existence, and though they were anxious to link Holden directly with it, they did not uncover any evidence that he belonged to the Heroes. Nevertheless, Vance newspapers attempted to associate the disloyal Heroes, or Red Strings, as they were usually known, with Holden's candidacy. The Raleigh *Confederate* provided the campaign charge when it asserted that "every member of the order is expected to vote for Mr. Holden—who, though not a member, is a beneficiary of the organization." [51]

Holden hotly denied that he knew anything about the Heroes of America "or any other secret political party." He dismissed the report of the society's existence as "one of the thousand and one

50. William T. Dortch to Zebulon B. Vance, March 5, 1864, in Vance Papers; Samuel F. Phillips to William A. Graham, February 26, 1864, in Hamilton and Williams (eds.), *Graham Papers,* VI, 35; Jonathan Worth to A. M. Tomlinson, July 13, 1864, in Hamilton (ed.), *Correspondence of Worth,* I, 322–23.

51. Jonathan Worth to J. J. Jackson, May 30, 1864, in Hamilton (ed.), *Correspondence of Worth,* I, 309; William T. Auman and David D. Scarboro, "The Heroes of America in Civil War North Carolina," *NCHR,* LVIII (1981), 346; Kruman, *Parties and Politics in North Carolina,* 264. After the war Holden joined the Heroes of America and in 1869 was elected grand chancellor of the state society.

popgun charges started against the strait Conservatives" by the Vance-"Destructive" forces. Despite his rebuttal and evidence that the organization was "as harmless as Masonry," the publicity given to the Heroes of America and the implication that they were tied to Holden reinforced the belief that the editor of the *Standard* was "dyed with treason as black as night," as one Conservative put it.[52]

The battle front and northern political developments also contributed to Holden's undoing. Although Federal armies had penetrated deep into the South, with Sherman near Atlanta and Grant near Petersburg, Union victory appeared remote by midsummer, and reports were widespread that northern morale was faltering. A wave of renewed hope swept the South, with many Confederates believing that if their armies could hold out until the fall, the Republicans would be hurled from power in the presidential election and Confederate independence achieved.[53] In North Carolina, Governor Vance reflected this upbeat sentiment, while Holden, in the minds of the majority, represented the forces of defeatism. Unfortunately for Holden and the peace movement, the election occurred when the new wave of optimism was at its height; one month later the fall of Atlanta and other military setbacks would shatter the illusion of Confederate success for most North Carolinians.

On July 28 North Carolina troops in the field gave Holden an early defeat at the polls. Vance won 13,209 of the 15,033 votes cast by the soldiers; in a few regiments he received a unanimous vote. Holden, with some justification, excitedly charged that fraud and intimidation had occurred in the balloting. He claimed that officers either threw out ballots cast for him or directed pro-Holden soldiers not to vote in the election. In some units, he declared, officers placed Holden men on guard duty to prevent their voting. "My heart sickens at the memory of what occurred" in the army election, Holden wrote a friend. "Never before in the annals of American history did such voting take place." Despite the irregularities, he was mistaken in believing that most of the troops supported

52. Raleigh *Standard*, July 6, 13, 1864; Raleigh *Conservative*, as reported in Raleigh *Standard*, June 29, 1864; Auman and Scarboro, "Heroes of America," 362.

53. Larry E. Nelson, *Bullets, Ballots, and Rhetoric: Confederate Policy for the United States Presidential Contest of 1864* (University, Ala., 1980), Ch. 5.

him. Even if the election had been fair, Vance still would have won a comfortable majority of the army vote.[54]

The army results presaged what was to follow in the state balloting on August 4. Vance won reelection by capturing 77.2 percent of the civilian votes. Holden polled only 14,432 of a total vote of 72,305 in the army and at home.

Holden's enemies exulted in the magnitude of his defeat. "Such a victory over Holden," the Fayetteville *Observer* joyously announced, "is worth several victories in the field." Former Governor Charles Manly, who was the victim of Holden's poisoned pen in the election of 1850, crowed that his old enemy was like a "dead cock in a pit. Did ever man or beast get such a beating?" The outcome of the election, Manly said, was "not only a most gratifying achievement personally, but a great public triumph of patriotism & order over disloyalty & lowbrowed treachery." Another foe exclaimed, "Holden is *down, forever* down, and our glorious state redeemed from the foul reproach and deep damnation which would have resulted" if he had won the election.[55]

Most of his antagonists, both inside and outside the state, proclaimed that the election results had saved North Carolina for the Confederacy. As Vance put it: "It had been supposed that there was much disaffection in this State particularly, but the recent election contradicts it. My competitor, a bold and popular demagogue, made the issue distinctly of peace on terms less than independence, and I have beaten him worse than any man was ever beaten in North Carolina."[56] Even General Lee sent his congratulations to Vance, indicating that his victory would "cheer and sustain the people of the Confederacy . . . [and] dissipate the hopes that our enemies had cherished of a division of our efforts and councils." The results of the election, Lee told Vance, should convince northerners "that three years of war have in no degree shaken the reso-

54. Yates, *The Confederacy and Vance*, 106; W. W. Holden to Calvin J. Cowles, July 29, 1864, in Holden Papers, NDAH; Raleigh *Standard*, August 3, 10, 1864; Raper, "Holden and the Peace Movement," 514; Bailey, "North Carolina Politics During the Civil War," 215.

55. Raleigh *Standard*, August 17, 1864; Bailey, "North Carolina Politics During the Civil War," 215; E. B. Liles to Zebulon B. Vance, August 7, 1864, in Vance Papers.

56. Yates, *The Confederacy and Vance*, 106. See also A. S. Merrimon to Vance, August 8, 1864, in Vance Papers.

lution of our people to resist, as long as they present them no alternative but that of degrading submission." The election's "effect upon the northern mind will be salutary in demonstrating the futility of force as a means of adjusting the pending controversy," Lee concluded.[57]

The reaction of Holdenites was naturally one of bitter disappointment. Robert P. Dick of Greensboro, a leader in the state convention movement, wrote Holden that he was "perfectly astounded by the result of the recent elections. I can not account for so universal and so sudden revulsion in public sentiment." Dick, like Holden a former Democrat, suspected, however, that "the old spirit of Whiggery was in some degree resurrected" to defeat the man who more than anyone else had destroyed that party in the state. Holden himself, though proclaiming the election "a mere farce," professed to be "neither dismayed nor depressed by the results," and he promised to continue the fight for an honorable peace and for the cause of "true Conservatism" in North Carolina.[58] Indeed, he was soon back at his desk composing peace editorials.

Historians have long concluded that northern military victories and Lincoln's reelection in the fall ended the possibility of a negotiated settlement of the war.[59] Holden and many of his supporters, however, believed that through immediate negotiations southerners could yet avoid Federal suppression of their rights—always a central concern of Holden—and the sudden emancipation of the slaves. But it was now understood that they would have to agree to reconstruction of the Union in order to obtain these terms. "If there is a strong probability that, in the end, we will be overrun and subjugated, and held down by our enemy at his mercy," Holden argued, "would it not be wise to avoid that unspeakable evil by compromising our difficulties at once, on the best terms that can be obtained. For our part—and we believe we utter the sentiments of a large majority of our people—as anxious as we have been for Confederate

57. R. E. Lee to Zebulon B. Vance, August 12, 1864, in Vance Papers. Lee, of course, had misjudged the effect of the election on the "northern mind."

58. Robert P. Dick to W. W. Holden, August 20, 1864, in Holden Papers, DU; Raleigh *Standard*, August 17, September 7, 21, 1864.

59. See, for example, Allan Nevins, *The War for the Union: The Organized War to Victory, 1864–1865* (New York, 1971), 198–201, 254.

success, we would prefer a restoration of the old government to the subjugation of the South." In another issue of the *Standard*, he declared that "we would rather live with the Northern people as equals than live *under* them." Aware of Lincoln's mild terms for the South, Holden assured his readers that neither property confiscation nor mass proscription or punishment for southerners would occur if the South agreed to reconstruction.[60]

When the legislature met in late November, 1864, Holden demanded the appointment of commissioners, to be joined by those from other southern states, for the purpose of initiating peace negotiations. He assured the legislators that he was not suggesting "hasty action" or "separate state action." A peace proposal similar to what Holden recommended was soon introduced into the state senate by John Pool. But after a sharp debate it was rejected by a close vote, with Vance Conservatives joining "Destructive" members to defeat it. Holden now revived the proposal for a state convention to institute peace negotiations, but he was unsuccessful in his attempt to have the legislature submit the question to the voters.[61] With this defeat he gave up hope for a negotiated settlement.

While General Sherman marched through South Carolina toward North Carolina in early 1865, Holden devoted a great deal of attention in the *Standard* to denouncing the Confederate proposal to free the slaves and arm them to fight the invaders. The scheme "is not merely an abolition measure," he stormed, "it is a confession of subjugation. It surrenders the great point upon which the two sections went to war." At the same time, Holden did not want to see any more white men die to preserve slavery, though "we regret the loss of our property [and] think the policy of sudden emancipation is injurious to society and cruel to the slaves." He reminded North Carolinians that "if our humble advice had been heeded and taken eighteen months ago, the States could have secured the privilege to themselves of perpetuating slavery as long as they pleased."[62]

Sherman's invasion of North Carolina in early March frightened

60. Raleigh *Standard*, January 18, February 1, 1865.
61. *Ibid.*, November 23, 1864, January 11, February 15, 1865. Under the Pool proposal, President Davis would still have a role in the negotiations, but it was vaguely defined.
62. *Ibid.*, February 8, March 1, 1865. See also issues of February 1, 15, 1865.

Holden, causing him, strangely enough, to have one last illusion that the enemy might be stopped and the state saved from "Yankee bummers." On March 22 he declared: "Nothing but an undying concurrent resolution" to use all available men and resources "can save us." "We must continue this struggle to a successful issue, or make abject cowardly submission" to the Federal forces. Even if the Confederacy fell, "we would counsel no base submission to the enemy." One week later he was buoyed by news of a "brilliant victory for Confederate arms" at Bentonville. Confederate General Joseph E. Johnston, Holden claimed, was now in a good position to "deal blow after blow on the enemy," sparing Raleigh from Sherman's devastating march.[63] The battle of Bentonville, however, was not a Confederate victory; instead it sounded the death knell for southern resistance in North Carolina and opened the road to Raleigh for Sherman's army. On April 5 Holden published the last Civil War issue of the *Standard*, still hoping for a miracle that would save North Carolina and "our beautiful little City."

The miracle did not occur, but Raleigh was more fortunate than most southern towns in Sherman's path. It was saved from destruction. On April 13 the end of the war came for the citizens of North Carolina's capital. From his home one block away, Holden could hear Sherman's cavalry clatter up deserted Fayetteville Street toward the capitol, where former Governor David L. Swain, then president of the University of North Carolina, waited alone to surrender the town and its state buildings to the invaders.[64]

63. *Ibid.*, March 22, 29, 1865.
64. Barrett, *The Civil War in North Carolina*, 515–16; Raleigh *Progress*, April 15, 1865.

VIII
Provisional Governor

Four days after Sherman's army entered Raleigh, Holden resumed publication of the *Standard*. "The revolution has failed," he announced in this first issue. "Mr. Lincoln has made good his declaration that he would 'hold, occupy, and possess' the forts and other property of the United States, and that he would enforce the laws of the nation." Holden called on North Carolinians to submit immediately to national authority and thereby hasten the restoration of peace.[1] His flirtation with reconstruction in the peace movement and his desire to avoid a postwar military tyranny made it relatively easy for him quickly to abandon his defiance of the North and accept the realities of defeat.

That day, April 17, the shocking news reached Raleigh of the assassination of the president, filling Holden with alarm for the safety of the town and dismay for the future of reconstruction. Holden and other Raleighites, along with General Sherman himself, feared that the assassination would send enraged Union soldiers into the streets to exact revenge against helpless citizens. Rushing the news to press early the next morning, Holden assured his readers, who included Sherman's troops encamped in and around Raleigh, that

1. Raleigh *Daily Standard*, April 17, 1865. This was the first time that Holden published a daily edition of the *Standard*, a practice that would continue during Reconstruction. Except for 1865, when few extant issues of the *Weekly Standard* exist, I have used the weekly edition, since it was more comprehensive and designed for statewide circulation.

"North Carolina had no agency in the awful deed. . . . We call heaven to witness that we deplore it as the saddest event in the history of this continent." He appealed to the soldiers and their officers to exercise restraint in this moment of outrage. "Let the friends of the Union," he artfully declared, "bear [the assassination] as best they may, and let not the innocent be held responsible for the acts of the guilty." [2]

Late that afternoon a hurriedly organized body of apprehensive Raleighites met at the courthouse "to express the profound regret felt by all of our people at the announcement of the death of Mr. Lincoln." Resolutions, which were drafted by Holden and four other prominent wartime peace advocates, were adopted deploring "the atrocious deed" and denouncing "any affiliation or sympathy with such outrages and atrocities." [3]

This important expression of public sympathy for the martyred Lincoln, followed by strong assurances of support for the Union by the *Standard*, calmed emotions in Sherman's camps. A friendly relationship soon developed between the soldiers and many Raleigh residents. After two weeks of the military occupation, Holden, writing in the *Standard*, praised the "nearly perfect" discipline of the troops and their respect for property and personal rights. "From Gen. Sherman to the humblest private we have witnessed nothing but what has been proper and courteous," Holden observed. "Our city has been thoroughly protected against stragglers. Every house is guarded, and the most perfect order prevails." [4] At the same time, northern soldiers were writing home and proclaiming the virtues of "the City of Oaks," its people, and, on occasion, its most famous citizen, Holden. "The Union element in Raleigh is very strong," an Ohioan happily wrote. "The most conspicuous Unionist is the fearless Holden, the well known editor of the *Standard*. When his history is fully known, he will become one of the most popular men in the nation." This writer also reported that Raleighites, influenced

2. Raleigh *Daily Standard*, April 18, 1865; General William Tecumseh Sherman to General Henry W. Halleck, April 18, 1865, in OR, Ser. I, Vol. XLVII, Pt. 3, pp. 243–44.

3. Raleigh *Daily Standard*, April 19, 1865; Raleigh *Daily Progress*, April 20, 1865.

4. Raleigh *Daily Standard*, April 24, 1865.

by Holden's newspaper, had displayed no discourtesies toward
Union soldiers: even the ladies, unlike those in other southern
communities, had been hospitable to the men in blue.[5]

Meanwhile Holden fretted that Sherman might permit the return
of Vance and his associates to power. Sherman, in a meeting with
President Lincoln in late March, had gained the impression that he
should recall state officials and permit them to lead the movement
back into the Union. He was to meet with Confederate General
Joseph E. Johnston near Durham Station on April 18 to arrange a
peace. Holden probably knew of Sherman's intention to offer Johnston generous terms, including the restoration of rebel governments.[6] On the day of the meeting Holden in the *Standard* reminded federal authorities that the Vance "Destructives," in fleeing
the capital upon the approach of the army, had "abdicated" their
offices and abandoned all responsibility for state governance. Furthermore, he claimed, the Vance administration did not "reflect the
wishes or the will of the people," because it "was elected by force
and fraud" and was only an appendage of the Davis despotism. The
people had no use for the "Destructives," he added. "Politically
they are doomed men for all time to come. We ask no further or
greater punishment" for them, he concluded.[7]

If Sherman read Holden's editorial, he ignored the admonition.
The Sherman-Johnston agreement of April 18 went beyond what
Lincoln had intended and what victorious northern Republicans
would tolerate. It was soon repudiated by the new administration
in Washington. Holden, though strongly objecting to the participation of Vance officials in reconstruction, favored Lincoln's mild wartime policies that were designed to restore the southern states to
the Union quickly. He expected Lincoln's plan to be implemented in
North Carolina by the old peace party. The president's assassination, however, chilled Holden's hopes for an early restoration of

5. Raleigh *Daily Progress,* April 27, 1865. See George W. Nichols, *The Story of
the Great March* (New York, 1866), 295–300, for similar observations by an occupying officer regarding unionist sentiment in Raleigh.

6. Herman Belz, *Reconstructing the Union: Theory and Policy During the Civil
War* (Ithaca, 1969), 278–79. By implication the Sherman-Johnston accord re-
stored slave property. Burke Davis, *Sherman's March* (New York, 1980), 263–64;
John M. Gibson, *Those 163 Days: A Southern Account of Sherman's March from
Atlanta to Raleigh* (New York, 1961), 270–71.

7. Raleigh *Daily Standard,* April 18, 1865.

civil government in the state. The northern cry for vengeance, Holden reasoned, might push Lincoln's successor, Andrew Johnson, and Congress toward a harsh reconstruction program, prolonging military control and continuing the war-bred disintegration of the state.

On April 24 Holden recommended in the *Standard* a reconstruction plan for the new president to follow. Drawing upon Lincoln's earlier policies, he proposed that Johnson appoint a provisional governor for North Carolina "whose duty it shall be, in co-operation with the regular military power, to restore order among the people, to enforce the laws, and to suppress that terrible guerrilla warfare which is already afflicting the State, and which unless suppressed by the strong hand, will complete the ruin of every neighborhood."[8] The provisional governor, "as one of his first duties" under the plan, would "issue a call for the election of delegates to a State Convention"; the assembled delegates would then meet the national requirements for reconstruction and also provide for the election of officials to the restored state government and to membership in Congress. "By this mode," Holden declared, "order will be maintained, the people will be consulted, the institution of slavery will be promptly disposed of, a new State government will be established deriving its existence immediately from a Union people, and the State will have her members of Congress in readiness to take their seats even before that body shall meet in December, 1865."[9]

In order to demonstrate North Carolina's loyalty, Holden soon after the surrender urged the assembling of Union meetings throughout the state. Such meetings, he said, should begin the work of organizing a Union party in North Carolina, one that by implication would be loyal to him and would control reconstruction once President Johnson had announced his plan for the defeated South. Following this advice, self-proclaimed unionists held rallies through-

8. Holden's somber view of conditions in North Carolina was accurate. Interior areas of the state tottered on the brink of anarchy as Confederate authority collapsed. John Pool to David M. Carter, April 15, 1865, Lewis Thompson to John Pool, April 15, 1865, in David Miller Carter Papers, SHC; Mrs. E. J. Thompson to Benjamin S. Hedrick, May, 1865, in Benjamin S. Hedrick Papers, DU.

9. Raleigh *Daily Standard,* April 24, 1865. There is no evidence that Johnson saw this editorial, though later, when he conferred with Holden, he was given the North Carolinian's views on reconstruction.

out North Carolina during the first few weeks after the surrender and sent reports of their proceedings to the *Standard*.

Holden himself addressed a large Union rally at Raleigh in which, partly to impress the victors present, he sang paeans to the Union and demanded the punishment of former Confederate leaders, though he did not say what form the punishment should take. In his remarks he followed closely his expansive antebellum praise of the Union. He proclaimed that with the end of the war "the stars on the [national] banner will never go out, and the sun of American liberty will never go down." He continued: "The war has resulted in the utter extinction of African slavery. . . . It remains for the people of this State in Convention and by legislative action to de-fine the state of the emancipated race. I, for one, have no fear in this regard. I am willing to see the alphabet, the Bible and the school book placed in their hands, and to recognize among them the mar-riage relations heretofore so culpably disregarded. The extent of their further elevation belongs legitimately to the governing race." What North Carolina needed, Holden told his audience, was labor and capital to rehabilitate the state's economy and develop its var-ied resources. "To our brethren of the North and East and West we say, come over and help us. Bring your capital, your muscle, your intelligence, your industry, your ingenuity, and settle among us." [10]

Many of the Union meetings adopted almost verbatim Holden's words in the *Standard* calling for a state convention "to repeal the abominable and detestable ordinance of secession" and restore the state to its proper place in the Union. They also praised Holden for his wartime defense of the constitutional rights of the people, re-ferred to him as their "great Conservative champion," and recom-mended that Johnson appoint him military governor of North Carolina.[11] Most of these participants had supported Holden and the peace movement in 1863–1864; only a minority had remained true to the Union throughout the war, though after the surrender many more attempted to give the impression that they had done so.

10. *Ibid.*, May 12, 1865; William W. Holden, *Memoirs of W. W. Holden* (Dur-ham, 1911), 52–55.
11. Raleigh *Daily Standard*, May 2, 3, 11, 12, 1865; Raleigh *Daily Progress,* issues of May, 1865; New Bern *North Carolina Daily Times*, May 5, 11, 16, 22, 1865; proceedings of Union meeting in Surry County, June 6, 1865, in William La-fayette Scott Papers, DU.

Meanwhile President Johnson was grappling with the reconstruction problem, specifically with the reestablishment of national
authority in North Carolina. Probably because of the state's near-
ness to Washington, where the history of the North Carolina peace
movement was well known, Johnson was determined to make his
native state the model for his reconstruction program. The plan
that emerged in mid-May, despite the initial fears of many former
Confederates, generally followed the mild policy laid down by Lincoln for Louisiana, and it conformed even closer to Holden's April
24 proposal. Indeed, as will be seen, the Raleigh editor probably
had a hand in the final shaping of Johnson's plan of reconstruction.

On May 8 Johnson and his cabinet first considered the issue of
reconstruction in the Old North State. Secretary of War Edwin M.
Stanton proposed in broad outline the creation of a military government for North Carolina. Stanton's plan also provided, though
somewhat vaguely, for the appointment of a provisional governor
and the election of delegates to a constitutional convention. The
purpose of the convention would be to reestablish a republican
form of government in the state. When the question of black suffrage was raised in the cabinet discussion, the president postponed
the consideration of the plan and called for a further study of the
whole reconstruction problem. The next day, evidently without
consulting his cabinet, he telegraphed Holden, asking him to go
immediately to Washington and confer with him on North Carolina affairs. The president also invited Holden to bring along any
political friends he desired.[12]

Holden quickly assembled four Raleigh associates and Robert P.
Dick of Greensboro for the trip to Washington. On May 18 they
arrived in Washington and immediately met with the president at
his temporary office in the Treasury Building.[13]

The substance of this first discussion is unknown, but apparently
the North Carolinians, after reporting on the grim social and economic conditions in the state, impressed Johnson with the need for

12. Benjamin P. Thomas and Harold Hyman, *Stanton: The Life and Times of
Lincoln's Secretary of War* (New York, 1962), 444–45; OR, Ser. 1, Vol. XVVII, Pt.
3, p. 453.
13. General John M. Schofield to President Andrew Johnson, May 15, 1865, in
Andrew Johnson Papers (on microfilm), LC (unless otherwise noted, all citations
are to Series I); Holden, *Memoirs*, 45, 75.

the state's early return to the Union. It is likely that what Holden told the president was similar to a report on the situation that he had sent to Washington a few days earlier. "The condition of affairs in this state is cheering," he had written Johnson on May 13. "A large majority of the people are delighted on immediate emancipation and are ready for civil Government as soon as can be conveniently established." He did not, however, call for the removal of Federal troops, who were engaged in restoring order.[14] The conference at the Treasury broke up without reaching a decision, but in parting, the president asked the North Carolinians to meet with him again.

At home, Conservatives of the old Vance faction viewed the Holden mission with dismay. They dispatched a delegation to Washington for the purpose of countering Holden and securing a lenient reconstruction settlement. The delegation consisted of University of North Carolina President David L. Swain, Raleigh attorney Bartholomew F. Moore, and William Eaton—all of whom had been prestigious unionists in the secession crisis of 1860–1861. They met with the president four days after his first session with the Holden party. Johnson had his secretary read to them the draft of a reconstruction proclamation for North Carolina, the details of which he evidently had worked out with Holden and his friends in earlier meetings. The Swain delegation argued vigorously against the proclamation on the grounds that it represented unnecessary federal intrusion into the affairs of the state. They told the president that the last Confederate legislature—not Johnson's provisional governor, as provided for in the proclamation—should initiate the process of reconstruction. The president, however, would not budge from his position, and the delegation left the meeting with the disquieting knowledge that Holden had gained Johnson's confidence and would be given control of reconstruction in the state.[15]

14. Holden to Johnson, May 13, 1865, in Johnson Papers.
15. This account of the Washington meeting has been pieced together from B. F. Moore to the editors, Raleigh *Daily Standard*, June 19, 1865; David L. Swain to William A. Graham, July 4, 1865, in J. G. de Roulhac Hamilton and Max R. Williams (eds.), *The Papers of William Alexander Graham* (7 vols. to date; Raleigh, 1957–), VI, 318; and David L. Swain to Thomas Ruffin, September 15, 1865, in J. G. de Roulhac Hamilton (ed.), *The Papers of Thomas Ruffin* (4 vols.; Raleigh, 1918–20), IV, 28.

On May 25 both North Carolina delegations met with Johnson, but only to discuss his proposed amnesty proclamation and the revival of the state's commerce. The next day Holden's friends addressed a note to the president recommending that he appoint the *Standard* editor provisional governor of North Carolina. Johnson quickly agreed, and in a final meeting with Holden the draft of the reconstruction proclamation was carefully read and approved. In the course of the discussion, Johnson startled Holden by announcing his intention to confiscate the property of unpardoned rebels and divide it among unoffending yeoman whites. When Holden protested such a drastic plan, the president, the North Carolinian later wrote, backed down and agreed not to press the issue. Holden's arguments were probably not decisive in changing Johnson's mind, since the president had a habit of vacillating in conversation, leaving the appearance of ambiguity when in fact his position had already been decided.[16] On this issue it seems that after becoming president, Johnson never seriously considered a policy of confiscation and was perhaps only toying with the idea to see what Holden's reaction would be. He also might have been warning Holden that unless North Carolinians cooperated with him, the Radicals in the North would overturn his lenient reconstruction plan and succeed in confiscating southern property.

On May 29 Johnson issued his proclamation appointing Holden provisional governor of North Carolina and launching the reconstruction process in the state.[17] The proclamation became the model for presidential reconstruction in other southern states. Essentially, it gave Holden "all the powers necessary and proper" to enable loyal North Carolinians to reestablish a republican form of government and restore the state to "its constitutional relations to the Federal Government." Johnson indicated that his definition of republicanism broadly included the creation of a unionist state government that would ensure justice, domestic tranquillity, and the protection of life, liberty, and property.

16. Robert P. Dick *et al.* to Johnson, May 26, 1865, in Johnson Papers; Holden, *Memoirs,* 55. On Johnson's habit of vacillating in private conversation, see Albert Castel, *The Presidency of Andrew Johnson* (Lawrence, Kan., 1979), 27.

17. Johnson's North Carolina proclamation may be found in James D. Richardson (comp.), *A Compilation of the Messages and Papers of the Presidents* (11 vols.; Washington, D.C., 1896–99), VI, 310–12.

The proclamation did not specifically direct the state to abolish slavery or invalidate North Carolina's 1861 ordinance of secession, two obvious requirements, given the results of the war. Holden clearly understood that these actions were necessary before Johnson would approve the work of reconstruction. In his conversations with the president, Holden evidently advised Johnson against their inclusion in the proclamation, since they would represent, as he saw it, an unnecessary federal involvement in the affairs of the states and would conflict with the president's desire to encourage voluntary state action in reconstruction. Holden had earlier insisted that a large majority of the people "will recognize and carry out the emancipation views of the national administration" when they formed a new state government. The invalidation of the secession ordinance, Holden believed, would be quickly done by a state convention dominated by "straitest-sect" conservatives or unionists, even if the president's plan did not explicitly require such action.[18]

The May 29 proclamation directed Holden to arrange as soon as possible for the election of a loyal state convention to bring North Carolina's constitution into line with the results of the war. The president, temporarily checking the Radical Republican drive for black suffrage as a part of the reconstruction settlement, indicated that only persons who had been qualified voters before the passage of the 1861 secession ordinance could participate in the election or serve as delegates to the convention. Each voter and delegate also had to subscribe to the oath of allegiance contained in the president's amnesty proclamation issued on the same day as his North Carolina edict. The oath simply required future loyalty to the United States; fourteen classes of Confederate leaders, including large property holders, however, were excluded from the oath until they had petitioned and received pardons from Johnson for their rebellion against the government.[19] The requests for pardon were to be processed through Holden, who would make a recommendation to the president in each case.

18. Raleigh *Daily Standard*, May 2, 12, 15, 1865. On Johnson's commitment to state voluntarism in his reconstruction policy, see Michael Les Benedict, *A Compromise of Principle: Congressional Republicans and Reconstruction, 1863–1869* (New York, 1974), 126–27.

19. Richardson (comp.), *Messages and Papers of the Presidents*, VI, 310–13; Benedict, *A Compromise of Principle*, 106–108, 117.

Johnson's North Carolina proclamation also directed federal troops in the department to aid Holden and refrain from "hindering, impeding or discouraging the loyal people from the organization of a State government." No mention was made of the role that the recently organized Freedmen's Bureau or the military should play in the protection of black freedom. The proclamation also provided for the reestablishment of federal functions (courts, postal services, and revenue collection) in the state.[20]

On June 3 Holden returned home from Washington. Two days later, after turning over control of the *Standard* to his son Jo and to Joseph S. Cannon, he launched his provisional government. In assuming office, Holden was not required, as were other Johnson governors, to take the ironclad oath swearing unblemished wartime loyalty. Secretary of State William H. Seward, who gave him his commission, later claimed that the omission was an oversight, which, if true, was fortunate because Holden could not honestly swear that he had not aided the rebellion.[21]

The task that Holden undertook in early June was formidable, and to guide him, he had only those precedents established by Lincoln's wartime military governors in southern unionist enclaves. A substantial body of North Carolinians, though demoralized by Confederate defeat and concerned mainly with survival, seethed with resentment at Holden's appointment as provisional governor. The snobbish Catherine Ann Edmondston reflected the bitterness of many diehard Confederates and anti-Holdenites when she wrote that the conquerors had "taken the lowest, most abject, & degraded man they could find amongst us—one Holden—& exalted him to the post of provisional Governor. A base born bastard with neither the breeding or the instincts of a gentleman, is placed over us—& in utter defiance of the fact that six months since he [was] utterly repudiated, and almost to a man," in the race for governor. A. M. McPheeters, a Union Whig who supported Vance during the war, moaned that with Holden's elevation North Carolina "has fallen into *bad* hands. I regard Holden now, as I have done for years past, as a bad man, entirely devoid of principle." David Schenck, a

20. Richardson (comp.), *Messages and Papers of the Presidents*, VI, 312–14.
21. New Bern *North Carolina Daily Times*, June 5, 1865; Raleigh *Daily Standard*, June 6, 1865; William H. Seward to President Andrew Johnson, March 1, 1866, in *Senate Executive Documents*, 39th Cong., 1st Sess., No. 26, p. 2.

western North Carolina lawyer, confided to his diary that Holden would immediately institute a "reign of terror and persecution" against his old foes. Anti-Holdenites seemed genuinely baffled by the president's appointment of a man who had supported secession and had demonstrated, at least to their satisfaction, a political unreliability and duplicity unmatched in North Carolina history. They believed that from the moment that Holden launched the peace movement in 1863, he possessed a morbid ambition to preside over the state's return to the Union and its reconstruction.[22] Holden's quickness after the surrender in disassociating himself from the Confederate cause and embracing the Union confirmed in their minds this judgment of him.

Holdenites, though a minority of the white population, made no apologies for the appointment of their hero as provisional governor. Unionists in the West held meetings at Hendersonville and Asheville and expressed "the great satisfaction of a large majority of the people" with Holden's appointment. Having experienced "the force of bayonets" during the war, western friends appealed to the new provisional governor for a speedy restoration of civil authority with native unionists in control. They also warned him against radical policies, particularly the enfranchisement of blacks, which many northern Republicans demanded.[23]

Farther east, supporters found it necessary to provide a more vigorous defense of the appointment. Eastern friends admitted that "many loud and fierce denunciations have been made against Mr. Holden by his enemies," especially on the ground that he had been a leading secessionist before the war. They argued, however, that his opposition to the "Destructives" during the war had made his antebellum past irrelevant. One defender wrote that Holden, before any other North Carolina leader, realized "that secession and rebellion was destined to be a failure . . . and he at once united all the energies of mind and body to bring about a speedy termination

22. Catherine Ann Edmondston Diary, 1860–1866, June 26, 1865 (Ms in NDAH); A. M. McPheeters to R. L. Patterson, June 10, 1865, in Rufus L. Patterson Papers, NDAH; David Schenck Diary, June 7, 1865 (Ms in SHC); H. H. Helper to Benjamin S. Hedrick, June 21, 1865, John Graham Tull to Benjamin S. Hedrick, August 25, 1865, in Hedrick Papers.
23. Raleigh *Daily Standard*, June 29, 1865.

of the war and reunion of the States. This is why he has influence with the President" and why he was placed in charge of the state's reconstruction. Another supporter claimed that Holden deserved the appointment because he had "aided the cause of Union more than any other man in the State," and was intelligent and eminently qualified to manage the intricate problems of postwar adjustment.[24]

Harsh economic and social conditions in North Carolina provided an ominous setting for Holden's reconstruction work. The state's economy lay in ruins, and little hope existed for an early recovery. Stark poverty confronted many people, and only the continued distribution of army rations prevented hundreds of them from starving. Throughout the state, money was almost nonexistent, banks were closed, and though the army had partially restored railway service, transportation and commerce were virtually at a standstill. Stock animals—a prerequisite for agricultural recovery—and the state's infant industries had been almost completely destroyed by foraging military and guerrilla units. The war and its disruptive aftermath had caused property to be reduced to less than one-half of its former value. Public institutions like the University of North Carolina, the common school system, the insane asylum, and the county poorhouses had all gone down in the general ruin.[25]

Despite some success by the military in suppressing the lawless, security for persons and property continued to be precarious. In the West, unionists and brigands stalked their wartime persecutors when the army was not looking. The freed slaves especially felt the heavy hand of a society tottering toward anarchy. The objects of

24. Salisbury *Union Banner*, October 28, 1865; New Bern *North Carolina Daily Times*, June 5, 1865. See also excerpts from pro-Holden newspapers quoted in the Raleigh *Daily Standard*, June 10, 12, 1865, and the Raleigh *Daily Progress*, July 19, 1865.

25. Kenneth Rayner to President Johnson, July 8, 1865, in Johnson Papers; Benjamin S. Hedrick to Secretary of Treasury Hugh McCulloch, May 29, 1865, W. C. Kerr to Benjamin S. Hedrick, June 28, 1865, in Hedrick Papers; David L. Swain to Zebulon B. Vance, September 12, 1865, in Zebulon B. Vance Papers, NDAH; Schenck Diary, June 7, 1865; Raleigh *Daily Standard*, June 1, 1865; Mayor Arch McLean of Fayetteville and Cumberland County Commissioners to Governor W. W. Holden, June 8, 1865, in Provisional Governor William Woods Holden Papers, NDAH.

mistreatment by embittered whites, many blacks hovered in and around towns like Wilmington, Raleigh, and New Bern, where they could find protection and exercise their new freedom.[26]

On June 12 Holden outlined in a proclamation his plan for the early restoration of civil government and constitutional rights in the state. He announced that he would arrange "at as early a period as practical" for the election of a convention to meet the president's terms for reconstruction. Probably because Johnson's reconstruction requirements were still not entirely clear, Holden did not specify what actions the convention should take. He reminded North Carolinians of Johnson's requirement that only those persons who had subscribed to the amnesty oath could vote in the election or serve as delegates to the convention. Holden indicated that individuals "not well-affected towards the Federal Government," including those in the excepted classes who were unpardoned, were barred from the oath. He also directed the convention to submit all changes in the constitution to the voters for ratification. Finally, he said, the convention should provide for the election of a restored government under the constitution.[27]

Meanwhile, since no regular government existed in the state, Holden informed North Carolinians that he would reinstitute civil authority by the appointment of a host of officials, including judges, justices of the peace, and state railroad directors. Under Holden's plan the new justices of the peace would initiate the reconstruction process in the counties. He directed them to appoint sheriffs and county court clerks, try nonjury cases, and "exert themselves to maintain the laws and promote the peace of society." He also instructed the justices to oversee the election of delegates to the state convention. Holden insisted that only "loyal men" should be appointed to office, but he required them to subscribe only to the president's amnesty oath pledging future loyalty to the United States and

26. Sidney Andrews, *The South Since the War: As Shown by Fourteen Weeks of Travel and Observation in Georgia and the Carolinas* (Boston, 1866), 112–19; Howard N. Rabinowitz, *Race Relations in the Urban South, 1865–1890* (Urbana, 1980), 21–22.

27. Holden's proclamation was repeatedly published in the Raleigh *Daily Standard* in late June, 1865, and in other newspapers. There is a printed broadside of the proclamation in the William Woods Holden Papers, DU.

Holden as a young man
Courtesy North Carolina Division of Archives and History

Holden in 1865
Courtesy North Carolina Division of Archives and
History

Louisa Virginia Harrison Holden
Courtesy Manuscript Department, William R. Perkins
Library, Duke University

Joseph W. Holden in about 1860
Courtesy North Carolina Division of Archives and History

Holden's home in Raleigh from 1852 to 1892
Courtesy North Carolina Division of Archives and History

John W. Ellis, governor of North Carolina,
1859–1861
Courtesy North Carolina Division of Archives and History

Zebulon B. Vance, governor of North
Carolina, 1862–1865
Courtesy North Carolina Division of Archives
and History

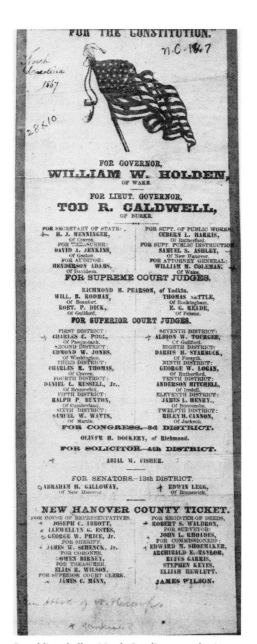

Republican ballot, North Carolina state election, 1868

Courtesy Department of Rare Books, William R. Perkins Library, Duke University

Holden in 1868, the year he was elected to the governorship
Courtesy Manuscript Department, William R. Perkins Library, Duke University

FACTS FOR THE PEOPLE

To Read, Ponder and Digest, if they can.

For the benefit of those who really desire information, and to show in proper light the Extravagance, Wastefulness, and utter disregard for the people's best interests, shown by the Radical party, we submit the following comparison of the expense of one year of Democratic rule, under Gov. Bragg in 1857 & '58 ; and one year ending Sept. 30th, 1869, under the Radical rule of William W. Holden :

	Expenditures 1857, '58	Expenditures 1868, '69
Adjutant General,	$ 200 00	$ 1965 56
Capitol Square,	1277 82	3687 73
Executive Department,	2550 00	7752 65
Treasury Department,	2750 00	6082 96
Keeper of Capitol,	266 00	1054 19
Auditor's Department,	1000 00	4010 54
Binding Laws,	1073 25	6596 96
Copying Laws,	348 50	1608 60
State Department,	800 00	3903 25
Public Printing,	5240 57	28,685 10
Judiciary,	28,163 15	54,130 50
General Assembly,	49,113 54	191,102 10
Fugitives from Justice,	572 75	6,834 00

Contingences for 1868, '69, $76,506 64

☞ Among the expenditures for 1868, '69, may be found such items as these :—

D. D. Colgrove, one copy of "How to Make the Farm pay,"	$ 4 50
L. D. Wilkie, Holden's detective,	1042 90
L. H. Mowers, " "	949 75
State Militia, (to outrage Jones County,)	1864 91
Newbern Republican, for adv. duties S. C. C.,	250 00
Newbern Times, printing Badges for Militia,	18 80
Douglass Bell, for Toilet Soap,	6 00
Geo. W. Nason, jr., Drawer locks, Chairs and Water Coolers,	130 20
Phil. Thiem, 6 Baskets, 1 Corkscrew,	9 00
Half doz. ostrich feathers, water bucket and dipper,	16 75

OTHER FACTS FOR THE CITIZENS OF CRAVEN COUNTY ESPECIALLY.

The entire tax for this County levied for all purposes in 1867, under a Democratic State Government was $18,000. This, deducting the tax on Polls, was only 3-4 of one per cent on the assessed value of property.

The tax for this year, under Radical rule, will reach $47,000. Deduct the Poll tax and the tax levied on real and personal property as assessed, will reach 2 1-2 per cent.

Citizens of Craven, how like you this picture of increase in the short space of two years ?

Again—It is a fact worthy of note, that the principal officials, County Commissioners, Legal Adviser of the Board, (R. F. Lehman, Esq., $500,) have all been paid dollar for dollar of their claims, while the jurors, witnesses, &c., have their tickets on hand, or have been subjected to a shave of seventy per cent. to get the money for them.

☞ This is Radical justice—Radical love and care for the poor white and colored man, with a vengeance !

☞ Next week we will show you other iniquities of the party in power.☜

Conservative-Democratic party broadside, 1870
Courtesy Department of Rare Books, William R. Perkins Library, Duke University

Josiah Turner, Jr., Holden's nemesis
Courtesy North Carolina Division of Archives and History

John W. Stephens, the Republican state senator whose murder triggered the Kirk-Holden War
Courtesy North Carolina Division of Archives and History

not the 1862 ironclad oath that consistent unionists alone could legitimately take.

Holden could not resist the opportunity in his June 12 proclamation to recount the wrongs that North Carolinians had suffered under Confederate domination. "You have just been delivered by the armies of the Union from one of the most corrupt and rigorous despotisms that ever existed in the world," he told the people in his typical and exaggerated editorial fashion. He insisted that their liberties would now be well guarded by the United States. "Remember," he declared, "that all that you have, and all you can hope to be, and all of good that is reserved for your children, are indissolubly bound up with the American Union." To Holden the reconstruction of the Union was not merely the acceptance of the results of the war; it meant the restoration of a virtuous republic, one committed to the principles of liberty, constitutional rights, and local autonomy.

Holden's proclamation approached black liberty and rights in a far different way. Like most white North Carolinians, Holden conceived of black rights as something to be earned rather than something acquired by virtue of emancipation. He informed blacks that they were beginning their freedom with the same rights, "regulated by law, that others have, to enter upon the pursuit of prosperity and happiness," including security for their person and property and remuneration for their labor. Advancement in freedom, he told them, depended upon their careful practice of the virtues of industry, temperance, and frugality. He indicated that as a result of freedom they could learn to read and educate others of their race, but he made no promise that public support for their schools would be forthcoming. In justifying this program of gradualism based on future performance, the provisional governor paternalistically informed blacks that since "your race has been depressed by your condition of slavery . . . it is not to be expected that you can comprehend and appreciate . . . the wise provisions and limitations of Constitutions and laws; or that you can now have that knowledge of public affairs which is necessary to qualify you to discharge all the duties of the citizen." Either the forthcoming state convention or the new legislature, Holden maintained, should determine the status of blacks in postwar North Carolina. In any event, he found the northern Radical proposal for black political rights unworthy of comment and unlikely to be imposed on the South.

Holden also warned the freedmen against idleness, which he saw as the blacks' greatest weakness in freedom. "If you are idle you will become vicious and worthless," he declared; "if vicious and worthless you will have no friends, and will at last perish." Holden, like many white southerners during the blacks' "year of jubilee," predicted that the race would become extinct in the South if they did not go to work. To prevent it in North Carolina, he promised to set his face "against those of you who are idle and dissipated" and vowed to promptly punish blacks who violated the law. "I will be your friend as long as you are true to yourselves, and obedient to the laws, and as long as you shall labor, no matter how feebly, if honestly and earnestly to improve your condition."

Holden's first priority as provisional governor was clearly not to deal with the real issues involving black freedom. His main purpose was to bring about an early restoration of civil government under the control of members of his unionist faction, almost all of whom, like himself, viewed emancipation as a hardship caused by the folly of secession and war and not a central concern of the victorious North. Having announced his intentions to restore civil government as soon as possible, Holden obtained the consent of General John M. Schofield, commander of the occupation forces, to the replacement of military officers in the towns with loyal civil officials appointed by the provisional governor. At the same time, he issued a call for unionists to compile and forward to him lists of "none but loyal men" for appointment as justices of the peace in the counties. Instead of systematically holding public meetings to make nominations, he permitted small groups of unionists to draw up their own lists of suitable candidates for office. In some cases he wrote friends who evidently had supported him during the war, asking them to make recommendations for office.[28] Frequently unionists, or self-styled unionists, went to Raleigh to obtain appointments for themselves or their friends, and almost as frequently, when they

28. Raleigh *Daily Standard*, June 14, 29, 1865; W. W. Holden to R. L. Patterson, June 18, 1865, in Patterson Papers; W. W. Holden to Thomas D. McDowell, June 28, 1865, in Thomas D. McDowell Papers, SHC.

appealed to the governor, they inveighed against their "disloyal" local opponents.

Throughout late June and early July, Holden's office in the state capitol swarmed with office seekers and their friends. The governor was so busy with such matters and with the reorganization of local governments that some state officials complained that even on pressing public business they felt uncomfortable asking to see him. Ultimately he was driven to physical exhaustion and for more than a week was unable to work. By mid-July, Holden had appointed three thousand justices of the peace and town officials, and civil governments were in operation in all but the most remote counties, where the absence of mail service after the war had delayed the reconstruction process.[29] Unlike other provisional governors, he sought a thorough reorganization of local governments, but this policy did not necessarily mean placing only untainted unionists in power.

The governor's hastily conceived method of selection and haphazard appointments of justices of the peace and town officials inevitably produced mistakes. By late June, Holden was receiving complaints from "true Union men" that former rebels had misrepresented themselves to him and been appointed to county offices. He usually reacted to such protests by immediately selecting a new corps of officers, but in some counties he failed to act before the original group of justices had appointed sheriffs, county clerks, police forces, and other officials who reportedly were hostile to local unionists. More frequently, Holden knowingly selected men who, like himself, had favored Confederate independence but had opposed the Davis administration and supported the peace movement in 1863–1864. Some of these ultra Conservatives, whom Holden misleadingly referred to as "straitest-sect Unionists," had little credibility with either the Vance Conservatives or the unstained loyalists.[30]

29. Jonathan Worth to W. W. Holden, June 16, 1865, Holden to N. Dunn, July 12, 1865, in Provisional Governor Holden Papers; Holden to President Johnson, July 17, 1865, in Letterbook of Provisional Governor William Woods Holden, NDAH; New Bern North Carolina Daily Times, July 1, 1865; Holden, Memoirs, 58–59.
30. R. H. Northrop to W. W. Holden, June 26, 1865, Holden to R. Swann, July

Although only a small minority of Holden's local appointees had been secessionists or "Vance Destructives," to the true unionists they stood out like a sore thumb. These unionists believed that the provisional governor was permitting local rebels to worm their way back into power, foretelling an early revival of Confederate influence. By August complaints from North Carolina and elsewhere were reaching Washington that Holden and the other provisional governors had deserted the cause of unionism. Stunned by these charges, the president on August 22 dispatched a circular telegram to the governors, informing them of the unionist complaints but assuring them that "I place no reliance in such statements." He claimed that the purpose of the reports "is to embarrass the Government in its reconstruction policy," and he advised each governor of "the importance of encouraging & strengthening to the fullest extent the men of your State who have never faltered in their allegiance to the Government."[31]

Holden, along with other provisional governors, bristled with indignation when he received Johnson's telegram. He immediately wired the president, vigorously denying that in his appointments he had "shown any preference for persons who have participated in the rebellion." On the contrary, he said, "I have been very careful to prefer and to appoint persons who were originally Union men, and persons who were in favor of restoring the authority of the federal government." Doubtless in the four thousand appointments he had made, Holden told the president, "some have been appointed who ought not to have been," but these exceptions did not mean that he was turning the state over to the rebels.[32]

Nevertheless, Holden admonished his handpicked justices of the peace to select only loyal men for office. Although he disclaimed any desire to proscribe staunch Confederates, he insisted that "original secessionists and ultra war men," presumably of the Vance faction, should take back seats and permit Union men to lead in the

19, 1865, in Provisional Governor Holden Papers; A. B. Griggs *et al.* to Holden, July 14, 1865, Holden to W. A. Albright, August 31, 1865, in Letterbook of Provisional Governor Holden.

31. Johnson to Holden, August 22, 1865, in Letterbook of Provisional Governor Holden.

32. Holden to Johnson, August 26, 1865, in *ibid.*; Eric L. McKitrick, *Andrew Johnson and Reconstruction* (Chicago, 1960), 165–66.

work of reconstruction. President Johnson, who viewed Holden's administration as a prototype for reconstruction in other southern states, reassured the North Carolina governor of his support and indicated that the purpose of his August 22 message was not to criticize but to call attention to rumors in the North that sought to discredit the progress that had been made in reconstructing the South.[33]

Holden's reorganization of the state government, in which he exercised more direct control, was much smoother and less controversial than the process of local reconstruction. In selecting state officers, judges, solicitors, executive aides, and directors of the railroad companies, the governor turned to old associates in the Conservative party, most of whom had been unionist Whigs before the war and peace advocates during it. Despite his hostility toward the "Vance Destructives," a few of the more than forty men whom he appointed to state positions had voted for the war governor in 1864, but after the surrender all of them had gracefully accepted defeat and indicated their support for Holden.[34] Only the distinguished Matthias E. Manly, who was retained on the supreme court, had been a secessionist Democrat; at the other extreme, none of the appointees to state offices was a proscriptive unionist who demanded the expulsion of former rebels from political life or the confiscation of their property. Few were politically unknown, and even anti-Holdenites admitted that the provisional governor had acted wisely in making his selections.[35]

33. Holden to W. A. Albright, August 31, 1865, in Letterbook of Provisional Governor Holden; Andrew Johnson to W. W. Holden, August 27, 1865, in *Senate Executive Documents*, 39th Cong., 1st Sess., No. 26, p. 222; David L. Swain to William A. Graham, July 4, 1865, in Hamilton and Williams (eds.), *Graham Papers*, VI, 320.

34. A convenient table of Holden's state appointees, which includes their past political affiliations, may be found in James L. Lancaster, "The Scalawags of North Carolina, 1850–1868" (Ph.D. dissertation, Princeton University, 1974), 73–76. On Holden's purposes in these appointments, see Raleigh *Daily Standard*, October 2, 1865.

35. Harvey M. Watterson to President Johnson, June 29, 1865, Kenneth Rayner to Johnson, July 8, 1865, in Johnson Papers; Henry E. Colton to Holden, July 4, 1865, in Provisional Governor Holden Papers; Raleigh *Daily Standard*, October 2, 1865.

Despite the rapidity in which officials were appointed and installed in office, the continued presence of the federal army created an air of uncertainty about the civil authority. Nevertheless, only in cases involving white violence against blacks did serious conflict occur between the provisional government and military officers. Before the reorganization of the courts, the military, with Holden's approval, had exercised jurisdiction over whites charged with offenses against blacks. But once the courts were revived in midsummer, Holden expected the army and its adjunct, the Freedmen's Bureau, to turn over such cases to the civil authorities. Conflict erupted in late July when army officers arrested and held for military trial three Person County whites charged with assaulting a freedman. When General Thomas H. Ruger, commanding in North Carolina, refused to release the prisoners to the regular courts or grant jurisdiction to the state in instances of white violence against blacks, Holden appealed to President Johnson for support.[36] Although Johnson sympathized with his provisional governor's desire to restore full civil authority and gain control of race relations, he refused to act. There were probably two reasons for this. First, his reconstruction plan had not yet been completely implemented in the state, and in addition, he did not want to do anything that, in the North, might adversely affect the outcome of the process in North Carolina or in any other southern state.

Holden had no choice but to acquiesce in Ruger's intervention on behalf of blacks. He subsequently made an arrangement with the general "by which civil courts shall try all cases of breach of the peace where white persons *only* are concerned, and the military courts shall try all cases in which freedmen or free persons of color are concerned." The agreement, however, provided that black suspects could be arrested by civil officers and held in jail for military trial. Holden left it to the state convention to take action on the old North Carolina statute prohibiting black testimony in court against

36. W. W. Holden to General J. D. Cox, June 21, 1865, Cox to Holden, June 22, 1865, in Provisional Governor Holden Papers; Major Clinton A. Cilley to W. W. Holden, July 8, 1865, in Records of the U.S. Army Continental Commands, 1821–1920, Department of North Carolina and Army of the Ohio, Letters Sent, Correspondence of Major Clinton A. Cilley, Record Group 393, NA (on microfilm in NDAH); W. W. Holden to General Thomas H. Ruger, July 27, August 8, 1865, Ruger to Holden, August 1, 1865, in Letterbook of Provisional Governor Holden.

whites, a law that soon became the main barrier to the restoration of civil jurisdiction in cases involving the freedmen.[37]

A greater concern for Holden was the continued presence of Negro troops in North Carolina. When most of the white troops were mustered out during the summer of 1865, blacks constituted a majority of the nine-thousand-man federal force remaining in the state. They were mainly stationed in military posts in the East, where white citizens, a minority in that region's population, were most fearful of racial strife. Although the discipline of these soldiers was on a par with that of the white troops, eastern whites bombarded Holden's office with exaggerated complaints about their conduct and their "pernicious" influence upon local blacks, including the fomentation of rebellion. After the governor appealed to the president and General Ruger for the removal of the black troops, the army in late September began transferring them to forts and other isolated installations on the coast where they would have little contact with whites or with the freedmen.[38]

Despite his differences with the military, Holden's relations with army officers, including General Ruger and officials of the Freedmen's Bureau, were generally good. In several towns where troops were stationed, military commanders, acting on the provisional administration's request, prohibited the sale of alcoholic beverages to soldiers and disciplined their men for infractions of the civil law. At the Raleigh post troops were even required to have passes to visit in town.[39] In 1865 the presence of bluecoats served more as a source

37. General George Meade to Holden, September 22, 1865, Holden to General Oliver Otis Howard, September 26, 1865, in Letterbook of Provisional Governor Holden. Ruger later permitted blacks to be tried in courts where no racial distinction was made in punishment. But not until 1866 did the state courts again obtain exclusive jurisdiction over all criminal cases. Jesse P. Bogue, Jr., "Violence and Oppression in North Carolina During Reconstruction" (Ph.D. dissertation, University of Maryland, 1973), 29.

38. Roberta Sue Alexander, "North Carolina Faces the Freedmen: Race Relations During Presidential Reconstruction, 1865–1867" (Ph.D. dissertation, University of Chicago, 1974), 136, 138–40, 143; Harvey M. Watterson to President Johnson, June 20, 1865, in Johnson Papers; A. M. Waddell to W. W. Holden, June 18, 1865, Holden to President Johnson, August 10, 1865, in Provisional Governor Holden Papers; W. W. Holden to General O. O. Howard, September 26, 1865, Holden to General Thomas H. Ruger, September 23, 1865, in Letterbook of Provisional Governor Holden.

39. General George Meade to W. W. Holden, September 22, 1865, in Letter-

of security in communities tottering on the brink of anarchy than as a cause of resentment. Although Holden opposed the army's intervention in civil matters, he was constrained from demanding an early end of the military occupation by the necessity of restoring law and order.

During the first few weeks of his administration Holden moved vigorously to regain state property and revive the government's finances. He first sought to halt the United States Treasury's seizure and shipment from North Carolina of a large quantity of cotton and naval stores in the state's possession that had accumulated during the war. On June 13 he wired President Johnson that the provisional government depended upon these valuable commodities to meet its expenses. "In view of the destitute condition of our people" and their inability to pay taxes, Holden wrote, "I beg you not to enforce confiscation of state property." When no action was forthcoming, Holden dispatched State Treasurer Jonathan Worth to Washington to meet with the president and his cabinet and appeal for the return of the property. He also sent along a personal note to Johnson, reiterating the importance of the cotton and naval stores to the state's financial reconstruction.[40]

This time Holden was successful. The Johnson administration on July 8 authorized North Carolina officials to resume possession of the state's property. By his quick action, Holden saved for the North Carolina treasury approximately $300,000 in cotton and naval stores. This success contrasted with developments in other southern states where United States Treasury agents stripped state and local governments of most of their property before President Johnson could intervene and stop the seizures. As required by Johnson, Holden applied the income from the cotton and naval stores to the support of the provisional state government. After

---

book of Provisional Governor Holden; W. L. Scott to W. W. Holden, July 29, 1865, Major C. A. Cilley to Lieutenant John B. Shissler, August 10, 1865, in Scott Papers; Raleigh *Progress*, July 26, 1865.

40. W. W. Holden to President Johnson, June 13, 1865 (telegram), in Johnson Papers; Richard Zuber, *Jonathan Worth: A Biography of a Southern Unionist* (Chapel Hill, 1965), 193–94.

meeting these expenses, he still had enough money left to pay the costs of the constitutional convention that met in the fall.[41]

He also obtained Johnson's promise to suspend the collection of the federal tax on cotton of two and one-half cents a pound. Although the relief from this levy was temporary, it enabled North Carolina farmers and planters, the major producers of wealth in the state, to market their wartime cotton without having to pay the burdensome tax on it. Again Holden's influence with the president had achieved an important concession, evidently for North Carolina alone. The tax relief kept scarce agricultural income in the state and improved the chances of cooperation by sullen ex-Confederates in the president's reconstruction program.[42]

Holden's good standing in Washington also contributed to an early restoration of the state's railroads. Seized by the Union army during the war, the major railroads, except for the Western North Carolina line, continued for several months after the surrender to be operated by military authorities. In order to facilitate the return of these railroads to local control, Holden appointed men whom he called "straitest-sect" unionists as presidents and state directors of the roads and required that only pardoned stockholders could vote for the companies' private directors. He left to the new presidents the task of negotiating the return of the roads. Most of these executives had long-standing railroad interests and would prove to be able administrators; one, Tod Robinson Caldwell of the Western North Carolina Railroad, would later serve as a successful Republican governor of the state.[43]

The provisional governor experienced no similar success in his efforts to revive North Carolina's banking institutions and recover the

41. William H. Seward to W. W. Holden, July 8, 1865, in *Senate Executive Documents*, 39th Cong., 1st Sess., No. 26, p. 17; Raleigh *Daily Standard*, August 30, 1865; New Bern *Daily Times*, October 20, 1865.

42. Raleigh *Daily Standard*, July 3, 6, 1865; Harvey M. Watterson to President Johnson, July 8, 1865, in Johnson Papers.

43. Charles L. Price, "Railroads and Reconstruction in North Carolina, 1865–1871" (Ph.D. dissertation, University of North Carolina, Chapel Hill, 1959), 138–39, 143; List of State Appointments to the Board of Directors of the Atlantic and North Carolina Railroad and the North Carolina Railroad, July 7, 1865, in Provisional Governor Holden Papers; Lancaster, "The Scalawags of North Carolina," 76.

public's interest in the state's two largest banks, the Bank of North Carolina and the Bank of Cape Fear. On July 29 Holden issued a proclamation appointing two state and nine private directors for the institutions. He also directed State Treasurer Worth to investigate the condition of the school system's Literary Fund, which before the war had been worth about $2.5 million and had been placed in the possession of the two banks. Worth sadly reported that the fund was virtually worthless because the banks had unwisely invested most of it in repudiated Confederate and state securities. Even the September reorganization of the once prosperous Bank of North Carolina as a national bank with George W. Swepson, a shrewd financial wheeler dealer, as president and Joseph S. Cannon and Jo Holden, the governor's son, as vice presidents, failed to save much of the Literary Fund.[44] The Bank of North Carolina, along with other state banks, floundered because of a lack of capital and the continuation of postwar economic doldrums, a condition beyond Holden's power to correct.

The insolvency of the Literary Fund and the impoverishment of the taxpayers convinced Holden that no effort should be made to revive the common school system until a permanent government had been established and financial prospects had improved. When Calvin H. Wiley, the holdover state superintendent of common schools and a wartime political opponent of Holden, sought to retain control of the crippled system, Holden refused to recognize him and subsequently had the office declared vacant by the state convention that met in October, 1865.[45]

Holden showed more interest in the revival of the state university at Chapel Hill than he did in the restoration of the common schools.

44. List of Appointments of Directors to the Bank of North Carolina, July 29, 1865, Appointment of Jonathan Worth as Public Treasurer, June 10, 1865 (including Holden's instructions to him), June 10, 1865, in Provisional Governor Holden Papers; business notice of the Raleigh National Bank of North Carolina in Raleigh *Daily Standard*, October 10, 1865; State of North Carolina, *Executive Documents, Convention, Session 1865: Constitution of North Carolina, with Amendments, and Ordinances and Resolutions Passed by the Convention, Session, 1865* (Raleigh, 1865), Doc. No. 1, pp. 17, 19–20, 103, 106.

45. Calvin H. Wiley to W. W. Holden, June 12, 1865, in Calvin H. Wiley Papers, SHC; Wiley to Holden, September 14, 1865, in Letterbook of Provisional Governor Holden; J. G. de Roulhac Hamilton, *Reconstruction in North Carolina* (New York, 1914), 610.

The university had been a hotbed of conservative Whigs who had long viewed Holden with contempt and late in the war had quietly supported the Vance faction of the Conservative party. Nevertheless, Holden refrained from removing President David L. Swain and the faculty lest he be charged with partisan intervention in the affairs of the institution. After the venerable president and faculty members had demonstrated proper contrition for their support of the war, Holden presided over a meeting of the university's trustees that provided for the reopening of the institution in August. Only twenty-two students, however, registered for the first semester after the war.[46]

Having accomplished a modest revival of the university, Holden let other public institutions (for example, the insane asylum) await the restoration of civil government for their rehabilitation and reform. His main interest lay in the realm of politics, not in institutional reconstruction. He was convinced that the general recovery of North Carolina from the ruins of war, including the restoration of a stable labor system, depended upon the state's early return to the Union. The relationship of economic recovery to political reconstruction became increasingly apparent to him as winter approached and hundreds of impoverished people visited his office and related "tales of sorrow and suffering, of hunger and want." He told North Carolinians that "we can entertain no hope that confidence and activity in business will be revived, or that our people can ever begin to renew their former prosperity until the State shall have been fully restored to her place in the Union."[47] During the summer and early fall of 1865 Holden devoted most of his waking hours toward the achievement of this paramount objective. The task at hand—to reconcile all the state's various political elements, including his old foes, to the cause of unionism—would tax both his physical endurance and his manifold political skills.

46. "Delphi Papers" in Raleigh *Daily Standard,* August 10, 1865; Spencer Journal, August, 1865, in Hope Summerell Chamberlain, *Old Days in Chapel Hill: Being the Life and Letters of Cornelia Phillips Spencer* (Chapel Hill, 1926), 115; entry for meeting of September 19, 1865, in Minutes of the Executive Committee of the University of North Carolina, January 2, 1835, to November 29, 1873, SHC.

47. Raleigh *Daily Standard,* October 2, 1865; State of North Carolina, *Legislative Documents, 1865–1866,* No. 1, pp. 1–2.

IX
Johnsonian Champion

Holden's main task as provisional governor was to pre-pare for the election and assembly of a state convention that would meet President Johnson's requirements for North Carolina's return to the Union. The first step in that direction—and a matter closely entwined with the whole issue of loyalty and political regenera-tion—was the implemention of the president's amnesty proclama-tion of May 29. Johnson required that, in order to qualify to vote in the election, a person must take the amnesty oath pledging future loyalty. Members of the excepted classes must have been pardoned by Johnson and also must have been administered the oath before they could participate in the election or hold seats in the convention.

In his proclamation of June 12 Holden promised that arrange-ments would be made "as early as practicable" for the adminis-tration of the amnesty oath to the great body of North Carolina citizens. He moved, however, with greater caution than most provi-sional governors to implement this part of the president's policy and arrange for the election of convention delegates. On June 23 John-son, through an assistant attorney general, had warned Holden against "a loose or indiscriminate exercise of Executive clemency," specifically advising him to exercise caution in recommending mem-bers of the excepted classes for pardon. At first the North Carolina governor seemed determined to follow this advice, and during the early summer he spent more time in listening to appeals for am-nesty and investigating pardon petitions than he did on any other public business. When he left his office in the capitol in late afternoon, he frequently took petitions home with him, and working until after midnight, he wrote out his recommendation to the president on each application. By late July, Holden had reviewed and forwarded to Washington more than five hundred petitions, many of which were lengthy and embraced several of the exception clauses in Johnson's amnesty proclamation.[1]

Mainly in order to control the pardoning process after the petitions had left Raleigh, Holden appointed Robert J. Powell as the state's agent in Washington. Powell, a native of North Carolina who had lived in Washington since 1840 and had known Johnson for many years, was ideal for the task. When the president became overwhelmed with petitions and began issuing pardons to many southerners who did not have the endorsements of their provisional governors, Powell interceded in North Carolina cases and prevented the erosion of Holden's role in the process. As a result only a handful of North Carolinians managed to obtain pardons without the provisional governor's consent.[2]

Historians, as well as Holden's contemporary detractors, have charged that he deliberately used his pardoning authority to develop a political party in the state that would guarantee his election as governor.[3] Holden certainly was not immune to political considerations, the importance of which varies with time and circumstances.

1. *Proclamation by William W. Holden, Provisional Governor, to the People of North Carolina* (June 12, 1865), broadside in William Woods Holden Papers, DU; Assistant U.S. Attorney General J. Hubley Ashton to W. W. Holden, June 23, 1865, in Provisional Governor William Woods Holden Papers, NDAH; Raleigh *Daily Standard*, July 26, October 2, 1865.

2. R. J. Powell to W. W. Holden, August 15, September 6, 1865, in Letterbook of Provisional Governor William Woods Holden, NDAH; Peter W. Hairston to "My dear Fanny," September 30, October 5, 1865, in Peter W. Hairston Papers, SHC; James M. Leach to William A. Graham, July 4, 1865, in J. G. de Roulhac Hamilton and Max R. Williams (eds.), *The Papers of William Alexander Graham* (7 vols. to date; Raleigh, 1957–), VI, 315–16.

3. Jonathan T. Dorris, *Pardon and Amnesty Under Lincoln and Johnson: The Restoration of the Confederates to Their Rights and Privileges, 1861–1898* (Chapel Hill, 1953), 194; Eric L. McKitrick, *Andrew Johnson and Reconstruction* (Chicago, 1960), 150; James L. Lancaster, "The Scalawags of North Carolina, 1850–1868" (Ph.D. dissertation, Princeton University, 1974), 69–70; Roberta Sue Alexander, "North Carolina Faces the Freedmen: Race Relations During Presidential Reconstruction, 1865–1867" (Ph.D. dissertation, University of Chicago, 1974), 166, 171–72.

His long tenure as editor of a partisan newspaper made it virtually impossible for him, however well meaning he may have been, to avoid political motivation in his conduct as provisional governor. Furthermore, the memory of the war's bitter political battles, which had culminated in his defeat for governor in 1864, would surely have taxed the charity of a St. Paul toward his adversaries. Even if he could have restrained his resentment of the secessionists, whom he believed had precipitated the war, and the Vanceites, whom he felt had prolonged it to a disastrous end, most "straitest-sect Conservatives" of his faction would have vehemently opposed a pardoning policy that threatened to return the "Destructives" and apostate Conservatives to power. Holden would have found it extremely difficult to resist for long the demands of his supporters or his own political instincts to use his authority as provisional governor to check the resurgence of the old war party.

But in the beginning of his administration the political motive appears to have been secondary in Holden's pardon recommendations. In his mind the great issues of the late war—liberty, constitutional rights, and the shape of the peace—transcended ordinary political concerns; these issues involved the survival of a free people and the welfare of the civil community, in this case the state of North Carolina. On the pardoning question his main purpose was to secure a speedy restoration of citizenship rights to as many people as would honestly accept the Johnson-defined results of the war, a course that would make possible an early reinstitution of civil government. But Holden had more demanding requirements for the leaders of the war party; he wanted them to show penance for their sins of misleading the people and prolonging the conflict, though he was unclear what form this penance should take. He soon discovered, or so he professed, that the radical secessionists of 1860–1861 were more contrite than the Vance Conservatives and thus more deserving of pardon. "I find, what is a little singular," he reported to Johnson, "that the ultra original secessionists who profess to have repented, appear to be more penitent than the ultra partisans of Vance who were once Union men."[4] At first he did not ask the president to withhold pardons from all of this class of politicians;

4. Holden to Johnson, July 24, 1865, in Andrew Johnson Papers (on microfilm), LC (unless otherwise noted, all citations are to Series I). See also W. B. Gulick to

he only recommended the disapproval or suspension of the petitions of the most prominent "Vance Destructives," including William A. Graham, John A. Gilmer, and Vance himself. The erratic former Whig Josiah Turner, Jr., was added to this list because of his postwar criticism of presidential reconstruction and Holden's administration. The governor charged that Turner, who had supported him during the war, was seriously undermining the Union cause in the state after it.[5]

The provisional governor's efforts to prevent a pardon for Graham went far toward reopening old political wounds and reviving charges that an embittered Holden sought vengence against those who were responsible for his defeat in the election of 1864. Graham, the state's most prominent old-line Whig, replaced Vance immediately after the war as the recognized leader of what Otto H. Olsen refers to as the "Conservative-Confederate" faction.[6] Led mainly by old Whigs, these Conservatives insisted, like the Holdenites, that they had opposed secession until no alternative remained and then had cast their lot with the Confederacy. They indicated that during the war they had vigorously resisted Confederate encroachments on the rights and liberties of North Carolinians, but that, unlike the Holdenites, they had done the honorable thing and stood by the South until the bitter end. After the war these Conservatives admitted no guilt for the catastrophe that had befallen North Carolina and thus saw no need to repent for their past conduct. Nevertheless, they believed that Holden, for political reasons, was determined to link them in the minds of the people with the secessionists and the tragic consequences of the war. Their ability to disassociate themselves from the war would largely determine their success or failure in overcoming the advantage that President Johnson had given Holden in postwar politics. Conversely, the skill with which

---

William B. Rodman, September 24, 1865, in Rodman Family Papers, East Carolina Manuscript Collection, East Carolina University Library, Greenville, North Carolina.

5. Holden to Johnson, June 29, 1865, in North Carolina Petitions for Pardon, 1865–68 (photostat copies), Civil War Collection, NDAH; Holden to Robert J. Powell, October 5, 1865, in Johnson Papers; William W. Holden, *Memoirs of W. W. Holden* (Durham, 1911), 59–60.

6. Otto H. Olsen (ed.), *Reconstruction and Redemption in the South* (Baton Rouge, 1980), 162.

Holden could use the war issue against them would greatly influence the course of reconstruction and determine whether he could build a majority party in the state.

Early in the reconstruction process Graham gave Holden good cause to oppose his pardon. The former Confederate senator claimed that President Johnson possessed no authority to abolish the constituted (wartime) government of the state and free the slaves without compensation. When informed of this statement, Holden wrote Johnson, recommending that he defer clemency in Graham's case, though Graham had not yet submitted a request for pardon. Holden told the president that Graham, along with John A. Gilmer, was "largely responsible for the ultra course of Vance while Governor" and for the failure of the state convention movement of 1864.[7] His determination to prevent the pardoning of Graham increased when he received Graham's petition and discovered that it contained no expression of regret for his role in the war.

During the summer of 1865 Holden slowly came to believe that Graham was not only a threat to a smooth return by the state to the Union but that he was also the logical choice to lead a revived "rebel" party. Since Vance had been arrested and was high on the federal list of traitors, Graham was the only prominent Conservative left who could mount a successful challenge against the Union party that was emerging under Holden's direction. Holden was soon strenuously urging President Johnson not to pardon Graham, because, he explained, to do so "would be to open in this state bitter division and would strengthen the faction now being secretly organized against the administration." Even after the Union party's defeat in the fall election and Graham's selection to the United States Senate, a mortified Holden continued to thwart his rival's efforts to obtain a pardon. Writing later, the wily David L. Swain concluded, perhaps accurately, that Holden's greatest mistake in 1865 and the main reason for his failure to win the fall election was his partisan treatment of Graham. Whig Conservatives, who never had any love for Holden but had been willing to follow his lead in reconstruction, especially resented his failure to recommend

7. Holden to Johnson, June 29, 1865, in North Carolina Petitions for Pardon; James M. Leach to Graham, July 4, 17, 1865, in Hamilton and Williams (eds.), *Graham Papers*, VI, 315–16, 328; Holden, *Memoirs*, 58.

a pardon for Graham while approving those for prominent seces-sionists who were no longer political threats.[8]

His nonpartisan mask removed, Holden, as reconstruction elec-tions approached, began using the pardoning power to aid the Union party. In August, through his agent Powell, he submitted to Johnson 290 applications for pardon. He recommended that 40 of them be suspended and the others be quickly granted in order to ensure the eligibility of "friends" for election as delegates to the forthcoming state convention. When Johnson did not move with alacrity on his request, Holden sent Powell back to the White House to plead for immediate action on the applications of Union party candidates. Overwhelmed by personal appeals for clemency and by other government business, Johnson apologetically told the gover-nor's agent that he would sign the pardons as soon as possible.[9] A few days later Holden, having received no word from Washington, again instructed Powell to see the president about the pardons. He wanted Johnson informed that "we are losing from the fact that pardons are granted on personal application at Washington while the cases of special friends for whom appeals are made are not finally acted upon." This time the president granted the pardons, prompting Holden later to report that "the exercise of the pardon-ing power has been of a material benefit" in aiding the Union party in the convention election.[10]

On August 9, 1865, Holden issued a proclamation announcing that the election for delegates to the state convention would be held on September 21 and that the convention would assemble on Oc-tober 2. Since mail service had not been completely restored, the

8. Holden to R. J. Powell, October 5, 1865, in Johnson Papers; W. W. Holden to President Johnson, September 22, 1865, in Provisional Governor Holden Papers; David L. Swain to Benjamin S. Hedrick, April 26, 1866, in Benjamin S. Hedrick Papers, DU. Holden also declined to recommend Vance for a pardon, but his deci-sion was understandable because of Vance's prominent role in the war and the fact that he had been imprisoned in Washington. W. H. Battle, Jr., to Zebulon B. Vance, November 2, 1865, in Zebulon B. Vance Papers, NDAH.

9. Holden to Robert J. Powell, August 15, 1865, Powell to Holden, Septem-ber 6, 1865, in Letterbook of Provisional Governor Holden; Dorris, *Pardon and Amnesty Under Lincoln and Johnson*, 195.

10. Holden to Powell, September 15, 1865 (telegram), in Letterbook of Provi-sional Governor Holden; Holden to Powell, October 5, 1865, in Johnson Papers.

governor dispatched messengers throughout the state to circulate his proclamation and encourage eligible voters to take the amnesty oath required by the president for participation in the reconstruction elections. No organized political party emerged to nominate candidates for the convention, and little campaigning occurred. Unionists of every prewar and wartime persuasion, however, were alert to the first signs of a "vile secessionist" revival. Discredited by the death and ruin that their policies had produced, most original secessionists chose not to participate in the campaign. In some counties they supported Graham "unionists" in order to defeat the Holdenites. The main issue in the campaign was the candidates' records on secession and unionism. In only a few contests were Johnson's requirements for the convention's action discussed or the question of the status of the freedmen in North Carolina raised. Because of his peculiar role in arranging the election, Holden did not participate in the campaign. Nevertheless, when asked, he advised that only "straitest-sect Unionists"—*i.e.*, Holdenites—be chosen for the convention.[11]

The election returns delighted Holden. Despite the election of about twenty ardent ex-Confederates, he happily reported to President Johnson that the "ultra Union" faction had won a large majority of the convention seats. At least 46 of the 120 elected delegates had been unionists during the secession winter of 1860–1861; all 46 would later become Republicans, which suggests that they were strong and persistent supporters of Holden. Most of the remaining delegates were "good and true Vance men" who had been wartime Conservatives and now supported Holden.[12] Although Holden had announced that only men already pardoned should run for the convention, after the election he telegraphed the president asking him to approve the pending applications of eleven victorious candi-

---

11. *A Proclamation by William W. Holden, Provisional Governor to the People of North Carolina* (August 8, 1865), broadside in Holden Papers, DU; Raleigh *Daily Progress*, September 7, 1865; William Pickens to W. W. Holden, August 17, 1865, in Provisional Governor Holden Papers; W. C. Kerr to Benjamin S. Hedrick, October 13, 1865, in Hedrick Papers; New Bern *Daily Times* and Raleigh *Daily Progress*, issues of August–September, 1865; W. W. Holden to J. M. S. Rogers, September 19, 1865, in Letterbook of Provisional Governor Holden.

12. W. W. Holden to President Johnson, September 25, 1865, in Letterbook of Provisional Governor Holden; Lancaster, "The Scalawags of North Carolina," 94; R. H. Battle, Jr., to Zebulon B. Vance, October 6, 1865, in Vance Papers.

dates, "all but one or two ultra Union men," he claimed. Johnson complied, and when the convention met a few days later, the newly pardoned delegates had been notified of the president's action.[13]

In ability and political experience, the "Holden convention" of 1865 was comparable to earlier state conventions. The body included such able and experienced leaders as Edwin G. Reade (who presided), Bedford Brown, Robert P. Dick, Alfred F. Dockery, John Pool, Nathaniel Boyden, Matthias E. Manly, Edward Jenner Warren, Samuel Field Phillips, Bartholomew F. Moore, Tod R. Caldwell, and the young Thomas Settle, an ardent Holdenite who had already served as speaker of the state House of Commons. On the second day Holden told the delegates, "Your duties are too plain to require suggestions from me." The provisional governor did indicate to the convention that North Carolina had "entered the rebellion a slave-holding State, and she emerged from it a non-slaveholding State. In other respects, so far as her existence as a State and her rights as a State are concerned, she has undergone no change."[14] In addition to abolishing slavery, Holden and the delegates clearly understood that the convention must invalidate the secession ordinance.

Under the driving direction of Bartholomew F. Moore, an antebellum state attorney general and a wartime unionist, the convention on October 9 unanimously passed an ordinance declaring slavery "forever prohibited" in North Carolina. Without comment, Holden sent the delegates the address of a black convention, then meeting in Raleigh, that asked for legal rights and fair treatment for the freedmen. The address was referred to a committee headed by John Pool, which reported that the matter "could be more appropriately acted on by the Legislature than by this Convention." The Pool report, which was adopted by the convention, proposed that Governor Holden appoint a three-member commission to recommend to the next session of the General Assembly "a system of

13. W. W. Holden to President Johnson, September 23, 25, 29, 30, October 2, 1865, in Letterbook of Provisional Governor Holden. This correspondence is also in *Senate Executive Documents*, 39th Cong., 1st Sess., No. 26, pp. 223–25.

14. *Journal of the Convention of the State of North Carolina, at Its Session of 1865* (Raleigh, 1865), 11–13; Sidney Andrews, *The South Since the War: As Shown by Fourteen Weeks of Travel and Observation in Georgia and the Carolinas* (Boston, 1866), 159–61; John Richard Dennett, *The South as It Is* (1865; rpr. New York, 1965), 161; *Senate Executive Documents*, 39th Cong., 1st Sess., No. 26, pp. 48–55.

laws" for the freedmen. The governor responded by selecting Moore and two other members of his faction to serve on the committee. (In early 1866 the Moore committee recommended to the legislature a relatively mild black code for the freedmen.) Almost simultaneously with the passage of the slavery ordinance, the convention, after a debate over wording, overwhelmingly pronounced the secession ordinance null and void. Both ordinances, as Holden required, were to be submitted to the voters for ratification.[15]

The provisional governor dutifully reported to the president the convention's actions on these ordinances. At the same time, he indicated to Johnson that the convention "will, in all probability, ignore [repudiate] the rebel State debt."[16] As with the secession and slavery ordinances, Holden expected the convention to act promptly and without a divisive debate on the war debt.

With Holden's wishes in mind, Thomas Settle on October 7 introduced a resolution prohibiting the state from paying any debt incurred either directly or indirectly in aid of the rebellion. Settle's proposal immediately triggered a lively debate. Many unionist delegates, including the influential Moore, argued that the problem of differentiating between the war debt and regular state obligations was too complex to settle in a short session of the convention. They believed that the financial solvency of the state and the fate of the common schools' Literary Fund, which had been invested in war-

15. *Ordinances Passed by the North Carolina State Convention, at the Sessions of 1865–'66* (Raleigh, 1867), 4, 10–11; Samuel F. Phillips to William A. Graham, October 10, 1865, in Hamilton and Williams (eds.), *Graham Papers*, VI, 390; *Journal of the Convention of the State of North Carolina, 1865*, pp. 12, 23, 28–29; *Senate Executive Documents*, 39th Cong., 1st Sess., No. 26, p. 40.

16. W. W. Holden to President Johnson, October 6, 7, 1865, in Johnson Papers. Holden incorrectly reported that the ordinance invalidating secession passed by a unanimous vote. Actually, nine delegates voted against it. *Journal of the Convention of the State of North Carolina, 1865*, p. 23. Historians have incorrectly assumed that when Holden used the word *ignore* in his message to Johnson he meant that he wanted the convention to avoid the debt issue. Later in an October 17 telegram to the president, he used the same word and clearly meant "repudiate." Johnson Papers, Series II. This revelation throws an entirely different light on Holden's role in the war debt controversy. For the old interpretation, see J. G. de Roulhac Hamilton, *Reconstruction in North Carolina* (New York, 1914), 129–30; Alexander, "North Carolina Faces the Freedmen," 198–99; Horace W. Raper, *William W. Holden: North Carolina's Political Enigma* (Chapel Hill, 1985), 78–79; and Dan T. Carter, *When the War Was Over: The Failure of Self-Reconstruction in the South, 1865–1867* (Baton Rouge, 1985), 74–75.

time state securities, hinged on the outcome. Since the president
had not asked the Alabama and Mississippi conventions to repudiate their war debts, they concluded that he would not insist upon
immediate action by North Carolina on the issue.[17] An earlier motion to ask Holden "whether he has received any information"
from Johnson "relative to the State's assuming the debt contracted
during the rebellion for the prosecution of the war" failed to pass,
and without such a request the provisional governor declined to
offer official guidance in the matter.[18]

When it appeared that Settle's repudiation resolution would be
defeated, Holden excitedly wired the president that "contrary to
my expectation, the convention has involved itself in a bitter discussion of the State debt made in aid of the rebellion." The continuance of the debate, he informed Johnson, "will greatly excite the
people and retard the work of reconstruction. Our people are believed to be against assuming the debt by a large majority. Is it not
advisable that our convention, like that of Alabama, should positively ignore [repudiate] this debt now and ever? Please answer at
once."[19]

The next day Johnson gave Holden the answer he wanted. He
sent a message directing that "every dollar of the debt created to
aid the rebellion against the United States should be repudiated
finally and forever."[20] For the first time, the president had issued
specific instructions to a southern state regarding the Confederate
debt. The message from Johnson had an instantaneous effect upon
the North Carolina convention: that evening the Settle resolution

17. *Journal of the Convention of the State of North Carolina, 1865,* p. 26;
Samuel F. Phillips to William A. Graham, October 10, 1865, in Hamilton and
Williams (eds.), *Graham Papers,* VI, 385–86, 388; Jonathan Worth to "Mr. Jackson," September 9, 1865, in J. G. de Roulhac Hamilton (ed.), *The Correspondence
of Jonathan Worth* (2 vols.; Raleigh, 1909), I, 413–14; Andrews, *The South Since
the War,* 172. Although the Alabama convention was not required to repudiate the
war debt, it did so. Michael Perman, *Reunion Without Compromise: The South
and Reconstruction, 1865–1868* (New York, 1973), 75–76.

18. *Journal of the Convention of the State of North Carolina, 1865,* p. 15; Andrews, *The South Since the War,* 168–69.

19. W. W. Holden to President Johnson, October 17, 1865, in Letterbook of
Provisional Governor Holden.

20. Johnson to Holden, October 18, 1865, in *ibid.* The telegrams between the
two men on the debt issue are reprinted in *Senate Executive Documents,* 39th
Cong., 1st Sess., No. 26, pp. 226–27.

was revived, and the following morning it passed by a voice vote. An effort to have the resolution submitted to the voters for approval, as was done for the ordinances invalidating secession and ending slavery, failed to pass.[21]

On October 20 Holden happily informed President Johnson that the convention had completed its work by repudiating "the rebel debt" and binding "all future legislatures, not to pay any of it." The final act of the convention was to call for the election of a new state government, as provided for in Johnson's reconstruction plan. The date chosen for the election was November 9, which allowed only three weeks for campaigning.

Even before the convention adjourned, political intrigue gripped the capital as preparations were made for the campaign. Most of the maneuvering centered on the contest for governor. Holdenites wanted their man elected governor, claiming that his rejection by North Carolinians would be injurious to President Johnson's reconstruction program and would delay the state's readmission to the Union. On October 14 Holden supporters in the convention signed a letter asking him to become a candidate for governor in the November election. Not unexpectedly, Holden agreed to run for the office. In his acceptance letter, which was designed for publication and would be his only campaign statement, he tried to stave off opposition by declaring that "faction and bitter party spirit [had been] the bane of the Republic" and the cause of "the evils we are now suffering." He claimed that as provisional governor "I have known no party but the sincere friends of the Union" and that "it is not agreeable to my feelings in a crisis like the present, when everything dear to us depends upon union and harmony among ourselves, to speak of parties." Seemingly oblivious to the contradiction, he told North Carolinians that "the only party to which I belong is the National Union party, composed of the best elements of all the old parties, of which Andrew Johnson is the head."[22]

Holden's attempt to forestall competition did not work. Former secessionists and Graham-Vance Conservatives interpreted his po-

21. Perman, *Reunion Without Compromise,* 76; Andrews, *The South Since the War,* 171–72; *Journal of the Convention of the State of North Carolina, 1865,* pp. 84, 87, 92; *Ordinances Passed by the North Carolina State Convention, 1865–'66,* p.30.
22. Raleigh *Daily Standard,* October 18, 1865.

litical disclaimer as the height of hypocrisy and effrontery. To these opponents, he had used his power as provisional governor to develop a political party that would at last enable him to realize his great ambition—to be elected governor of North Carolina.[23] Calvin H. Wiley observed that hostility to Holden's candidacy ran deeper than the mere rancor of politicians. He reported to Graham the existence of "a powerful desire among the masses for an opposition candidate" who was "more conservative, more liberal, & more identified in history with the love of Union, than Mr. Holden." Wiley, the longtime state superintendent of the common schools, found "a general feeling of disgust" with Holden's administration. He charged that Holden as provisional governor, despite his frequent professions, "has shown the powerful bent of his nature in breaking thro' all temptations to a generous policy, & spending his precious time in petty intrigues to insure his own promotion, and to gratify old animosities." From Washington, Benjamin S. Hedrick, Holden's old antagonist, reported to Graham that, contrary to what the provisional governor's defenders had claimed, the election of "this infamous charlatan and demagogue . . . will be regarded all over the country as evidence that the people of the State desire to unite with what are known as the copperheads of the North. . . . Holden's record in support of secession will all come up before Congress, and his election would be a curse to the State." What Hedrick recommended to Graham was the election "of an honest, conservative man, of fair record" who "would place the people of N.C. in sympathy with the great Union party of the Nation."[24]

Already Graham's associates in Raleigh were moving rapidly to nominate a "conservative man, of fair record" to oppose Holden. After Alfred Dockery, a former Whig candidate for governor, refused to run, they asked State Treasurer Jonathan Worth to become a candidate. Worth was an ex-Whig of "sterling honesty" who, though supporting the goals of the peace movement during the

23. James Graham Ramsay to William A. Graham, October 13, 1865, in Hamilton and Williams (eds.), *Graham Papers*, VI, 393; R. H. Battle, Jr., to Benjamin S. Hedrick, November 6, 1865, in Hedrick Papers; Peter W. Hairston to his wife, September 30, 1865, in Hairston Papers.

24. Calvin H. Wiley to William A. Graham, October 10, 1865, Benjamin S. Hedrick to William A. Graham, October 12, 1865, in Hamilton and Williams (eds.), *Graham Papers*, VI, 383–84, 392.

war, had remained aloof from the Vance-Holden struggle. Although he was viewed by some Graham Conservatives as politically weak, especially among old secessionists who had long been targets of his acid attacks, Worth was the best candidate available. Graham himself was unpardoned and refused to become a candidate.[25] The anti-Holden wire-pullers believed that secessionists, despite old differences, would surely vote for Worth in preference to the despised Holden. They also assumed that, since Worth's unionist credentials were stronger than Holden's, President Johnson would not object to their man's candidacy.[26]

Both Holden and Worth stayed at home during the brief campaign. The burden of the canvass was carried by the newspapers and the numerous aspirants for Congress and the legislature, many of whom wisely avoided endorsing a gubernatorial candidate. Neither Holden nor Worth developed a campaign organization, though Holdenites in several counties formed what they called the National Union party.[27]

In addition to the *Standard*, which was edited by Jo Holden and an aide to his father, the provisional governor received the support of several prominent newspapers. The Salisbury *Union Banner*, the Wilmington *Herald*, and the Charlotte *Western Democrat*, all of which had opposed Holden in 1864, endorsed him in 1865 mainly because they believed that he had the confidence of President Johnson and Congress and that his election would ensure the immediate restoration of the state to the Union. Reconstruction under Holden, these journals as well as ardent Holdenites insisted, would restore civil law, revive the state's economy, and end the Radical Republican threat of black equality. The Charlotte *Western Democrat* claimed that Holden had served ably as provisional governor and,

25. Richard L. Zuber, *Jonathan Worth: A Biography of a Southern Unionist* (Chapel Hill, 1965), 201; Calvin H. Wiley to William A. Graham, October 10, 1865, David L. Swain to Graham, October 14, 1865, James Graham Ramsay to Graham, November 25, 1865, in Hamilton and Williams (eds.), *Graham Papers*, VI, 383, 394, 449; Jonathan Worth to John Pool and Lewis Thompson, October 16, 1865, in Hamilton (ed.), *Correspondence of Worth*, I, 429–30; Salisbury *Union Banner*, October 18, 1865.

26. Andrews, *The South Since the War*, 173–74; Greensboro *Patriot*, October 21, 1865; Jonathan Worth to A. M. Tomlinson, October 18, 1865, in Hamilton (ed.), *Correspondence of Worth*, I, 435–36.

27. New Bern *Daily Times*, October 13, 17, 19, 1865.

contrary to the charges of the Worth faction, had "shown a disposition to let by gones be by gones. By his wise management and conciliatory course, peace and quiet have reigned within our borders," unlike in other states.[28] The *Standard* declared that, since Worth had the support of the old war party, his victory "would perpetuate disunion" and cause federal authorities in Washington to "fasten upon our people for years all the rigors of military rule." The bottom line in the election, the *Standard* contended, was "W. W. Holden and GO BACK to the Union, or Jonathan Worth and STAY OUT of the Union." The *Standard* also repeatedly claimed that Worth, if elected, would seek payment of the repudiated war debt, a charge that he denied.[29]

Worth's campaign managers concentrated on Holden's ill-starred record and their own candidate's unionist credentials. They issued a broadside excerpting past *Standard* editorials—many of which were taken out of context—in an attempt to demonstrate Holden's inconsistency and perfidy. The broadside, as well as the Worth press, warmed over the old chestnut of Holden's support for secession. It asked rhetorically, "Does such a man, whose sole aim appears to be to continue himself in power, and to atone for his past secession proclivities and teachings by a zealot vindictiveness towards those whom he lured to destruction, deserve the suffrages of the people of North-Carolina?"[30] The answer obviously was no.

In stressing Holden's secession record and contrasting it with their candidate's unionism, the Worth forces sought to persuade North Carolinians that their man's election would be entirely acceptable to President Johnson and the people of the North. The Charlotte *Daily Carolina Times* claimed that the difference between the two candidates was that Worth "resisted secession to the utmost and to the last extremity," whereas Holden "was a secessionist and voted [North Carolina] out of the Union." The editor of

28. Raleigh *Daily Standard*, October 18, 1865; Salisbury *Union Banner*, October 18, 20, November 2, 1865; Wilmington *Daily Herald*, October 18, 19, 27, 28, 1865; Charlotte *Western Democrat*, quoted in the Raleigh *Daily Standard*, October 28, 1865.

29. Raleigh *Daily Standard*, October 19, 23, 24, 26, 1865, and issues of November, 1865.

30. *Facts for the People! Record of W. W. Holden* (N.p., 1865). See also the Raleigh *Daily Sentinel*, issues of late October, 1865.

this newspaper assured uneasy voters that "the election of Mr. Worth will be hailed by the North as proof of our loyalty."[31]

Despite their public show of confidence, Worth leaders feared that President Johnson would undercut their campaign by announcing his support for Holden. Worth himself pleaded with Benjamin S. Hedrick, his political lobbyist in Washington, "to counteract the impression, which Holden's friends mainly rely upon, that my election over him would be disagreeable to the Prest & the North." Although Hedrick was unable to see the president, Attorney General James Speed assured him that the administration would remain neutral in the contest.[32]

Holden did not give much credence to Speed's declaration when it was published in the Worth newspapers. But he was sufficiently aroused to wire the president and urge him to make a public announcement supporting his candidacy. In his appeal he shrewdly touched upon all the points that were sure to trouble Johnson. "I am morally certain of my election," he professed to the president, "but I cannot tell what will happen. All the rebel debt interest of the state is against me. The money power is making a last desperate effort to commit the state to the treason of assuming the state rebel debt after the state gets back" into the Union. In addition, Holden reported, "a powerful effort" was being made "to rally the old Whig party against me, and this is succeeding to some extent. Traitors and malcontents have grown bold & insolent because the hand of power has not been placed upon them. If I am beaten a powerful party will at once exist against your administration." But, Holden told Johnson, "a few lines from you would place [the election] beyond all doubt," and in that case, "I would as soon the triumph should be considered Andrew Johnson's as my own."[33]

The president, however, refused to endorse Holden, probably because he feared the nationwide conservative reaction that would follow if he intervened in a state election. Such an action would

31. Alexander, "North Carolina Faces the Freedmen," 210.
32. Jonathan Worth to Benjamin S. Hedrick, October 18, 21, 1865, in Hedrick Papers; Patrick H. Winston, Jr., to William A. Graham, October 23, 1865, in Hamilton and Williams (eds.), *Graham Papers,* VI, 421; Jonathan Worth to J. J. Jackson, November 2, 1865, in Hamilton (ed.), *Correspondence of Worth,* I, 446.
33. W. W. Holden to President Johnson, November 5, 1865, in Johnson Papers, Series II.

also conflict with his emphasis on the voluntary reconstruction of the southern states. Despite Johnson's inaction, Holden remained confident that he would win the election. His friends in Raleigh predicted a majority of thirty thousand for him at the polls, and even some prominent Worth supporters believed that Holden would win because of his close association with President Johnson, whose mild plan of reconstruction was popular in the state.[34]

But Worth won the election with a majority of 5,939 out of 57,616 votes cast; he carried fifty-three counties to Holden's thirty-five. Most of the Holden counties were in the sparsely populated West and in his home district, both areas where the wartime peace movement had been popular. The election returns stunned Holden and sent him to bed for almost three weeks in what apparently was another attack of neuralgia.[35]

The Worth victory was mainly a vote against Holden and had little to do with loyalty to the Union or with reconstruction issues. A northern traveler in North Carolina wrote that former secessionists, as well as Graham-Vance Conservatives, voted for Worth, "not that they love him, but that they hate Holden." An editor who supported Holden also believed that "the vote in the State was leveled at Governor Holden—there was every shade of opposition to him brought to bear upon the election. The Whigs opposed him because he denounced Vance—the War democrats because he had turned upon them in 1860 and destroyed them."[36] Many North Carolinians, even those who sympathized with Holden's policies, simply did not trust him, and in voting for Worth, they were prepared to risk the wrath of President Johnson and the possibility that the state's return to the Union would be delayed.

As might be expected, Holden reported a different story to

34. John A. Gilmer to Zebulon B. Vance, November 7, 1865, in Vance Papers; H. H. Helper to Benjamin S. Hedrick, November 7, 1865, John A. Hedrick to Benjamin S. Hedrick, November 6, 1865, in Hedrick Papers; New Bern *Daily Times*, November 2, 1865; Wilmington *Daily Herald*, November 1, 1865.

35. New Bern *Daily Times*, December 1, 1865.

36. Andrews, *The South Since the War*, 174; Salisbury *Union Banner*, November 20, 1865. See also the New Bern *Daily Times*, November 14, 1865, and R. H. Battle, Jr., to Benjamin S. Hedrick, November 25, 1865, in Hedrick Papers. As in 1864, Holden's opponents gloated over his defeat and predicted his political demise. "After such a rebuke," an old Holden foe wrote Vance, "Holden will never be able to hold up his head again in North Carolina. He is dead forever, however

Johnson. "The late election in this State was shaped by secession votes and the rebel debt," he wrote the president a few days after leaving his sickbed. He complained that "more than half of those who voted for Mr. Worth were original secessionists and Vance men." They are "still more or less unsubdued, and are disposed to return to the Union only under their chosen leaders." Bitterly, he told Johnson that he had been deceived into believing that the rebel leaders had been destroyed politically. "In May and June last these rebellious spirits would not have dared to show their heads even for the office of constable; but leniency has emboldened them, and the copperhead now shows his fangs. If these men had supreme power in this State the condition of the real Union men and of the freedmen would be exceedingly disagreeable."[37]

Holden obviously wanted the president to intervene and delay, if not prevent, the inauguration of the Worth government. At first Johnson seemed agreeable. Through Secretary of State William H. Seward he directed Holden to continue the functions of provisional governor, suggesting, however, that he would be relieved of his duties when the new legislature ratified the Thirteenth Amendment. On November 26 Holden, while sick, had his Washington agent, Robert J. Powell, who was then visiting in Raleigh, wire the president that "the rebellious element" was continuing to deceive the masses regarding Johnson's views on reconstruction. In order to check their ambitions, Holden wanted Johnson to send a telegram to North Carolina supporting him. Powell, evidently at Holden's direction, even recommended the wording of the message.[38]

Apparently without much thought, President Johnson agreed to send the message. He immediately wired Holden thanking him for "the noble and efficient manner in which you have discharged your duty as Provisional Governor" and promising that "you will be sustained by the government." Then, following verbatim Powell's suggested wording, Johnson declared: "The results of the recent elec-

much he may be galvanized with manifestations of vitality by those in power." Edward Jenner Warren to Zebulon B. Vance, November 14, 1865, in Vance Papers.
  37. W. W. Holden to President Johnson, December 6, 1865, in Johnson Papers.
  38. William H. Seward to W. W. Holden, November 21, 1865, in Holden Papers, DU; R. J. Powell to President Johnson, November 26, 1865, in Johnson Papers.

tions in North Carolina have greatly damaged the prospects of the
State in the restoration of its governmental relations. Should the action and spirit of the legislature be in the same direction, it will
greatly increase the mischief already done and might be fatal." [39]

Buoyed by this show of support, Holden wrote the president, "I
will do all in my power to prevent bad men from ruining our poor
old state." The immediate battleground for the Holden unionists
and the "bad men" of the Graham-Worth faction was the newly
elected General Assembly, which convened on the day that the
president's stunning message was received. Most of the legislators
had been elected, not because they had supported Holden or Worth,
but because they had been Union Whigs in the secession crisis of
1860–1861. The majority, however, looked to Graham or Worth
for leadership, and they planned to elect Graham and a political
ally, perhaps Vance, to the United States Senate. The president's
message supporting Holden shocked Conservatives in the legislature, since they had come to believe that North Carolina, under
the leadership of old Union Whigs, was on the right course toward
reconstruction. [40]

With Johnson's criticism ringing in their ears, the legislators
sought to placate the president by quickly ratifying the Thirteenth
Amendment to the Constitution and reappointing Holden's provisional judges. They also attempted to satisfy Holden by offering
him the short senatorial term, provided he would recommend a
pardon for Graham. Holden refused to cooperate, because, as he
claimed, the former Confederate senator would not announce his
support for presidential reconstruction. But Holdenites in the General Assembly agreed to vote for Graham for the long term in ex-
change for the election of John Pool to the other seat. [41]

After his election Graham immediately left for Washington with

39. Holden immediately had the message published in the Raleigh *Daily Standard*, November 29, 1865.

40. W. W. Holden to President Johnson, November 27, 1865, in Johnson Papers, Series II; New Bern *Daily Times*, December 4, 18, 1865; William E. Pell to
Zebulon B. Vance, November 22, 1865, in Vance Papers.

41. R. H. Battle, Jr., to Benjamin S. Hedrick, December 1, 1865, in Hedrick
Papers; W. W. Holden to President Johnson, December 1, 1865, R. J. Powell to
Johnson, December 2, 1865, in Johnson Papers, Series II.

a petition from the legislature asking the president to pardon him. An irate Holden wired Johnson denouncing the action of the legislature and declaring, in reference to Graham, that "if I were a northern member of Congress, I doubt whether I would sit with any member of the so-called Confederate Congress." Johnson was caught between a desire to accommodate his provisional governor, whom only a few days before he had pledged to sustain, and his aim to bring reconstruction closer to an end by granting pardons to newly elected representatives from the South, such as Graham, who needed executive clemency to qualify for seats in Congress. He chose to sign Graham's pardon but not to send it to him until later. Inexplicably, Graham did not receive it until 1867.[42]

The issue of a seat in the Senate for Holden's rival was soon a moot one. Distressed Republicans in Congress, when they convened in early December, 1865, refused to recognize any of the southern representatives or senators who owed their elections to presidential reconstruction.

Anticipating further congressional opposition, Johnson defiantly moved to complete the work of reconstruction by dismantling the provisional governments in the southern states. On December 4 the president instructed Secretary of State Seward to notify Holden that he should turn over the control of North Carolina affairs "to the constitutional authorities chosen by the people." On December 23 Seward informed the disappointed provisional governor by telegram of the decision and conveyed to him "the President's acknowledgement of the fidelity, the loyalty and the discretion which has marked your administration." Holden, still expressing his confidence in Johnson and in his plan of reconstruction, on December 28 relinquished his authority and gave Jonathan Worth the keys to his office in the state capitol. His many enemies breathed a sigh of relief that "North Carolina's malicious prince of Demagoguism," as Worth deliciously referred to Holden, was no longer in power.[43] But

42. W. W. Holden to President Johnson, December 1, 1865, in Johnson Papers, Series II; Kemp P. Battle to William A. Graham, December 15, 1865, in Hamilton and Williams (eds.), *Graham Papers*, VI, 463; Jonathan Worth to President Johnson, March 29, 1867, in Hamilton (ed.), *Correspondence of Worth*, II, 926–27; Dorris, *Pardon and Amnesty Under Lincoln and Johnson*, 200–201.

43. Michael Les Benedict, *A Compromise of Principle: Congressional Republi-*

they were terribly mistaken if they believed that reconstruction was over or that they had seen the last of Holden.

---

cans and Reconstruction, 1863–1869 (New York, 1974), 144; William H. Seward to W. W. Holden, December 23, 1865, *Senate Executive Documents,* 39th Congress, 1st Sess., No. 26, p. 47; Jonathan Worth to Benjamin S. Hedrick, December 16, 1865, in Hedrick Papers.

X
Moderate
Reconstructionist

On January 31, 1866, Holden, demoralized by political defeat and contemplating moving to Washington, halfheartedly resumed control of the *Standard*. Two former secessionists, Thomas L. Clingman and William B. Rodman, proposed to ease their old adversary out of the state by purchasing the newspaper, but Holden informed them that he would relinquish ownership only "to men of a more conservative [unionist] record."[1] When no suitable "conservative" stepped forward to buy the *Standard*, Holden abandoned his efforts to sell and moved vigorously to reestablish his preeminence as an editor and state political leader.

In early 1866 his interest, as well as that of many other southerners, focused on the struggle between President Johnson and the Republican-dominated Congress over reconstruction policy. The overwhelming majority of North Carolinians, including Holden, continued to support the president's mild but sidetracked plan for a quick restoration of the southern states to the Union. Holden, however, significantly differed from the Worth conservatives on the reason for the reconstruction impasse. Governor Worth and his followers believed that the real cause for conflict in Washington and

1. Raleigh *Standard*, January 31, February 7, 1866; R. H. Battle, Jr., to Benjamin S. Hedrick, February 6, 1866, in Benjamin S. Hedrick Papers, DU. Actually, Holden became the senior editor of the newspaper; his son Jo continued as the junior editor. Editorial policy was determined by the father, and he wrote almost all of the commentaries, as was clear from the numerous personal allusions that were made.

the delay in completing reconstruction was the bitter northern hatred and distrust of the South that had been inculcated by Radical Republican politicians like Thaddeus Stevens and Charles Sumner. According to this view, Congress and the North, with an assist from local malcontents like Holden—not the president and defeated Confederates—were the real obstacles to reconstruction of the Union. These conservatives insisted that North Carolinians had demonstrated their loyalty by repudiating secession, abolishing slavery, and electing old unionists to the highest offices. What more could be reasonably and constitutionally expected of the state? they asked.[2] To them the answer was clear: nothing further was needed except the admission of their representatives to Congress.

Holden blamed the Worth conservatives, or "latter-day war men," as he preferred to call them, for the failure of North Carolina to be restored to the Union. According to Holden, these obstructionists had not met the president's requirements for reconstruction in any important matter. They had failed to step aside and permit true unionists, or Holdenites, to direct the course of reconstruction. As he had done before, Holden neatly merged his partisan interests with the larger unionist cause. He soon discovered that the Worth administration was replacing most of the unionists whom he had appointed with men of doubtful loyalty to either the Union or to President Johnson. "This is not done," he declared, "by original secessionists, but by renegade Union men, who fell in love with Davis and the Confederacy in 1864 and 1865 [1863 and 1864?], and who are more untrustworthy, if possible, than the original war men. The latter are so odious to the people that they are obliged to work through these renegades, who have only an odor of Unionism about them, and who claim, with an impudence that would startle Satan himself, that they are the truest and best Union men in the South."[3]

President Johnson, Holden argued, had "repeatedly declared"

2. Richard L. Zuber, *Jonathan Worth: A Biography of a Southern Unionist* (Chapel Hill, 1965), 214; Roberta Sue Alexander, "North Carolina Faces the Freedmen: Race Relations During Presidential Reconstruction, 1865–1867" (Ph.D. dissertation, University of Chicago, 1974), 333–34; J. G. de Roulhac Hamilton and Max R. Williams (eds.), *The Papers of William Alexander Graham* (7 vols. to date; Raleigh, 1957–), VI, 467–68.

3. Raleigh *Standard*, April 18, 1866. See also issues of March 14, 28, April 4, June 13, July 25, 1866.

that the southern states "must be reorganized through the agency of 'unmistakably loyal men.'" Furthermore, he claimed that the northern people demanded this concession. They "have a right to expect that the States will return to the Union in good faith, through the instrumentality of loyal men." Acting through their representatives in Congress, northerners would never approve of southern reconstruction until this fundamental requirement was met, he said. Because of its recalcitrance, the South was rapidly losing the support of northern conservatives, who held the key to reconstruction policy. Unless Johnson's program was fully sustained by the southern states and restoration to the Union achieved soon, a radical settlement would be demanded by the majority in the North and imposed by Congress. "The longer we are delayed in this work, the greater is the danger," Holden told North Carolinians. He raised the specter of property confiscation, military government, and "rigid test oaths" for holding office if reconstruction remained in limbo. Furthermore, he maintained, "the material interests of our people" would continue to suffer until the state had returned to the Union.[4]

Holden was vague on a practical plan for breaking the reconstruction impasse. Throughout the first half of 1866 he continued to praise Johnson, though privately he must have been disappointed at the failure of the president to sustain him against the Worth faction. He repeatedly called for cooperation between Johnson and Congress in completing the presidential program for the South lest a division among unionists give Democrats the opportunity to regain national power. He believed that an accommodation could be reached even after the president had alienated the Republican majority with his veto of the civil rights bill, a veto that Holden approved. At this time he wrote that "the only just, safe and practical plan is that of the President."[5]

Holden's opposition to the civil rights bill, which was designed to end the flagrantly discriminatory treatment of the freedmen, demonstrated clearly that he understood the issue of reconstruction almost exclusively in terms of loyalty and political power in the South. Although he was not as unsympathetic to the plight of the

4. *Ibid.*, March 14, April 4, 25, 1866.
5. *Ibid.*, March 28, April 4, 11, 1866.

freedmen as were the Worth conservatives, he viewed the status of blacks after emancipation as a matter for the states to decide. He especially warned Congress against approving "any plan by which the insurgent States should be coerced to establish" black suffrage or other rights for the freedmen. Holden believed that the national authorities should "place all power in these States in the hands of the truest Union men that can be found." If this were done, he maintained, "Not only will the rights and interests of the freedmen be fully protected, but the Union itself will be safe against any combination that may be formed of Southern secessionists and Northern copperheads."[6]

He believed that, despite the Republican outrage over the South's black codes and the agitation for black suffrage by some Radicals, most northerners considered Negro rights to be of secondary importance in reconstruction. He was not far wrong on this point. But in 1866, when the issue of southern loyalty was merged with the question of bona fide black freedom, the rights of blacks became a serious concern of northerners, affecting their attitudes toward reconstruction policy and their position in the conflict between Johnson and Congress.

In July, 1866, Holden went to Washington to press his views on national leaders and to learn at first hand the direction that the reconstruction struggle was taking. The ostensible purpose of the trip, which lasted ten days, was to attend Senate confirmation hearings on his nomination by Johnson as minister to El Salvador. The president had offered him the position out of gratitude for his support and perhaps because he felt some guilt for having failed to endorse him in the 1865 election. Holden was not enthusiastic about a Latin American appointment, but he was eager for any sign of administration support that could aid him and his unionist faction at home. Furthermore, with the reconstruction dispute undecided, he did not want to risk offending Johnson by showing a lack of interest in the position. In any event, he probably understood (correctly) that because he could not take the ironclad oath, he would not be confirmed by the Senate.[7] He talked to the president on four

6. *Ibid.*, March 28, 1866.
7. Benjamin S. Hedrick to Jonathan Worth, June 20, July 8, 1866, in J. G. de Roulhac Hamilton (ed.), *The Correspondence of Jonathan Worth* (2 vols.; Raleigh, 1909), I, 639, II, 695.

occasions, to Charles Sumner and Thaddeus Stevens twice each, and to various other leaders. He painted a dismal picture of North Carolina affairs under Governor Worth. In a conference with the president, the substance of which Johnson asked him to put in writing, the former provisional governor complained that under Worth true unionists had been replaced in office by "leading war men and rebels" who were now engaged in undoing reconstruction and proscribing Union men and wartime peace advocates. "Treason and disloyalty are promoted and honored," Holden pointedly told the president, "while loyalty is evinced at the hazard of political, social, and pecuniary proscription." When it became clear to Holden that Johnson would not directly intervene to remove the Worth faction from office, he drafted a public letter for the president's signature expressing the administration's support for the North Carolina unionists.[8] But the president, probably suspicious of Holden's motives, refused to sign the letter.

Although politically no better off than when he had left Raleigh, Holden's Washington trip did provide him with a keener insight into the national conflict over reconstruction and the growing determination of the Republicans to take charge of southern policy. He was heartened by the fact that he could detect "no present purpose on the part of Congress . . . to reduce the States to the condition of Territories, or to force negro suffrage upon them." Even Radicals such as Sumner and Stevens in their discussions with him, he reported in the *Standard*, did not mention black suffrage as a requirement for southern reconstruction. They seemed content to await southern action on the Howard amendment (later the Fourteenth Amendment to the Constitution). The proposed amendment, as Holden accurately concluded, was the moderate Republicans' reconstruction plan, which was designed to retain the largely voluntary features of Johnson's program but at the same time correct its flaws.[9]

8. Raleigh *Standard*, July 18, October 10, 1866; W. W. Holden to President Johnson, July 11, 1866, in Andrew Johnson Papers (on microfilm), LC (unless otherwise noted, all citations are to Series I). Holden had appointed the state judges.

9. Raleigh *Standard*, July 18, August 8, 15, October 10, 1866. For an excellent account of the purposes behind the Fourteenth Amendment, see Allen W. Trelease, *Reconstruction: The Great Experiment* (New York, 1971), 60–64.

Holden was convinced that the Howard amendment offered the South the last opportunity to control reconstruction and avoid a radical settlement. Before his trip to Washington he had announced that if the president's "plan cannot be carried out as an entirety, we would accept Mr. Howard's plan as the next best we can get." After his visit—and despite the president's strong objection to the amendment—Holden filled the columns of the *Standard* with arguments in favor of its ratification by the southern states. He pleaded with North Carolinians to accept the amendment "as the *only* course left them to escape future and greater evils." With typical hyperbole he predicted that if they rejected "the Congressional plan" contained in the Howard amendment, "the result will be the reorganization of the State government, confiscation, executions for treason, negro suffrage, and the exclusion of rebels, so-called, not only from office but from the ballot-box as long as they live. . . . We are most anxious to avoid these results." [10] Whether he would admit it or not, Holden had separated himself from Johnson and his discredited plan of reconstruction.

Not until the legislature met in the late fall would North Carolina make a decision on the proposed Fourteenth Amendment. Meanwhile Holden saw in the work of the state convention, meeting in mid-1866 to write a new constitution, a test of reconstruction fidelity. The convention, which in 1865 had been elected with a unionist majority sympathetic to Holden, framed a document whose main changes were the relaxation of the discriminatory black code passed a few weeks earlier by the legislature and the establishment of the white basis of representation in the House of Commons. [11] Otherwise, the constitution retained the undemocratic fea-

10. Raleigh *Standard,* June 6, September 19, October 10, 1866. See also issues of August 8, 15, 1866.

11. Historians have usually ignored the state convention's invalidation of the most controversial features of the black code. This action was motivated by the unionist majority's desire to meet congressional concerns about the basic rights of the freedmen. For the traditional account, see J. G. de Roulhac Hamilton, *Reconstruction in North Carolina* (New York, 1914), 172–76; Samuel A'Court Ashe, *History of North Carolina* (2 vols.; Raleigh, 1925), II, 1036–37; and James L. Lancaster, "The Scalawags of North Carolina, 1850–1868" (Ph.D. dissertation, Princeton University, 1974), 140–42. On the repeal of some of the discriminatory laws, see Alexander, "North Carolina Faces the Freedmen," 325–36.

tures of the antebellum document, specifically the taxation basis for apportionment of senatorial seats, the legislative election of numerous officers, and property qualifications for governor and for members of the General Assembly. Holden supported the new constitution, but he indicated his disappointment that it did not eradicate the undemocratic parts of the old document.[12]

When the constitution was rejected by the white voters for a variety of reasons, Holden wrongly attributed its defeat to "hostility to the national government." He now pronounced presidential reconstruction a failure, blaming it on conservative "traitors" and "secession demagogues," not Johnson. These "oligarchs and traitors," with "complete control of the State government," had "thrown away . . . the magnanimity and kindness of the President" and by "appeals to prejudice and passion" had inflamed the people against a true reconstruction. "If justice were done in their cases," Holden thundered, "they would be tried and executed for treason, or at least banished to Brazil or the Dry Tortugas."[13]

The fate of North Carolina and the South now lay with Congress, Holden declared, and he expected the northern elections in the fall to return a more radical membership to that body. "The people of the United States who suppressed the rebellion [will] say on what terms the government shall be restored. . . . Our sympathies are with those who are most devoted to the Union, and who are determined to restore it on a loyal basis, without the dictation of Northern copperheads or Southern traitors."[14]

Holden, however, clung to the notion that North Carolina could escape the full fury of northern indignation. He still believed that it could do so, like Tennessee, by ratifying the Fourteenth Amendment and electing a unionist governor in the fall. With this in mind, in early September he issued a call for a "Mass Convention" of "Loyal Union men" of the state to assemble in Raleigh on the twen-

12. Raleigh *Standard,* June 20, 27, July 25, 1866. Historians have mistakenly interpreted the constitution as the product of postwar democratic reform. See Lancaster, "The Scalawags of North Carolina," 141–42; and Otto H. Olsen (ed.), *Reconstruction and Redemption in the South* (Baton Rouge, 1980), 163. Unionism and the desire of many, for largely political reasons, to correct the sectional imbalance in the legislature did not necessarily reflect democratic impulses.

13. Raleigh *Standard,* August 8, September 12, 1866.

14. *Ibid.,* August 15, 29, 1866.

tieth of the month. Mainly because of the short notice, only twenty men, representing nine counties, attended the "convention" held at the *Standard* office.[15]

Holden chaired the session and delivered an address to the people of North Carolina that was designed more for publication than for the edification of his audience. The president's plan, he declared, "has been marred and destroyed by malcontents and traitors at this end of the line." He devoted most of the address to arguing that the Fourteenth Amendment did not differ significantly from the president's original plan of reconstruction. They both required loyalty as a test of governance in the reconstructed South and left the matter of black suffrage in the hands of the states, he explained. He contended that the federal guarantee of rights for all citizens, including blacks, contained in the first section of the amendment could not be reasonably contested by supporters of presidential reconstruction. It simply gave blacks the same liberties and legal rights that they already held by virtue of the Civil Rights Act of 1866. Furthermore, he said, the Fourteenth Amendment did not propose to abolish the Johnson state governments but only to purge them of their disloyal elements. With an eye on the forthcoming congressional elections in the North, Holden insisted that North Carolina should ratify the amendment and be restored to the Union before northern opinion forced a harsh settlement upon the South.[16]

Holden ended his address by appealing, as he had before, to the material interests of North Carolinians. "Our capacity to discharge our [financial] obligations, whether public or private," he indicated, "is greatly restricted by our exclusion from the Union. . . . The longer we remain out of it, the poorer we shall become, and the heavier will be our burdens as a State and as individuals." Upon the state's restoration to the Union, he said, "we shall at once enter on a new career of prosperity."[17]

15. W. W. Holden to David M. Carter, September 3, 1866 (printed), in David Miller Carter Papers, SHC; *Union Meeting in Raleigh: Alfred Dockery of Richmond, Nominated for Governor* (Raleigh, 1866), 1–2; Perrin Busbee to Benjamin S. Hedrick, September 21, 1866, Lewis Hanes to Hedrick, September 22, 1866, in Hedrick Papers.

16. *Union Meeting in Raleigh*, 7, 8–13. Holden's address was also published in several sympathetic newspapers, including the Raleigh *Standard*, September 26, 1866.

17. *Union Meeting in Raleigh*, 15–16.

After Holden's address, the small unionist gathering nominated Alfred Dockery for governor on a platform calling for the ratification of the Fourteenth Amendment. The "Union party" meeting also expressed its support for "any further action that in the wisdom of Congress and the Executive may be deemed necessary to guarantee the State of North-Carolina a Republican [republican] form of government, and restore the Union."[18] Given his bitter defeats in the 1864 and 1865 elections, Holden knew that he could not be elected in 1866 and did not seek the gubernatorial nomination. Instead, he agreed to serve as chairman of the Union party's state executive committee, which would be a strategic position if Congress imposed a loyal political order upon the state. In fact, this committee became the embryo of the state Republican party, which was founded in 1867 after Congress assumed complete control of reconstruction.

The main issues in the brief campaign were the Fourteenth Amendment and, as before, Holden. Like Dockery, Governor Worth, the conservative candidate, did not campaign, but in numerous letters to his supporters and to sympathetic newspapers he proclaimed his strong opposition to the proposed Fourteenth Amendment. "No full-blooded North Carolinian will humiliate and degrade himself by favoring this amendment, whatever may be the consequence of refusing to ratify it," he wrote a friend. Conservative newspapers charged that the amendment was only the entering wedge for the Radical Republicans. "The adoption of the Howard amendment," the Raleigh newspaper organ of the Worth forces declared, "will remove every barrier in the Constitution to the full consummation of the Stevens and [Parson] Brownlow programme," namely black suffrage. Several conservative campaigners claimed (incorrectly) that the amendment itself imposed Negro suffrage upon North Carolina and the South. Some conservatives defiantly announced that, before accepting reunion under such terms, the state should remain a territory and thereby avoid groveling before the Radicals.[19]

18. *Ibid.*, 1–2.
19. Jonathan Worth to C. C. Clark, October 1, 1866, in Hamilton (ed.), *Correspondence of Worth*, II, 807 and 805–17 *passim;* Raleigh *Semi-Weekly Sentinel,* September 15, 1866; David Hodgin to Benjamin S. Hedrick, October 20, 1866, in Hedrick Papers. There was no official party name for the conservative Worth faction.

Conservative spokesmen reserved their deadliest arrows for their homegrown nemesis, Holden. The Raleigh *Sentinel*, edited by William Pell, a Methodist minister who during the war had worked in the *Standard* office, led the attack on his former employer. The good parson denounced the Union party leader as an "utterly unscrupulous Radical" who since his 1865 defeat for governor "has not ceased to pour his anathemas upon the people." The intemperate *Sentinel* editor even professed that "Providence wanted [him] in this position" solely "to expose the vileness of W. W. Holden."[20] Conservative extremists denounced not only Holden but also his allies, like Robert P. Dick, as "mortal enemies to the South . . . scheming for her ruin and disgrace." Governor Worth erroneously claimed that "loyal leagues of the North" had been organized in North Carolina and were vigorously cooperating with Holden in the campaign. But "the support of Holden will beat any man in North Carolina," a Worth associate contended. Conservative leaders, however, still feared that the "imprudent zeal" of friendly editors could lead President Johnson to intervene on the side of the Union party.[21]

In a long letter to Johnson on September 15 Worth sought to forestall any such presidental intervention in the election. He recounted Holden's checkered political past and claimed that the president had been grievously misled by the *Standard* editor's professions of support. Despite Holden's "unceasing reiteration" of "his supposed intimacy with you," Worth told Johnson, "the true Union men despised him" and would vote for the conservatives in the election.[22]

The governor need not have worried about Johnson's position. The president had already become disenchanted with Holden and had no intention of intervening in the politics of a state that he had already pronounced fully restored to the Union. In an election marked by voter apathy, mainly because of the uncertainty over re-

20. Raleigh *Semi-Weekly Sentinel*, July 9, October 15, 1866; Raleigh *Sentinel*, quoted in the Raleigh *Standard*, June 6, 1866.
21. Lancaster, "The Scalawags of North Carolina," 149; Jonathan Worth to Benjamin S. Hedrick, June 16, 21, October 1, 1866, in Hamilton, (ed.), *Correspondence of Worth*, I, 629, 642, II, 805; Lewis Hanes to Benjamin S. Hedrick, September 22, 1866, in Hedrick Papers.
22. Jonathan Worth to President Johnson, September 15, 1866, in Johnson Papers.

construction, Worth and conservative candidates for the legislature swept to an easy victory over Dockery and Holden's Union party.[23] The congressional elections in the North with the Republicans trouncing Johnson's National Union party (composed mostly of Democrats) made it unlikely that the North Carolina conservatives would be able to enjoy the fruits of victory.

When the General Assembly met in November, it defiantly rejected the Fourteenth Amendment and replaced unionist John Pool in the United States Senate with a former secessionist.[24] After Pool's defeat but before the vote on the amendment, Holden abandoned any remaining pretension that the president should have a hand in reconstruction and called on Congress to begin anew the work of restoration. "We do not want the Howard amendment," he stormed on December 5. "It is not sufficiently stringent on traitors. We want something better. We want to see this State governed for years to come by unmistakably loyal men, and the Howard amendment . . . does not go far enough to effect this object."[25]

Almost simultaneous with the appearance of this editorial, Holden assembled four political friends, including Pool, and went to Washington to lay his reconstruction views before Congress. The delegation arrived in the national capital on December 8, and the next day, a Sunday, they met with Thaddeus Stevens, who they reasonably assumed was now in charge of reconstruction legislation. At the end of the meeting the powerful Pennsylvanian asked Holden and friends to draw up a bill incorporating their ideas. The North Carolinians returned to their hotel, where they drafted a bill "to establish civil government in North Carolina, and to enable it to resume its former relations" in the Union. On December 13 Stevens, "at the request of certain gentlemen from North Carolina," he said, introduced the measure into the House of Representatives, where it was immediately referred to the Committee on Territories.[26]

23. Raleigh *Standard*, October 31, 1866; David Hodgin to Benjamin S. Hedrick, October 20, 1866, in Hedrick Papers.
24. Governor Worth claimed that Holden's support was "fatal" to Pool's chances for reelection. Jonathan Worth to Benjamin S. Hedrick, November 29, 1866, in Hedrick Papers.
25. Raleigh *Standard*, December 5, 1866.
26. W. W. Holden to David M. Carter, November 1866, in Carter Papers; Holden to his wife, December 9, 1866, in William Woods Holden Papers, NDAH;

The "Holden bill," as the New York *Times* called it, provided for "a loyal Convention of the people of the State" to meet in Raleigh on May 20, 1867, for the purpose of framing a new constitution that would be "republican in form" and acceptable to Congress. All whites who had previously been eligible to vote could participate in the election of delegates; in addition, those blacks who were literate and owned one hundred dollars' worth of real property could vote in the election, which would be under the supervision of federal marshals and their agents. In order to qualify for a seat in the convention, a delegate had to swear that on or after March 4, 1864, he had opposed the rebellion and "earnestly desired the success of the Union."[27] March 4, 1864, had a special significance for Holden and other North Carolina unionists. It was the day Holden announced his candidacy for governor against Vance, an announcement, coming soon after the Confederate government's suspension of the writ of habeas corpus, that supposedly launched the reconstruction movement in North Carolina. The test oath was mainly designed to ensure that Holdenites, and not "latter-day war men" of the Worth-Graham political stripe, controlled the constitutional convention. The oath would also provide a more practical definition of unionism, one that would avoid the rigid ironclad test of loyalty and at the same time exclude Union men of 1860–1861 who later supported the Confederacy to the bitter end.

The acceptance by Holden and associates of the principle of qualified black suffrage reflected their realistic assessment of the changed reconstruction atmosphere in Washington following the national elections of the fall and the southern rejection of the Fourteenth Amendment. The politically astute Stevens in his first meeting with the North Carolinians had impressed upon them the point that the Republican majority in Congress was prepared to go to extreme lengths in its southern settlement. The North Carolina bill sought a formula that would be a compromise between the northern Radical demand for universal black suffrage (and possibly more stringent requirements) and the desire of North Carolina unionists and

---

John Pool, *Address of the Hon. John Pool to the People of North Carolina* (Raleigh, 1867), 9; *Congressional Globe*, 39th Cong., 2nd Sess., 109.

27. Pool, *Address*, 9; Greensboro *Patriot*, December 21, 1866; Raleigh *Standard*, December 19, 25, 1866.

many moderate Republicans in the North for a reconstruction in which only whites could vote. Several moderate northern Republican journals, including the Washington *Chronicle* and the *Nation*, immediately endorsed the bill. The *Nation* described it as "the most sensible and conservative plan yet submitted to the public" and predicted that it would be adopted not only for North Carolina but for all the wayward states.[28]

Private conversations with "leading Republicans" led the Holden delegation to believe that the North Carolina plan would be approved by Congress.[29] But despite this initial support and Stevens' willingness to introduce the bill as a favor to Holden and his friends, the proposal soon gave way to a more radical scheme. On January 3, 1867, Stevens introduced a reconstruction bill into the House that would take away the citizenship, including political rights, of former Confederate leaders for at least five years and would enfranchise all black male adults. Despite these radical provisions, the Stevens bill followed the North Carolina measure in exempting from the proscriptive clause all whites who could take an oath that they favored reunion on and after March 4, 1864. Stevens had accepted Holden's test oath rather than the earlier ironclad one affirming continuous wartime loyalty that had been required of federal officials and congressmen. The "noble old Roman," as Holden admiringly referred to Stevens, perhaps never realized that the March, 1864, date was peculiarly related to North Carolina's and to Holden's own political fortunes. A provision in the Stevens bill for a state convention to frame a new constitution acceptable to Congress was also strikingly similar to the North Carolina proposal.[30]

28. W. W. Holden to S. A. Ashe, December 6, 1881, Raleigh *News and Observer*, n.d., in Scrapbook, William Woods Holden Papers, DU; Raleigh *Standard*, December 25, 1866; *Nation*, December 20, 1866, p. 496. See also excerpts from several northern newspapers in the Raleigh *Standard*, January 9, 1867, and in the New York *Times*, December 31, 1866. The North Carolina conservative opposition to the proposal was vigorous. Governor Worth dispatched a "Union commission" to Washington to lobby against Holden and the North Carolina bill. The delegation failed to sway Congress. Jonathan Worth to Edwin G. Reade, December 5, 1866, Worth to Nathaniel Boyden, December 29, 1866, in Hamilton (ed.), *Correspondence of Worth*, II, 846–47; Kemp Battle to Benjamin S. Hedrick, January 3, 1867, in Hedrick Papers.

29. New York *Tribune*, December 15, 1866.

30. Holden, however, exaggerated when he wrote that Stevens' bill included "the main features of the North Carolina bill." A significant difference between the

Although the Stevens bill became the starting point for congressional reconstruction, the Pennsylvanian was forced to accept a number of changes before it became law. These changes included the abandonment of the North Carolina test-oath provision and the addition of a section imposing temporary military rule.[31] Before the debate on the floor began, the Holden delegation returned home, confident that Congress would soon reorganize the southern governments and place their faction in control of the state.

Holden moved quickly to gain the confidence of North Carolina blacks, who, he knew, would soon be enfranchised by Congress. Since the end of the war he had refrained from the typical white practice of disparaging or abusing blacks and, along with unionist members of the 1866 state convention, had successfully obtained a softening of the black code. Nevertheless, he had not championed black rights and had frequently lectured them about their responsibilities in freedom. As late as October, 1866, Holden, speaking before the state Colored Educational Convention, had warned blacks to avoid politics and to cultivate the goodwill of whites. He also told them that they were entitled to their rights as provided for in the 1866 Civil Rights Act and the proposed Fourteenth Amendment and that they should insist upon the education of their children. But he maintained that federal intervention was not necessary to secure their rights.[32] The December, 1866, trip to Washington and his discussions with prominent Republicans like Stevens con-

---

two bills was the Stevens bill's requirement that the new state constitutions be ratified by the voters before submission to Congress; the Holden proposal required no such voter approval. The Stevens measure was reported in the newspapers prior to its introduction on the floor of the House. Raleigh *Standard*, January 2, 1867; *Congressional Globe*, 39th Cong., 2nd Sess., 250.

31. For accounts of the debate and maneuvering in Congress following the introduction of the Stevens bill, see Michael Les Benedict, *A Compromise of Principle: Congressional Republicans and Reconstruction, 1863–1869* (New York, 1974), Ch. 10, and David Donald, *The Politics of Reconstruction, 1863–1867* (Baton Rouge, 1965), 65–70.

32. *Minutes of the Freedmen's Convention; Held in the City of Raleigh, on the 2nd, 3rd, 4th, and 5th of October, 1866* (Raleigh, 1866), 23–25. In his remarks to the convention Holden indicated that blacks were capable of much greater "mental improvement" than they had achieved. He blamed the lag partly on the dulling effects of slavery.

vinced Holden that the idea of federally guaranteed black rights, including suffrage, was more important in the reconstruction thinking of congressional leaders than he had supposed. It must have come as a shock to hear Stevens and other Radicals speak of black loyalty and rights on a par with those of white unionists like himself. Nevertheless, the Union party in the state had committed itself to whatever reconstruction plan emerged in Congress, and as black enfranchisement appeared inevitable, Holden and his white associates had little choice but to accept a political status for blacks. Furthermore, as Holden rather crudely argued, blacks would "attach themselves to Union men, and adhere to the Union cause, just as the animals of the desert seek for and find water, or as the child runs to its mother."[33]

Soon after his return to Raleigh in mid-December, Holden proclaimed his support for black rights. In the *Standard* he announced that "it is utterly idle for any citizen of the insurgent States to expect or hope that these States will ever be restored to their former places in the Union until they shall have provided in their fundamental law for absolute equality between the two races as to political and civil rights." On New Year's Day he made his first political contact with the black community when he appeared at a Raleigh meeting of a large number of black people and in a two-hour speech declared his unqualified support for their enfranchisement. He also introduced a resolution, which passed, asking Congress "to reorganize the government of North-Carolina on the basis of loyal white and black suffrage."[34]

A few days later Holden addressed another meeting of blacks. He reportedly told them that they would soon be relieved of their conservative oppressors and placed in the hands of white unionist friends.[35] Conservatives expressed outrage at Holden's audacity in promoting black political equality and in seeking the political support of the former slaves. Governor Worth indignantly wrote that "Holden, having lost the confidence of the white race, is co-

33. Raleigh *Standard,* January 9, 1867.

34. *Ibid.,* December 25, 1866, January 9, 1867; Kemp Battle to Benjamin S. Hedrick, January 3, 1867, in Hedrick Papers; Raleigh *Sentinel,* January 9, 1867.

35. Jonathan Worth to Bedford Brown *et al.,* January 12, 1866, in Hamilton (ed.), *Correspondence of Worth,* II, 865–66; Perrin Busbee to Benjamin S. Hedrick, January 8, 1866 [1867], in Hedrick Papers.

operating with our external foes, to engender animosity between the whites and blacks and to get into power through the agency of the poor deluded negro." The governor wrote a friend that Holden "has made much impression" on blacks in the Raleigh area and that he feared Holden would "delude the masses of them as he had often deluded and misled the more intelligent whites." Kemp Battle, a political associate of Worth, wondered, "Can this great [federal] government use its powers to reward such a man" as Holden?[36]

Before too long Battle and his conservative friends had their answer. Congress in February, 1867, awarded a public printing contract to the *Standard*. At almost the same time, it passed the military reconstruction bill that made possible the ascendancy of a new, Holden-led political party in the state. Even before the bill was enacted over President Johnson's veto, Holden, anticipating its passage, rejoiced that "the long night of misrule and oppression is departing, to be succeeded by a day of peace and prosperity under just and equal laws."[37]

Holden must have known that the political transformation would still be difficult. The foreboding presence of sectional animosity, racial prejudice and antagonism, military occupation, and postwar poverty, combined with the bitter heritage of intrastate political strife, strongly suggested that North Carolina's night of travail would not end soon. Under these circumstances Holden was hardly the best person to lead the new political order in the state. His political notoriety (though not universal), his repudiation at the polls in 1864 and 1865, and his self-righteous combativeness, in addition to the long list of political foes whom he had accumulated during his career as the editor of the *Standard,* would surely work against the success of a reconstruction plan that was viewed as radical by most North Carolina whites. Even some unionists who had supported the peace movement during the war believed that Holden, as D. Frank Caldwell of Greensboro expressed it, was a "most reckless and bad man" who was determined to rule or ruin. "He is odious

36. Jonathan Worth to Thomas Ruffin, January 7, 1867, in J. G. de Roulhac Hamilton (ed.), *The Papers of Thomas Ruffin* (4 vols.; Raleigh, 1918–20), IV, 42; Kemp Battle to Benjamin S. Hedrick, January 3, 1867, in Hedrick Papers; Raleigh *Sentinel,* January 9, 1867; Greensboro *Patriot,* January 11, 1867.

37. W. W. Holden to his wife, February 11, 1867, in Holden Papers, DU; Raleigh *Standard,* February 27, March 20, 1867.

and hated by everyone," Caldwell claimed, and if he became governor under congressional reconstruction, "dark days and troubles are before us."[38] Other "straitest sect" unionists could not forget—particularly since Worth conservatives would not let them—that Holden had been a southern-rights Democrat before the war.

Most unionists, however, were prepared to forgive Holden of his presumed antebellum sins, provided he continued on a straight and narrow course during Reconstruction. They responded with some enthusiasm to his leadership, remembering that he had fought the good fight to keep the state in the Union in 1860–1861, had taken a courageous stand against the secessionists and Vance forces during the war, and had been the driving force behind the Union party of 1866. Despite the increasingly bitter tone of the *Standard*, Holden possessed some attributes that would be advantageous in organizing a new political party in the state. He had a keen sense of reality about the postwar world, combined with the ability to adapt to new political conditions. He also possessed practical organizational skills and knew the political terrain of the state. Finally, he was North Carolina's ablest editor, despite his tendency to exaggerate, overreact to the opposition's challenges, and go for the opponent's jugular on slight provocation.

What the new order needed most was state and local leadership that would not only serve the interests of blacks but also secure the support of many whites, including former Confederates, without which congressional reconstruction would probably fail. Although this was a tall order, the time seemed ripe in early 1867 for a new beginning. After two years of political strife and continuing economic hard times that appeared worse in 1867 than before, most North Carolinians were anxious to end the uncertainty surrounding reconstruction. Despite their resentment of black suffrage, northern Republicans, and Holden, they recognized that if they continued the fight, a worse fate awaited them. Specifically, as Holden repeatedly warned, if they did not cooperate with Congress, they could expect to see property confiscated, poverty stalking the state, and social disorders erupting. A new frame of mind was emerging in

38. W. C. Kerr to Benjamin S. Hedrick, March 12, 1867, in Hedrick Papers; D. F. Caldwell to John Sherman, March 8, 1867, in James A. Padgett (ed.), "Reconstruction Letters from North Carolina, Part II: Letters to John Sherman," *NCHR*, XVIII (1941), 296.

North Carolina that would lead to important white support for re-construction if it were properly cultivated. A conservative of Davie County reported that the white people "will submit to anything—from President, Congress or Subalterns of either—in order to be reconstructed. The spirit of resistance is dead. . . . What they want is peace and to be let alone." [39] A man who had been a strong sup-porter of the Confederacy, but who now desired "immediate reor-ganization as the shortest road to re-union," wrote Holden: "Our highest interest and our first duty is to get out of this condition of uncertainty, which oppresses our energies and paralyzes our indus-try. The fact is, my ardent desire is to see all our fortunes rebuilt, my own among the number; and I know that this cannot be done while the present condition of affairs continue. I think the temper of our people—not the leaders—is improving." [40] In essence, the success of congressional reconstruction in North Carolina depended to a considerable extent upon the skill in which it was implemented by Holden and his associates. As would become increasingly clear, it also depended upon the willingness of federal authorities to pre-serve their handiwork and protect the new political order until it was able to stand firmly on its own feet.

39. John M. Clement to Edward McPherson, March 19, 1867, in James A. Padgett (ed.), "Reconstruction Letters from North Carolina, Part VII: Letters to Edward McPherson," *NCHR*, XIX (1942), 192. For additional evidence of the widespread desire for acquiescence to congressional reconstruction, see Kemp Battle to Benjamin S. Hedrick, March 3, 12, 1867, in Hedrick Papers; Charlotte *Western Democrat*, March 26, April 2, 23, July 2, 1867; John B. Odom to Thomas Settle May 18, 1867, in Thomas Settle Papers, SHC; and John Cunningham to Cal-vin H. Wiley, May 22, 1867, in Calvin H. Wiley Papers, SHC. Still, a large number of conservatives bitterly opposed and feared congressional reconstruction. David Schenck, an ex-secessionist lawyer of Lincolnton, confided to his diary (March 5, 1867 [Ms in SHC]) that the Military Reconstruction Act will "create a deadly feud between the races, and give rise to scenes of violence and disorder. . . . The white race will not suffer this outrage without bloody resentment, and if it cannot be done by force it will be done by assassinations and secret means of revenge."
40. Raleigh *Standard*, January 9, 1867.

XI
Republican Leader

The congressional reconstruction program, enacted on March 2 and 23, 1867, divided the former Confederate states, excluding Tennessee, into five military districts with an army general over each. Congress gave the military commanders broad authority "to protect all persons in their rights of persons and property, to suppress insurrection, disorder, and violence, and to punish or cause to be punished all disturbers of the public peace and criminals." The district commanders, however, might retain the Johnson governments for caretaking purposes. As the first step in the process of reconstruction, the commanders were to register a new electorate, including black male adults but excluding whites barred from holding office by the proposed Fourteenth Amendment. They were then to hold elections for delegates to state conventions that would frame constitutions guaranteeing black political equality. When the voters in each state ratified their constitution and the newly elected legislature approved the Fourteenth Amendment, Congress would readmit the state to the Union and lift military authority.[1]

North Carolina and South Carolina were placed in the Second Military District under the command of General Daniel E. Sickles. From his headquarters in Charleston, the one-legged Sickles estab-

---

1. *U.S. Statutes at Large*, XIV, 428–29, XV, 2–4. Even if a state ratified the Fourteenth Amendment, the reconstruction law provided that it could not be readmitted to the Union until the amendment had been approved by the necessary three-fourths of all the states.

lished eleven military posts in North Carolina. The officers in charge of these posts, located in geographically strategic towns, were to enforce the reconstruction laws as unobtrusively as possible. Contrary to legend, the state was never overwhelmed by military force; fewer than fifteen hundred troops were stationed in North Carolina during the sixteen-month period of military reconstruction.[2] The certainty of military intervention, along with the rejuvenation of the Freedmen's Bureau, was usually sufficient to check the fever of lawlessness and racial violence that had plagued the state since the war. General Sickles, however, permitted the Worth administration to remain in office, dismaying Holden and his friends, who feared that the old government, with encouragement from President Johnson, would undermine their chances in the reconstruction elections. Their fears proved unfounded. Sickles and his officers maintained a close supervision of the state government and the courts to ensure that neither the reconstruction process nor security for blacks and unionists would be impaired.[3]

Although the reconstruction laws did not require the ascendancy of a Union party like Holden's, Congress obviously expected its southern supporters to organize immediately and control the new governments. With most Confederate leaders temporarily disfranchised, blacks enfranchised, and the military available to provide protection for friends of Congress, the stage was set for a political transformation of the South. Holden and his associates in North Carolina moved rapidly to begin the process and also prevent other political claimants, either conservative or radical, from gaining the upper hand in congressional reconstruction. In early March the Raleigh editor assembled in his office a "caucus" of unionist legislators to prepare for a state convention of "loyal men." A total of 140 men were invited to attend the convention, which was to be held in Raleigh on March 27. All of the names on the list were white; only five of them were non-natives, or "carpetbaggers." The

2. For a revealing chart of troop strength in North Carolina and other southern states see James E. Sefton, *The United States Army and Reconstruction, 1867– 1877* (Baton Rouge, 1967), Appendix B.

3. General Orders No. 1, March 21, 1867, in *Senate Executive Documents,* 40th Cong., 1st Sess., No. 14, pp. 60–61; W. W. Holden to Edward McPherson, July 6, 1867, in James A. Padgett (ed.), "Reconstruction Letters from North Carolina, Part VII: Letters to Edward M. McPherson," *NCHR,* XIX (1942), 196.

caucus also agreed to consult with blacks in order to secure their "cooperation" with white unionists in the work of reconstruction. When a meeting of Raleigh blacks indicated an interest in attending the state convention, Holden through the columns of the *Standard* broadened the invitation to include representatives of the freedmen. He also assured blacks that their delegates would receive a cordial reception in the convention.[4]

On March 27 the first biracial political meeting in North Carolina's history opened in the capitol's Hall of Commons. In attendance were 148 delegates, representing 45 counties. Ninety-four of the delegates were native whites, including Daniel R. Goodloe and Benjamin S. Hedrick, who had fled the state before the war because of their antislavery views and had now returned to wrest control of reconstruction from Holden. Forty-nine blacks, a surprisingly large number, led by James H. Harris, a Raleigh Holdenite, served as delegates.[5] Most of the men who would lead the state for the next few years were present, and almost all of them had supported the peace movement during the war and the Union party in 1865–1866. Leading delegates John Pool, Alfred Dockery, Robert P. Dick, David M. Carter, James T. Leach, George Washington Logan, and Holden had been prominent in antebellum politics. Some of the delegates, including Pool, Dockery, Dick, Leach, William A. Smith, and Ceburn L. Harris, had been large slaveholders. Most of them, however, came from relatively obscure backgrounds, though few were young men. The convention was a "noble spectacle," Holden reported, in which "the former master met his former slave as his equal in all that pertains to manhood and the rights of self-government, and this meeting of freemen had no restraint in it, but was cordial, respectful, kind and confiding on both sides."[6]

4. Kemp Battle to Benjamin S. Hedrick, March 7, 1867, in Benjamin S. Hedrick Papers, DU; Raleigh *Standard*, March 13, 20, 1867; James L. Lancaster, "The Scalawags of North Carolina, 1850–1868" (Ph.D. dissertation, Princeton University, 1974), 202.

5. Lancaster, "The Scalawags of North Carolina," 206. For the convention's proceedings, see the Raleigh *Standard*, April 3, 1867, and the Greensboro *Patriot*, March 29, 1867. The *Standard* of April 3 identified the delegates by race.

6. Holden praised the abilities of the native whites in the convention and commented favorably on their backgrounds. Raleigh *Standard*, April 3, 1867. James L. Lancaster concludes that 62 percent of the state's Republican leaders during Re-

It was clear from the beginning that Holden and his lieutenants were in control of the convention. Under a banner proclaiming UNION, LIBERTY, EQUALITY, Holden associate Robert P. Dick moved the formal organization of the Republican party of North Carolina. Goodloe and Hedrick, who had a foot in the conservative camp of Worth and Graham, almost alone opposed Dick's resolution on the ground that the odium attached to the label "Republican" in North Carolina would prevent thousands of whites from cooperating with the party. They preferred the retention of the name "Union party." With a ringing affirmation, the convention adopted Dick's resolution, thereby giving birth to the Republican party of North Carolina.[7]

Rousing unionist speeches absorbed most of the convention's time. "Colored orators, as well as white orators," Holden approvingly reported in the *Standard*, "enchained the attention of vast audiences, the former vieing [sic] with the latter in humor, wit, logic, and eloquence." James H. Harris, the main black speaker, attempted to allay the fears of many white unionists that their alliance with blacks would destroy them. He assured them that blacks did not seek domination and would stand by their true white friends in the party. Most of the speeches of the white delegates reflected the ardent tone of the Holden editorials on reconstruction that had been appearing in the *Standard* since early 1866. They denounced the continuation of the spirit of rebellion and defiance in the state, attacked the Worth administration, sang paeans to the Union and Congress, and expressed their confidence in North Carolina blacks. But they also suggested that the motive of expediency may have been paramount in the white unionists' conversion to the cause of equal rights when they appealed to white North Carolinians to support

---

construction had participated in the Civil War peace movement. Lancaster, "The Scalawags of North Carolina," 362.

7. Raleigh *Standard*, April 3, 1867; John A. Hedrick to Benjamin S. Hedrick, April 19, 1867, in Hedrick Papers. For a good account of this convention, see Lancaster, "The Scalawags of North Carolina," 207–10. It is likely that few missed the irony of Hedrick's and Holden's positions in the 1867 convention. It was Hedrick's announcement of support for the Republican party in 1856 that led to Holden's campaign to drive him from the state; now, in 1867, Hedrick rejected the name "Republican" while Holden advocated it.

the congressional program and the Republican party in order to avoid a truly radical reconstruction settlement. After adopting a platform reflecting these views and specifically endorsing black rights, the Republican convention selected a state executive committee to coordinate the party's organization at the local level and provide overall direction to its members during the crucial months ahead. Holden was appointed to the committee, which contained a majority of his supporters, including the black members, and he was later elected its chairman.[8]

The convention was still in session when the conservative press began its campaign of vilification against the "Holden miscegenationists," as the Wilmington *Dispatch* deliciously branded the delegates.[9] The editor of the Weldon *State* raged that in the Raleigh convention "we see organized, under the vigilant direction of a disappointed politician [Holden], a set of unprincipled men, congregated for the purposes of vengeance, and reveling in the misfortunes of a ruined people."[10] William E. Pell, Holden's nemesis on the Raleigh *Sentinel*, claimed that the "ill-concealed design of many of [the delegates] is to disfranchise, if possible by the aid of the colored man, the greater portion" of North Carolina whites and then "inaugurate just such a Pandemonium here as curses and darkens the unhappy State of Tennessee. A more fiendish spirit never prompted human action." Despite their bitterness at the imposition of black suffrage, most conservative spokesmen avoided racial epithets in their campaign against the "Holden convention," since they hoped to persuade black voters that they were the black man's "best friends."[11] It was an illusion born of desperation, fueled by the unrealistic expectation that blacks would scorn the leadership of a former disunionist like Holden. Before the fall election—the first under congressional reconstruction—conservatives would be disabused of the illusion and would adopt a strategy of "masterly inactivity" that refused to recognize the enfranchisement of blacks.

8. Raleigh *Standard*, April 3, 17, June 12, 1867.
9. As reported in *ibid.*, April 3, 1867.
10. As reported in the Raleigh *Semi-Weekly Sentinel*, April 3, 1867.
11. Raleigh *Semi-Weekly Sentinel*, March 30, April 3, 1867; Greensboro *Patriot*, March 29, 1867. For reports of conservative efforts to win black support, see the Raleigh *Standard*, April 24, May 1, 1867.

Immediately after the March convention Holden and his allies went to work to organize the Republican party on the local level. Holden himself spoke at Republican organizational meetings in Wake County, and he was joined by representatives of all three elements in the new party—carpetbaggers, blacks, and scalawags. The local Republican rallies were frequently large, especially in predominantly black counties in the East. In the overwhelmingly white western counties the meetings were fairly small and attended mainly by whites. Following traditional patterns, the Republican meetings were open and often attended by curious conservatives.

Simultaneously with the regular organization of the party, secretive, oath-bound Union Leagues sprang up like mushrooms where the black population was relatively large. The main purpose of these legendary Republican auxiliaries was the formation of blacks into an unintimidated phalanx of voters that would support the Republican party during Reconstruction. The Union League, or Loyal League of America, appeared in the state in 1866, but it had made little progress until after the passage of the reconstruction acts in March, 1867. Holden himself served as president of the league's Grand Council for North Carolina and, with his customary energy and forcefulness, provided the leadership for the thorough organization of the league in the state. During his one-year tenure as president, Holden maintained a tight control of the local councils. He demanded that the officers submit reports on membership to him, insist on voter registration of all their members, and "guard well the passwords and signs of the order." Probably in no other state were the Republicans as successful in providing central direction for the Union Leagues as in North Carolina. The success of the society in the state was due not only to Holden's leadership. Blacks eagerly joined the order and participated in its political and social activities. Possessing a relatively small percentage of the state's total population (about one-third), North Carolina blacks welcomed the security of numbers and the discipline offered by the league in the face of numerous hostile whites.[12]

Despite the phenomenal success of Republicans in organizing at

12. W. W. Holden to Albion W. Tourgée, April 3, 25, 1867, printed letter from Holden to local presidents and officers of the ULA, July, 1867, in Albion W. Tourgée Papers (on microfilm), Roll 5, Nos., 713, 719, 739, SHC; Raleigh *Standard*, May 15, October 9, 1867; printed letter of W. W. Holden to officers and members of the

224 William Woods Holden

the grass roots, disaffection boiled among party leaders as they prepared for the convention election to be held in the fall of 1867. Not surprisingly, Holden was the cause of some of the discontent, though fundamental differences over the party platform also created serious divisions. Both Radical carpetbaggers like Albion W. Tourgée and conservative Republicans like Daniel R. Goodloe and Benjamin S. Hedrick seethed with resentment over Holden's preeminence in the party. They believed that he was a political charlatan and (in the case of Tourgée) no real friend of blacks or (in the cases of Goodloe and Hedrick) of the Union. They convinced themselves that Republican reconstruction would be jeopardized if the controversial Raleigh editor continued his leading role in the party.

At a meeting of the state executive committee in June the Goodloe-Hedrick faction made the first move against Holden. Instead of attacking him directly, Goodloe, who was a member of the committee, secured the passage of a motion calling for a second state Republican convention, to meet in Raleigh in September. Ostensibly its purpose would be to prepare for the fall election. Goodloe's real objective, however, was to end Holden's control by packing the convention with his opponents, who would dutifully dismiss him from the executive committee and adopt a conservative platform that would endorse only the minimum requirements of congressional reconstruction. Not incidentally, the reorganized party would also put Goodloe in the governor's office after the state was reconstructed.[13]

By the time of the convention Holden had beaten back the Goodloe challenge, but a more serious threat to his ascendancy had emerged. Carpetbaggers, though relatively few in number, as local party organizers during the spring and summer had developed impressive strength in the black communities of the East and the Piedmont. Their energy, their unspotted devotion to the Union, and their greater sympathy for the freedmen had given them an advantage over the often standoffish and Negrophobic scalawags.

ULA, October 18, 1867, in Calvin Cowles Papers, NDAH; Otto H. Olsen, *Carpetbagger's Crusade: The Life of Albion Winegar Tourgée* (Baltimore, 1965), 80, 83.

13. Kemp Battle to Benjamin S. Hedrick, June 12, 1867, in Hedrick Papers. For Goodloe's resolution, see Raleigh *Standard*, June 12, 1867, New Bern *Republican*, June 11, 1867, and Lancaster, "The Scalawags of North Carolina," 242–43.

Some of these transplanted northerners were determined to make their influence felt in the state party and root out scalawag leaders like Holden, who they characterized as "disfranchised rebels." To Holden, the emergence of the carpetbaggers not only threatened his leadership but also threatened to destroy the scalawag effort to win substantial white support for the party. Although carpetbaggers were not of one mind, they tended to be more radical than the scalawags, believing, along with some black leaders, that the confiscation of the property of prominent rebels was desirable if southern whites continued their contumacy toward reconstruction. Such men were viewed by most North Carolina whites, including many native unionists, as vindictive political adventurers who had little interest in the welfare of the state and were in fact determined to complete its ruin. Powerful scalawags such as John Pool, Robert P. Dick, and Alfred Dockery, more so than Holden, who had welcomed northerners to the state, resented the growth of carpetbagger influence and were determined to resist the radicalization of the party.[14]

Tension gripped the state Republican convention when it met in Tucker's Hall in Raleigh on September 4. David Heaton, a carpetbagger friend of the scalawags, was selected temporary president of the convention, and almost immediately, when debate erupted over the credentials of the delegates, he appointed Holden to chair a committee to recommend a solution. Holden reported that all claimants should be seated, which created some opposition on the floor, because it gave Wake and neighboring counties, Holden strongholds, a disproportionate share of the delegates. Of the 286 delegates in the convention, most of whom reportedly were black, Wake claimed 49 and nearby Johnston County claimed 22. The convention approved Holden's report, bolstering the Raleigh editor's strength as the struggle over control began.[15]

The main conflict occurred when carpetbagger Joseph C. Abbott was nominated for permanent president of the convention, the

14. John Pool to David M. Carter, September 31 (30?), 1867, in David Miller Carter Papers, SHC; David Hodgin to Benjamin S. Hedrick, September 20, 1867, John A. Hedrick to Benjamin S. Hedrick, September 22, 1867, in Hedrick Papers; Olsen, *Carpetbagger's Crusade*, 86.

15. For the proceedings of the Republican convention, see the Raleigh *Standard*, September 11, 1867.

position that dominated proceedings and controlled membership on the committees. Carpetbagger Byron Laflin, who like Heaton had a foot in the Holden camp, followed with the nomination of scalawag John B. Odom, explaining that because of understandable southern prejudices against newcomers like Abbott it would be wiser to elect as president "a Southern man of known Union proclivities" than a person of northern birth. When a carpetbagger of New Hanover County labeled Laflin a "white Northern Copperhead," the debate became intense, though powerful scalawags such as Pool and Holden remained silent. Finally, James W. Hood, a Fayetteville black leader and a native of Pennsylvania, proposed a compromise that a hurriedly called caucus of black delegates had already approved. The plan, which was adopted, called for the election of Abbott as president, Pool as chairman of the important Committee on Resolutions and Platform, and Holden as chairman of the state executive committee charged with directing the fall campaign. This arrangement seemed satisfactory to most delegates, and they settled back in their seats to hear speeches while awaiting the report on the platform.[16]

The delegates got more than they bargained for in the speeches. Holden took to the floor and unleashed a stinging tirade against his enemies, particularly those outside of the Republican party. He obviously wanted to demonstrate to critics the soundness of his Republicanism and his commitment to black equality. In the process he contributed, probably not by design, to the increasingly radical mood in the convention. He began his declamation by denouncing the "vile secessionists and rebels" who had recently published "an anonymous pamphlet" designed "to injure me in the eyes of my colored friends here and throughout North Carolina." The pamphlet printed excerpts from prewar Holden editorials defending slavery and vilifying free blacks. In a rare admission of inconsistency, he acknowledged that his views toward blacks had changed, though he lamely claimed that even during the antebellum period he had been in advance of other whites in asserting the slave's "absolute equality in matters spiritual." He continued, "I [now] heartily welcome them to the freedom which the Union arms have secured for them" and the political equality that Congress had enacted. He

16. *Ibid.*

reminded the convention's black delegates, whose support for him was uncertain in view of the emergence of the carpetbaggers and the increased political involvement of blacks themselves, that in his speech of New Year's Day, 1867, he "was the first public man in North Carolina to declare . . . for general negro suffrage."[17]

Holden also lashed out at those persons, both inside and outside the party, who charged that he had been a fiery rebel during the war. As he did repeatedly throughout Reconstruction, Holden explained—somewhat weakly—that during the war he was "so surrounded by rebels and Confederate enemies . . . as a matter, more or less, of moral coercion, I was obliged to take a certain position against the National Government." But "I kept all the while burning in my heart the vestal fires of Liberty and Union," and these were given an outlet in the peace movement of 1863–1864, which, he reminded his audience, he had organized and led.

Finally, Holden defended the Republican convention from the savage assaults of the conservative press. By this time even moderate opposition journals had abandoned their futile effort to win black votes and in order to defeat reconstruction had launched a blatantly racist campaign against the Republicans. Holden reported to the delegates that earlier in the day the Raleigh *Sentinel* had referred to the convention as "the blacks and albinos in council" and contemptuously described the black minister-delegate who opened the session with a prayer as "a molasses complexioned individual." Raising his voice to an angry pitch, Holden warned the *Sentinel* editor and his political associates that "if they desire to provoke the Republican party of this State by persistence in their infernal schemes of rebellion and by the perpetuation of those sentiments and principles which dragged this people from their lofty height of prosperity and honor, and involved all in a common ruin . . . so help me Heaven, I shall insist upon it that the nation shall hold them to the most rigid and terrible responsibility for their crimes." Later, in the debate on the party platform Holden indicated what punishment he would demand if "rebel" obduracy continued. If reconstruction were defeated in North Carolina, he

17. Holden's speech is in the Raleigh *Standard*, September 11, 1867, and the Asheville *Pioneer*, September 26, 1867. He justified his inconsistency in this way: "He who is consistent during the entire portion of his public life, and who prides himself on it is consistent for the most part in the mistakes of the past."

declared, Congress should confiscate the property of those who had opposed it.[18]

Holden, having stoked the embers of radicalism in the convention, succeeded in reclaiming the mantle of leadership in the Republican party, though many scalawags were dismayed by his course.[19] His salute to radicalism also contributed to the defeat of resolutions, reported by John Pool's platform committee, opposing property confiscation and supporting the removal of Confederate political disabilities "within just and safe limits." With Holden's endorsement, the convention substituted for the Pool committee's resolution a statement indicating that North Carolina Republicans would support any action by Congress on the confiscation issue. The committee's resolution opposing political proscription was simply tabled, and the delegates went home to face a perplexed if not hostile unionist constituency.[20]

The defeat of the Pool resolutions threatened to drive many scalawag founders of the state Republican party and their white supporters out of the party. Pool himself, with the backing of other moderate scalawags like Robert P. Dick and Thomas Settle, as well as conservative Republicans like Goodloe and Hedrick, published a "Republican Address to the People of North Carolina" attacking the rising tide of radicalism in the state party and specifically the work of the September convention. The address also denounced

18. Raleigh *Standard*, September 11, 1867. Earlier in the year he had published Thaddeus Stevens' "Confiscation Speech" as a warning of what might occur unless North Carolina accepted the congressional reconstruction acts. *Ibid.*, April 13, 1867.

19. This account of Holden's success in maintaining his control in the party, despite concessions to the new elements in the unionist coalition, rejects the prevalent interpretation of historians that carpetbaggers controlled the September convention. See Lancaster, "The Scalawags of North Carolina," 245; Horace W. Raper, *William Woods Holden: North Carolina's Political Enigma* (Chapel Hill, 1985), 97; J. G. de Roulhac Hamilton, *Reconstruction in North Carolina* (New York, 1914), 246–47. The fact that scalawags, most of whom were loyal to Holden, dominated the new state executive committee was another indication of Holden's strength in the party by the time of the convention's adjournment.

20. Raleigh *Standard*, September 11, 1867; Raleigh *Register*, September 6, October 11, 1867; Daniel R. Goodloe to Robert P. Dick, September 30, 1867, in Thomas Settle Papers, SHC; Daniel R. Goodloe to Benjamin S. Hedrick, September 18, 1867, in Hedrick Papers; Raleigh *Daily Progress*, October 5, 1867.

carpetbagger efforts to control the party and impose Negro supremacy upon the state.[21]

The bitter disaffection of his longtime allies stunned Holden. He
knew that if prominent scalawags like Pool, Dick, and Settle left the
party or continued to divide it, his political strength would be
undercut and the moderate, native white Republican fulcrum that
he wanted to control North Carolina would be destroyed. In order
to prevent such an eventuality, Holden sought to placate scalawag
dissidents but without repudiating the work of the state Republican convention, an action that would surely have alienated his new
carpetbagger and black friends. He played down the failure of the
convention to renounce the principle of confiscation, asserting that
fears of property seizures were "groundless." Neither the reconstruction acts nor the resolutions adopted by the state Republican
convention, Holden indicated, supported the confiscation of "rebel"
property. No specific denial of this fact was necessary, he claimed.
Yet he reaffirmed the convention's decision that the issues of confiscation and political proscription "are in the hands of Congress,
and that the Republicans of this State shall keep even step with that
body."[22] He understood that the overwhelming majority in Congress had no appetite for confiscation. Holden's continued threat of
confiscation was designed to frighten uneasy North Carolinians
into supporting the work of reconstruction and thereby avoid a
prolonged process that, as had occurred in presidential reconstruction, would work to the advantage of conservative elements and
against the success of the Union party.

Holden also obtained the approval of the party's state executive
committee, which he chaired, to a resolution deprecating any action that would array blacks against whites or scalawags against
carpetbaggers. The committee, in addition, announced that it favored the congressional removal of the political disabilities of all
North Carolinians who "avail themselves promptly and in good
faith of the reconstruction acts," a position that would soften the
political proscription pronouncements of the Radicals.[23]

21. Pool's address is in the Raleigh *Register,* October 15, 1867, and also in the
Carter Papers.
22. Raleigh *Standard,* September 18, 25, October 9, 1867.
23. *Ibid.,* October 9, 1867; Asheville *Pioneer,* October 17, 1867.

These resolutions, along with the repeated assurances of Holden
in the *Standard*, soothed the troubled minds of the moderate scalawags. Pool, who hated "rebels" and their Worth coadjutors more
than he did "strangers" from the North, made his peace with the
party leadership. He soon became Holden's chief lieutenant and the
first North Carolina Republican elected to the United States Senate.
On the other hand, conservative unionists like Goodloe, Hedrick,
Hardie H. Helper, and Bartholomew F. Moore, who bitterly resented the leadership of Holden and who feared the control of
Radical "blackguards" and Negroes more than they did former
Confederates, abandoned the Republican party. They carried some
unionists with them into a new conservative party, but their bolt
was not serious enough to damage Republican chances in the first
election held under congressional reconstruction.

Having forestalled a major schism in the party, Holden entered the
final days of the 1867 election campaign with a quiet sense of optimism about Republican prospects. The registration of voters, conducted under military supervision and completed in mid-October,
gave Holden and his friends good reason to believe that a constitutional convention would be approved and Republican delegates
elected to it. Blacks constituted more than one-third of the 179,653
enrolled voters, and they were expected to vote in a bloc for the
party. In addition, prominent scalawags like Pool, Dockery, and
Settle, now that the Republican platform had been clarified to their
satisfaction, were campaigning vigorously for the cause. Based on
encouraging reports from grass-roots campaigners, Holden predicted that at least one-third of the registered white voters would
support the party in the election.[24]

The fact that the conservative opposition was divided on whether
to vote also buoyed Holden's spirits as election day approached.
William A. Graham, the most influential opponent of reconstruction in the state, believed that Democratic victories in the early fall
elections in the North portended the end of congressional reconstruction, and he appealed to whites to go to the polls and vote
down the convention. At the same time, Governor Worth, finding
the imposition of congressional reconstruction "positively humiliating," urged conservatives not to participate in a process "which

24. Raleigh *Standard*, October 23, 1867.

must establish universal negro suffrage." According to his reasoning, if whites refused to vote, the majority for the convention required by Congress would not be obtained, and the state would remain under the relatively benevolent rule of the military commander, with the Worth administration in control of most governmental functions. A few conservative spokesmen, accepting the reality of congressional reconstruction, advised whites both to support the convention and run conservative candidates for seats in it.[25] Because of the confusion of tongues, no state conservative party was organized during the campaign, which virtually ensured a large majority for the convention and the election of Republican delegates.

Holden, remembering the misplaced optimism of his gubernatorial campaigns of 1864 and 1865, was taking no chances in the 1867 contest. From Raleigh, he cajoled local Republican leaders to work diligently to perfect the organizations of both the Union League and the regular county units of the party. He urged party workers to get out a full Republican vote on election day and ensure that conservatives did not place the wrong ballots in the hands of blacks, who would be voting for the first time. In the Raleigh area especially, blacks who had been educated in northern missionary schools eagerly read the *Standard* and were guided by it.[26]

As was his custom, Holden, who was not himself a candidate for a seat in the convention, confined his campaigning to Wake County. He reassured voters that the Republicans "will do nothing more [radical] than may be deemed absolutely necessary to restore the Union and maintain loyal rule." He declared that his party "honors the Working-man . . . and looks with the greatest abhorrence upon aristocratical or monarchical governments." It was also "the only organization that can redeem and build up [the] State, and save and perpetuate the Republic with its free institutions." He decried the conservative charge of confiscation against the Republicans and also insisted that "the cry against 'Yankees and negroes' ruling the

25. *Ibid.*; William A. Graham to his son William, November 8, 1867, in William A. Graham Papers, NDAH; Salisbury *Union Banner*, issues of October, 1867; Jonathan Worth to William A. Graham, October 28, 1867, Worth to James W. Osborn, October 29, 1867, in J. G. de Roulhac Hamilton (ed.), *The Correspondence of Jonathan Worth* (2 vols.; Raleigh, 1909), II, 1066–68; Charlotte *Western Democrat*, October 15, 22, 29, 1867.

26. Raleigh *Standard*, October 23, 30, November 6, 20, 1867; H. C. Thompson to Benjamin S. Hedrick, November 9, 1867, in Hedrick Papers.

country" was a false one. As for his own attitude toward the new-comers, Holden announced that he was "anxious for all the aid I can get in restoring" the Union. "The true test" for office, he told a large rally of Republicans in Raleigh, "is character—merit. We are all in one sense Yankees, for we are all Americans. . . . We ought to cultivate friendly feelings with our Northern brethren. We ought to bid them come down here, and bid them welcome when they do come." He also defended the blacks' capacity for politics, though avoiding the issue of racial equality, and he labeled as absurd the conservative prediction that congressional reconstruction would lead to "a war of races."[27]

The election results were all that Holden could wish. His party swept almost every county, winning a resounding approval for the calling of a constitutional convention and capturing 107 of the 120 delegate seats in it. The election, Holden crowed, "is a most impressive vindication of the reconstruction policy of Congress, and it renders certain the power of the loyal people in this State for years to come." He particularly exulted in the large Republican majorities cast by blacks in the East, where the Union Leagues were strongest. Blacks, he exclaimed, "have demonstrated to the world that they are possessed in a high degree of that chief requisite to manhood and citizenship, to wit, firmness and determination of character. No people in any civil contest have ever met and overcome greater temptations than they have. They have been equally unmoved by artifice, trickery, falsehood, persuasion, bribes, and threats." He admonished white Republicans to "keep faith to the uttermost with the loyal colored people who have given us their votes, and who would pile up their bodies, if necessary, as a sacred offering to the cause of Liberty, Union, and political Equality." He also praised "the free white men of the West, who, uninfluenced by prejudice or the hellish, contemptible cry about 'negro supremacy,' have stood like their own native mountains by the Republican cause!" "The two races together will govern," Holden announced, and the status of blacks "will run coeval and coequal with that of the white race" except in "social and domestic intercourse," in which, he claimed, even black leaders did not seek equality.[28]

27. Raleigh *Standard*, October 23, 30, November 6, 1867.
28. *Ibid.*, November 27, December 4, 18, 1867.

Conservatives were shaken to the marrow by the overwhelming success of the Republicans and by the somber realization that Holden and other so-called Radicals would soon be in control of North Carolina's affairs. On December 31 General Edwin R. S. Canby, who in August had replaced General Sickles in command of the district, directed that the constitutional convention should assemble in Raleigh on January 14, 1868. Many of the old citizens feared that the worst would happen when the convention met. The "blackguard" majority, they seriously believed, would enact "social equality" between the races, proscribe the political and civil rights of former Confederates, and confiscate property either by imposing heavy taxes and seizing the land for their nonpayment or adopting a policy of outright expropriation.[29] Few conservatives, however, would have agreed with Holden—or, for that matter, with late-twentieth-century historians of Reconstruction—that their refusal to recognize the legitimate concerns of the victorious Union had contributed immensely to the triumph of the new political order and moved North Carolina close to a radical political transformation.[30]

29. Otto H. Olsen (ed.), *Reconstruction and Redemption in the South* (Baton Rouge, 1980), 167; Raleigh *Semi-Weekly Sentinel,* December 4, 7, 1867, January 1, 1868; William L. Harris to Calvin H. Wiley, January 16, 1868, in Calvin H. Wiley Papers, SHC.

30. For the contribution of the southern resistance to the success of congressional Radicals, see Allen W. Trelease, *Reconstruction: The Great Experiment* (New York, 1971), 74, and Kenneth M. Stampp, *The Era of Reconstruction, 1865–1877* (New York, 1967), 118.

XII
Scalawag Governor: Part I

The convention that assembled in the state capitol on January 14, 1868, was not the Radical conclave of ignorant blacks and white scamps depicted by the opposition. As in most deliberative bodies, men of incompetence, immoral standing, and extreme views were present. But such delegates were not typical of the 1868 constitutional convention. Neither was the North Carolina convention dominated by alien carpetbaggers, as has been commonly assumed about many southern reconstruction assemblages.[1] Although the eighteen carpetbagger members exercised an influence in the deliberations greater than their numbers would indicate, it was the seventy-seven scalawag delegates, forty-eight of whom had been in the Holden-led peace movement, who controlled the convention. Calvin J. Cowles, a political ally of Holden and soon to be his son-in-law, presided over the convention, and he selected scalawags to chair eight of the thirteen committees that drafted the constitution. None of the fifteen black delegates chaired a major committee, but Negro leaders James H. Harris, James W. Hood, and A. H. Galloway, though differing on reconstruction priorities, consistently gave full voice to their ideas. The handful of conservative

---

1. For the traditional view of the convention see J. G. de Roulhac Hamilton, *Reconstruction in North Carolina* (New York, 1914), 264–78. On the South as a whole see E. Merton Coulter, *The South During Reconstruction, 1865–1877* (Baton Rouge, 1947), 134–36.

delegates served mainly to obstruct the proceedings and arouse white opposition to the new constitution.[2]

On the sidelines, Holden did not directly have a hand in the framing of the constitution. However, as the editor of the state party organ he influenced the mood of the delegates and the direction that they took on a number of important issues. He encouraged Republican delegates to refuse any compromise with their "enemies," while at the same time cautioning them not to go beyond the congressional requirement of equal political and civil rights for blacks. He interpreted the will of Congress to mean that "no man should be allowed to vote or hold office who will not solemnly swear to maintain the rights" of blacks.[3] The convention rejected Holden's advice on this voter requirement, probably because moderate scalawags viewed it as proscriptive and certain to lose white support for the Republican party. Unlike the case in several neighboring states and despite the constant abuse from the state conservative press, the North Carolina convention turned down all proposals for the disfranchisement of whites.

Holden also called upon the constitutional convention to provide relief for the large number of people who were suffering from the virtual collapse of the state's economy in early 1868. He reported that the failure of the 1867 grain crop and the sudden fall in the price of cotton—still the leading staple crop of North Carolina—had shattered the hopes of all groups for recovery. Because of the hard times, "judgments are pressed—execution sales are common—the [federal] bankrupt law is taking hold of estate after estate," and soon "thousands are likely to be stripped of all they have, while the large amount of property thus put upon the market must pass into the hands of the few who happen to have money or credit." He declared that "every sympathy of our nature is touched by the appeals that are reaching us by mail," and he asked the convention to stay the collection of debts "until the next crop is made and until the State can begin to realize some of the beneficial effects of its

2. Otto H. Olsen, *Carpetbagger's Crusade: The Life of Albion Winegar Tourgée* (Baltimore, 1965), 93–96; James L. Lancaster, "The Scalawags of North Carolina, 1850–1868" (Ph.D. dissertation, Princeton University, 1974), 281–82, 289.

3. Raleigh *Standard*, February 12, 1868.

restoration to the Union." Partly following Holden's advice, as well
as the demands of many people, the convention passed an ordinance suspending legal action on debts until July 1, 1868, or until
the new constitution went into effect.[4]

The scalawag editor also hotly defended the convention from the
intemperate attacks of conservatives. He referred to such tactics as
"low blackguardism" designed to defeat reconstruction, drive Republican leaders from public life, and perpetuate the "rebel" Worth
administration. "Never before," Holden exclaimed, "has there
been a legislative or Constitutional assembly in North Carolina
which has been characterized by greater merit or by a more exalted
patriotism." He specifically defended the carpetbaggers in the convention from the invective of the conservative press. "We are proud
to have such men among us as permanent settlers" and as members
of the constitutional convention, he said. He also denied that any
rivalry or antagonism existed between carpetbagger and scalawag
delegates, and falsely claimed that perfect harmony and good order
characterized the proceedings in the convention.[5]

The debate in the convention on racial separation in the public
schools caused Holden the greatest concern. When the conservatives assailed Republican delegates for their reluctance to require
the racial segregation of the new school system, Holden immediately recognized that the issue could become the Achilles heel of
the new political order. He understood that the convention must
placate whites on the matter in order to win support for the party
in the white community. At the same time, he knew that if the convention went too far in this direction it would alienate blacks from
the scalawag leadership and impel them to support the Radicals.
Black Republicans wanted at least to keep open the door for the
future integration of the schools. As a solution to the difficulty,
Holden proposed that the convention make "no distinction in the
organic law between the two races" in the schools while at the same
time assuring whites that de facto segregation would exist. In the
end the convention followed the wishes of Holden and almost all

4. *Ibid.*, January 8, 29, 1868; *Constitution of the State of North-Carolina, Together with the Ordinances and Resolutions of the Constitutional Convention, Assembled in the City of Raleigh, Jan. 14th, 1868* (Raleigh, 1868), 45–46.
5. Raleigh *Standard*, January 22, 29, February 5, 1868.

white Republicans when it ignored the question, presumably leaving the matter for the General Assembly to decide, provided it
chose to act.[6]

As in other southern states, the opposition to congressional reconstruction soon abandoned its policy of "masterly inactivity" and
organized a political party to defeat the ratification of the new constitution and its Republican sponsors. At first styling themselves the
"Constitutional Union party," a term that would appeal to old
Whigs without offending Democrats, more than three hundred opponents of Holden and the Republicans met in Raleigh on February 5 and formed what officially became known as the Conservative-
Democratic party. After listening to a bitter, uncompromisingly
white-supremacist speech by William A. Graham, the Conservative
convention adopted a resolution proclaiming that "the great and
all absorbing issue" in the forthcoming election was "negro suffrage and negro equality, if not supremacy." The Conservative platform called on North Carolina whites to unite against the threat
and save the state from a Radical despotism.[7]

The Conservatives' shrill strategy of seeking to divide the electorate along racial lines threatened to drive a wedge into the white
unionist ranks and undo the delicate coalition of whites and blacks
that Holden had forged. Republican success depended upon the
party's receiving a relatively large white vote (perhaps as high as
one-third of the total), which could not be achieved if many old
unionists and peace advocates followed the siren call of white supremacy into the party of their old enemies. Sensing the danger,
Holden, in an effort to forestall unionist defections on the race
issue, profusely recalled the calamitous war record of the Conservative kingpins. With stronger hyperbole than usual, he denounced
the Conservative leaders as a "desperate set of conspirators" who
during the war "shot and hung conscripts . . . whipped women and

6. *Ibid.*, March 11, 1868.
7. Edward H. McGee, "North Carolina Conservatives and Reconstruction"
(Ph.D. dissertation, University of North Carolina, Chapel Hill, 1972), 252; Raleigh
Semi-Weekly Sentinel, February 8, 1868. The party was more commonly referred
to as the Conservative party; however, it struck an early alliance with the national
Democratic party.

put their thumbs under the fence, or justified or ordered it, [and] opened smokehouses and corncribs" for rapacious Confederate impressment officers. He declared that the main purpose of the "Rebel" chiefs during the war was to perpetuate their political control. "It was to gratify their lust for power that this broad land was ridged with graves," he exclaimed. Now, after the bloodletting, "nothing will satisfy these Rebel leaders save their complete restoration to power, the extinction of every noble sentiment of freedom in the colored race," and the punishment of unionists. Their strategy for regaining power, Holden told North Carolinians, was "to excite the evil passions" of race, which had been "so nearly extinguished" by the congressional reconstruction program. They planned to produce "a war of races" that would fulfill their dreadful predictions regarding black equality and galvanize white support against the new regime.[8]

The scalawag leader also moved quickly to prepare the Republican party for the crucial election on the not-yet-completed constitution. As chairman of the state executive committee, he issued a call for the selection of delegates to a state Republican convention to be held in Raleigh on February 26. The main purpose of the convention was to nominate candidates for state office. Although Holden was a candidate for governor, he evidently made no effort to influence the choice of delegates except to urge Republicans in every county either to send "fresh delegates" or authorize members of the constitutional convention to act for them. Nevertheless, Holdenites, representing all three elements in the party (scalawags, carpetbaggers, and blacks), dominated the well-attended convention that met in Tucker's Hall. A number of delegates, including a few close political friends of Holden, fretted that the *Standard* editor's candidacy for governor might lead to the party's defeat in the election. In order to relieve their concerns and perhaps also satisfy Holden's ambitions, his associates tried to persuade him to forgo the gubernatorial nomination and accept a later election to the United States Senate. Holden, however, knew that he was now master of the party and could capture the nomination. He rejected the overtures of his friends and became a candidate. Placed in nomination by black leader James W. Hood, Holden was chosen by ac-

8. Raleigh *Standard*, February 12, 19, 1868.

clamation to head the Republican ticket, which also contained four other scalawags and two carpetbaggers.[9]

Members of the small Goodloe-Hedrick wing of the Republican party could not bear the thought of their old enemy becoming governor. They publicly denounced Holden's nomination and intrigued to put a conservative Republican ticket in the field. Wealthy unionist Israel G. Lash of Forsyth County was Goodloe's choice to head the ticket, but he refused to bolt the regular party, whereupon Hardie H. Helper, the editor of the Raleigh *Register*, brought out Goodloe for governor on a platform supporting the ratification of the constitution.[10] Helper also began publication of an ephemeral campaign sheet entitled *Holden's Record*, in which he, like other anti-Holdenites before him, extracted incriminating material from past issues of the *Standard*. But North Carolina Republicans refused to follow the Goodloe dissidents into revolt against Holden. They knew that a major division in the party, which could not be avoided if Holden were seriously challenged, would defeat the ratification of the constitution and result in the triumph of the reactionary Conservative party.

Even without a Republican division, Conservative leaders expected the inflammatory race issue and the disrepute of Holden to carry them to victory. "If Radical rule prevails in North Carolina," the Raleigh *Sentinel* told whites, "we shall have not only negro policemen, but negro mayors, negro magistrates, negro judges, and 'nigger everywhere.' . . . Arouse, white men . . . before the black rotters are irrevocably fixed upon you." Conservative spokesmen repeatedly charged that under the new constitution white children would be compelled to go to school with blacks and "social equality" would occur. The editor of the Greensboro *Times* passionately announced that "if it be treason to hate Holden and the other negro worshippers, then there will be room for a big hanging after the election is over. Holden has deceived every party he ever be-

9. *Ibid.*, January 29, February 5, 1868; Calvin Cowles to Alfred Dockery, February 15, 1868, Cowles to Tod R. Caldwell, March 6, 1868, in Letterbook P, Calvin Cowles Papers, NDAH; Asheville *Pioneer*, March 12, 1868; Daniel R. Goodloe to Benjamin S. Hedrick, March 27, 1868, in Benjamin S. Hedrick Papers, DU. The proceedings of the state Republican convention are found in the Raleigh *Standard*, March 4, 1868.

10. Daniel R. Goodloe to Benjamin S. Hedrick, March 8, 13, 27, 1868, John A. Hedrick to Benjamin S. Hedrick, April 3, 1868, in Hedrick Papers.

longed to, and his putrid carcus [*sic*] was so politically corrupt that
even the negroes loathe him." In what must have been the most un-
usual speech in the campaign, the condemned outlaw Tom Dula, as
he mounted the gallows, attacked Holden's credibility and predicted that ruin would accompany his control of the state.[11]

North Carolina whites found the issues of Holden and black
domination far more appealing than they did the Conservative candidates who were nominated for state office in case the constitution
was ratified. Bitter division existed in the party over the political
antecedents of prospective nominees. When Vance refused the nomination for governor because of conservative unionist opposition to
him, the state party executive committee selected Thomas S. Ashe,
whose secessionist credentials did nothing to improve the situation.
Twenty of the twenty-five Conservative candidates for state office
(including judgeships) were former Whigs, but unionists and Civil
War peace men, whose support was crucial to the success of the
white unity campaign, believed correctly that the old Vance-Graham
war faction dominated the new party.[12]

Holden, along with other Republican leaders, took to the stump
in March to drive the wedge deeper into Conservative ranks and
also rally blacks to the Republican standard. He went down the railroad to Morehead City, speaking to more than a thousand people
each at Goldsboro and New Bern and several hundred at Kinston
and Beaufort. The majority of these audiences were made up of
blacks. He returned to Raleigh with a severe cold but almost immediately departed on the North Carolina Railroad for a swing along
the Piedmont crescent to Charlotte. Despite the excitement of the
contest, only one threatening incident marred his western canvass.
At Charlotte anti-Holdenites, on the night before he was to speak,

11. Raleigh *Sentinel,* quoted in McGee, "North Carolina Conservatives and
Reconstruction," 260; Greensboro *Times,* April 16, 1868; Manly Wade Wellman,
Dead and Gone: Classic Crimes of North Carolina (Chapel Hill, 1954), 184;
Charlotte *Western Democrat,* May 19, 1868.

12. Zebulon B. Vance to Samuel McDowell Tate, March 1, 10, 1868, in Samuel
McDowell Tate Papers, SHC; Vance to William A. Graham, March 2, 1868, Wil-
liam E. Pell to Graham, March 5, 1868, in William A. Graham Papers, NDAH;
Charlotte *Western Democrat,* March 10, 1868; William H. Bagley to Benjamin S.
Hedrick, May 1, 1868, in Hedrick Papers; Jonathan Worth to Nathaniel Boyden,
May 4, 1868, in J. G. de Roulhac Hamilton (ed.), *The Correspondence of Jonathan
Worth* (2 vols.; Raleigh, 1909), II, 1194.

burned him in effigy, an act that apprehensive town fathers quickly condemned. A relatively large number of whites, in addition to blacks, heard him speak at Charlotte, Salisbury, Lexington, and High Point; at Charlotte he was introduced by former Confederate General Rufus Barringer, who had cast his lot with the Republican party.[13]

Everywhere Holden spoke, the theme was the same: neither the Republican party nor the new constitution was radical on the race issue. He castigated the "designing rebel demagogues" for raising the bugaboo of "social equality" against his party and the constitution, and he ridiculed the notion that "negro domination" would occur under Republican rule. Neither black nor white Republicans, he claimed, wanted the racial integration of the public schools or any state institution. He also asserted that, despite Conservative claims and despite the fact that the law did not prohibit it, interracial marriage would rarely occur. Although the *Standard* and the Charlotte *Union Republican* raised a class issue—i.e., that the white working class should unite behind the Republicans to prevent the restoration to power of the slaveholding aristocracy now represented by the Conservative party—Holden avoided the issue in his campaign. As had been his editorial custom, candidate Holden repeatedly recalled the state's tragic political history during the "rebellion" in order to demonstrate the perfidy of his foes and conversely to prove his own rectitude. The crisis of reconstruction had been reached, he proclaimed to his audiences. The issue was simple: "Are we to have peace and prosperity and a restoration of the Union, or are we to go out again upon a dark and stormy sea of revolution without knowing our bearings, or whither we may be drifted? It was to divert attention from this one issue," he insisted, "that the hue and cry against the black man had been raised."[14]

Returning home, Holden and his family were greeted as they walked to church the next morning by an effigy of him hanging on the Capitol Square. The incident precipitated a free-wheeling fight between Jo Holden and the vituperative anti-Republican editors of

13. Raleigh *Standard*, March 11, 18, 25, 1868. When he launched his campaign, Holden turned over the editorship of the *Standard* to his son Jo and William M. Coleman.

14. Charlotte *Union Republican*, March 24, 1868; Raleigh *Standard*, March 25, April 8, 1868.

the Raleigh *North Carolinian*; luckily no one was seriously injured in the affray. But Holden, still suffering from the cold that he had contracted in his eastern swing, limited his speaking engagements for the remainder of the brief campaign. In late April, one week before the election, he delivered his last campaign speech before an enthusiastic Republican audience in Raleigh.[15]

The contest ended on a tranquil note except for a few minor incidents caused mainly by the first appearance of the Ku Klux Klan in North Carolina. The presence of military units ensured a generally free election, and 84 percent of the registered voters cast ballots. The Republicans again swept to victory, though their success was not as great as in the fall election when the opposition employed its foolish strategy of "masterly inactivity." The constitution was ratified, Holden captured the governorship by a vote of 92,235 to Ashe's 73,593, the Republicans won the other state offices, and the party gained solid control of the General Assembly.[16]

Perhaps as many as thirty-five thousand whites, or almost 30 percent of the registered white voters, supported the Republican party in the election. This success in the white community reinforced the sanguine view of Holden and other scalawag leaders that a biracial party could succeed in the state despite the Conservatives' passionate appeal to white supremacy.[17] The Civil War issues and the need for a reconstruction peace, which Holden had emphasized during the campaign, had more importance than the race issue for the relatively large number of whites who voted Republican in the election. The white Republican vote was distributed throughout North Carolina and was not heavily concentrated in the West, as has been commonly assumed; indeed, twelve mountain counties voted against Holden in the election.

While Holden and associates proclaimed the beginning of a new era, forebodings of doom echoed through the Conservative camp. Governor Worth gloomily observed that the "dregs of society" had

15. Calvin Cowles to David Heaton, March 23, 1868, in Letterbook P, Cowles Papers, NDAH; Raleigh *Standard*, April 22, 1868.

16. Raleigh *Standard*, April 29, May 6, 1868; William J. Clarke Diary, April 23, 1868, in William J. Clarke Papers, SHC. For the election returns see John L. Cheney (ed.), *North Carolina Government, 1585–1979: A Narrative and Statistical History* (Raleigh, 1981), 1402–1403.

17. Raleigh *Standard*, May 20, 1868; William B. Rodman to W. W. Holden, May 5, 1868, in William Woods Holden Papers, NDAH.

triumphed in the state, and with these elements in power he trusted that "anarchy is not to supplant civilization, but I can give no reason for this hope." Editor David Frank Caldwell of the Greensboro *Patriot*, who prided himself on his Civil War unionism, announced that "freedom, whose cradle was first rocked in our beloved old State, will be known no more." North Carolinians, Caldwell lamented, were "to be pitied that God in his wrath" would permit "such an unblushing creature as W. W. Holden to be placed over them for a day." [18]

A few prominent Conservative editors, however, called on the people to give Holden a chance as governor. William J. Yates of the Charlotte *Western Democrat*, an antebellum associate of Holden, told his readers that "the great mass of the people want quiet and rest from excitement." Yates warned that unless Conservative editors and politicians ceased their abuse of Holden and recognized the validity of the new Republican order, political turmoil would continue, threatening the social order in every community of the state. [19]

Most Conservative spokesmen brusquely rejected Yates's advice. At least one leader, Governor Worth, joined with the Hedrick-Goodloe faction of Republican dissidents in a campaign to prevent the inauguration of their old antagonist. These frustrated diehards appealed to Congress to refuse Holden's petition for the removal of his Fourteenth Amendment office-holding disabilities. Referring to the Raleigh editor as "one of the bloodiest rebels in the state," Hedrick recounted to Republican congressmen Holden's record on secession and war and reminded them also of his anti-Republican policies during presidential reconstruction. This former university professor fallaciously claimed that Holden as provisional governor in 1865 had "endeavored to place nearly all power in the hands of the old rebel democracy, and to restore that party to power." When the reconstruction acts were passed, he "turned a short corner, denied all his acts of rebellion and treason, declared he was a republican, and at once went to organize the negroes to get their votes, but kept up his old hostility to the antislavery republicans in the state

18. Jonathan Worth to Benjamin S. Hedrick, May 11, 1868, in Hamilton (ed.), *Correspondence of Worth*, II, 1201; Greensboro *Patriot*, May 1, 29, 1868.

19. Charlotte *Western Democrat*, May 5, 26, 1868; Raleigh *Standard*, June 3, 1868.

and to the men who opposed him in his efforts to restore the old secession party." [20]

Despite the Hedrick-Worth campaign against him, the congressional leadership praised Governor-elect Holden as "a noble man" who "had fully renounced Secessionism and all the errors of his ways." On June 25 Congress removed his office-holding disabilities as well as those of seven hundred fellow North Carolina Republicans. On the same day Congress passed a bill, over President Johnson's veto, providing that, since the constitutions of North Carolina and five other southern states had met the readmission requirements of Congress, the newly elected governors could convene their legislatures for the purpose of ratifying the Fourteenth Amendment, the final requirement for reconstruction. Holden, who had gone to Washington in May to lobby for the immediate installation of his government, did not wait for the bill to be enacted; on May 15 he issued a call for the North Carolina legislature to assemble in Raleigh on July 1. On June 29 General Canby, the district commander, instructed Richmond M. Pearson, the newly elected chief justice, to take the oath of office and then administer it to Holden. Three days later Holden became governor of North Carolina, replacing Worth, who, under what he termed "military duress," bitterly surrendered the executive office. That same day the Republican legislature ratified the Fourteenth Amendment, and General Canby lifted military authority in the state, though he reserved the right to intervene if the new regime encountered resistance. [21]

July 4, 1868, was a banner day for Holden and North Carolina Republicans. It was inauguration day for the new political order, and combined with Independence Day festivities, it brought hun-

20. Benjamin S. Hedrick to John Covode, June 22, 1868, Hedrick to Senator Lyman Trumbull, June 8, 1868, in Hedrick Papers. See also Jonathan Worth to Senator James R. Doolittle, May 11, 1868, Worth to Benjamin S. Hedrick, May 22, 1868, Worth to Senator William P. Fessenden, May 26, 1868, in Hamilton (ed.), *Correspondence of Worth*, II, 1198–99, 1207–1208, 1211–12.

21. Frank Fuller to Benjamin S. Hedrick, May 8, 1868, in Hedrick Papers; Richard L. Zuber, *Jonathan Worth: A Biography of a Southern Unionist* (Chapel Hill, 1965), 286; Hamilton, *Reconstruction in North Carolina*, 289–90; Raleigh *Standard*, June 17, 1868; General E. R. S. Canby to W. W. Holden, June 29, 1868, in Holden Papers, NDAH; Canby to Holden, July 3, 1868, Jonathan Worth to Holden, July 1, 1868, in Letterbook of Governor William Woods Holden, 1868–1870, NDAH.

dreds of Republicans pouring into downtown Raleigh in the early morning. At nine o'clock a "vast procession" began to weave its way through the dusty streets, moving toward Capitol Square, where state Republican dignitaries had assembled to hear Holden's inaugural address. Before a crowd of five thousand people, the new governor delivered a speech that was both well-reasoned and well-received, even by some Conservatives.[22] Speaking in a tone strikingly different from the strident language of his editorials and campaign addresses, Holden proclaimed the final end of the "Great Rebellion" and announced that the Union "has been preserved not only on its former basis of liberty for one race" but also of liberty "for the whole people, of whatever origin, color or former condition." He sanguinely predicted that "the passions which the rebellion engendered and evoked . . . can neither inflict us hereafter nor retard the progress of free principles on this continent."[23]

He specifically underscored black political equality as a fundamental principle whose preservation was essential to political and racial peace. "There is no power that can deprive" southern blacks of their political rights "without plunging us into a protracted and terrible civil war," he told his audience. "Four millions of human beings who have once tasted the blessings of freedom, would not surrender those blessings without a struggle. They would find powerful friends here and elsewhere in the country," and in the end "liberty for all would again triumph." He indicated that racial conflict could be avoided "if every one will faithfully submit to the Constitution and laws, and follow the things that make for peace and good will among the people." He insisted that black suffrage would "operate beneficially for all, [and] the repugnance to it, which exists among many of our people, will gradually subside, when they shall be convinced by actual experience that none of the evils they anticipated have resulted from it."[24]

Holden also announced that "the injunction of the Constitution

22. J. S. Harrington to John M. Harrington, July 7, 1868, in John McLean Harrington Papers, DU; Raleigh *Standard*, July 8, 1868; Charlotte *Western Democrat*, July 14, 1868.

23. "Inaugural Address of Gov. W. W. Holden, Delivered in Capitol Square, Raleigh, July 4th, 1868," in State of North Carolina, *Executive and Legislative Documents, 1868*, Doc. No. 2, pp. 1–2.

24. *Ibid.*, 3–4.

regarding education should be faithfully observed. Colleges, high schools, normal schools for the education of teachers, and public schools for all, should be established at the earliest practicable period, and liberally sustained from the public treasury. . . . The first duty of a free State is to educate its children," since "the structure and perpetuity of free institutions depend on the intelligence and virtue of the people." As he had done during the campaign, Holden in his inaugural address sought to alleviate white fears of racial integration in the schools. "It does not follow, nor does the Constitution require," he declared, "that the white and colored races shall be educated together in the same schools. It is believed to be better for both, and more satisfactory to both, that the schools should be distinct and separate. But they should be equally calculated to impart instruction, and . . . should enjoy equally the fostering care of the State." [25]

In his inaugural address the new governor also put a high premium on the economic development of North Carolina. Reviving a major theme that he had promoted before the war, Holden maintained that "a vigorous and well-directed system of internal improvements, from the seashore to the Tennessee line," connecting the state with the Mississippi Valley, "would stimulate agriculture and the mechanic arts, build up our seaports, increase our commerce both foreign and coastwise, draw thither immigrants from the Northern States and from Europe, arrest emigration from the State, give employment to thousands of our people, and thus place us at no very distant day in the front rank of American States." He also proposed that the state seek northern capital and skilled labor to develop its resources. To attract northerners, he urged North Carolinians to discard their "prejudices growing out of nativity, or out of the rebellion," and receive settlers "with courtesy and kindness." [26]

As he had done in his 1856 Fourth of July oration, Holden ended his inaugural address by singing paeans to the Union. The Civil War, he declared, had brought the suppression of the rebellion, vitiated the extreme states' rights philosophy held by Calhoun and followers, consolidated American liberties, and made possible the future greatness of the nation. "How beneficent, how glorious, how

25. *Ibid.*, 5–6.
26. *Ibid.*, 9–10.

far-reaching will be the light [the Union] will dispense when it reaches its meridian. We shall not live to see it, but the generations to come after us will walk in that light, and be contented, prosperous and happy. In the fullness of their gratitude they will thank God, as we do, that the government of the United States, delivered from the perils of rebellion, and reconstructed on the basis of the equal rights of all, is as indestructible as the earth itself." [27]

Soon after his inauguration Holden, in order to devote full-time to his gubernatorial duties, sold the *Standard* to a group of Republicans headed by carpetbagger Milton S. Littlefield. He received fifteen thousand dollars for the newspaper, which he wisely invested in United States bonds. In addition to $10,000 in bonds that he already possessed and the relatively high value of his Raleigh real estate, the sale of the *Standard* made Holden one of the most affluent residents of the state capital and provided him with a financial cushion for his eventual retirement from public óffice. [28]

Holden chose not to move into the dilapidated Governor's Palace, citing the expense to the state for the repairs and furnishings that would be necessary to make it livable. He reported to the legislature that his home on Hargett Street was adequate for state functions, and he recommended that the mansion "be rendered suitable for school purposes or for public offices." The General Assembly did not take his advice; instead ten thousand dollars was appropriated to restore the building. [29] Holden, who in this and other ways shunned the trappings of power, never lived in the house that was the symbol of executive authority in North Carolina.

After assuming the reins of office, Holden moved quickly to consolidate the new order in the state. He persuaded General Canby to revoke Governor Worth's midnight appointments of new railroad directors and proxies for the state, though he had ample authority to rescind them himself. A few days later he selected Republicans to fill these positions and indicated to them his choice for the presidency of each company, the most important office under state pa-

27. *Ibid.*, 11–12.
28. Raleigh *Standard*, July 15, 1868; testimony of Ida Holden Cowles before Referee S. F. Mordecai, February 20, 1904, in *F. L. Mahler and Wife* v. *W. R. Henry and Wife*, W. W. Holden Folder, Wake County Estates Records, NDAH.
29. W. W. Holden to the General Assembly, November 28, 1868, in Letterbook of Governor Holden.

tronage. The private stockholders of the Western North Carolina Railroad, however, defied Holden and defeated his new son-in-law, Calvin Cowles, for the presidency of the road. Holden threatened to take legal action against the "rebel stockholders," but he backed down when another Republican was elected to the office, though with diminished authority.[30]

A more serious conflict occurred over the new governor's replacement of local Conservative officials with Republicans. Soon after the election but before the inauguration, John Pool had written Holden that secessionists and members of the old war party "must be made to feel that loyal men *will* be the masters in this State." Pool, who would emerge as the governor's foremost adviser and a United States senator, warned Holden against compromising with his old enemies as he had done in 1865. "If you suffer your natural exuberance of kind feeling and personal generosity to betray you into the errors that became so apparent in your administration as provisional governor," Pool wrote him, "it will result in your own destruction as well as ours." When he became governor, Holden, following Pool's advice, seized upon an ambiguous wording in the new constitution and, reinforced by the disabling clause in the Fourteenth Amendment, began a wholesale removal of county and town officials, replacing them with Republicans until elections could be held. In several counties sheriffs and other officials refused to surrender their offices. Within sight of the governor's office in Raleigh, violence broke out when Holden's appointees unsuccessfully attempted to take over city hall. Holden immediately wired General Canby in Charleston for military assistance to put his men in office, only to be told at first that the governor had no constitutional grounds for removing the incumbents. After other reports of resistance reached him, Canby, though still insisting that the issue was a legal matter for the state to resolve, yielded to Holden's demand and sent troops into several counties to install the new appointees. A few days later the General Assembly settled the conflict

30. General E. R. S. Canby to Governor W. W. Holden, July 3, 1868, Holden to Canby, July 16, 1868, in *ibid.*; Calvin Cowles to James J. Mott, July 11, 1868, Calvin Cowles to Calvin Cowles, Jr., and Josiah Cowles, August 30, 1868, Calvin Cowles to J. L. Henry, August 31, 1868, in Letterbook P, Cowles Papers, NDAH.

by declaring all town offices vacant and authorizing the governor to fill them until elections could be held in January, 1869.[31]

Anticipating trouble as the 1868 presidential campaign began, Holden asked the General Assembly for the authority to organize the militia and county police units. Conservatives in the legislature immediately charged that the governor's proposal was "unconstitutional, subversive of the rights and liberties of the people of North Carolina, and well calculated to invoke the country in a disastrous civil war." Even some unionists, who had fought alongside Holden in the wartime struggle for constitutional rights, questioned the governor's motives in proposing the organization of military forces on the eve of the presidential election. Bartholomew F. Moore, a unionist supporter of Holden until 1867, believed that the governor in advancing his militia scheme was "fatally bent on mischief. There is no need for such a measure. His own fears and a heart bent on vindictiveness lie at the foundation of his want of force."[32]

Despite the bitter criticism—perhaps because of it—the Republican General Assembly on August 17, 1868, authorized the creation of a state militia under Holden's command. The legislature, however, evidently with the governor's approval, rejected the highly controversial proposal for county police units and placed restrictions on the militia. It provided that the companies must be racially segregated and that militiamen must not interfere with voters at the polls.[33]

Holden acted immediately to organize the militia. By September he had appointed high-ranking officers for the force and had given them instructions to enroll county units but not to activate them except on his orders. His efforts to form local units soon ran into difficulty. In three-fourths of the counties Holden could not find cap-

31. John Pool to W. W. Holden, May 9, 1868, in Holden Papers, NDAH; W. W. Holden to General E. R. S. Canby, July 14, 15, 16, 1868, Canby to Holden, July 15, 16, 22, 1868, in Letterbook of Governor Holden; *Public and Private Laws of North Carolina, Special Session, 1868* (N.p., 1868), 5.

32. *Journal of the House of Representatives of the General Assembly of the State of North Carolina, at Its Session of 1868* (Raleigh, 1868), 154–55; B. F. Moore to Benjamin S. Hedrick, August 14, 1868, in Hedrick Papers. See also George W. Welker to William L. Scott, August 4, 1868, in William Lafayette Scott Papers, DU.

33. *Laws of North Carolina, Special Session, 1868*, pp. 35–38.

tains who were willing to accept commissions and enroll troops. In rejecting appointment as officers, local Republicans claimed that militia duty would take them away from their farms and businesses during the critical harvest season. But the main reason for their refusal to serve was probably community hostility to Holden's "Radical army."[34]

The governor also sent north for arms and equipment, obtaining three thousand rifles on loan from state authorities in Vermont. At the same time, reports reached him that anti-Republican "desperadoes" were obtaining arms and threatening violence against blacks and their white friends. Holden, instead of activating his ill-prepared militia units, asked General George G. Meade, the departmental commander, to dispatch federal troops to threatened communities in the state. Meade at first agreed to send units to a few towns, but he soon backed down when the governor asked for additional assistance as the presidential election approached. The general, perhaps persuaded that Holden sought military intervention for electioneering purposes, lectured the governor on the need for state authorities to preserve the peace and declared that his forces would intervene only "if any actual resistance to law which you cannot suppress occurs."[35]

Left largely to his own devices—and these were undependable—Holden on October 12 issued a proclamation "admonishing the people to avoid undue excitement, to be peaceable and orderly, and to exercise the right of suffrage firmly and calmly, without violence or force of any kind" in the November election. He promised that the state government would suppress the lawless and directed local officers to aid in the work. He also reminded county officials that militia units could be organized to maintain order, but he directed that such forces should be deployed only "in strict subordination to the civil power." Nevertheless, in 1868 Holden, probably remembering his own implacable opposition to military "tyranny" during

34. Report of Adjutant General A. W. Fisher, November 10, 1869, in State of North Carolina, *Executive and Legislative Documents, 1869–1870*, Doc. No. 10, pp. 24–25.

35. W. W. Holden to General George G. Meade, August 25, September 14, 1868, R. C. Drum, Meade's adjutant, to Holden, September 15, 1868, in State of North Carolina, *Executive and Legislative Documents, 1870–1871*, Appendix, 17–19.

the war, authorized the activation of militia units in only two counties, Halifax and Robeson, the latter county being the haunts of Henry Berry Lowry, the Lumbee Indian outlaw.[36]

The presidential campaign itself was one of the most exciting political contests in North Carolina history. The governor did not campaign himself; instead he remained in Raleigh, where he participated in Republican rallies and entertained party functionaries.[37] With emotions high, both sides seemed genuinely to believe that their liberties and the state's future welfare depended on the outcome of the contest. Holden and his associates with justification feared that the triumph of the Democrat Horatio Seymour would doom the congressional reconstruction settlement, the new state constitution, and the Republican ascendancy in North Carolina. Leading "rebels," like Vance, Republicans believed, would then be restored to power and the rights of unionists and blacks would be crushed.[38] On the other hand Conservatives assumed that the success of the Republican ticket, headed by General U. S. Grant, would fasten on North Carolina and the South a "Radical despotism," backed by an ignorant black electorate, that would ultimately snuff out free government in America. Racism and the concern for constitutional liberty, as before the war, were merged in the bitter and fearful minds of many white North Carolinians. "Is it possible," a friend of Vance asked, "that the American People who once was [sic] the most free people on earth will quietly and tamely surrender their rights and liberties to those Negro worshippers and scoundrels" of the Radical party.[39]

36. State of North Carolina, *Executive and Legislative Documents, 1870–1871*, Appendix, 1–5; Governor's message, November 17, 1868, in State of North Carolina, *Executive and Legislative Documents, 1868–1869*, Doc. No. 1, pp. 12–13; Hamilton, *Reconstruction in North Carolina*, 372.

37. Clarke Diary, September 16, 1868, in Clarke Papers.

38. On Republican fears, see the September–October, 1868, issues of the New Bern *Republican* and the Raleigh *Standard;* Thomas Settle to R. M. Pearson, August 8, 1868, in Thomas Settle Papers, SHC; and William B. Rodman to his wife, n.d., 1868, in Rodman Family Papers, East Carolina Manuscript Collection, East Carolina University, Greenville, North Carolina.

39. J. C. Whitson to Zebulon B. Vance, October 19, 1868, in Tate Papers. For other shrill expressions of the Conservative position, see August 13, 1868, and October, 1868, in David Schenck Diary (Ms in SHC); Jonathan Worth to William Clark, October 1, 1868, in Hamilton (ed.), *Worth Correspondence*, II, 1247–58; and Raleigh *Semi-Weekly Sentinel*, September 19, October 1, 28, 1868.

Despite forebodings of violence, the election passed off quietly. The only significant exception was a racial clash in Asheville that left one black man dead. The presence of federal troops in various parts of the state, and General Nelson A. Miles's orders, following Governor Holden's request, that they be used to assist civil authorities in maintaining the peace, went far toward cooling election day ardor. In addition, Republican officials in Charlotte, Raleigh, Greensboro, Wilmington, and other hotly contested towns demonstrated a surprising ability to preserve the peace and ensure a free ballot. Coming so soon after the Civil War catastrophe, white moderates were frightened by repeated threats in the press of another war, and a number of their leaders quietly worked to prevent violence at the time of the election.[40]

Grant won the state with 53 percent of the votes, and his party captured six of the state's seven seats in Congress.[41] The Hero of Appomattox received 4,704 more votes than Holden had won in April, suggesting that Conservative intimidation and violence did not play a significant role in the election. Seymour, the Democratic candidate for president, however, polled almost 11,000 more votes than Holden's Democratic opponent in the gubernatorial contest, as the white Conservative masses continued to shake off their lethargy and vote for the party opposed to black political equality.

Holden and his Republican friends preferred to see only the bright side of the election results. Since Grant and the Republican party had triumphed nationally, they concluded that the contest had settled the issue of reconstruction with a ringing endorsement of the congressional program. National Republicans now seemed firmly in control and firmly committed to the cause of southern unionism and black political rights. At a giant victory celebration in Raleigh, Holden confidently announced that the Republican triumph had laid the foundations of the Republic "so securely on the principles of Freedom and Justice that hereafter we may fear

40. Charlotte *Western Democrat,* November 3, 10, 1868; *Speeches of Governor William Holden and Gen. Nelson A. Miles, in Raleigh, N.C., November 6, 1868, at the Grant and Colfax Celebration* (New York, 1869), 8; Raleigh *Standard,* August 19, November 11, 1868; R. M. Pearson to W. L. Scott, July 16, 1868, in Scott Papers.

41. Election returns are in Cheney (ed.), *North Carolina Government,* 1332–33.

nothing." He even taunted the Ku Klux Klan for its ineffectiveness in resisting the new political order. "The Ku Klux—nobody is afraid of them now. The truth is, we never were afraid of them here in North Carolina." Turning to the black majority in the crowd, Holden declared that "this election for the first time has given you practical assurance of your freedom. If it had gone against us . . . you would have [become] peons, serfs, with no substantial rights as citizens," a condition worse than slavery.[42]

In the afterglow of victory Holden was touted for a position in the Grant cabinet. Vice-President-elect Schuyler Colfax announced that the North Carolina governor would be offered a cabinet post, and Senator John Pool reported from Washington that he could have the position of secretary of the navy if he wanted it. But Pool probably expressed Holden's sentiments when he wrote a mutual friend, "I really feel that his services as Governor are necessary to the preservation of our party in the State."[43] At any rate Holden did not encourage the talk of a cabinet position for himself, and Grant soon dropped the idea.

In North Carolina Holden was heartened by reports of a sharp lessening in political tension after the fall election. A number of Conservative leaders and editors grudgingly acknowledged the legitimacy of Republican rule, acquiesced in black suffrage, and moderated their attacks on the national Republican leadership. "The State is quiet and tranquil," Holden informed the legislature when it met for its 1868–1869 session, and "there is no ground for apprehending . . . that the peace of the country will be disturbed." Based on a "richly crowned" fall harvest, he concluded that material prospects were propitious for the complete economic recovery of the state and for the success of Republicanism.[44]

Despite the upturn in the economy—which proved to be temporary—and the relative political peace that had followed the impres-

42. *Speeches of Holden and Miles at Grant and Colfax Celebration,* 3–4, 7.

43. Charlotte *Western Democrat,* December 15, 1868; John Pool to Thomas Settle, December 12, 1868, in Settle Papers.

44. Charlotte *Western Democrat,* December 1, 1868; Greensboro *Patriot,* May 20, 1869; Goldsboro *Daily Messenger,* July 2, 1869; Governor's message. November 17, 1868, in State of North Carolina, *Executive and Legislative Documents, 1868–1869,* Doc. No. 1, pp. 1–2; W. W. Holden to the North Carolina Land Company, April 19, 1869, in Little-Mordecai Collection, NDAH.

sive triumph of the Republican party in the 1868 elections, Holden knew that the ultimate fate of the new order would be largely determined by the success or failure of his administration to carry out the tenets of Republicanism and set the course for the state's permanent recovery from the harsh economic and social effects of the war. Racial tension and hostility to his government, he realized, remained a fact of life, but these destructive forces could be controlled by the wise implementation of the Republican program in North Carolina. This program, as outlined in the constitution of 1868, the state Republican platform, and Holden's inaugural address, called for the rehabilitation and expansion of public institutions, the creation of a comprehensive educational system for both races, state aid for economic development, and security for the rights of all citizens. Its realization, Holden believed, would ensure a permanent biracial democracy in North Carolina and eradicate completely the blighting incubus of sectionalism and war.

XIII
Scalawag Governor: Part II

Holden and his colleagues entered upon their tasks of rehabilitation and reform in an expansive and confident mood. They believed that, given an end to political turmoil, they could redeem the state from the destructive policies and inattention of the past, though they proposed no radical social reforms. A great deal needed to be done simultaneously if they were to implement the provisions of the constitution and fulfill the promises of Republican reconstruction. Requiring their immediate attention was the resuscitation and expansion of the state's institutions in order to accommodate the needs of a citizenry that had increased by one-third with the freedom of blacks. In addition to the insane asylum and the institution for the care of the deaf and blind, both created before the 1860s and neglected during and after the war, the new constitution provided for the establishment of a state penitentiary and the creation of a "Board of Public Charities, to whom shall be intrusted the Supervision of all charitable and penal State institutions, and who shall annually report to the Governor upon their condition, with suggestions for their improvement."[1]

Although interested in the development of the penal and charitable institutions, Holden rarely played an active role in their management. The board of public charities accumulated a massive amount of data on the appalling conditions in the county jails and

1. John L. Cheney (ed.), *North Carolina Government, 1585–1979: A Narrative and Statistical History* (Raleigh, 1981), 866.

poorhouses and, when it finally reported in 1870, recommended that the state revamp the system. But Governor Holden and the General Assembly, with other financial priorities to serve, ignored its findings, as did subsequent Conservative governments.[2]

On the other hand Holden took an active interest in the care of mentally ill North Carolinians. When the facilities in the asylum at Raleigh proved inadequate to meet the increased postwar needs, the governor appealed to the General Assembly for money either to expand the institution or to build a new one. "It is now crowded to repletion with the unfortunate," he told the legislature in 1870, "and there are hundreds of insane who should be cared for, and who cannot be received into the institution for the want of room." He declared that it was "a sacred duty which we owe to these unfortunates, to their families, to society and to ourselves, to make provision for every person within our borders who is thus afflicted." But neither the Republican legislature of 1869–1870 nor the Conservative one of 1870–1871 responded to his appeal, and the insane asylum continued to languish.[3]

Holden permitted the General Assembly to take the initiative in planning for a much-needed state penitentiary. A legislative committee selected a site on the Deep River, but before contracts were let, reports of fraud in the purchase of the land began to circulate. Under fire from all sides, the General Assembly abandoned the Deep River site and located the prison in Raleigh. Once the issue of the location had been settled, Holden sought to galvanize legislative support for the early completion of this "indispensable establishment," and he wrote county sheriffs seeking information on prisoners who could be transferred to the penitentiary as soon as adequate facilities were available. Although the prison was not completed until 1884, there were 220 convicts incarcerated in tem-

2. State of North Carolina, *Executive and Legislative Documents, 1869–1870,* Doc. No. 26; State of North Carolina, *Executive and Legislative Documents, 1872–1873,* Doc. No. 22, pp. 5–7.

3. Governor's message, November 16, 1869, in State of North Carolina, *Executive and Legislative Documents, 1869–1870,* Doc. No. 1, p. 12; Third annual message of Governor W. W. Holden, November, 1870, in State of North Carolina, *Executive and Legislative Documents, 1870–1871,* Doc. No. 1, p. 10; message of Governor Tod R. Caldwell, 1871, in State of North Carolina, *Executive and Legislative Documents, 1871–1872,* Doc. No. 1, pp. 25–26.

porary log-cabin cell-blocks there when Holden left office in 1870.[4]

The most distinctive feature of congressional or Republican reconstruction was its recognition of blacks as citizens possessing many of the rights and privileges of whites. Holden vigorously proclaimed his support for civil and political rights for blacks, but like other southern unionists, he had done so only after Congress had settled upon the policy as a means of undoing the damage that Johnson had caused in permitting the war party to return to power in the South. Like the majority of northern Republicans, he disapproved of laws requiring the racial integration of public facilities, a radical position advocated by Senator Charles Sumner of Massachusetts and favored by only a handful of white North Carolina Republicans. Holden warmed to the support of black suffrage and civil rights when blacks demonstrated their faithfulness to the Republican party by accepting his leadership in 1867–1868 and voting as a bloc for the party in the elections of those years. But he continued to believe that blacks needed "training in the art or habit of self-government" before they could participate equally with whites in public affairs.[5] Holden assumed that white Republicans would be their teachers.

The cautious position of Holden and other white Republican leaders on black equality was also influenced by a fear of losing white votes. A radical implementation of the principle of equality could drive from Republican ranks thousands of whites who, despite their antipathy for rebels, had been wary from the beginning of affiliating with a party that championed the cause of the Negro. Holden and associates believed that the new political order could not endure for long without substantial white support, which could only be secured through a circumspect policy on black rights. In practice this meant that blacks were excluded from high state office,

4. Horace W. Raper, *William Woods Holden: North Carolina's Political Enigma* (Chapel Hill, 1985), 116; State of North Carolina, *Executive and Legislative Documents, 1868–1869*, Doc. Nos. 7, 16, 19; Governor's message, November 17, 1868, in State of North Carolina, *Executive and Legislative Documents, 1868–1869*, Doc. No. 1, p. 14; Third annual message of Governor W. W. Holden, November, 1870, State of North Carolina, *Executive and Legislative Documents, 1870–1871*, Doc. No. 1, p. 11.

5. Governor W. W. Holden to the General Assembly, March 4, 1869, in Letterbook of Governor William Woods Holden, 1868–1870, NDAH.

including railroad positions, though black leader James W. Hood was appointed assistant state superintendent of public schools. Nevertheless, the doors of political opportunity were opened, with Holden's support, to many blacks. Holden himself broke the ice soon after his inauguration by appointing two blacks to the Raleigh city council. Many blacks also served as county and town officials, especially in the East, where fear of a white Republican backlash was not so great, and others played important roles in state and local Republican conventions. Nineteen blacks served in the General Assembly in 1868–1869, and one of them, James H. Harris, a Holden associate in Wake County politics, exercised considerable influence in the House of Representatives and in the party. Negro leaders in North Carolina, unlike their brethren in the Lower South, where black voters constituted a higher percentage of the voters, understood that if they pressed for advanced civil rights and for greater political recognition for their race, they risked defeat for the party. They appeared satisfied with Holden's moderate leadership and valued him as a true friend of their race.[6]

In a number of nonpolitical ways Holden demonstrated a keen interest in black welfare and progress. Before he became governor, he served on a three-member committee to administer the Boston Fund, a northern aid program for the relief of the acute sufferers of the southern crop failures of 1866–1867. Although some white farmers received assistance from the fund, the committee, with Holden as its de facto head—Colonel Nelson A. Miles, the Freedmen's Bureau chief in the state, was its chairman—distributed most of the provisions to blacks, who because of their lowly status were most affected by the economic collapse. Holden selected subcommittees in the counties to identify the needy and to purchase food locally for those whom the state committee approved. Although most of the local agents were Republicans, Conservatives surpris-

6. Elizabeth Balanoff, "Negro Legislators in the North Carolina General Assembly, July 1868–February 1872," NCHR, XXXVI (1972), 25–31. For the moderation of North Carolina blacks, see *ibid.*, 23, 32, 35, and James H. Harris' speech in the Raleigh *Standard,* September 4, 1867. Even Abraham H. Galloway of Wilmington, who was widely viewed as a "Jacobin," opposed the confiscation of rebel property and other radical proposals. W. McKee Evans, *Ballots and Fence Rails: Reconstruction on the Lower Cape Fear* (Chapel Hill, 1966), 111. For evidence of strong black support for Holden, see Mrs. L. N. Brown to Alexander M. McPheeters, September 15, 1868, in Alexander M. McPheeters, Sr., Papers, DU.

ingly did not raise a political cry against the relief program. The scalawag leader also responded directly to individual pleas for aid, and in May, 1868, when the committee became overwhelmed by requests for assistance, Holden, who had recently been elected governor, sent James H. Harris and radical carpetbagger Albion W. Tourgée to the Northeast to solicit additional relief funds. He also called for voluntary community assistance until the General Assembly could meet and act upon a plan of relief that he promised to submit. Little aid was forthcoming, but with the harvesting of late spring vegetables, followed by a bountiful grain crop in the fall, the crisis ended. Holden, who like other Republicans was leery of using public means for direct poverty relief, never unveiled an aid program for legislative approval. One month before he became governor, he resigned from the Boston Fund committee, but he continued to take an interest in its work.[7]

He also promoted the virtues of frugality and saving among the few blacks who, despite economic handicaps, were able to accumulate money. Holden, along with black leader Harris, entrepreneur George W. Swepson, and other Raleigh citizens of both races, in 1867 organized the Freedmen's Savings Bank, and he was selected its first president. Blacks constituted a majority of the board of trustees, which did not seem to bother the mildly paternalistic Holden. The bank did not prosper, but Holden maintained an interest in it after he resigned its presidency to become governor.[8]

He also developed a close relationship with officials of the much-maligned Freedmen's Bureau in North Carolina. He could frequently be seen in the company of Colonel Miles, the state Freedmen's Bureau chief, and the families of the two men became staunch friends.[9]

7. Colonel Jacob L. Chur to Gray Williams, July 16, 1867, W. W. Holden to Chur, June 5, 1868, statement of W. W. Holden recommending James H. Harris and Albion W. Tourgée, n.d., endorsements of Holden on requests for aid, February 28, April 18, 21, 23, May 5, 8, 12, 1868, in Records of the Assistant Commissioner for the State of North Carolina, Bureau of Refugees, Freedmen, and Abandoned Lands, 1865–1870, Microfilm Publication M843, Roll 19, NA, hereinafter cited as Records of the Freedmen's Bureau, North Carolina.

8. Raleigh *Standard*, October 30, 1867; Carl R. Osthaus, *Freedmen, Philanthropy, and Fraud: A History of the Freedmen's Savings Bank* (Urbana, 1971), 67, 75.

9. Laura Holden to Ida Holden Cowles, August 9, 1868, in Calvin J. Cowles Papers, SHC.

Although in other southern states the bureau ceased operations when the Republican governments were installed, Holden as governor permitted its agents to continue some of their civil functions. He mainly allowed them to oversee planter-labor relations until the courts were firmly established and black workers protected. Although the effectiveness of the bureau varied from place to place, the agency did not close its North Carolina office until May, 1869. Even then, with Holden's encouragement the bureau continued to support black schools in the state.[10]

In addition, Holden sought legislative action to protect "mechanics" and laborers of both races in their arrangements with "capitalists and employers." He maintained that the state should assure the workingman that "the reward of his labor will be realized; and, to enact this, there should be a lien in every case until he is paid." "Being a working man myself," he told the General Assembly, "I feel a deep interest in whatever concerns the workingmen of the State. Our present and future prosperity must be based on labor. Labor should not only be honored, it should be protected and promoted by every practical means." Since the governor's proposal held out the hope that the rights of black laborers would be safeguarded by the state, black leaders rallied to its support. A few weeks later black Representative James H. Harris introduced a bill in the House to implement Holden's recommendation. The amended bill, which provided a lien on related property to protect laborers and mechanics, became law on April 6, 1869. It was the first North Carolina statute specifically designed to protect the rights of the laboring man.[11]

As governor, Holden also insisted on equal justice for blacks in the enforcement of criminal law. In a number of cases in which

10. Colonel Nelson A. Miles to General Oliver O. Howard, September 26, 1868, in Registers and Letters Received by the Commissioner of the Bureau of Refugees, Freedmen, and Abandoned Lands, 1865–1872, Letters Received, July–December, 1868, Microcopy No. 752, Roll 60, NA; Raleigh *Standard*, May 18, 1868; introduction to Records of the Freedmen's Bureau, North Carolina, Roll 7; W. W. Holden to Oliver O. Howard, March 26, 1870, in Oliver Otis Howard Papers, Bowdoin College Library, Brunswick, Maine.

11. Governor's message, November 17, 1868, in State of North Carolina, *Executive and Legislative Documents, 1868–1869*, Doc. No. 1, pp. 9–10; *Public and Private Laws of North Carolina, 1868–1869*, pp. 305–309; Raleigh *Daily Telegram*, April 4, 1871.

a white man murdered a black, he offered the maximum award allowed by law (four hundred dollars) for the apprehension of the culprit. He admonished county officials to put blacks on juries, especially in cases involving members of their race. In addition, he lectured local officers on the need to protect blacks from white violence. "The habit which some of our people have of taking their guns to be used against colored people" for supposed offenses "must be put down," he wrote the sheriff of Warren County, where a black man had been murdered by a white man. The life of the murdered black man, he told the sheriff, "was as sacred and as valuable in the eye of the law, and in the sight of God," as that of the murderer "or any other man." The governor also promised to remove officials who failed to act against whites guilty of assaulting blacks.[12] When the Ku Klux Klan began to attack blacks in 1869–1870, it seemed the governor's admonitions had had no effect.

A comprehensive system of public schools was designed to be the centerpiece of Republicanism in North Carolina as well as in other southern states. Soon after becoming governor, Holden asked Superintendent of Public Instruction Samuel S. Ashley to study carefully the educational resources of the state and to bring in a detailed plan for the organization of the schools. Carpetbagger Ashley enthusiastically undertook the task. Although he had earlier opposed the creation of the dual system of education that Holden wanted, Ashley drew up an organizational plan that provided for racially separate schools.[13]

Finance, not Conservative opposition, proved the main barrier in the Republican effort to establish a viable school system in North Carolina. Based on Ashley's study, Holden reported to the General Assembly in November, 1868, that the antebellum Literary Fund had been lost, and he called on the legislature to find the money to launch the new system of schools. "We must have free schools for all the children of the State, at whatever cost," he told the Gen-

12. Proclamations of Governor W. W. Holden, July 16, 18, August 5, 1868, Holden to the sheriff of Warren County, November 30, 1868, in Letterbook of Governor Holden; New Bern *Republican*, September 22, 1868.

13. Marion N. O'Quinn, "Carpetbagger Samuel S. Ashley and His Role in North Carolina Education, 1865–1871" (M.A. thesis, North Carolina State University, 1975), 61–62, 92, 99.

eral Assembly. "This is a duty which can neither be postponed or evaded."[14]

In urging the legislature to act, the scalawag governor expanded on his earlier justification for education. Not only did he say that the perpetuation of free institutions depended upon public education, as he had emphasized in his inaugural address, but he also argued that it was "the light which distinguishes refined and civilized from barbarian races." In addition, he maintained that education provided the human resources for the material progress of society. He claimed that property holders, who would pay most of the taxes for the support of the schools, should be "specially interested in promoting education," since through the inculcation of "good morals," schooling becomes "the strongest bulwark that can be erected to protect the rights of property. . . . Taxes for such a˙ purpose should be cheerfully and promptly paid." Furthermore, "industrious and worthy immigrants" would settle in North Carolina if a comprehensive school system were established. "If we do not put in operation as good public schools as there are in other portions of the country," he told the legislators, "we cannot hope to attract to the State any considerable number of immigrants."[15]

Despite Holden's plea, the Republican General Assembly of 1868–1869 failed to appropriate the necessary funds for the establishment of an adequate school system. The legislature approved Ashley's plan for the central administration of the system, but it left the main burden of school finance in the hands of local authorities. Lacking adequate state funds, the system had a fitful beginning, causing Holden in his 1869 annual message to the legislature to renew his appeal for a substantial appropriation for the schools. But with the state finances in worse straits than before, the lawmakers again refused to fund the ambitious system of public education that Holden and Ashley desired. By late 1870, on the eve of Holden's removal from office, only 49,000 children (approximately 12,000 of whom were black) out of a school-age population of 330,000 were attending the public schools. This enrollment compared unfavorably with the 105,048, including 45,558 girls, attending public and private schools on the eve of the Civil War. In

14. Governor's message, November 17, 1868, in State of North Carolina, *Executive and Legislative Documents, 1868–1869,* Doc. No. 1, pp. 7–8.
15. *Ibid.,* 7–8.

despair Holden pleaded with Congress to "establish a national system of public education," a step, he said, that "would confer immeasurable benefits on the people of the Southern States" and would strengthen their devotion to the Union. Although few congressmen would go so far as to support a federal school system, a bill to aid education by applying the proceeds from the sale of federal lands to state schools passed the House of Representatives in 1872 but failed in the Senate.[16] Despite the disappointment of Holden and his associates in the results of their efforts to achieve their educational objectives, they had laid the foundations for a system of public schools in North Carolina that would ultimately be one of the best in the South.

The Republican effort on behalf of higher education achieved no such modest success. As provisional governor in 1865, Holden had assisted in the shaky revival of the University of North Carolina at Chapel Hill, the only public institution of higher learning in the state. When he became governor in 1868, the university was again floundering on the shoals of financial stringency, with fewer than one hundred students in residence (as compared with an average annual enrollment of about four hundred during the late antebellum period). Furthermore, the university had become embroiled in the political divisions of war and reconstruction, creating bitter strife over the control of the institution. Republicans were appalled by the continued presence of "rebels" on the board of trustees and on the faculty and also by the defiant spirit toward congressional reconstruction that pervaded the university community. Although proclaiming himself a champion of the university and disdaining any political interference in its operations, Holden as early as 1866 attacked the administration for inviting Jefferson Davis, Zebulon

16. Daniel Jay Whitener, "Public Education in North Carolina During Reconstruction, 1865–1876," in Fletcher M. Green (ed.), *Essays in Southern History Presented to Joseph Gregoire de Roulhac Hamilton, Ph.D., LL.D., By His Former Students at the University of North Carolina* (Chapel Hill, 1949), 83–84; Governor's message, November 16, 1869, in State of North Carolina, *Executive and Legislative Documents, 1869–1870*, Doc. No. 1, p. 5; O'Quinn, "Carpetbagger Samuel S. Ashley," 153; *Executive and Legislative Documents, Session 1860–1861* (Raleigh, 1861), Doc. No. 10, p. 18; Third annual message of Governor W. W. Holden, November, 1870, in State of North Carolina, *Executive and Legislative Documents, 1870–1871*, Doc. No. 1, p. 9; William C. Harris, "The Creed of the Carpetbaggers: The Case of Mississippi," *JSH*, XL (1974), 211.

Vance, and other "insurgent leaders" to serve as honorary managers of the commencement ball. Vance was also asked to deliver the commencement address, an invitation that he accepted. "The people of this State," Holden warned President David L. Swain, "will not be taxed to support a political University, or an institution which does not inculcate respect for the government of the United States and the most thorough submission to its authority." One of his charges against the university was that a "loyal" professor had been forced to resign from the faculty because of a unionist speech he had made late in the war, a charge reeking with irony in view of Holden's role in driving Professor Benjamin S. Hedrick from the university faculty in 1856 after he had spoken in favor of the Republican candidate for president.[17]

As soon as he became governor in July, 1868, Holden used his authority under the new constitution to reconstruct the university. Although it was the prerogative of the state Board of Education to appoint the university's board of trustees, Holden in effect appointed the new board, which included a large number of university alumni sympathetic to the Republican reform program. The board met in late July, removed President Swain and the faculty from their positions, suspended the university's operations, and chose members for the board's executive committee. This committee had authority to reorganize and reopen the school.[18] Meeting on a regular basis in the governor's office with Holden presiding, the executive committee appointed Solomon Pool, the brother of Senator John Pool, president of the university, established "chairs or Departments of Instruction," and selected four professors to head the departments. Although the old guard at Chapel Hill and Conservatives elsewhere scorned the new appointments, President Pool actually had solid academic credentials (he had taught mathematics

17. Solomon Pool to W. W. Holden, December 4, 1867, in Raleigh *Standard*, December 11, 1867; entries for meetings of May 9, 1866, January 26, April 4, 1867, in Minutes of the Executive Committee of the University of North Carolina Board of Trustees, January 2, 1835, to November 29, 1873, SHC; Raleigh *Standard*, May 23, 1866, August 21, 28, 1867; Solomon Pool to Benjamin S. Hedrick, June 16, 1866, in Benjamin S. Hedrick Papers, DU.

18. Kemp P. Battle, *History of the University of North Carolina* (2 vols.; Raleigh, 1907–12), II, 4–5; Raleigh *Standard*, May 12, 1869. Apparently no blacks were appointed to the board of trustees; only one carpetbagger, the influential Samuel S. Ashley, has been identified as a member of the board.

at the university), and the four professors, including two northerners, were qualified to instruct at the college level. On March 3, 1869, the university reopened its doors, but only ten students enrolled for classes. Later, during the spring, the number of registrants rose to thirty-five, only one of whom was a returning student.[19]

An unrelenting Conservative campaign of defamation against the "bogus president and faculty" virtually ensured the failure of the reconstructed university. Student enrollments remained low, and the university's buildings and grounds continued to deteriorate. On February 1, 1871, the board of trustees reluctantly closed the institution.[20] It would not reopen until 1875, after the Conservatives had regained control of it.

The question of the admission of blacks to the university also troubled Holden and the Republican trustees. Although Republicans had settled upon a segregation policy for the public schools, a few members of the full board of trustees desired the racial integration of the university not only as a matter of principle but also to avoid the expense of constructing a separate college for blacks. At a meeting of the board on November 19–20, 1868, chaired by Holden, a compromise was arranged. The board decided to create a Negro branch of the university at a separate location, and the executive committee of the board was directed to find the site. This branch would have the same administration, institutional affiliation, and citations on its graduates' degrees as the Chapel Hill school.[21]

Several sites for the "colored department" were proposed, but the Republican-dominated legislature, meeting in early 1869, showed little enthusiasm for the project. When the lawmakers reconvened

19. Entries for meetings of August 21, 28, 1868, January 1, 1869, in Minutes of the Executive Committee of the University of North Carolina Board of Trustees; Charlotte *Western Democrat*, November 24, 1868; Raleigh *Standard*, January 6, 18, March 24, 1869.

20. Governor W. W. Holden to the General Assembly, January 21, 1870, in Letterbook of Governor Holden; State of North Carolina, *Executive and Legislative Documents, 1869–1870*, Doc. No. 14; Annual Message of Governor Tod R. Caldwell, 1871, in State of North Carolina, *Executive and Legislative Documents, 1871–1872*, Doc. No. 1, p. 13.

21. Entries for meetings of January 18, 19, 1869, in Minutes of the Executive Committee of the University of North Carolina Board of Trustees; Raleigh *Standard*, January 13, February 3, 1869; Archibald Henderson, *The Campus of the First State University* (Chapel Hill, 1949), 194.

in the fall, Holden urged them to provide the necessary funds for the branch. "This department is not only a matter of justice, but of necessity," he told the legislators. "Our colored fellow-citizens are entitled in proportion to their number to equal consideration in this respect with the whites," and he admonished members of the General Assembly to "make as thorough provision" for the Negro branch as for the university at Chapel Hill. On another occasion, in promoting the cause of black higher education, Holden avowed that "education knows no color or condition of mankind" and that blacks should be treated equally but separately with whites in dispensing its benefits. The legislature, whose financial priorities centered on railroad development and paying off a huge state debt, did not heed the governor's appeal, and the plan for a black branch of the university died a silent death.[22]

A major part of Holden's program was public assistance for the economic rehabilitation and development of the state. Holden believed that the attraction of capital and immigrants was a prerequisite to the complete economic recovery of North Carolina. The state had lost heavily in the migration of whites to the Lower South before the war, and it had also suffered a tremendous loss of manpower in the war. Like other Republicans, Holden, in promoting immigration to the state, downplayed any purpose of replacing reputedly undependable black farm labor with white workers. He insisted that what he wanted was to develop a landholding class in North Carolina consisting of men of energy who would build up the country and not become dependent laborers.[23]

With such a purpose in mind, the governor in late 1868 asked

22. Entry for meeting of March 18, 1869, in Minutes of the Executive Committee of the University of North Carolina Board of Trustees; Governor's message, November 16, 1869, in State of North Carolina, *Executive and Legislative Documents, 1869–1870*, Doc. No. 1, p. 6; Raleigh *Standard*, June 23, 1869. Holden's request for normal schools to train teachers for both white and black classes was also rejected by the General Assembly.

23. "Inaugural Address of Gov. W. W. Holden, Delivered in Capitol Square, Raleigh, July 4th, 1868," in State of North Carolina, *Executive and Legislative Documents, 1868*, pp. 9–10; Governor's message, November 16, 1869, in State of North Carolina, *Executive and Legislative Documents, 1869–1870*, Doc. No. 1, p. 11; W. W. Holden to Allan Rutherford, June 5, 1870, in Letterbook of Governor Holden.

the General Assembly immediately to adopt measures to attract immigrants to North Carolina. However, he advanced no plan to obtain settlers except for a recommendation, which the legislature refused to act on, that a Bureau of Statistics, Agriculture and Immigration be established. Lacking executive direction and with other interests to serve, the legislature never seriously considered Holden's request for a state program to secure settlers. The General Assembly, however, did charter, but without direct state aid, the North Carolina Land Company, which announced the ambitious purposes "of aiding in the transportation and location of Northern and European settlers coming to North Carolina, and [selling] lands of all descriptions, suited to the wants of the agriculturist, the vine and fruit grower, the truck farmer, the miner and manufacturer." The company also proposed to sell town lots to immigrants "and to render all possible assistance to persons who desire to invest their funds in this State."[24]

Holden eagerly aided the land company by writing letters endorsing its work and proclaiming the virtues of North Carolina for settlers. He especially sought to allay outside fears that postwar conditions in North Carolina were unpropitious for settlement. In a letter written for the North Carolina Land Company's promotional tract, he reported that "the State is now thoroughly reconstructed politically and civilly, and is pushing forward its work of improvement with commendable energy. Large expenditures are being made on this account, thus affording employment to labor and developing our resources." He told prospective immigrants that with the completion "at an early date" of a railroad trunkline to the Mississippi Valley, the wealth of the West would pour into North Carolina's seaports, and the interior communities along the path of the road would benefit immensely.[25]

The North Carolina Land Company, however, did not succeed. Because of a revival of political and social turmoil in the state in late 1869 and continued economic stagnation, relatively few immi-

24. Governor's message, November 17, 1868, in State of North Carolina, *Executive and Legislative Documents, 1868–1869*, Doc. No. 1, p. 6; *A Guide to Capitalists and Emigrants* (Raleigh, 1869), 2–3.

25. W. W. Holden to the North Carolina Land Company, April 19, 1869, Holden to W. F. Gray, December 13, 1869, in Little-Mordecai Collection, NDAH; *Guide to Capitalists and Emigrants*, 94–95.

grants, either from the North or from Europe, sought opportunity in the Tarheel State.[26]

No program for the material rehabilitation and growth of North Carolina attracted as much Republican support as railroad development. Even before Holden took office, the constitutional convention of 1868, responding to the popular clamor for the completion of the state's railroad system and persuaded that the railroads promised future prosperity, had launched the Republican aid program. It granted $2,150,000 to finance the completion of five railroads. When the legislature met in July, 1868, it continued on a more massive scale the program of state assistance for railroad construction. Before the floodgates were closed in 1869, the reconstruction government had extended $27,830,000 in the form of stock subscriptions and bonds to eighteen railroad companies.[27]

It was mainly zeal for internal improvements that accounted for the generosity of the legislators in granting state aid to the railroads. But some of the more extravagant and ill-advised bills owed their passage to the nefarious activities of a railroad "ring" that employed bribery and manipulation to gain support in the General Assembly. The ring was headed by George W. Swepson, an erstwhile banker and speculator in the Carolinas who schemed to establish a railroad empire in the Southeast similar to what Tom Scott and Cornelius Vanderbilt were then creating in the North. Beginning in 1868, Swepson plotted to control the impoverished North Carolina railroads and also to obtain state financial assistance and charter privileges for the completion of the links in the systems. An important part of his plan was the use of state bonds and credit to manipulate companies and individuals in order to gain control.

26. Gath Nemakey to David F. Caldwell, December 7, 1869, in David Frank Caldwell Papers, SHC.

27. Charles L. Price, "Railroads and Reconstruction in North Carolina, 1865–1871" (Ph.D. dissertation, University of North Carolina, Chapel Hill, 1959), 361–62. The 1868–1869 authorization of aid compared with $8,378,200 extended to the railroads before the war. An indeterminate but rather modest amount of aid was given to the railroads during the war. Governor's message, November 16, 1869, in State of North Carolina, *Executive and Legislative Documents, 1870–1871*, Doc. No. 4, Table D. The conservative government of 1865–1867 had chartered several railroad companies and had extended $3,015,000 in aid. Perrin Busbee to Benjamin S. Hedrick, February 22, 1867, in Hedrick Papers; J. G. de Roulhac Hamilton, *Reconstruction in North Carolina* (New York, 1914), 427.

Swepson's associates in the ring included North Carolina railroad men, politicians of both parties, and lawyers (frequently these groups were interchangeable), though not all of them stooped to corrupt practices. His chief lobbyists before the General Assembly were two transplanted northerners—Milton S. Littlefield, a suave and affable former Union army officer, and Byron Laflin, one of the founders of the state Republican party. They wined, dined, and bribed legislators to the tune of about $200,000 to ensure the success of Swepson's ventures and also those of minor entrepreneurs whose interests did not conflict with the ring's.[28] Republicans, whether bribed or not, were the main supporters of Swepson's railroad program; the overwhelming majority of Republican legislators voted for the railroad bills while the majority of Conservatives voted against them.[29]

As Swepson, Littlefield, and other members of the ring realized, Governor Holden's support was crucial to the success of their railroad schemes. Swepson made himself right politically by indicating during the 1868 presidential campaign, which occurred precisely at the time when the ring was launching its lobbying effort, that he planned to vote for Grant. Nevertheless, he maintained a low political profile, thereby avoiding the albatross of scalawaggery. When Holden sold the *Standard* upon his elevation to the governorship, Littlefield provided most of the fifteen thousand dollars for the purchase—a generous but not unreasonably high amount in hard United States currency. The new proprietors insisted that the editors proclaim the virtues of the Holden administration as well as promote railroad development. On one occasion Swepson, by his own admission, "proposed to let Gov. Holden have $25,000 [in state bonds] at cost," but the governor, citing the impropriety of

28. For a good summary of Swepson's schemes and methods, see Charles L. Price, "The Railroad Schemes of George W. Swepson," in *East Carolina College Publications in History* (2 vols.; Greenville, N.C., 1964), I, 32–50. See also Price's "Railroads and Reconstruction in North Carolina," Chs. 11–13. For the extensive documentation of the railroad frauds, see State of North Carolina, *Report of the Commission to Investigate Charges of Fraud and Corruption, Under Act of Assembly, Session 1871–1872* (Raleigh, 1872), hereinfter cited as *Shipp Commission Report*, its common name.

29. Allen W. Trelease, "Republican Reconstruction in North Carolina: A Roll-call Analysis of the State House of Representatives, 1868–1870," *JSH*, XLII (1976), 329; Price, "Railroads and Reconstruction in North Carolina," 373.

the transaction, turned down what he otherwise considered to be "a good investment."[30] No evidence exists that Holden, who took pride in his personal honesty, ever accepted any money from Swepson and his lieutenants for backing their schemes. Even his enemies never charged him with benefiting financially from his association with the railroad ring.

Swepson and his collaborators succeeded in gaining the governor's support by projecting an attractive vision of the material development of North Carolina based on the approval of their railroad program. This vision, in its promise of prosperity once the state was laced with railroads and connected to the Mississippi Valley, closely resembled the one Holden had painted of North Carolina under Republican leadership. Swepson, one of the new breed of resourceful, unscrupulous entrepreneurs produced by the age of enterprise, carefully concealed his real motives, which were financial self-aggrandizement and domination of the railroads.[31] A political editor for most of his adult life, Holden was a babe in the woods in dealing with the smooth-talking Swepson on intricate postwar railroad matters. Holden took him at his word, and he was soon the governor's main adviser on railroads.

The governor, however, was not alone, at least in the beginning, in succumbing to Swepson's wiles. Many North Carolinians, including prominent westerners like Thomas L. Clingman and Augustus S. Merrimon, believed that his railroad schemes would benefit the state and finally open the mountain region to economic development. Even the archconservative Raleigh *Sentinel*, before revelations of the ring's corruption became widespread, expressed confidence in Swepson's railroad leadership.[32]

The keystone of Swepson's railroad schemes was the Western North Carolina Railroad. This strategically located road, running from Salisbury to the mountains and beyond, had not been completed west of Morganton, and since the company was experienc-

30. *Shipp Commission Report*, 200.
31. For early and revealing evidence of Swepson's unscrupulous designs, see George W. Swepson to Samuel McDowell Tate, February 23 1868, in Samuel McDowell Tate Papers, SHC.
32. George W. Swepson Papers, SHC, 1867–1868 *passim;* Price, "Railroads and Reconstruction in North Carolina," 401; Jonathan Daniels, *Prince of Carpetbaggers* (Philadelphia, 1958), 183; *Shipp Commission Report*, 250.

ing financial difficulties, the likelihood of its early completion was remote. When the Republicans assumed power in 1868, Swepson saw an opportunity to gain control of the road. But problems abounded. Since the state, in this case the Holden administration, did not control the railroad, though it owned a majority of the stock, Swepson was forced to move cautiously to avoid a struggle with the private stockholders before he was strong enough to defeat them. He had learned early of the private stockholders' strength when they blocked an attempt by Holden to secure the election of Calvin Cowles, his son-in-law, to the presidency of the company.[33] Swepson soon ingratiated himself with the irate governor by proposing a scheme to circumvent the control of the "rebel" stockholders. The plan, which both Holden and the General Assembly accepted, split the railroad into two divisions, providing the state with the opportunity to control the organization of the western division and isolating the private stockholders in the eastern company.

With Holden's approval, Swepson's lobbyists also persuaded the General Assembly to appropriate $4,000,000 to each division of the Western North Carolina Railroad. The aid would be in the form of state bonds that were to be issued when construction contracts were awarded. (The amount was later increased to $6,666,666.) The state also subscribed to two-thirds of the capital stock of the companies with the stipulation that the private stockholders had to pay for 5 percent of the remainder before the state would take up its shares.[34]

Holden then, through the appointment of state directors sympathetic to Swepson, aided in the election of the wily entrepreneur as president of the Western Division of the North Carolina Railroad. Swepson's election, however, became a reality only after Littlefield, his man Friday, through financial skullduggery became the majority stockholder, though he had actually invested no money in the company.[35] Having secured control of the Western Division,

33. Calvin Cowles to James J. Mott, July 11, 1868, Calvin Cowles to Henry Cowles, July 13, 14, 1868, Calvin Cowles to Josiah Cowles and Calvin Cowles, Jr., August 30, 1868, in Letterbook P, Calvin Cowles Papers, NDAH.

34. Price, "Railroads and Reconstruction in North Carolina," 285–86; *Shipp Commission Report*, 14–15.

35. *Shipp Commission Report*, 212–14, 234. The charters of the two divisions of the Western North Carolina retained the arrangement whereby the private

Swepson let bogus construction contracts to Littlefield and Samuel McDowell Tate, another associate, in order to fulfill the requirements of the law for the acquisition of the state bonds. When Swepson applied to the governor for the bonds, Holden, without questioning the legitimacy of the contracts, promptly signed and issued $6,367,000 of the securities to the railroad. Holden later admitted that he might have "stretch[ed] the law a little" in issuing the paper, but he did so "because I wanted the Western people to have these bonds" to complete their railroad.[36] But Swepson squandered the bonds in an effort to gain control of other railroads, including a Florida company, and the Western road was not completed until after Reconstruction.

Fortunately for the state's interests, Governor Holden provided little direct assistance to Swepson and the ring in its schemes to dominate the other railroads of the state. In the case of the Eastern Division of the Western North Carolina Railroad, there was no need for state intervention beyond the issuance of the bonds to complete the road. Tate, a member of the ring, dominated the Eastern Division, and he used Swepson's banks to handle the funds of the company. He also made available the company's state bonds for Swepson's ventures to gain power over other railroads.[37]

In addition to the western railroads, the only other major road still under construction, and thus a prime target for Swepson's manipulation, was the Wilmington, Charlotte, and Rutherford Railroad, which traversed the southern part of North Carolina. To obtain $4,000,000 in special tax bonds, the private directors of this company, at Holden's insistence, had to agree to state control. Holden immediately chose Republicans to represent the state's majority interest on the board, and they dutifully appointed his choice for president of the company. The man selected for the position had been recommended to the governor by Swepson. But the new president failed to do Swepson's bidding, and the ring, using the bonds

stockholders, though in a minority, would hold a majority of the votes at the annual meetings.

36. *Ibid.*, 213; Price, "The Railroad Schemes of Swepson," 46; William K. Boyd, "William W. Holden," *Trinity College Historical Society Papers*, Series III (1899), 115.

37. Price, "The Railroad Schemes of Swepson," 44–45.

and assets of other companies, began to purchase large amounts of Wilmington, Charlotte, and Rutherford mortgage bonds for the purpose of forcing the railroad into bankruptcy. Swepson's scheme to win control of the company, however, ended with his financial failure on Black Friday, 1869.[38]

Even if the state's financial interest in the railroads had been managed properly, the generous extension of public aid for internal improvements, which doubled the state debt, came at an inopportune time. Despite a brief upsurge in the economy in late 1868 and early 1869, the state's financial structure remained weak, with assets still greatly reduced as a result of the war and the disarray of the tax revenue system. Although Holden became increasingly concerned as the public debt mounted with the passage of each piece of the railroad aid program, he expressed confidence that the necessary taxes could be raised to finance the projects. In his 1868 annual message to the General Assembly he predicted that the new property assessment, to be completed in 1869, would reveal a value of $250,000,000 in real estate. This property—the main source for public revenue—would be sufficient, he claimed, to support a tax of $1,000,000. Based on these calculations, he contended that "the people of the State are fully able to carry on their government and at the same time provide for the payment of the interest on their debt. . . . The people will cheerfully pay whatever amount may be necessary to meet the interest" when it fell due. Holden insisted that in order to honor "our solemn obligation" to creditors and protect the financial standing of the state, the General Assembly must immediately pass a tax bill that would provide the money for the prompt payment of the interest on the bonds that were already due.[39]

Holden's view of property values soon proved to be entirely too optimistic. Instead of the $250,000,000 value that he had predicted, the 1869 assessments totaled $79,557,344 and produced only $448,023 in tax revenues, a sum that fell far short of the $1,032,902

38. Price, "Railroads and Reconstruction in North Carolina," 306–12, 434–36; W. T. J. Miller to W. W. Holden, April 15, 1869, in Letterbook of Governor Holden.

39. Governor's message, November 17, 1868, in State of North Carolina, *Executive and Legislative Documents, 1868–1869,* Doc. No. 1, pp. 4–5.

needed for interest payments alone.[40] The General Assembly, though willing to commit the state to a large debt, showed little enthusiasm for finding the necessary taxes to finance it. Not until April, 1869, almost a year after the launching of the ambitious aid program, did the legislature finally pass a revenue bill to finance the regular functions of the government and pay the interest on both the old and the new railroad bonds. But it was too little and too late to save the state from defaulting on its interest payments. This failure caused the railroad bonds to plunge to 50 percent of par value by June and to 28 percent by the end of the year, severely damaging the state's credit standing and creating a financial crisis in the state government.[41]

Conservatives, with a mixture of partisan glee and genuine concern for the fate of the state's financial and economic development, railed against the railroad excesses in Raleigh. They warned that when their party gained control of the state government, it would repudiate the "unconstitutional" bond issues, a pronouncement that further weakened state credit. Conservatives nevertheless agreed with Holden's position that "the credit of the State is of paramount importance, [and] it should be maintained. In no other way can our good name be preserved untarnished; in no other way can we hope to prosecute those works of internal improvement on which it is believed our prosperity in the future materially depends."[42] Both the governor and his political foes, however, opposed the improper legislative approval of special tax bonds designed to assist the construction of several lines. When the companies sought the issuance of these bonds, Republicans such as Senator John Pool and Radical carpetbagger Albion W. Tourgée, who were shocked by

40. State treasurer's report, November 16, 1869, in State of North Carolina, *Executive and Legislative Documents, 1869–1870*, Doc. No. 4, pp. 2–3. For the 1869 property assessment values and the amount of state taxes paid, see state auditor's report for 1869, in *ibid.*, Doc. No. 23, p. 6. Because of the heavy private debts, the difficulties of recovering from the war, and a general skepticism of the way tax revenues would be used, many property holders undervalued their land, a practice that was frequently winked at by county assessors and other authorities. State auditor's report, November 16, 1870, in State of North Carolina, *Executive and Legislative Documents, 1870–1871*, Doc. No. 3, pp. 1–2.
    41. Price, "Railroads and Reconstruction in North Carolina," 366, 393.
    42. Greensboro *Patriot*, March 11, 1869; Charlotte *Western Democrat*, January 5, November 9, 1869; Governor W. W. Holden to the General Assembly, January 6, 1869, in State of North Carolina, *Executive and Legislative Documents, 1868–1869*, Doc. No. 17, p. 1.

revelations of corruption and worried that the railroad scandals would destroy the party in the state, pleaded with Holden to withhold the bonds. He responded by refusing to issue $8,000,000 in the special bonds, an action that sent a chill through Wall Street, causing further damage to the state's credit standing and to the bonds that were already on the market.[43]

In a desperate effort to salvage the remaining bonds, Holden went to New York, where he joined Swepson and other railroad presidents, some of whom were members of the ring, in a plan to sell North Carolina's securities. Using the St. Nicholas Hotel as their headquarters, the North Carolinians unsuccessfully attempted to raise the prices on all these bonds by forming a pool and agreeing to sell when prices peaked. In September, 1869, a similar scheme by Swepson alone, evidently with the naïve Holden's approval, ended in disaster for North Carolina's interest when the Jay Gould–Jim Fisk attempt to corner the gold market backfired, plunging Wall Street into a financial crisis. Swepson was compelled to forfeit hundreds of state bonds worth several hundred thousand dollars at face value (the exact figure is still unknown).[44]

Swepson's failure also administered a final setback for North Carolina's railroad bonds in the Reconstruction period. Still, Holden's faith in him remained unshaken. One month after the collapse of the bond market he wrote the wily entrepreneur: "I sincerely trust that your affairs are not seriously embarrassed. I have the greatest confidence in your wisdom and energy, and I feel sure that you will extricate yourself from any trouble that may surround. Happen what may I am your friend, and will never desert you."[45] In his

43. Charlotte *Western Democrat*, December 22, 1868, January 5, 1869; Price, "Railroads and Reconstruction in North Carolina," 553–57, 592; Report of State Treasurer David A. Jenkins, January 5, 1869, in State of North Carolina, *Executive and Legislative Documents, 1868–1869*, Doc. No. 17, p. 4.

44. *Shipp Commission Report*, 320–22, 501; Price, "Railroads and Reconstruction in North Carolina," 458–62; Daniels, *Prince of Carpetbaggers*, 210–19.

45. W. W. Holden to George W. Swepson, November 1, 1869, in Swepson Papers. See also W. W. Holden to "My Dear Mr. Swepson," October 6, 1869, in *Shipp Commission Report*, 336, for a similar expression of support. Even after Reconstruction and the *Shipp Commission Report*'s confirmation of the venality of the railroad ring, Holden retained his friendship with Swepson. In 1880–1881 the two men planned a banking partnership in Raleigh, but it was aborted when Swepson died. Testimony of F. L. Mahler before Referee S. F. Mordecai, March 22, 1904, in *F. L. Mahler et al. v. W. R. Henry and wife*, W. W. Holden Folder, Wake

letter to Swepson, Holden made no mention of the losses that the
state had suffered because of his friend's nefarious activities. Of the
$17,640,00 issued to the railroads in 1868–1869, only $4,345,000
was returned to the state in 1870 after the General Assembly passed
a law to recover the bonds. For the state's investment, only seventy-
two miles of track were completed during Holden's administration,
though additional miles of roadbeds were graded and almost ready
for track by the end of the Republican era.[46]

Criticism of Holden's association with the railroad ring intensified when he refused to support efforts in the General Assembly
to investigate the railroad scandals. Even some Republicans joined
Conservatives in attacking the governor. The Rutherfordton *Star*,
the organ of Superintendent of Public Works Ceburn L. Harris,
whose schemes to control the state's railroad interests Holden had
thwarted, maintained a constant barrage of criticism against the
governor for his favoritism toward "men who had fed worse than
vultures upon the poor and impoverished laborers of North Carolina."[47] Preferring to believe that charges of fraud against Swepson
and associates were politically motivated, Holden provided no
encouragement or assistance to two legislative committees formed
in 1869–1870 to investigate charges against the ring. His lack of
enthusiasm for the investigations reinforced the determination of
Republicans in the General Assembly, some of whom had been
involved in the railroad corruption, to limit the scope of the committees' work and prevent a thorough inquiry of the frauds. As expected, the committees—headed by carpetbagger William H. S.
Sweet and former Governor Thomas Bragg—failed to prove con-
clusively the existence of fraud in the railroad schemes of Swepson
and his friends.[48]

County Estates Records. Although efforts were made by the Republican administration of Governor Tod R. Caldwell to bring Swepson, Littlefield, and their associates to justice, they eluded prosecution.

46. For a table of the bonds issued and returned, see Hamilton, *Reconstruction
in North Carolina,* 448. On the miles of track completed during the Republican
era, see Price, "Railroads and Reconstruction in North Carolina," 550. It should
be noted that because of the rugged terrain in western North Carolina, some of the
construction was unusually expensive.

47. Rutherfordton *Star,* November 27, December 4, 11, 1869, January 22, 29,
February 5, 1870.

48. Thomas B. Keogh to Thomas Settle, December 3, 1868, in Thomas Settle

The scandals and the financial failures of the state government, however, severely divided the Republican party and stigmatized it in the minds of many North Carolinians with mismanagement and corruption, a burden that the new political order could ill afford to bear before it had an opportunity to establish itself firmly in the state. As reports of corruption grew and financial difficulties multiplied, so did the problems encountered by Holden and other Republican officials in their efforts to maintain law and order and the rights of their supporters against an increasingly militant and often violent Conservative opposition.

Papers, SHC; Report of Committee on Bribery and Corruption, in State of North Carolina, *Executive and Legislative Documents, 1868–1869,* Doc. No. 20; William L. Scott to his wife, February 18, March 4, 1870, Scott to H. M. Miller, March 24, 1870, in William Lafayette Scott Papers, DU; State of North Carolina, *Executive and Legislative Documents, 1869–1870,* Doc. No. 33.

XIV
Defender of the
New Order

As in other southern states, in North Carolina the acid test for Republican leaders was their ability to protect themselves and their supporters from the violence and intimidation of incorrigible whites. Throughout the South in 1868–1869 the spread of secret night-riding organizations, known collectively as the Ku Klux Klan, threatened to destroy Republican reconstruction. The success of these night riders, however, was not inevitable, especially in North Carolina, where almost a third of the white population supported the Republican party in the 1868 elections and could be expected to provide strong opposition to the Klan. Furthermore, a number of Conservative leaders eschewed violent tactics. They believed that such methods would create further labor problems, threaten the social fabric, and prevent the success of a moderate campaign, like the one in Virginia, to attract blacks to the Conservative party. The fact that several North Carolina Conservative leaders, soon after their Virginia counterparts captured that state on a platform accepting black political equality, sought to quiet the vitriolic Josiah Turner by replacing him as editor of the party newspaper at the state capital suggested that the forces of moderation might yet prevail in the Conservative party.[1] Even if the militant Turner faction gained control of the party and violence spread,

---

1. Greensboro *Patriot*, August 12, 1869; Charlotte *Western Democrat*, June 22, September 21, 1869; Asheville *Pioneer*, September 2, October 30, 1869; Goldsboro *Daily Messenger*, July 2, 1869.

North Carolina Republicans—particularly Holden—expected the
national administration, now safely in the hands of the Republican
Grant, to intervene to aid state authorities in suppressing the lawless. As time would prove, much depended upon the course of
events, Holden's reaction to these events, and the perception of
people, outside as well as inside the state, to the situation.

The Ku Klux Klan emerged slowly in North Carolina and never
possessed a central directory or a coordinated plan for the overthrow of Republicanism. Its elements included an amalgam of postwar lawlessness, vigilantism against alleged black criminals, and
violent political activity against local Republicans, with the latter
becoming most important by 1870. A few disturbing acts of Klan
terror occurred during the 1868 political campaigns and in early
1869, but these did not involve a widespread conspiracy. On April
16, 1869, Holden appealed to "the great body of the people of the
State [who] are submitting quietly and peacefully to established authority . . . to unite with me in discountenancing and repressing"
such criminal activity. In making his plea, the governor maintained
that "public opinion properly embodied and expressed will be
more effectual in repressing these evils . . . than the execution of
the law itself against offenders in a few individual cases." [2]

Holden only slowly came to realize that public opinion was not
sufficient for the task of breaking the fever of Klan intimidation
and violence that spread through North Carolina in 1869–1870.
One month after his appeal to the public for aid against the lawless, the first political murders occurred when carpetbagger Sheriff
O. R. Colgrove of Jones County and a black companion were as-
sassinated. Appalled by the killings and by increasing reports of
depredations in this eastern county, Holden dispatched a white militia company to the area. But when it was withdrawn a few weeks
later, M. L. Shepard, another local carpetbagger leader who had
organized a black self-defense force, was gunned down by Klans-

2. Proclamation of Governor W. W. Holden, April 16, 1869, in *Third Annual
Message of W. W. Holden, Governor of North Carolina* (Raleigh, 1870), Appendix
6–7. This pamphlet, containing not only his 1870 annual message but also documents relating to his actions against the Klan, is found in North Carolina Governors' Addresses and Messages, Government Documents Section, NDAH. This
proclamation, as well as others by Holden, are also in the Letterbook of Governor
William Woods Holden, 1868–1870, NDAH.

men. At the same time, Holden received disturbing news of wide-spread Klan activity in neighboring Lenoir County and in Chatham and Orange counties in the Piedmont.[3]

Instead of dispatching militia units immediately into the areas of Klan activity, Holden on October 20 issued another proclamation appealing to North Carolinians to check the tide of violence. He informed the people of the lawless conditions in the four afflicted counties and warned that he would proclaim a state of insurrection and "exert the whole power of the State to enforce the law" unless the depredations ceased and the perpetrators were brought to justice. He also sent numerous messages to local officials and citizens "urging the necessity of repressing the outrages and enforcing the law." Finally, he dispatched two dozen detectives into several counties to aid Republican officials in ferreting out offenders against the peace. This last action resulted in the arrest of eighteen men on a variety of charges, most of whom were charged with the murder of Sheriff Colgrove. But because of sympathy or fear, either grand juries failed to indict or trial juries refused to convict, with only a few exceptions. Nevertheless, the governor's action in highlighting the disorders and obtaining the arrests of the Klansmen brought peace to Jones and Lenoir counties and a lull in night-riding attacks in Chatham and Orange.[4]

Elsewhere in late 1869 violence spread and Klansmen became bolder in their operations and public appearances. They openly marched through the streets of several towns, including sedate Chapel Hill, where they galloped around the university, whipped

3. Allen W. Trelease, *White Terror: The Ku Klux Klan Conspiracy and Southern Reconstruction* (New York, 1971), 190–91; *Appleton's Annual Cyclopaedia, 1869*, p. 492; Raleigh *Standard*, June 9, 1869; Sheriff John Turner of Orange County to Governor W. W. Holden, August 12, 1869, in *Third Annual Message of W. W. Holden*, Appendix, 27–28.

4. Third annual message of Governor W. W. Holden, November, 1870, State of North Carolina, *Executive and Legislative Documents, 1870–1871*, Doc. No. 1, pp. 14, 17; Proclamation of Governor W. W. Holden, October 20, 1869, in *Third Annual Message of W. W. Holden*, Appendix, 7–10; R. T. Berry to Governor W. W. Holden, September 3, 1869, in William Woods Holden Papers, DU; New Bern *Daily Times*, issues of September, 1869. For a fascinating account of Holden's use of detectives in lawless areas, see Stephen E. Massengill, "The Detectives of William W. Holden, 1869–1870," *NCHR*, LXII (1985), 448–87. Of the other southern states, only Mississippi employed detectives to combat Ku Klux Klan activity during Reconstruction. The Mississippi experiment with a detective force also failed.

and threatened blacks, and drove whites from their homes. Although sympathetic editors, such as Josiah Turner of the Raleigh *Sentinel*, ignored or rationalized Klan activities, moderate opponents of the Republican regime, along with fearful Republicans, called for an end to the violence. Several Conservative newspapers—none, however, in the hotbed of Klan activity—praised Governor Holden for his efforts to put down the Klan short of armed intervention, though they were careful to suggest that he give the same attention to the Union League and black arsonists.[5] In a few counties where the Klan attempted to establish a foothold, the intervention of leading moderates like David S. Reid, whom Holden had once made governor, prevented its success. Holden himself eventually turned to a policy of employing prominent Conservatives in Chatham and Orange counties to pressure the Klan to disband. In both cases he was successful, suggesting that, though its success everywhere was problematical, he should have tried this policy in other Klan areas.[6]

By the end of 1869 the main focus of attention had become Alamance and Caswell counties, where insurrection was brewing. These two Piedmont counties, with a population about equally divided between the races, had been bitterly contested in reconstruction elections. In both counties the Conservatives had won control of most of the local offices, including that of sheriff, but the Republicans were well organized and had elected T. M. Shoffner of Alamance and John W. Stephens of Caswell, both native sons, to the state Senate. As the crisis unfolded in the Piedmont, Holden slowly learned that unless an outright insurrection occurred, the administration in Washington would not intervene against the

5. Trelease, *White Terror*, 195–97; Third annual message of Governor W. W. Holden, November, 1870, in State of North Carolina, *Executive and Legislative Documents, 1870–1871*, Doc. No. 1, p. 16; Greensboro *Patriot*, October 28, 1869; Charlotte *Western Democrat*, October 26, 1869, February 1, 22, 1870; Hillsborough *Recorder*, January 26, 1870.

6. A. W. Tourgée to W. W. Holden, July 3, 1869, in Letterbook of Governor Holden; Thomas Settle to Holden, July 28, 1869, Pride Jones to Holden, March 4, 1870, in Holden Papers, DU; Third annual message of Governor W. W. Holden, November, 1870, in State of North Carolina, *Executive and Legislative Documents, 1870–1871*, Doc. No. 1, p. 17; Thomas A. Donoho to W. W. Holden, May 16, 1870, in *Third Annual Message of W. W. Holden*, Appendix, 51–55; *Senate Reports*, 42nd Cong., 1st Sess., No. 1, p. xvi.

Klan. He lamented that the government and the northern people did not understand "our real situation," and he especially criticized Congress for failing to provide the means for the garrisoning of an adequate number of troops in the South. Holden wrote that in North Carolina "the presence of a regiment of infantry, and four companies of cavalry, stationed at different points, would have a most salutary effect in suppressing these outrages and maintaining the peace." Although he did not doubt that "in an emergency any number of federal troops that might be required would be promptly furnished" by President Grant, Holden knew that for the present the main responsibility for the suppression of the Klan rested with him.[7]

With this in mind, the scalawag governor in his annual message of November 16, 1869, and again one month later, asked the General Assembly to strengthen the militia law. He explained to the legislature that in some communities "many good citizens are in a constant state of terror" and that, though he had adopted all measures under the civil law to suppress the violence, Klan activity was increasing. As was his custom in other matters, Holden left the specific provisions of the law to the General Assembly. He did indicate that it "would not be advisable to employ colored militia only" in the disorderly Piedmont counties where whites generally outnumbered blacks. "To call out the colored militia alone in these Counties would be unjust to the colored race, and would give a pretext for increased exasperation among certain whites against the colored people."[8]

On December 16 Senator Shoffner introduced a bill to implement Holden's request for a stronger militia law. In January, after a bitter debate and the deletion of an unconstitutional clause authorizing the suspension of the writ of habeas corpus, the bill passed

7. W. W. Holden to Secretary of War William W. Belknap, November 16, 1869, in State of North Carolina, *Executive and Legislative Documents, 1869–1870,* Doc. No. 1, p. 10. During 1869 the War Department drastically reduced federal troop strength in North Carolina. The total went from 939 in late 1868 to only 366 soldiers in late 1869 and early 1870, when the Klan neared its high-water mark. James E. Sefton, *The United States Army and Reconstruction, 1865–1877* (Baton Rouge, 1967), Appendix B.

8. W. W. Holden to the General Assembly, December 16, 1869, in Letterbook of Governor Holden; Governor's message, November 16, 1869, in State of North Carolina, *Executive and Legislative Documents, 1869–1870,* Doc. No. 1, p. 10.

the legislature. Conservatives attacked it as a Radical attempt to "blot out in this State the last vestige of chartered rights and civil liberty." But as historian Allen W. Trelease has observed, the Shoffner act did not significantly expand the governor's power to preserve law and order. It permitted him to proclaim a state of insurrection "whenever in his judgment the civil authorities in any county are unable to protect its citizens in the enjoyment of life and property . . . and to call into active service the militia of the state" to suppress the insurrection. The constitution of 1868 had given the governor these powers, and Holden had already dispatched small militia detachments into Jones and Alamance counties to aid local civil officials. He had also threatened to declare a state of insurrection in several areas if the night riders did not cease their depredations.[9] The Shoffner act, however, did reinforce, at a critical junction in the Ku Klux Klan upheaval, Holden's authority to use the militia on a large scale to put down the Klan and impose temporary military rule. The law also authorized the governor to call upon the president for assistance if necessary to restore order.

Even with renewed authority, Holden drew back from using militia forces. The state treasury lacked money to finance a large-scale military operation. Furthermore, Holden did not believe that in the Klan-infested Piedmont counties he could muster a "white militia of the proper character" to confront the night riders. The governor also wanted to avoid military intervention because he knew from experience that North Carolinians would not take lightly such interference in their affairs. He hoped that the mere passage of the Shoffner act, supplemented by the work of his detective force and the calming influence of prominent local men, would prove sufficient to restore law and order in the afflicted counties.[10] He was soon grievously disappointed. On February 28 he received the

9. *Trial of William W. Holden, Governor of North Carolina, Before the Senate of North Carolina, on Impeachment by the House of Representatives for High Crimes and Misdemeanors* (3 vols.; Raleigh, 1871), Pt. 1, pp. 990–91; Wilmington *Semi-Weekly Post*, January 27, 1870; Greensboro *Patriot*, December 23, 1869; Trelease, *White Terror*, 209; *Public Laws of the State of North Carolina, Passed by the General Assembly at Its Session 1869–1870* (Raleigh, 1870), 64–65.

10. W. W. Holden to Lieutenant Governor Tod R. Caldwell, February 23, 1870, in Letterbook of Governor Holden; Holden to President U. S. Grant, March 10, 1870, Holden to S. A. Ashe, November 29, 1881 (newspaper clipping), both in Scrapbook, Holden Papers, DU.

shocking news from Alamance that Wyatt Outlaw, the leading black Republican in the county, had been hanged on the courthouse square in Graham by a large body of Klansmen, who had also run roughshod through the town and left a note threatening the white Republican mayor with a similar fate.[11]

Stunned by this brutal incident in the Piedmont, Holden proclaimed a state of insurrection in Alamance. He also had forty federal troops sent to the county, but they could do little more than show their colors. Holden wanted more, and on March 10 he sent an urgent appeal to President Grant for sufficient federal aid "in repressing these outrages and in restoring peace and good order." The angry governor told Grant that "if Congress would authorize the suspension, by the President, of the writ of *habeas corpus* in certain localities, and if criminals could be arrested and tried before military tribunals, and shot, we would soon have peace and order throughout all the country. The remedy would be a sharp and a bloody one, but it is as indispensable as was the suppression of the rebellion." He also wrote North Carolina's representatives in Congress beseeching them to obtain congressional approval for the suspension of the writ of habeas corpus in Alamance County. Although Congress was becoming concerned about reports of Klan terror in the South, neither its leadership nor President Grant was sufficiently aroused at this time to come to Holden's assistance. "Is it possible," Holden incredulously asked carpetbagger Senator Joseph C. Abbott, that the federal government "will abandon its loyal people to be whipped and hanged" by the Ku Klux Klan?[12]

Instead of raising a militia force, Holden during the spring of 1870 renewed his campaign to have county officials and prominent local citizens assert themselves against lawless bands. He was only partly successful. As the violence escalated, blacks in some communities struck back by pillaging and burning the houses and barns of

11. Henry A. Badham *et al.*, to W. W. Holden, February 28, 1870, in Letterbook of Governor Holden. The governor received this message the same day it was written.

12. W. W. Holden to President U. S. Grant, March 10, 1870, Holden to the senators and representatives in Congress from North Carolina, March 14, 1870, in Holden Papers, DU; W. W. Holden to Senator Joseph C. Abbott, March 17, 1870, in Letterbook of Governor Holden.

suspected Klansmen. Excited Conservatives charged that blacks initiated the action for the criminal purpose of plundering the countryside. When reports reached Holden of black reprisals against the Klan, he denounced such activity. "Retaliation for violence greatly aggravates the evil, and is calculated to increase strife," he wrote. Despite his frequent lament that indictments against Klansmen could not be secured, he told his supporters that the proper redress for wrongs was in the courts.[13]

The forthcoming August election to choose a new legislature and a state attorney general ensured that the situation would become worse and that the fate of Republicanism would hang in the balance. All along, many Conservatives had assumed that Holden's campaign against the Ku Klux Klan was designed to win the election by suppressing a free ballot. Holden and his Radical friends, the Greensboro *Patriot* charged, "intend to resort to every possible means, either fair or foul to carry the election next August." The Shoffner or "military bill," according to Conservatives such as the *Patriot* editor and Josiah Turner of the Raleigh *Sentinel*, was the first step in the Radical campaign to overawe the opposition at the polls and continue "their ill gotten power in order that they may be better enabled to rob and plunder the people and State."[14] Many Conservatives seemed sincerely to believe that Holden would not permit a fair election in 1870. Regardless of the prospects, they were bitterly determined to wage a relentless campaign for the "redemption" of North Carolina from "Radical misrule." "Never was more at stake," former governor and Conservative leader Thomas Bragg wrote to a

13. W. W. Holden to James Sinclair, April 1, 1870, Holden to Thomas A. Donoho, April 22, 1870, Holden to N. A. Ramsay, May 7, 1870, Holden to W. P. Bynum, May 7, 1870, in *Third Annual Message of W. W. Holden*, Appendix, 50–51, 55, 58; Pride Jones to Holden, April 19, 1870, Holden to Jones, April 22, 1870, in Letterbook of Governor Holden.

14. Greensboro *Patriot*, February 10, 1870. See also J. G. de Roulhac Hamilton (ed.), *The Papers of Randolph Abbott Shotwell* (3 vols.; Raleigh, 1929–36), II, 330, and the Tarboro *Southerner*, June 9, 1870. Although most historians now agree that Holden's war on the Ku Klux Klan was motivated primarily by his desire to maintain law and order and the rights of citizens of both races, some still subscribe to the traditional interpretation that he resorted to military force in order to win the 1870 elections. See, for example, William Gillette, *Retreat from Reconstruction, 1869–1870* (Baton Rouge, 1979), 90–91.

friend. "If we beat them, all is gained. If beaten by them, all is lost and adieu to anything like civil liberty in N.C. during this generation at least."[15]

Despite a rising tide of opposition to Holden and the Republicans, the Conservative party entered the 1870 campaign in disarray. Old political divisions between former Whigs and Democrats, as well as recent quarrels over control of the party, plagued the Conservatives. Each faction was suspicious that the other would gain the upper hand in the coalition.[16] In addition, conflict had broken out among Conservatives over the tone and methods of the anti-Republican campaign. Moderates, who were more numerous and influential than recent historians have judged, were disturbed, as one editor wrote, by "the fierce partizan excitement of the time and the want of confidence felt by so many in the officers whose duty it is to administer justice." These "respectable men" called for the reorganization of the Conservative party on "a new departure" platform that would exclude Turner and extremists of his ilk and unite "the great body of the best and most respectable" North Carolinians, including anti-Holden Republicans like the Dockerys, in a movement to redeem the state from the corruptionists. The new departure platform would also cautiously seek the votes of blacks.[17]

Hopes for the success of the moderates continued into the spring. In early April the Conservative members of the legislature issued a long, moderate address appealing for support in the election against "Radicalism, reckless extravagance, corruption, and partizan tyranny." Pronouncing the reconstruction laws "a finality," they acknowledged that "the question of colored suffrage and the civil rights of the colored race . . . have been decided upon by the people of the United States," and they proposed to accept the verdict "in

15. Thomas Bragg to David Schenck, August 1, 1870, in David Frank Caldwell Papers, SHC.

16. William A. Graham to William A. Graham, Jr., April 16, July 1, 1870, in William A. Graham Papers, NDAH; Greensboro *Patriot*, August 12, 1869; Raleigh *Daily Telegram*, March 14, 1871; A. W. Ingold to David F. Caldwell, May 15, 1870, George Mathes [?] to Caldwell, June 9, 1870, in Caldwell Papers; David Schenck Diary, June 25, 1870 (Ms in SHC).

17. Salisbury *Old North State*, March 11, 1870; Charlotte *Western Democrat*, January 25, February 1, 25, March 1, 23, 1870; Salem *People's Press*, March 18, 25, 1870; William H. Battle to the public, March 23, 1870, in Graham Papers, NDAH.

good faith." In June the Conservative state executive committee, avoiding the divisive issue of a party name, nominated William M. Shipp, a moderate and a former Whig, as the coalition's candidate for attorney general, the only high state office to be filled by the election. Shipp launched a new departure campaign that, in addition to stressing the issues of Republican corruption, heavy taxes, the railroad bond frauds, and Holden, denounced violence of all kinds and announced support for black rights.[18]

Whatever chance for success the true moderates had was dashed by events in Caswell County. There, in the courthouse at Yanceyville on May 21, "the most diabolical affair of these wicked times" occurred.[19] This was the brutal Klan murder of state Senator John W. Stephens. The governor's hand was now forced in his policy toward the Ku Klux Klan, and his response, and the train of events that quickly followed, would greatly affect the August election and Holden's own fate.

When news of the assassination reached Raleigh, Holden hurriedly called a meeting of about thirteen leading Republicans to advise him on what action to take in Caswell and also in adjoining Alamance County. In a critical session at his office on June 8, the governor mainly listened while Senator John Pool, black leader James H. Harris, and several other Republicans discussed the crisis and considered the options open to the state. The issue of military intervention was no longer debatable: the question was what form it should take. A related question was whether captured Klansmen should be tried by military commissions or by the regular courts. Because the federal government had been timid in responding to the governor's appeals for assistance, most of the participants in the meeting agreed that a state military force should be immediately sent to the two counties and should supersede the authority of the local governments. The Republican leaders were divided on the issue of trials for arrested Klansmen. The influential Pool at first advised that military courts should be formed to try them. Richard C. Badger, another close confidant of Holden's, objected to such a course be-

18. Charlotte *Western Democrat*, April 5, June 14, July 5, 12, 1870; Salem *People's Press*, April 1, July 8, 15, 29, 1870.
19. Calvin Cowles to W. W. Holden, May 28, 1870, in Letterbook R, Calvin Cowles Papers, NDAH.

cause "trial by military court was too dangerous an experiment for [the governor] to undertake." He proposed that a special judge be appointed to try the prisoners in the regular courts, perhaps after moving the trials to other counties, as provided by the Shoffner act. Later, in a corner of the office and evidently out of the governor's hearing, Pool admitted to Badger, according to the latter's account, that the establishment of military tribunals would be unwise.[20] Whether Pool informed Holden of his change of mind is unknown, but the governor adopted the senator's original suggestion that military courts should try Klansmen.

In preparation for the military action, Holden dispatched scala-wag William J. Clarke of New Bern, who was to command eastern troops, to Washington in order to obtain the administration's support. The governor specifically asked for military equipment and supplies, since the state treasury could not pay such a large expense. President Grant assured Clarke of his support and, in his own handwriting, directed the War Department to give the state the necessary provisions to equip a regiment. He also expressed his willingness to send additional troops to North Carolina for deployment in case the state operation failed.[21]

Holden wanted a westerner, who could recruit white troops in the area, to command the military force in the West, specifically the operation in Caswell and Alamance counties. His first choice was Wallace W. Rollins of Marshall, who, incredibly, had served in both the Confederate and Union armies during the war. Rollins, however, declined the appointment and recommended instead George W. Kirk, sometime sojourner in western North Carolina but then a resident of East Tennessee.[22] Kirk had commanded a North Carolina Union regiment during the war, and his raids from East Ten-

20. The only contemporary account of the meeting at the governor's office was given by Badger in 1871 to a legislative committee investigating the events of the preceding year. None of the participants disputed his account. *The Holden-Kirk War! Secret History of the Holden-Kirk War* (Broadside in the North Carolina Collection, University of North Carolina, Chapel Hill).

21. William J. Clarke to W. C. Meigs, January 17, 1870, U. S. Grant to General William Tecumseh Sherman, June 17, 1870, William J. Clarke to W. W. Holden, June 18, 1870, in Papers of Governor William Woods Holden, 1868–1870, NDAH, hereinafter cited as Governor Holden Papers.

22. W. W. Holden to W. W. Rollins, June 8, 1870, in Letterbook of Governor Holden.

nessee had created terror among Confederates and given him a reputation as a brigand.

In mid-June, Holden invited Kirk to Raleigh and offered him the command of the force, which he accepted. While Kirk was in the capital, the governor printed a handbill calling for the enlistment of one thousand Union men to avenge "the horrible murders and other atrocities committed by rebel K.K.K. and 'southern chivalry' on grayhaired men and helpless women." The troops would be mustered at Asheville, Marshall, and Burnsville, virtually assuring that the regiment would be largely composed of Kirk's former troops and sympathizers. Although many of them probably welcomed the opportunity of striking another blow at the "rebels," most of the 670 men who answered the call, including a relatively large number of youths who had not served in the war, were primarily motivated to join by the fact that they would receive the same pay, clothing, and rations as regular federal troops. A small detachment of black troops were enlisted as teamsters and stablemen. As required by the militia act of 1868, these blacks were kept separate from the white troops, though their officers were white.[23]

While Kirk's troops mustered and began their slow movement toward the Piedmont, Governor Holden went to Washington for consultation with Grant on the crisis. On June 30 Holden and Senator Pool "had a long and satisfactory interview with the President," Stephen A. Douglas, Jr., the governor's aide, reported from the scene. Grant reaffirmed his approval of Holden's military operation and, according to Douglas, pledged "the moral, and if necessary, physical support of the Government to maintain law and order in North-Carolina." Buoyed by this report and by news of the dispatch of additional federal troops to the state, Jo Holden, the governor's son and editor of the *Standard*, proclaimed in the columns of the newspaper that "the nation is with us" and that the Ku Klux Klan would soon be suppressed and punished for their atrocious acts.[24]

In mid-July, Colonel Kirk's troops began to arrive in Alamance

23. The handbill was reproduced in *Impeachment Trial of Holden*, Pt. 1, p. 283. For the composition of Kirk's force, see *ibid.*, Pt. 2, pp. 2167, 2171, 2306.

24. John Pool to W. W. Holden, June 28, 1870, in Governor Holden Papers; Raleigh *Standard*, July 6, 1870.

County. Their reputations preceded them. Incidents of rowdiness en route to their destination seemed to confirm the fears of many people that a brutal despotism was about to be imposed on the people of the Piedmont. Kirk himself went to Raleigh, where he received final instructions from Holden and obtained a list of men to arrest and hold for military trials. The governor directed him to leave Lieutenant Colonel George B. Bergen, a northern wartime comrade of the colonel's, in charge of affairs in Alamance while Kirk occupied Caswell County and apprehended the murderers of state Senator Stephens.[25]

At the same time, Holden dispatched small detachments of troops to other areas where local Republicans had asked for help. He sent units of Kirk's forces to Shelby, Asheville, and Gaston County in the West "to preserve order and to secure a fair and free election" on August 4. For the same reason the governor also ordered white troops from Colonel Clarke's eastern regiment to Hillsborough, Chapel Hill, and Carthage, all in the turbulent Piedmont. He brought to Raleigh two detachments of Clarke's troops, one containing one hundred blacks and the other sixty whites, to be available if disorders erupted.[26] When rumors of assassination plots against him reached Raleigh, Holden had a squad of state troops assigned to his residence, where they lived in an outside kitchen house. One plot was real, though it never endangered the governor.[27]

These reports heightened Holden's anxiety and caused him to seek more federal soldiers. On July 22 he dispatched a frantic message to Grant charging that former President Andrew Johnson was at the head of the Ku Klux Klan and indicating that the organiza-

25. Charlotte *Western Democrat*, July 18, 1870; J. G. de Roulhac Hamilton, *Reconstruction in North Carolina* (New York, 1914), 504; Trelease, *White Terror*, 216–17.

26. W. W. Holden to President U. S. Grant, July 20, 1870, in Governor Holden Papers; James B. Mason to Holden, June 27, 1870, Holden to George W. Kirk, July 28, 1870, in *Impeachment Trial of Holden*, Pt. 1, pp. 232–33. Historians have suggested that Holden could find reliable troops only in the unionist West. But Clarke had little trouble recruiting eastern men of both races for his regiment. William J. Clarke to W. W. Holden, July 3, 1870, in Governor Holden Papers.

27. Raleigh *Standard*, July 13, 1870; testimony of Daniel A. Graham, ex-Klansman, 1870 [?], misfiled in North Carolina Legislative Papers, 1865–1866, NDAH; deposition of Mrs. L. V. Holden, March 12, 1891, before a Wake County commissioner, in W. W. Holden Folder, Wake County Estates Records.

tion might be too powerful to be suppressed by state troops and the small federal force in North Carolina. He asked Grant to send immediately a regiment of troops. The request was partially granted, but as in the case of the federal units that were already in the state, the purpose of the additional federal troops was to back up Holden's men and not to become actively involved in preserving the peace.[28]

Meanwhile, in Alamance and Caswell counties Kirk and his ragtag army were busy rounding up suspected Klansmen. At first the colonel expected pitched battles between his forces and the Klan. Upon spotting "two companies" of Klansmen near Camp Holden (Yanceyville), Kirk excitedly asked the governor for reinforcements and two pieces of artillery "so I can beat off 5000" hostiles. But his fears of battle and bloodshed, which were shared by Holden, did not materialize. Only minor incidents of resistance occurred when he apprehended Klansmen and clamped military control over the two counties. Within a week or two about one hundred arrests had been made, and other suspects had fled the state. The governor ordered the prisoners held for military trials and instructed Kirk to ignore writs of habeas corpus from the courts.[29]

Cries of indignation against Holden's military operation reverberated throughout North Carolina, accompanied by tales of atrocities and outrages supposedly committed by Kirk's troops. David Schenck, a Lincolnton lawyer, referred to Kirk as "a guerilla bandit from East Tennessee" and charged that Holden's sole purpose in occupying Alamance and Caswell counties was "to overawe and terrify the people, so as to carry the elections for the Radical party." The Greensboro *Patriot* bitterly assailed the governor's military intervention and his suspension of the writ as "the last desperate act of his official insanity," a move calculated "to stifle the voice of the people and prevent the free expression of their will at the coming election." For his actions, the Wilmington *Journal* reviled the gov-

28. W. W. Holden to President U. S. Grant, July 20, 1870, Grant to Holden, July 22, 1870, in Governor Holden Papers.
29. George W. Kirk to W. W. Holden, July 24, 1870, in Governor Holden Papers; Kirk to Holden, August 1, 1870, Holden to W. J. Turrentine, August 2, 1870, in Holden Papers, DU; Otto H. Olsen, (ed.), *Reconstruction and Redemption in the South* (Baton Rouge, 1980), 182; W. W. Holden to Chief Justice Richmond M. Pearson, July 19, 1870, in *Third Annual Message of W. W. Holden*, Appendix, 61–62.

ernor as "one of the most unscrupulous despots and vindictive tyrants that ever disgraced the annals of modern history."[30]

Denunciation of Holden and his military movement reached into the North. As might be expected, the Democratic press raged against the "reign of terror" in North Carolina. Illustrative of the northern Democratic outrage was a Washington newspaper's characterization of Holden as "a demagogue, trickster, and political desperado."[31] Republican journals were scarcely less restrained in their criticism of the governor and his military commander. Colonel Kirk's "antecedents are odious," the New York *Times* announced, and his actions in the North Carolina Piedmont "display the license, recklessness, and cruelty, of an unbridled partisanship." As for Holden, who was responsible for Kirk's "infamies," the events in the state "exhibit [him] as the enemy of the law, and as the arbitrary, unrestrained military ruler of a State in which civil authority should be supreme." The *Times* admitted that crimes had been committed, but "there is no reason whatever to suppose that the State, or any part of it, is in a condition of anarchy or that any necessity existed for the employment of extra-judicial measures." Both this newspaper and the Springfield *Republican* concluded that the governor's timing of the military operation, following months of inactivity against the Klan, left one with the "not unreasonable suspicion that he was using the militia to control the election." President Grant was also severely criticized for sending federal troops to North Carolina, since Holden was making them "the instruments of a cruel tyranny" for the purpose of retaining power.[32]

The incidents that marked the military occupation of Alamance and Caswell counties hardly constituted "a cruel tyranny," though Kirk's forces, operating among hostile whites, did commit some wrongs and improprieties. According to the federal post commander at Ruffin, militiamen roamed the countryside, pillaging and insulting the people with impunity. But this officer's view was prejudiced by a rock-throwing incident between his troops and Kirk's men. At Yanceyville state troops scattered the county court records in

30. Schenck Diary, July 10, 1870; Greensboro *Patriot*, July 14, 1870; Wilmington *Daily Journal*, July 23, 1870.

31. Quoted in Hamilton, *Reconstruction in North Carolina*, 520–21n.

32. New York *Times*, August 2, 1870; Spingfield *Republican*, quoted in Gillette, *Retreat from Reconstruction*, 92–93.

the streets and sometimes threatened townsmen. Kirk and his officers also did not always distinguish between lawful "Democrats" and Klansmen. Kirk himself attempted to arrest John M. Leach, the Conservative candidate for Congress, during a joint debate with William L. Scott, his scalawag opponent. Scott intervened to prevent the detention of Leach and other Conservatives in the crowd.[33] The most serious incident occurred when Lieutenant Colonel Bergen partially hanged three prisoners in an effort to extract information. Holden immediately denounced Bergen's conduct and warned Kirk that "all prisoners, no matter how guilty they may be supposed to be, should be treated humanely." Bergen was later arrested for the offense but was never tried.[34]

Bergen's arrest of Josiah Turner, Jr., Holden's most abusive critic, created far more trouble for the governor than the torture incidents. Turner, recognizing an opportunity to goad his old foe into a serious mistake, went home to Orange County, near the scene of Kirk's operations, and began sending back to his Raleigh newspaper inflammatory reports and editorials that the governor would be certain to read. He characterized Holden as "the devil incarnate" and a "wicked rascal who . . . has wronged, robbed, despoiled, and plundered the people." The hot-tempered Turner raged that "the governor has been lying on us for twelve months" and that Jo Holden, "his profligate son" and editor of the *Standard*, "lies on us to-day by calling us a Ku Klux. If we are, why don't the pumpkin-faced rascal arrest us? We defy and dare him to arrest." Again, in another editorial Turner cried out to Holden: "You say you will handle me in due time. You white-livered miscreant, do it now."[35]

Despite Turner's provocative invitation, Holden refrained from ordering his arrest, since he was not in one of the insurrectionary counties where martial law had superseded civil authority. But on August 5, the day after the election, a detachment of state troops,

33. Captain George B. Rodney to Lieutenant J. W. Powell, August 14, 1870, in *Senate Reports*, 42nd Cong., 1st Sess., No. 1, p. lxxx; H. F. Brandon to W. W. Holden, August 31, 1870, in Governor Holden Papers; William L. Scott to his wife, July 18, 1870, Scott to "My Dear Payne," July 18, 1870, in William Lafayette Scott Papers, DU.

34. W. W. Holden to George W. Kirk, August 3, 1870, Holden to W. L. Bond, August 29, 1870, in Letterbook of Governor Holden; Trelease, *White Terror*, 218.

35. Raleigh *Sentinel*, July 28, August 1, 3, 1870.

acting under orders from Lieutenant Colonel Bergen and without Kirk's knowledge, entered Orange County and arrested the *Sentinel* editor. When queried by a Republican official why he had arrested Turner, Bergen replied that he knew Holden wanted it done but did not have the nerve to order it.[36] After the arrest Holden declined to have Turner released; instead he was held for military trial on the grounds that he was "King of the Ku Klux" and had incited his followers to resist lawful authority. As a prisoner of the "petty tyrants" that ruled North Carolina, Turner, whom "new-departure" Conservatives had recently characterized as "mentally deranged," instantly became a martyr to the cause of civil liberty. However, he was hardly put to the rack during his three weeks of incarceration in the Yanceyville courthouse, ironically in the same room where state Senator Stephens had been murdered by the Klan. Upon his release he received a hero's welcome at every station en route to Raleigh.[37] In the aftermath of his ordeal, Turner's demand for vengeance against Holden, as will be seen, could not be easily satisfied.

Nothing aroused such bitter opposition to Holden as the arbitrary arrests and retention for military trials of suspected Klansmen in Alamance and Caswell. His refusal to turn Kirk's prisoners over to civil authorities in effect constituted a suspension of the writ of habeas corpus, an action plainly prohibited by the constitution of 1868. Another course, which would not have violated the letter of the constitution, was open to him. He could have had suspects arrested by the military and, to prevent their release, transferred them out of the insurrectionary counties for trial. Because of the conflict over the writ during the war, which had led to the insertion of the nonsuspension provision in the 1868 constitution, Holden

36. Captain Robert Hancock to Colonel William J. Clarke, August 7, 1870, R. T. Berry to Holden, November 82, 1870, in Holden Papers, DU. Previous historians have assumed that Holden had a hand in Turner's arrest, but the evidence suggests that he did not. For the view that Holden either ordered the arrest or sanctioned it beforehand, see Hamilton, *Reconstruction in North Carolina*, 522; Trelease, *White Terror*, 218; Horace W. Raper, *William W. Holden: North Carolina's Political Enigma* (Chapel Hill, 1985), 187; and Edgar E. Folk and Bynum Shaw, *W. W. Holden: A Political Biography* (Winston-Salem, 1982), 220–21.

37. George W. Kirk to W. W. Holden, August 7, 1870, in Holden Papers, DU; Theodore N. Ramsey to Josiah Turner, Jr., August 21, 1870, N. S. Winder to Tur-

could ill afford to defy a court order of this kind, at least until other alternatives had been tried. But he rejected alternatives because he feared that Klansmen would be freed by the regular courts.[38] In the end the writ issue proved to be Holden's Achilles heel.

Almost immediately after their arrest, the suspected Klansmen applied, through their attorneys, to Chief Justice Richmond M. Pearson for release on writs of habeas corpus. Pearson, though sympathetic with Holden's efforts to suppress the Klan, believed that his hands were tied by the constitutional prohibition against the suspension of the writ—a cause for which he had fought along-side Holden during the war. But when he issued the writs for the prisoners, Holden refused to deliver the men to the court. The attorneys for the Alamance prisoners quickly petitioned Pearson for a court order commanding the sheriff to seize the men from Kirk and bring them before the court, even if it required the assistance of a posse. Realizing that bloodshed would probably result if he issued the order, the chief justice wisely refused to act. In a lengthy statement he lamely explained that, though he could not consent to the suspension of "the sacred writ of habeas corpus," he had exhausted his power in the matter, and now "the responsibility must rest on the Executive."[39]

In his wildest imaginings, Holden never dreamed that the national government would provide his foes with a victory on the writ issue that they could not obtain otherwise. But both the federal judiciary and President Grant did just that. On August 6 United States District Judge George W. Brooks, an old unionist who had been appointed to the court in 1865, ironically on Holden's recommendation, issued a writ of habeas corpus for the appearance of all of Kirk's prisoners, including Turner. He based his decision on the federal habeas corpus act of 1867 and the due process clause in the Fourteenth Amendment—a further irony, since both measures had been designed to protect friends of reconstruction, not its enemies.

---

ner, September 2, 1870, in Josiah Turner, Jr., Papers, SHC; William A. Graham to his son William, August 20, 1870, in Graham Papers, NDAH.

38. W. W. Holden to Richmond M. Pearson, July 19, 1870, in *Third Annual Message of Governor W. W. Holden*, Appendix, 61–62.

39. Opinion of Chief Justice Richmond M. Pearson in the habeas corpus case of A. G. Moore, in *ibid.*, Appendix, 64–67.

Brooks, however, did not indicate what court should indict or try the suspects.

Holden, confident that the president would sustain him in the matter, hurriedly sent a message to Grant explaining the situation and denying that the federal courts had jurisdiction in murder and assault cases. He plainly told Grant that he would not surrender the prisoners to Brooks "unless the Army of the United States, under your orders, shall demand them." The next day Attorney General Amos T. Akerman issued an opinion that Grant, without comment and probably without much thought regarding its implications, telegraphed to Holden. In his statement Akerman, himself a scalawag, announced: "I do not see how the United States district judge can refuse to issue the writ if the [prisoner's] petition makes out a case for it. . . . I advise that the state authorities yield to the United States judiciary."[40]

Stunned by Akerman's opinion, Holden concluded that he could not risk defying federal authority on the issue, though it is not altogether clear that Grant would have used federal troops to force compliance. The governor now instructed Kirk to deliver the prisoners to Pearson and Brooks as previously ordered. State Attorney General Lewis P. Olds, Holden's unstable son-in-law, bungled the prosecution of the suspected Klansmen in the federal court by not presenting evidence against them, and Judge Brooks, believing that he had no choice, released them from confinement. The governor fared somewhat better in the state court, where enough evidence was presented to cause Chief Justice Pearson to hold forty-nine prisoners for trial by the local courts. But as Holden had repeatedly predicted, none was ever convicted in Alamance and Caswell counties. The power of the Klan, however, had been broken, and in September the governor ended the military occupation of the two counties. Although the Klan would spring up again in 1871 in scattered western communities, Holden could report in November, 1870, in his last annual message to the legislature, that "peace and good

40. W. W. Holden to U. S. Grant, August 7, 1870, Amos T. Akerman to Grant, August 8, 1870, in *ibid.*, 80–82. Grant directed Secretary of War William W. Belknap to forward Akerman's opinion to Holden. Belknap to Holden, August 8, 1870, in *Impeachment Trial of Holden*, Pt. I, p. 214.

order have been restored to all parts of the State" except Robeson County, where non-Klan brigands held sway.[41]

Holden's military movement, accompanied by the suspension of the writ, cost the party dearly at the polls. A number of Republican leaders, principally in the overwhelmingly white West, foresaw this result and pleaded with the governor to avoid military action, at least until after the election, and to use a commander other than the notorious Kirk if it had to be undertaken. But all along, Holden had insisted that his war on the Klan would not be influenced by political considerations, a claim that his enemies found incredible. As he wrote William R. Albright when he sent Kirk's forces into the Piedmont, "I do not care how the State goes" in the election "if by what I am doing I shall save one human life." He was not oblivious, however, to the fact that Republican reconstruction and his own future were at stake. On the eve of the election Holden was encouraged by reports of Republican steadfastness against the "Ku Klux Democracy," and with the Klan under control he expected his party to win the contest.[42]

Even many Conservatives were startled by the magnitude of the Republican defeat. Although the Conservative candidate for attorney general, William M. Shipp, defeated Samuel F. Phillips, the Republican nominee, by only 4,221 votes, the Conservatives swamped the Republican legislative candidates by a two-to-one margin and elected most of their congressional candidates. In the predominantly white Piedmont and upland counties the Republican party suffered its greatest losses. Phillips, an old Union Whig and a member of a family prominent in the university—his sister was the out-

41. Olsen (ed.), *Reconstruction and Redemption in the South*, 183; Trelease, *White Terror*, 222; Third annual message of Governor W. W. Holden, November, 1870, in State of North Carolina, *Executive and Legislative Documents, 1870–1871*, Doc. No. 1, p. 19.
42. William M. Moore to W. W. Holden, June 24, 1870, David Proffitt to Holden, June 27, 1870, Albert Darvell to Holden, June 27, 1870, Marcus Erwin *et al.* to Holden, June 27, 1870, George H. Brown to Holden, July 1, 1870, in Governor Holden Papers; W. W. Holden to S. A. Ashe, November 29, 1881, quoting an 1870 letter from Holden to William R. Albright, newspaper clipping from Raleigh *News and Observer*, 1881, in Scrapbook, Holden Papers, DU; Thomas B. Keogh to William L. Scott, July 27, 1870, in Scott Papers.

spoken Conservative Cornelia Phillips Spencer—won only seven counties west of the fall line. In the East, which contained a predominantly black population, the party remained strong, and in a number of these counties, including Wake, where Josiah Turner's *Sentinel* had belched forth its tirades against Holden, Republicans actually gained votes in the election.[43] Statewide, Republican strength dropped by some 13,000 votes from the party's showing in the presidential election of 1868; yet the Conservative Shipp won only about 2,000 more votes than the defeated Democratic presidential candidate in 1868.

In view of the bitter political and racial climate, the intimidation of some voters, the railroad scandals, and, most important, the reaction to Holden's "military experiment," the Republicans did remarkably well in the 1870 election. Certainly Holden exaggerated when he claimed that Ku Klux violence had defeated his party. The state Republican party, under Holden's vigorous leadership and with the issues of the war and the realities of congressional reconstruction and economic stagnation influencing political attitudes, had established a surprisingly strong base in North Carolina. As events would demonstrate, this base, though severely shaken, had not been destroyed by the election of 1870. The most conspicuous victim of the Republican defeat would be Holden himself.

Holden's postelection troubles began immediately after the votes were counted. Republicans, particularly those outside the hotbed of Ku Kluxism, blamed the governor for their party's defeat. A western Republican declared that in his region "Governor Holden's military experiment" was too "monstrous a load to carry" in the election, and he was joined in this view by other westerners. Other Republicans charged that the railroad scandals, the deplorable condition of state finances, and the increasing tax burden to meet the bond obligations—all of which were partly laid at the scalawag governor's feet—were also important reasons for the party's defeat. Alfred F. Dockery, though a Republican stalwart in reconstruction, could never forgive Holden for causing his defeat for governor in

43. Official election returns for the attorney general's contest are in the Raleigh *Standard*, September 7, 1870. Alamance County, which was occupied by Kirk's troops, was one of the seven counties west of the fall line that the Republicans carried. But because of its military occupation, Caswell County was not included in the state election count.

1854, and after the election he bluntly confided to a friend, "Well, hasn't Holden played hell generally." He thought "the unprincipled scoundrel" should be impeached and removed from office.[44]

Northern newspapers reinforced the bitter internal criticism of Holden. "The Republican defeat in North Carolina," the New York *Times* pontifically concluded, "was due in a great degree to the odium fastened upon the party by the high-handed doings of the Governor. In his eagerness to make sure of victory, he rendered success impossible."[45]

Triumphant Conservatives did not wait for the new General Assembly to convene in November before launching a campaign to remove their archenemy from the governor's office. One week after the election the Tarboro *Southerner* called for the impeachment of Holden. The governor, this newspaper rancorously exclaimed, "is the vilest man that ever polluted a public office and his crimes are now crying in trumpet tones against him. Impeach the traitor, the Apostate, and the Renegade, and drive him into the infamous oblivion which is so justly his due." A western Conservative leader exulted: "Holden is now execrated by all parties and his quondam friends are deserting him in his misfortunes, until the miserable wretch now presents a forlorn and forsaken spectacle. Impeachment will certainly follow and his political and everlasting downfall will soon take place." New departure Conservatives like William J. Yates of the Charlotte *Western Democrat*, however, urged caution in dealing with Holden lest he and his Republican associates "induce Congress to again reconstruct the state." Yates, Zebulon B. Vance, and others also warned Conservatives against any action that would cause blacks to believe that their constitutional rights would be abridged or that the Conservative promise of peace would be broken.[46]

44. W. H. Wheeler to William L. Scott, September 25, 1870, in Scott Papers; Greensboro *Patriot*, August 11, 18, 1870; Rutherfordton *Star*, August 13, 20, 27, September 10, 1870; O. H. Brocker to Tod R. Caldwell, January 6, 1871, in Tod R. Caldwell Papers, SHC; R. T. Berry to W. W. Holden, November 25, 1870, in Holden Papers, DU; "Dockery" to David F. Caldwell, October 2, 1870, in David Frank Caldwell Papers, SHC.

45. New York *Times*, December 28, 1870. See also New York *Journal of Commerce*, quoted in Charlotte *Western Democrat*, August 16, 1870; and Gillette, *Retreat from Reconstruction*, 93.

46. Tarboro *Southerner*, August 11, 1870; Schenck Diary, September 27, 1870;

Meanwhile, Josiah Turner could hardly wait for his release from military confinement to have the governor jailed for ordering his arrest. Immediately upon his return to Raleigh, Turner applied to the state supreme court for a bench warrant against Holden and his militia officers. Justices Robert P. Dick and Thomas Settle, both friends of Holden, refused to issue the order, but they did sign warrants for the arrest of Kirk and Bergen provided they were found outside of the insurrectionary counties. The irrepressible Turner then applied to several superior court judges in an attempt to have the governor arrested for arbitrarily detaining him. All of the judges were Republicans, and they declined to issue the warrants, though one of them, the Radical Albion W. Tourgée, showed the cloven foot to Holden by recommending indictments against Kirk and his officers. Turner did obtain a summons for Holden and his secretary, Stephen A. Douglas, Jr., to appear in the Orange County court to answer charges of false arrest and assault against him, but the Wake County sheriff refused to serve the papers on the two men.[47]

When the new Conservative-dominated legislature met in the late fall, the final scene in Holden's long history at the center of political life in North Carolina was enacted. Perhaps in an attempt to derail the Conservative impeachment effort, the governor was unusually circumspect in his public statements. In a dispassionate annual message to the General Assembly, he dwelled on the inability of his administration to achieve its goals in educational reform, railroad construction, and agricultural improvements. These failures, he reported, occurred because of the impecunious condition of the people and the inability of the state treasury to meet its obligations. He admitted that the government had made mistakes in issuing a large amount of bonds to the railroads and then having them thrown

---

Charlotte *Western Democrat*, August 9, 16, October 11, 1870; Zebulon B. Vance to Cornelia Phillips Spencer, August, 1870, in Phillips Russell, *The Woman Who Rang the Bell: The Story of Cornelia Phillips Spencer* (Chapel Hill, 1949), 137.

47. Charlotte *Western Democrat*, September 6, 1870; copy of decision of Judge S. W. Watt, Superior Court of Johnston County, September 22, 1870, in Holden Papers, DU; William A. Graham to his son William, October 7, 1870, in Graham Papers, NDAH; summons for William W. Holden and Stephen A. Douglas, August 29, 1870, Orange County Superior Court, in Turner Papers. Douglas was the son of the prominent antebellum Democratic leader and the cousin of Thomas Settle, a leading Holdenite.

on the market at one time, which had driven the price down and made recovery virtually impossible. But he ignored the charges of corruption, manipulation, and favoritism in the Republican railroad policies. Still in a moderate tone, he outlined the history of the Ku Klux Klan in North Carolina and his actions to suppress it. He reported that, since "peace and good order" had been restored, on November 10 he had revoked his insurrection proclamations for Alamance and Caswell counties. Holden ended the address by decrying the existence of "partizan rancor and bitterness" and promising members of the legislature that he would cooperate with them in measures "to promote the prosperity and happiness of our people."[48]

The time for conciliation, however, had passed. The Conservative leadership in the legislature, with an eye on Washington, where an attempt was being made in the Senate to launch an investigation of the "outrages" in North Carolina, carefully moved toward the impeachment of the governor. Some legislators feared that action against Holden at this time would provoke Congress into overturning the 1870 election and reimposing reconstruction on the state. But most of them were willing to risk the ire of federal authorities to rid North Carolina of Holden. In a Conservative legislative caucus in early December, the majority, after considerable wrangling, agreed to impeach the governor. On December 9 a resolution to impeach Holden of "high crimes and misdemeanors in office" was introduced in the House and referred to the judiciary committee, which quickly approved it. On December 19 the full House adopted the resolution by a vote of 60 to 46. On the same day the House majority agreed to eight articles of impeachment. In summary, they charged Holden with unlawfully sending state troops into Alamance and Caswell counties, forcing the state treasurer to pay these troops, refusing to obey the writ of habeas corpus, and illegally arresting Josiah Turner in Orange County.[49]

In drawing up the articles, Conservatives avoided the issue of the

48. Third annual message of Governor W. W. Holden, November, 1870, in State of North Carolina, *Executive and Legislative Documents, 1870–1871,* Doc. No. 1.

49. William A. Graham to his son William, December 10, 1870, April 3, 1871, in Graham Papers, NDAH; Bartholomew F. Moore to his daughter, December 25, 1870, in Bartholomew F. Moore Papers, NDAH; Victor C. Barringer to Tod R.

railroad and bond scandals. They did so not because they feared
members of their party would be implicated if the matter were
pressed, as historians have assumed, but rather because they believed that the case against the governor on the issues related to the
"Kirk-Holden War" was stronger and more clear-cut.[50] Furthermore, whatever the reality, Conservatives genuinely believed that
Holden's actions in the Piedmont had been a high-handed usurpation of constitutional authority, subversive of true republican government and the liberties of the people, and that these issues should
take precedence over all others. These were matters of intense concern to North Carolinians who were schooled in the lore of the
Founding Fathers and chastened by their wartime experience with
the Davis "despotism." As the prominent Raleigh lawyer Bartholomew F. Moore, an associate of Holden's in the wartime peace movement and the Union party of 1865–1866, expressed it to his daughter, the governor's "impeachment is demanded by a sense of public
virtue, and [he] ought to be placed before the people as a public
example of a tyrant condemned and punished."[51]

Immediately upon the House's adoption of the impeachment articles, Lieutenant Governor Tod R. Caldwell, a Republican, assumed
the duties of governor, as provided by the constitution. Both sides
prepared for the trial, which was to begin in the Senate in late January. The governor's defense was led by William N. H. Smith, a Conservative and former Whig member of both the United States and
the Confederate congresses, and the brilliant Edward Conigland, a

Caldwell, January 5, 1871, in Tod R. Caldwell Papers; *Impeachment Trial of Holden*, Pt. 1, pp. 1–17.

50. While the trial in the Senate was in progress, an additional article charging Holden with railroad-bond frauds was introduced in the House, but it was sent to the Committee on Impeachment. Holden excitedly wrote George W. Swepson, "I am about to be impeached on account of issuing bonds to your Road," and he asked for evidence indicating that there was no collusion between the two in the matter. Hamilton and other historians have erroneously indicated that the impeachment article was adopted by the House, but the vote that they cite was on the decision to send the proposed article to the Committee on Impeachment. W. W. Holden to George W. Swepson, February 10, 1871, in George W. Swepson Papers, SHC; Hamilton, *Reconstruction in North Carolina*, 550; *North Carolina House Journal*, 1870–1871, pp. 311–12.

51. Bartholomew F. Moore to his daughter, December 25, 1870, in Moore Papers.

native of Ireland. In terms of prestige, Holden's attorneys could not measure up to the impeachment managers—former Governors William A. Graham and Thomas Bragg, and Augustus S. Merrimon, a rising Conservative leader from western North Carolina. The impeachment lawyers represented the full spectrum of Conservative opinion in the state.

Holden also prepared for the trial by being baptized into the First Baptist Church in Raleigh. When he joined the church, he reviewed at length his religious experience since childhood, recalling that he had been a member first of the Methodist church and then of the Episcopal church in Raleigh.[52] Like the Watergate conspirators a century later who humbled themselves in religious piety as they ignobly fell from power, Holden also turned to the solace of the church in the crisis of his political fate, though the circumstances of his troubles were different and the depth of his spiritual commitment was probably greater. "I have done a great deal of wrong in my life," he confessed to the Baptist congregation when he joined the church, "but I will, with Heaven's help, endeavor to do better hereafter." Under the circumstances, this act of religious contrition created a sensation both in North Carolina and elsewhere. The New York *Herald* commented that "Governor Holden goes to impeachment as if he were going to be hanged," and the *Nation* amusingly reported "no record of any similar preparation for impeachment is, we believe, to be found in the books." Some members of the church were not amused: Aunt Abbie House recommended to the pastor that Holden be baptized in concentrated lye rather than water.[53]

Holden also found comfort in reports of renewed Republican support for him as he faced the impeachment trial. The seventeen black representatives in the General Assembly, realizing that Holden's ordeal was also their own, issued an address to members of their race asking them to set apart January 13 as a day of "fasting and prayer on behalf of the Governor and our suffering people." Holden's only

52. Charlotte *Democrat*, January 17, 1871. During the war, about the time when he launched the peace movement, Holden rented a seat in Christ Church, the supposedly aristocratic Episcopal church in Raleigh. Certification of Vestry and Trustees of Christ Church, June 1, 1863, in Holden Papers, DU.

53. Hamilton, *Reconstruction in North Carolina*, 545n; Josephus Daniels, *Tar Heel Editor* (Chapel Hill, 1939), 282–83.

offense, they told their black followers, "is that he thwarted the designs of a band of assassins, who had prepared to saturate this State in the blood of the poor people" in order to win the 1870 election. "When Gov. Holden is disposed of, those whom he protected will be the next victims." Even many white Republicans—some of whom had been critical of the governor's railroad policies and his handling of the 1870 political crisis—rallied to his support, though not with the enthusiasm of old. Most white Republicans were more interested in defeating the Conservative effort to call a convention for the purpose of emasculating the constitution of 1868 than in saving Holden. An indication of this indifference toward the governor's fate, and also an attempt to put distance between the party and Holden, was the state Republican newspapers' policy of virtually ignoring the impeachment proceedings and concentrating on the convention bill then under consideration in the General Assembly. Indeed, reports from Washington soon indicated that the president and Congress were more concerned about the passage of this bill than about Holden's fate. Obviously, such news emboldened Conservatives in the state Senate in their determination to remove the governor from office.[54]

On January 23 Holden officially answered the impeachment charges against him. As before, he denied any wrongdoing in the Kirk-Holden episode, and he reiterated why he had proclaimed a state of insurrection in Alamance and Caswell counties. Holden insisted that, in sending troops into these counties, he was "actuated by the purest motives, by a sincere desire to restore the efficiency of the civil authority, to protect life and property, and to promote the welfare of the people of the whole State." He also insisted that his refusal to honor the writ of habeas corpus issued by Pearson in behalf of the prisoners was motivated solely by his desire to preserve "the safety of the State." He explained the dilemma that he faced in using his power under the constitution to suppress insurrection

54. *Address to the Colored People of North Carolina, December 19, 1870* (Broadside in the North Carolina Collection, University of North Carolina, Chapel Hill); J. N. Bunting to W. W. Holden, January 4, 1871, V. C. Barringer to Holden, December 19, 1870, A. C. Davis to Holden, March 6, 1871, in Holden Papers, DU; W. P. Bynum to Tod R. Caldwell, February 4, 1871, V. C. Barringer to Caldwell, January 5, 1871, in Tod R. Caldwell Papers; Rutherfordton *Star* and Wilmington *Semi-Weekly Post,* issues of January–March, 1871.

while at the same time sustaining inviolate the right of the writ: "It would be mockery in me to declare that the civil authority was unable to protect the citizens against the insurgents, and then turn the insurgents over to the civil authorities." He also claimed that he had intended to surrender the prisoners to the civil courts after order had been restored—a claim of questionable veracity in view of his decision to institute military trials as soon as possible after the arrests. Holden was more truthful when he told his Senate judges that he had ordered the arrest of Turner only if he entered an insurrectionary county, an intrusion that the bombastic editor did not make (he was arrested by the military in an adjoining county).[55]

At noon on January 30 Holden's impeachment trial began in the Senate chamber with Chief Justice Pearson presiding. Despite the fact that Pearson himself had been close to impeachment, the senators and managers treated him with deference and rarely overrode his rulings on procedure and evidence. Unlike the impeachment proceedings against President Andrew Johnson three years earlier, a courtroom formality prevailed during Holden's trial. Decorum broke down only once; not surprisingly it was when Turner was testifying. When asked about his personal feelings toward the governor, Turner answered that they "are just those which a good man would have for a bad man." Holden, who had been attending the sessions, rose from his seat and angrily protested against the court's permitting the witness to insult him. When a Conservative senator challenged his right to appeal from the floor, and before Pearson had an opportunity to warn Turner against such insolence, Holden picked up his cane and stalked from the chamber. He never returned.[56]

Despite the considerable Conservative bitterness toward Holden, the decision to remove was not a foregone conclusion. Some of the senators, including John A. Gilmer, an antebellum foe of Holden's, carefully weighed the testimony and pondered the question of the governor's guilt on each article of impeachment. Although the legis-

55. *Impeachment Trial of Holden*, Pt. 1, pp. 1–45. The quotations are on pp. 25, 33, 37.
56. Ida Holden Cowles to Calvin Cowles, February 17, 1871, in Cowles Papers, NDAH; Raleigh *Daily Telegram*, February 17, March 15, 1871; *Impeachment Trial of Holden*, Pt. 1, p. 907; William W. Holden, *Memoirs of W. W. Holden* (Durham, 1911), 165–66.

lative caucus had voted for impeachment, the Conservative party, which in 1871 was still only a loose coalition of factions, could hardly compel compliance of its members in the Senate. The bare two-thirds Conservative majority might not hold firm in the vote on removal. Partly with that in mind, the majority in the Senate continued, even while the trial was in progress, to juggle credential claims of prospective members in order to increase the Conservative margin in the Senate. The final membership stood at thirty-six Conservatives and fourteen Republicans, or three more than the necessary two-thirds to remove Holden from office.[57]

The attorneys for the impeachment managers brought 61 witnesses to the stand in an effort to prove the charges against Holden; the defense answered with 113 witnesses. Early in the proceedings the governor's counsel won an important point when Chief Justice Pearson ruled that evidence of Klan terror in Alamance and Caswell counties was admissible in the trial if it attempted to prove the existence of an insurrection as defined by the Shoffner act, the governor's authority for the military intervention. The act defined *insurrection* broadly—as a disorderly condition that local civil authorities would not or could not suppress. To establish the existence of an insurrection, then, the defense was not bound by the Conservatives' contention that it consisted only of rebellion against the United States. Although the impeachment lawyers disputed Pearson's decision, they did not seek to have it overturned by the Senate.[58]

Holden and his supporters were buoyed by this victory. Some of them—and perhaps Holden himself, despite a sinking feeling of futility—believed that the admission of the massive evidence of Klan activity would lead to the governor's acquittal. But it was a double-edged sword. The testimony regarding violence in Alamance and Caswell did convince a few senators that an insurrection in fact had existed in these counties and that Holden was justified in proclaiming it as such, though not necessarily in sending in Kirk's troops. More important, the testimony publicized to the nation the depredations of the Ku Klux Klan and ultimately aroused President

57. Raleigh *Daily Telegram*, March 7, 1871; Calvin Cowles to John Pool, February 16, 1871, in Cowles Letterbook S, Cowles Papers, NDAH; *Impeachment Trial of Holden*, Pt. 1, pp. 77–78.
58. *Impeachment Trial of Holden*, Pt. 1, pp. 300–303, 314–19, 457–77.

Grant and Congress to act against it in the South. Unfortunately for Holden, the evidence also revealed, at least to the complete satisfaction of most North Carolinians, including five or six Republican senators who would help decide his fate, that the governor was guilty of authorizing the unlawful arrest and detention of suspects.[59]

Holden, anticipating defeat as the trial entered its final days, rushed to Washington to seek assistance. His purpose was to enlighten Grant and congressional Republicans about the plight of reconstruction in North Carolina, and he hoped that if they did not intercede in his behalf, they would at least intervene to check the counterrevolutionary forces in the state. Upon his arrival in Washington he wrote his wife, Louisa, that "if Congress does not do its duty there will be no safety for loyal people in the South." He told her that his main concern was not his own political future but the future of the country, "for we are all involved in it."[60]

In the company of Senator Pool and other members of the state's congressional delegation, Holden lobbied extensively on Capitol Hill. Everywhere among Republicans he received sympathetic attention and promises that strong legislation would be enacted to suppress the Klan in the South. He also met with President Grant on Capitol Hill; he reported to Louisa that "there was no mistaking the cordial grasp of his hand" and the fact that "he is thoroughly with us." A few days later Holden visited Grant at the White House and impressed upon the president the importance of sending a firm message to Congress recommending immediate action against the Klan, a course other Republicans were also urging upon the president. On March 24 Holden was elated when the president sent a message to Congress asking for the passage of "severe laws to put down the Ku Klux." In the congressional debate on the Klan legislation, he listened with satisfaction as Senator Pool and northern Republicans defended his course in the Kirk-Holden affair. When

59. Calvin Cowles to Joseph W. Holden, February 9, 1871, Cowles to Henry Cowles, February 14, 1871, Cowles to W. W. Holden, February 15, 1871, all in Cowles Letterbook S, Cowles Papers, NDAH; W. W. Holden to his wife, March 18, 25, 1871, in Holden Papers, DU; Charlotte *Democrat,* February 21, 1871; New York *Times,* March 17, 1871; New York *Tribune,* March 23, 1871; Raleigh *Daily Telegram,* March 7, 1871.

60. W. W. Holden to his wife, March 2, 1871, in Holden Papers, NDAH; Holden to his wife, March 15, 1871, in Holden Papers, DU.

the Ku Klux Klan act passed on April 21, he took pride in the effusive comment of national Republicans that because of his ordeal he had "saved the country in 1872, and from a terrible civil war." [61]

Federal action, however, came too late to influence the impeachment proceedings in Raleigh. On March 22, before packed galleries, the North Carolina Senate rendered its verdict. On the first two articles, charging the governor with unlawfully proclaiming Alamance and Caswell counties in a state of insurrection, Holden was found not guilty, with half a dozen Conservatives joining the Republican minority in voting for acquittal. But on the articles charging him with raising an illegal military force and wrongfully directing it to arrest and detain Josiah Turner and other suspected Klansmen, he was found guilty, with four Republicans in one case and five in the other voting with the Conservative majority. The Senate then passed a resolution removing Holden from office and prohibiting him from ever again holding a state office. [62]

The reaction in North Carolina to Holden's removal from office— the first for a governor in American history—was restrained. "There is a general feeling of gladness that this long and tedious trial is at an end," the Raleigh *Telegram* reported. "The majesty of the law in North Carolina has been re-vindicated," and the state had "re-asserted and re-proclaimed the SUPREMACY OF CIVIL LAW in America. This is an event in which the whole country may well rejoice." The Greensboro *Patriot* simply referred to the Senate's decision as "a vindication of the people and of Constitutional liberty." In the western part of the state, lawyer David Schenck, when removal seemed inevitable in early March, recorded in his diary the judgment that "a more righteous punishment never fell on a more deserving wretch." [63]

The northern press generally approved of the removal of the gov-

61. W. W. Holden to his wife, March 4, 1871, in Holden Papers, NDAH; Holden to his wife, March 25, May 1, 1871, in Holden Papers, DU. For Pool's especially effective defense of Holden in the Senate, see the *Congressional Globe*, 42nd Cong., 1st Sess., 167–78.

62. Raleigh *Daily Telegram*, March 23, 1871; *Impeachment Trial of Holden*, Pt. 3, pp. 2536–60.

63. Raleigh *Daily Telegram*, March 23, 24, 1871; Greensboro *Patriot*, March 23, 1871; Schenck Diary, March 7, 8, 1871.

ernor while expressing concern about "the deplorable state of affairs in North Carolina which must have provoked him to arbitrary acts." Almost all northern newspapers, including Republican, criticized Holden for his unwise appointment of officers such as Kirk and Bergen to suppress the violence. "Had he been judicious in the selection of the militia," the Washington reporter of the New York *Tribune* claimed, "nothing probably would have been heard of his impeachment." [64] The New York *Telegram*'s verdict was a great deal harsher. Rejoicing that Holden had been removed from office, the editor of this newspaper claimed that the governor "was one of the most bitter and unrelenting of the numerous despots called into power by the reconstruction acts of Congress. Louis Napoleon never dared treat Frenchmen as he treated Americans." The New York *Sun*, a Republican newspaper, hoped that Holden's removal would be "an encouragement [to] the subjects of carpet-bag rule in other States" to replace the rogues in their governments with honest men. [65]

From Washington, Holden notified Louisa that he faced the bad news with a "calm and thoughtful" attitude, and he promised to return home. But disturbing reports soon reached him from North Carolina. As a result of the state Senate's action, which gave a claim of legitimacy to the charges against him, Turner and others sought again to have him jailed for the violation of their rights in the Kirk-Holden War. Warned by his attorneys not to return to North Carolina until the matter had been settled, Holden remained in Washington and brooded over his situation. Meanwhile, in Orange County, Turner secured an indictment against him, but Governor Caldwell refused to issue a requisition for his return to North Carolina. [66]

Holden was also plagued by civil suits instituted against his property for past claims. Most of these cases involved defaulting associates whose loans he had endorsed. While Holden was gover-

64. New York *Tribune*, March 23, 1871. See also New York *Times*, March 24, 1871.
65. For these two quotations and excerpts from other northern newspapers, see Raleigh *Daily Telegram*, March 26, 28, 1871. See also Chicago *Tribune*, March 26, 1871.
66. W. W. Holden to his wife, March 22, 25, April 24, May 1, 1871, in Holden Papers, DU.

nor, no movement had been made against his property, but once he had fallen from power and his financial prospects were uncertain, claimants rushed to court to obtain settlements before it was too late. Anticipating such actions, Holden in 1869 had transferred thirty thousand dollars in United States bonds to Louisa, with whom they would be legally safe from the "malicious" assaults of his foes.[67] The following year he deeded the home place in Raleigh to his wife. The claimants of 1871 were unable to touch these assets, but a few did secure judgments against the remaining property in his name, principally real estate in Orange County, where officials were hostile to Holden and willing to assist in the legal actions against him. In more friendly Wake County his attorneys, with Louisa's astute assistance, defeated most of the civil suits against his property.[68]

In addition to the threat of arrest in North Carolina, he had another reason for remaining in Washington: he sought a federal office. Not until May, however, was Holden able to obtain an interview with President Grant, who upon receiving him was surprised that he "had been all this time in the City!" When informed of the "bonds and imprisonment" that Holden faced if he went home, the taciturn Grant remarked, "That is very hard." Holden, however, did not obtain an office, because, as he wrote Louisa, Grant "no doubt feels that he ought not to tender me any subordinate position, and he has no chief position to offer." Probably a better reason for his failure to receive an important office was the damage that his appointment would do to the Republican party in the North. Although Republican stalwarts in Washington were aware

67. Edward Conigland to W. W. Holden, May 2, 1871, Holden to his wife, May 15, 1871, in *ibid.*; William A. Graham to his son William, April 3, 1871, in Graham Papers, NDAH. Evidence of Holden's motivation in transferring the bonds and property to Louisa came out later when Josiah Turner sued Holden for damages. *W. W. Holden* v. *Josiah Turner,* 1894, in W. W. Holden Folder, Wake County Estates Records, NDAH.

68. Deposition of Fitz L. Mahler, March 22, 1904, in *Fitz L. Mahler and wife* v. *W. R. Henry and wife,* 1904, Holden Folder, Wake County Estates Records; William A. Graham to his son William, May 8, 1871, in Graham Papers, NDAH; judgment order of Judge S. W. Watts, Superior Court of Wake County, 1871, court executive order against the property of W. W. Holden, May 8, 1871, Holden to his wife, April 12, 1871, in Holden Papers, DU.

of the circumstances of his impeachment and sympathized with him, most northerners viewed him as a prime example of a disreputable southern scalawag who had been imposed upon the South by a flawed reconstruction policy. Having failed to obtain an office, Holden concluded that "everything seems to point to a final retiring on my part from public life," an eventuality, that, he told Louisa, he would not regret.[69]

After a summer visit to Niagara Falls with his family, Holden changed his mind about retirement. He returned to Washington and entered into negotiations with the national Republican executive committee to become the political editor of the party's newspaper the Washington *Chronicle*. Although by this time he believed that he could safely go home, Holden leaped at the prospect of editing a national newspaper and also at the opportunity of having a regular income. With the backing of his friend Pool, he obtained the job in late August at a fairly substantial annual salary of five thousand dollars. But he did not regard the position as permanent, because, as he told his daughter, "I do not intend to abandon North Carolina." In October he moved his family to a comfortable house in Washington, which he rented while retaining his home in Raleigh.[70]

It had been three years since Holden had edited a newspaper, and his *Chronicle* editorials lacked the sparkle of his earlier *Standard* commentaries. Nevertheless, he relished the opportunity to strike hard at the Ku Klux Klan, which was now undergoing its own crisis in federal courtrooms throughout the South. In his first editorial he tersely announced that he would continue his "zealous efforts to expose and defeat the Ku Klux Democracy." In subsequent issues of the *Chronicle* he exhorted federal judges and officials in the South to be relentless in their enforcement of the Ku Klux Klan act. He repeatedly reminded his readers, who included northerners, that the Klan was "a great and dangerous conspiracy against the Constitution, against the Union, against the Government itself." He

69. W. W. Holden to his wife, May 15, June 5, 1871, and *ca.* May, 1871, in Holden Papers, DU. In late May he met Grant on the street and had a friendly conversation; evidently this was the last time he saw him during his Washington exile. Holden to his wife, May 25, 1871, in *ibid.*

70. Joseph W. Holden to Mary Holden, August 12, 1871, W. W. Holden to his daughter [Mary?], August 28, 1871, Holden to his wife, October 12, 1871, in *ibid.*

claimed that "the secret springs of this organization" were "worked by northern Democrats" for the benefit of Tammany Hall, "copperheads," and "nearly all late Southern leaders."[71]

Although the *Chronicle* prospered during his tenure, he continued to long for home. In late February, 1872, he resigned his position and a few weeks later ended his exile from North Carolina.[72] When Holden and his family arrived in Raleigh, they received a warm welcome from their old neighbors. The Conservative press ignored him, but not for long. In future political contests Conservatives, later Democrats, would roll out the sins of Reconstruction and of Holden, which were frequently synonymous, and parade them before the people for election purposes. As in other southern states, the legend of Reconstruction took root in North Carolina and became accepted dogma by the turn of the century.

Yet, in North Carolina the baleful image of the Republican party took longer than in other southern states to gain full acceptance and achieve the political objectives of its Democratic propagators. The party that Holden had founded in the state would continue to be strong and would win some important victories at the polls, including the election of 1872, only one year after the impeachment adversity and the apparent demise of reconstruction in the state. Although Holden had failed as governor, he had established, with the assistance of such able associates as Pool, Caldwell, James H. Harris, Abbott, and Dick, an enduring Republican party that by the logic of Reconstruction politics and the force of southern racism should have been buried after the 1870–1871 debacle. But partly because Holden had been such a visible target of anti-Republicans and such a perceived threat to the liberties and virtues of the people—ironic in view of the fact that as an antebellum and wartime editor he had helped inculcate North Carolinians in these values—his political eclipse eliminated an important unifying theme for the Conservatives and reduced the bitter partisan tension in the state from which these opponents of Republicanism had greatly profited.

71. Washington *Daily Chronicle*, September 13, 16, 20, 25, November 30, December 2, 1871.

72. *Ibid.*, February 29, 1872. Before he left Washington, Grant, perhaps out of gratitude for Holden's editorial support for his reelection, offered the North Carolinian an appointment as minister to Peru. Holden declined it. Raleigh *Tri-Weekly Carolina Era*, March 9, 1872.

Epilogue

After returning to Raleigh in 1872, Holden spent several months arranging his personal affairs and reestablishing himself in the community. He had suffered considerable financial loss from his sojourn in Washington and the legal expense involved in his impeachment trial and court suits against his property. Nevertheless, he was still relatively affluent, possessing several town lots and his home, which were assessed at ten thousand dollars in 1872; he also held thirty thousand dollars in United States bonds. As in the case of the bonds, he had put his real estate in Louisa's name as a precaution against court judgments.[1]

He had good reason to fear that the legal threat to his property had not ended. His old nemesis Turner, having failed in his efforts to have Holden arrested on criminal charges, in 1873 instituted a civil suit against him for false arrest during the Kirk-Holden War. After two changes of venue the case against Holden was dismissed in the Warren County superior court in 1874. Still not to be denied his revenge, the volatile Turner in 1879 sued Holden in the Chatham county court. This time he was awarded eight thousand dollars in damages, but, inexplicably, he asked the state supreme court to remand the case to the Chatham court because his lawyer had failed to follow his instructions. The supreme court granted the request,

1. W. W. Holden to George W. Swepson, September 25, 1871, in George W. Swepson Papers, SHC; Deposition of Dr. Eugene Grissom, February 20, 1894, in *Josiah Turner* v. *L. V. Holden and C. A. Sherwood*, 1894, and *Mahler and wife* v. *W. R. Henry and wife*, 1904, both in W. W. Holden Folder, Wake County Estates Records, NDAH; tax list for city of Raleigh, 1872, in William Woods Holden Papers, DU.

but Turner delayed so long in pursuing the case that the judge dismissed it on the ground that the statute of limitations had expired.[2]

Holden also was troubled during the 1870s by his son Jo's addiction to alcohol. The problem had existed for several years; however, Jo seemed to have conquered it at the time of his father's exile in Washington. In 1871 he went west to serve as assistant editor of the Leavenworth *Times* but returned to Raleigh the following year. His drinking problem also returned, creating emotional pain for his family. Holden, through a boardinghouse keeper in Raleigh, supported his son, and with the assistance of his family Jo underwent another period of rehabilitation. All along Jo had remained active in the Republican party, and in 1874, at the age of thirty-one, he was elected mayor of Raleigh. He served for only a few months. On January 21, 1875, with his grieving father at his bedside, this brilliant young politician and writer died.[3]

Gradually during the mid-1870s Holden reentered politics, in part because of Jo's involvement. The resurgence of the state Republican party under the leadership of such old Holden stalwarts as Governor Tod R. Caldwell and Thomas Settle further encouraged him to return to the cauldron of party politics. Although prohibited from holding state office, he could again be a force in the Republican organization, and if his party regained control of the General Assembly, he had reason to believe that his disability would be removed and the impeachment conviction reversed.[4] In 1872 the state Republican convention, controlled by his old friends, adopted a resolution expressing to him the delegates' "deepest gratitude for his manful and bold defense of them in 1869–70 from the assaults of the Ku Klux Democracy; for his uniform and consistent defense of the poor and humble when he was Governor; and his faithful

2. *Josiah Turner, Jr., v. Stephen A. Douglas, William W. Holden, and George Bergen,* in Warren County Court Records, Civil Action Papers, 1873–1875, NDAH; *C. A. Sherwood, Administrator for W. W. Holden, v. Josiah Turner,* 1894, in Holden Folder, Wake County Estates Records.

3. Thomas Settle to W. W. Holden, July 28, 1869, W. W. Holden to Joseph W. Holden, August 11, 1871, April 9, 1873, W. W. Holden to Mrs. L. P. Olds, January 22, 1875, in Holden Papers, DU; Ettie Holden to Ida Holden Cowles, May 28, 1873, in Calvin Cowles Papers, SHC.

4. William C. Harris, "William Woods Holden: In Search of Vindication," *NCHR,* LIX (1982), 362–63.

and ceaseless maintenance of Republican principles." The fact that
the party had endorsed his administration so soon after the ignominy of impeachment and immediately before a crucial state election deeply affected Holden and made him anxious to work for its
success. He was still, however, an easy target for Conservative attacks. To avoid damaging Republican chances, he maintained a low
profile, refusing to speak at Republican rallies but writing letters
and buttonholing people in Raleigh in behalf of the party. When
the Raleigh postmastership became vacant in 1873, he visited Grant
in the White House and came away with an appointment to the
position.[5]

In 1876 Holden supported Rutherford B. Hayes for the Republican nomination for president, and after the Ohioan was elevated to
the office, he flooded the White House with letters of support for
the president's conservative southern strategy. Although Hayes abandoned Republican stalwarts in other southern states in favor of conservative Democrats, North Carolina scalawags generally retained
their influence in federal patronage matters. Holden continued as
Raleigh's postmaster, and he also obtained the appointment of some
of his Republican friends to federal positions in North Carolina.[6]

Holden's political restoration never approached the lofty heights
of his earlier influence. His main ambition, however, was no longer
to hold political power per se; he now sought political acceptance
as a sign of vindication for his actions in Alamance and Caswell
counties during Reconstruction. He almost obtained a measure of

5. Raleigh *Tri-Weekly Carolina Era*, April 20, 1872; W. W. Holden to Thomas
Settle, April 21, 22, 1874, in Thomas Settle Papers, SHC; Holden to Ralph P. Bux-
ton, August 12, 1874, in Ralph P. Buxton Papers, NDAH; Holden to his wife,
March 2, 1873, August 5, 1875, in Holden Papers, DU. Briefly, before he became
postmaster, Holden attempted to earn a livelihood handling southern claims against
the federal government, but he did not prosper in this business. Advertisements in
Raleigh *Daily Era,* issues of February, 1873; Calvin Cowles to W. W. Holden,
March 30, 1873, in Cowles Letterbook W, Calvin Cowles Papers, NDAH.

6. W. W. Holden to Kenneth Rayner, August 1, 1877, in Kenneth Rayner Pa-
pers, SHC; W. W. Holden to Rutherford B. Hayes, June 16, 1876, January 1, 13,
February 20, March 8, 25, April 25, May 15, 1877, in Rutherford B. Hayes Papers,
Rutherford B. Hayes Memorial Library, Fremont, Ohio. North Carolina Republi-
can friends of Holden privately condemned Hayes's southern strategy. Thomas B.
Keogh to Thomas Settle, March 16, 1877, R. C. Badger to Settle, March 9, 1877,
W. A. Smith to Settle, October 17, 1877, in Settle Papers.

vindication in the constitutional convention of 1875 when his Republican friends came within four votes of having his office-holding disabilities removed.[7]

But the fight had gone out of Holden. When the issue of Reconstruction was raised in a political campaign, he ignored it. By the 1880s Holden, now in his sixties, had gradually lost interest in party politics and was devoting most of his time to family and church matters. His final political mistake occurred in 1880, when he supported his old benefactor Grant for the Republican presidential nomination, an action that contributed to his replacement as Raleigh's postmaster when James A. Garfield won the nomination and the election. Incensed by his dismissal, Holden in 1883 abandoned the Republican party, publicly justifying his action on the grounds that the party was discriminating against the South in its federal policies and had also succumbed to the doctrine of "negro equality."[8] Holden, however, never rejoined the Democratic party.

He never expressed regret for his role in the Civil War or in Reconstruction, though he played down the central feature of postwar Republicanism—black political equality. Holden continued to take pride in his suppression of the Ku Klux Klan during Reconstruction and the protection that he had given to the rights and liberties of all North Carolinians. He admitted that he had made tactical blunders in the military movement of 1870 but insisted that "there is truth in the old adage, 'Desperate diseases require desperate remedies.' And I again declare that all I did in that movement was done with a purpose to protect the weak and unoffending of both races, to maintain and restore the majesty of the civil law, and not to gratify personal feeling on my part, or to promote party interests or party ascendancy."[9]

7. For a fuller account of Holden's effort to defend his Reconstruction record and secure a reversal of the impeachment conviction, see Harris, "Holden: In Search of Vindication."

8. W. W. Holden to Thomas Settle, October 1, 1879, in Settle Papers; Holden to "the President" (Garfield), April, 1881, Holden to his wife, April 20, 25, 1881, in Holden Papers, DU; clipping from Raleigh News and Observer, August 31, 1883, in Scrapbook, Holden Papers, DU. By "negro equality," Holden meant the racial integration of the public schools, which he said that Republicans in Virginia were seeking.

9. W. W. Holden to Raleigh News and Observer, November 29, December 6, 1881, in Scrapbook, Holden Papers, DU.

He condemned the bitter partisan warfare that had afflicted North Carolina during the Civil War era. He even confessed his own guilt in it. "For one, I am heartily ashamed of the part which I bore in the matter of treating public men," he wrote in 1886. "It is born solely of that accursed thing, party spirit." He proposed to write a lengthy history of the Civil War–Reconstruction era that would "do justice to all of the public men of the State, living and dead." He added: "I believe neither in Union nor in Confederate histories. True history is many-sided," and his history would not "favor one class more than another" or champion his own partisan views.[10] Because of his feeble health, including strokes that partially paralyzed him in 1882 and 1889, Holden never wrote the proposed history. The only products of his study were several newspaper sketches of prominent prewar North Carolinians and his *Memoirs*, a disappointing work which he dictated to his daughter in 1889–1890.[11] The book, which was not published until 1911, reveals little of his critical faculties or the history of the period, though it provides in episodic form generally factual information on some of the events in which he played an important role.

Although many North Carolinians, particularly away from the state capital, never forgave him, a reconciliation with his most prominent living adversaries of the Civil War era occurred during the 1880s. A major step in that direction was his 1881 address to the state press association on the history of journalism in North Carolina. He prepared a first-rate account of the state press that was free of the acerbic political and personal rivalries of the past. His address was well received by members of the guild, most of whom had previously thought of Holden "as the meanest of men and worst of governors." He even became reconciled with Vance, who was still the leader of North Carolina conservatives. In Raleigh society his humility, religious piety, concern for the poor, and fine poetic tastes

10. W. W. Holden to Raleigh *State Chronicle*, April 30, 1886, Holden to Raleigh *News and Observer*, November 24, December 6, 1881, in *ibid.*; Holden to Zebulon B. Vance, November 21, 1884, in Zebulon B. Vance Papers, NDAH.
11. W. W. Holden to Ida Holden Cowles, September 10, 1884, in Cowles Papers, SHC; deposition of Dr. Eugene Grissom, February 20, 1894, in *C. A. Sherwood, Administrator of W. W. Holden, v. Josiah Turner,* 1894, in Holden Folder, Wake County Estates Records; clippings from Charlotte *Democrat*, February 11, 18, 1881, in Scrapbook, Holden Papers, DU.

enamored him with his neighbors, many of whom, like Aunt Abbie House, had shunned his company during Reconstruction.[12]

But one old foe never forgave him. As Holden lay partly paralyzed during the last few years of his life, Josiah Turner made a final attempt to obtain the vengeance that the courts had earlier denied him. Turner revived his suit against the former governor for false arrest during the Kirk-Holden War, and though Holden's mental powers were still largely intact, he was incapable of defending his estate against the new assault. In late 1889 the Wake County superior court awarded Turner $12,821 in damages, which shocked members of the Holden family and threatened to impoverish them. The family obtained a reconsideration of the case on the grounds that a similar suit in 1886 had been dismissed by another superior court. But before the issue was settled in favor of the Holden estate, the old political warrior, no longer in contact with the outside world, on March 2, 1892, at the age of seventy-four quietly died.[13]

Holden's death produced a brief wave of belated recognition of his contribution to the history of North Carolina. Without expressing regret for his impeachment and removal from office, newspapers throughout the state eulogized Holden for his powerful political influence during the Civil War and Reconstruction era, his literary attainments as editor and poet, and his religious and humanitarian services late in life. A Raleigh newspaper cautiously predicted, "History will doubtless do his memory justice."[14]

12. *Address on the History of Journalism in North Carolina, Delivered by W. W. Holden, at the Ninth Annual Meeting of the Press Association of North Carolina, Held at Winston, June 21, 1881* (2nd ed.; Raleigh, 1881); clipping from Raleigh *Evening Visitor*, n.d., clipping of letter to Raleigh *News and Observer*, June 21, 1881, Robert H. Whitaker, "William W. Holden, the Governor and the Man," clipping, n.d., in Scrapbook, Holden Papers, DU; W. W. Holden to Zebulon B. Vance, April 28, 1881, Holden to Vance, January 30, 1889, in Vance Papers; Vance to Holden, February 7, 1889, in Holden Papers, NDAH; Raleigh *State Chronicle*, March 2, 1892.

13. Charles F. Deems to W. W. Holden, April 12, 1890, John W. Hinsdale to Mrs. W. W. Holden, August 5, 6, 1890, in Holden Papers, DU; *C. A. Sherwood, Administrator of W. W. Holden, v. Josiah Turner*, 1894, in Holden Folder, Wake County Estates Records.

14. Harris, "Holden: In Search of Vindication," 372. More than forty newspaper eulogies and articles on Holden's death are conveniently collected and preserved in a separate scrapbook in the Holden Papers, DU. The quotation is from the Raleigh *Evening Visitor*.

Governor Thomas M. Holt, Chief Justice Augustus S. Merrimon, and other prominent North Carolinians attended the funeral at the Edenton Street Methodist Church.[15] Also present in the galleries of the packed church were numerous blacks, many of them old people who had come to show their last respects to the man who more than any other white North Carolinian had championed their rights during the hopeful days of Reconstruction. As the long procession passed by the state capitol en route to Oakwood Cemetery for burial, the flag on the dome was lowered to half-mast, a gesture of respect for the man who during North Carolina's most turbulent era had been at the center of the upheaval. Holden would have been pleased.

15. Accounts of the funeral appear in the Raleigh *State Chronicle*, the Durham *Daily Globe*, and the Raleigh *Biblical Recorder*, newspaper clippings in Eulogy Scrapbook, Holden Papers, DU.

Bibliographical Essay

It would probably not be a fruitful exercise to comment on all of the materials consulted for this biography. The most pertinent information on the sources may be found in the footnotes. Marc W. Kruman, in *Parties and Politics in North Carolina, 1836–1865* (Baton Rouge, 1983), 281–96, has provided an excellent survey of the secondary sources for the study of antebellum and wartime North Carolina. Allen W. Trelease has written a more descriptive account of the historical literature for the war and for the Reconstruction era. The Trelease essay appears in Jeffrey Crow and Larry E. Tise (eds.), *Writing North Carolina History* (Chapel Hill, 1979), 133–55. Because of the thoroughness of these accounts, I have chosen to comment only on the main primary sources used in this study. See the citations in the footnotes for the less important primary sources and for the secondary materials that were consulted.

MANUSCRIPTS

The most important manuscript collection was the William Woods Holden Papers in the Manuscript Department, William R. Perkins Library, Duke University (DU). This collection, consisting of 773 items and including scrapbooks and miscellaneous materials, was invaluable for the postbellum period. Only a few items in these papers, however, pertained to Holden's antebellum life. The small collections of Holden materials in the North Carolina Division of Archives and History (NDAH), Raleigh, and the Southern Historical Collection (SHC), University of North Carolina Library, Chapel Hill, revealed important information that could not be found elsewhere.

Because of Holden's prominence, the extant papers of many North Carolinians contained letters from Holden or references to him. Especially valuable for the antebellum period were the David S. Reid Papers, NDAH, which are being edited by Lindley S. Butler for subsequent publication. The Branch Family Papers, DU, the Mrs. Lawrence O'Bryan Branch Papers, NDAH, the Archibald H. Arrington Papers, SHC, and the Abraham W. Venable Papers, SHC, though frequently biased, provided important information on Holden's role in the political conflict of the 1850s. The papers of John H. Bryan, NDAH, Henry T. Clark, DU, William A. Jeffreys, NDAH, Katherine C. P. Conway, NDAH, and Calvin H. Wiley, SHC, were also useful for the antebellum era. The two Holden letters in the Stephen A. Douglas Papers, University of Chicago Library, and one Holden letter in the Daniel Moreau Barringer Papers, SHC, gave revealing insights into Holden's position in the critical presidential campaign of 1860.

For the war years, the most valuable manuscript collections were the Edward Jones Hale Papers, NDAH, and the Zebulon B. Vance Papers, NDAH. The Battle Family Papers, SHC, and the Thomas Settle Papers, No. 2, SHC, also contained nuggets of information on Holden's role in the war.

Manuscript materials for Holden's Reconstruction career are especially rich. The voluminous Governors' Papers, NDAH, were indispensable for information on postwar conditions and affairs and on Holden's reaction to developments. Important letters and telegrams, both outgoing and incoming, were frequently copied in Holden's letterbooks when he was provisional governor (1865) and later when he served as the state's first Republican governor (1868–1871). The Andrew Johnson Papers (on microfilm), Library of Congress, and the North Carolina Petitions for Pardon (photostat copies), NDAH, were valuable sources for Holden's provisional governorship and his political transformation in 1866. The papers of several Holden lieutenants illuminated the early history of the state Republican party and Holden's important role in postwar affairs. Those of Holden's son-in-law, Calvin Cowles, in both the NDAH and the SHC were especially revealing for Holden's intimate reflections and for information on his family life. The papers of Thomas Settle, Albion W. Tourgée (on microfilm), William J. Clarke (particularly his diary), and Tod R. Caldwell, all in SHC, and the papers of William Lafayette Scott and John M. Harrington, both in DU, also provided important information from the perspective of Holden and other Republicans. The large Rodman Family Papers, in the East Carolina Manuscript Room, East Carolina University, Greenville, North Carolina, contained valuable material on the Reconstruction period, though direct references to Holden were few. Smaller manuscript collections of Republicans James H. Harris and Ralph P. Buxton, both in NDAH, were also used.

Holden's relationships with blacks and federal authorities in North

Carolina were revealed in the Records of the Assistant Commissioner for the State of North Carolina, Bureau of Refugees, Freedmen, and Abandoned Lands, 1865–1870, Microfilm Publication M843, NA, and the Records of the U.S. Army Continental Commands, 1821–1940, Department of North Carolina and Army of the Ohio, Letters Sent, Correspondence of Major Clinton A. Cilley, Record Group 393, NA. Both collections are on microfilm in NDAH. On Holden's railroad policies and the intrigue involved in postwar railroad affairs, the George W. Swepson Papers and the Samuel McDowell Tate Papers, both in SHC, were extremely useful. Holden's role in the postwar development of the University of North Carolina was partly disclosed in the Minutes of the Executive Committee of the University of North Carolina, January 2, 1835, to November 29, 1873, SHC.

The perspective and tactics of the conservative opposition to Holden and Republican reconstruction are well recorded in the voluminous Benjamin S. Hedrick Papers, DU, the David Frank Caldwell Papers, SHC, the Zebulon B. Vance Papers, NDAH, the David Schenck Diary, SHC, the Josiah Turner, Jr., Papers, SHC, the William A. Graham Papers, NDAH, the Bartholomew F. Moore Papers, NDAH, and the David Miller Carter Papers, SHC.

Well-organized court records in the NDAH shed considerable light on Holden's home life, his financial assets and property, and Josiah Turner's suits against Holden after Reconstruction. The Wake County Estates Records were particularly significant, though other county court records were also consulted. The Rutherford B. Hayes Papers, Rutherford B. Hayes Memorial Library, Fremont, Ohio, contained several important letters from Holden on his reaction to President Hayes's southern strategy and to post-Reconstruction politics in North Carolina. The Thomas Settle Papers and the Kenneth Rayner Papers, both in SHC, also provided information on the North Carolina Republican party and Holden after the scalawag governor's impeachment and removal from office.

PRINTED PRIMARY MATERIALS

Published primary sources relating to Holden are abundant. By far the most useful printed source was, of course, the Raleigh *North Carolina Standard*. Holden owned and edited the *Standard* from 1843 to mid-1868, except for the period of June–December, 1865, when his son Joseph W. Holden and an associate controlled the newspaper. During these years the *Standard* was truly the mouthpiece of Holden, since he rarely permitted others to write the editorials. Holden's printed works also include *Memoirs of W. W. Holden* (Durham, 1911), a disappointing book that was dictated to his daughter in 1889–1890 while he was bedridden after a paralyzing stroke. Several of his public addresses were published in pamphlet form, and others were reported, though not always verbatim, in the *Standard*. These printed addresses, including his important Fourth of July oration of 1856 and his speech before the Union party convention of 1866, may be found in the North Carolina Collection, University of North Carolina, Chapel Hill. Although Holden wrote several poems, including his popular ode to John C. Calhoun, his most noteworthy literary effort was his *Address on the History of Journalism in North Carolina, Delivered by W. W. Holden, at the Ninth Annual Meeting of the Press Association of North Carolina, Held at Winston, June 21, 1881* (2nd ed.; Raleigh, 1881).

The North Carolina executive and legislative documents, 1865–1873, issued with varying titles after each legislative session, also provided a wealth of information on Holden during Reconstruction. These printed documents include Govenor Holden's messages to the General Assembly and the annual reports of state officials. The *Third Annual Message of W. W. Holden, Governor of North Carolina* (Raleigh, 1870), contains not only his last message to the legislature but also an appendix that conveniently includes his gubernatorial proclamations, 1868–1870, extensive correspondence and testimony on Ku Klux Klan violence, and the scalawag governor's communications with state and federal authorities regarding the Kirk-Holden War. This printed collection is filed in the Governor's Addresses and Messages, North Carolina State Library. Another valuable source of information on Holden in the 1870–1871 crisis was the *Trial of William W. Holden, Governor of North Carolina, Before the Senate of North Carolina, on Impeachment by the House of Representatives for High Crimes and Misdemeanors* (3 vols.; Raleigh, 1871). The *Public and Private Laws of North Carolina* and the journals of the state conventions of 1865 and 1868, as well as those of the General Assembly (printed for various sessions), were also useful. Important material on Holden and railroad affairs, including his relationship with George W. Swepson, was found in State of North Carolina, *Report of the [Shipp] Commission to Investigate Charges of Fraud and Corruption, Under Act of Assembly, Session 1871–1872* (Raleigh, 1872).

Federal printed documents for the Reconstruction era also shed light on Holden and the postwar problems that he confronted. *Senate Executive Documents,* 39th Cong., 1st Sess., No. 26, "Provisional Governors of States," and *Senate Executive Documents,* 40th Cong., 1st Sess., No. 14, "Correspondence Relative to Reconstruction," were especially valuable. Conveniently located source materials on the Ku Klux Klan and the Kirk-Holden War were found in *Senate Reports,* 42nd Cong., 1st Sess., No. 1,

"Condition of Affairs in the Southern States." Pertinent documents on the Civil War and the immediate postwar period were extracted from *The War of the Rebellion: A Compilation of the Official Records of the Union and Confederate Armies* (73 vols., 128 parts; Washington, D.C., 1880–1901). The *Congressional Globe* was also used for information on Holden and the events of Reconstruction in North Carolina.

The published papers of prominent nineteenth-century North Carolinians, most of whom were adversaries of Holden, provided a mine of information for this biography. Noble J. Tolbert (ed.), *The Papers of John Willis Ellis* (2 vols.; Raleigh, 1964), illuminated the rivalry between Holden and Ellis during the late antebellum period. J. G. de Roulhac Hamilton (ed.), *The Papers of Thomas Ruffin* (4 vols.; Raleigh, 1918–20), was valuable for political and social conditions during the Civil War. The attitude toward Holden of an ardent Confederate and plantation mistress has been preserved in Beth Gilbert Crabtree and James W. Patton (eds.), *"Journal of a Secesh Lady": The Diary of Catherine Ann Devereux Edmondston, 1860–1866* (Raleigh, 1979). J. G. de Roulhac Hamilton and Max R. Williams (eds.), *The Papers of William Alexander Graham* (7 vols. to date; Raleigh, 1957–), was especially important for insights on events and men during the Civil War and early Reconstruction periods. For the same period and until Worth's death in 1869, J. G. de Roulhac Hamilton (ed.), *The Correspondence of Jonathan Worth* (2 vols.; Raleigh, 1909), contained valuable information from the perspective of a bitter anti-Holdenite and his political allies.

During the 1940s James A. Padgett compiled and edited letters from North Carolinians to northern Republicans found in manuscript collections in the Library of Congress. These were published in the *North Carolina Historical Review*. Especially useful for political conditions in the state as they related to Holden were the letters to John Sherman (*NCHR*, XVIII [1941], 278–300) and to Edward M. McPherson (*NCHR*, XIX [1942], 187–208). A useful source of information on the immediate postwar period by a Holdenite who later affiliated with the anti-Republicans was the correspondence of state Senator Leander Sams Gash. These letters have been ably edited by Otto H. Olsen and Ellen Z. McGrew and appear in the *NCHR*, Vol. LX.

Travel accounts provided physical descriptions and perspectives on the state that could not be found elsewhere. Frederick Law Olmsted's description of late antebellum Raleigh in *A Journey in the Seaboard Slave States, with Remarks on Their Economy* (New York, 1856), was especially valuable, while the postwar accounts of John Richard Dennett in *The South as It Is* (1865; rpr. New York, 1965), and Sidney Andrews in *The South Since the War: As Shown by Fourteen Weeks of Travel and Observation in Georgia and the Carolinas* (Boston, 1866), provided insightful, though biased, commentaries on political conditions during presidential Reconstruction.

In addition to Holden's published speeches, there were other printed addresses and reports of meetings that were important sources for this study. Many of them were also published in the partisan press. Especially illuminating for the ideology of Holden Republicans was the lengthy and well-structured *Address of the Hon. John Pool to the People of North Carolina* (Raleigh, 1867). Holden's relationship with blacks during Reconstruction was partly revealed in *Minutes of the Freedmen's Convention, Held in the City of Raleigh, on the 2nd, 3rd, 4th, and 5th of October, 1866* (Raleigh, 1866) and in the black leadership's *Address to the Colored People of North Carolina, December 19, 1870* (Broadside in the North Carolina Collection, University of North Carolina Library).

In addition to the *Standard*, the main newspapers used in this study were the following: Charlotte *Western Democrat*, 1858, 1862, 1867–1870; Greensboro *Patriot*, 1858, 1865, 1867–1871; Raleigh *Register and North Carolina Gazette*, 1843–1844, 1848, 1858, 1862, 1867; and Raleigh *Sentinel*, 1865–1870.

Index

NCB
Holden

8   00157 16

NORTH CAROLINA ROOM
NEW HANOVER COUNTY PUBLIC LIBRARY